The Age of Enlightenment

Volume 1

The Age of Enlightenment

Edited by Simon Eliot
and Beverley Stern

Volume 1

Ward Lock Educational
in association with
The Open University Press

ISBN 0 7062 3921 0 paperback
      0 7062 3955 5 hardback

First published 1979

Set in 10 on 11 point Garamond by
Jubal Multiwrite Ltd London SE13
and printed by Biddles of Guildford
for Ward Lock Educational
116 Baker Street, London W1M 2BB
A member of the Pentos Group

CONTENTS

ACKNOWLEDGMENTS

We would like to thank all those members of the Course Team who helped in the preparation and writing of the various introductions and notes, in particular: Stuart Brown, Colin Cunningham, Roger Day, Clive Emsley, Francis Frascina, David Goodman, Lorna Hardwick, Pat Howard, Rosalind Hursthouse, Arnold Kettle, Tony Lentin, Graham Martin, Gill Perry, Aaron Scharf, Gerald Steele and Belinda Thompson. We would also like to thank our secretaries, Ann Hulme and Wendy Macey, for their heroic efforts on what to them (and us) seemed a never-ending series of drafts and redrafts.

Most of all, we want to express and record our thanks to Nick Furbank, Course Team Chairman, for all his judicious guidance, advice and practical help, without which this book would have been much poorer and more incoherent.

Before the tempering experience of editorial work we had thought that such acknowledgements were merely formal academic gestures. We are now much wiser.

The Open University and the Publishers would like to thank the following for permission to reproduce copyright material. All possible care has been taken to trace ownership of the selections included and to make full acknowledgement for their use.

George Allen & Unwin for the translation of Quesnai's *General Maxims for Economic Government* (1768) from *The Economics of Physiocracy* by Professor R.L. Meek (1962); Collier-Macmillan for the revision of David Hume Section X *Of Miracles* by P.N. Nidditch (1975); MacGibbon and Kee / Granada Publishing Ltd for the extract from *Samuel Johnson on Shakespeare* edited by W.K. Wimsatt (1960).

INTRODUCTION

One day in the late 1780s Goethe happened to be holding a prism and, remembering that Newton in his *Optics* had claimed that, by means of a prism, it was possible to divide light into individual colours, he turned the glass towards a whitewashed wall. Behold, there was no play of colours, the wall remained as white as before. In a flash, Goethe knew that Newton had been wrong, and for the next eighteen years he laboured, in his own *Theory of Colours*, to prove it. What he became eager to prove was that Newton had been wrong in the profoundest possible way, and a way which had infected the whole eighteenth century. For what had Newton been doing with his prism and his technique for resolving white light into the primary colours of the spectrum? He had been *torturing* that holy thing, 'Light', he had been, 'putting Nature on the rack'. The prism was the epitome of all that was wrong with Rationalism and so-called 'Enlightenment'; it was a way of dividing up, of separating and categorizing, of violating the living unity of Nature. Its chief instrument was mathematics, and this too was a dangerously overrated science, which made false abstractions from nature and which discovered nothing – merely elaborated a tautology. The need, he told himself, was to overthrow this whole evil fortress, this 'Bastille' of Newtonianism. Thus by a curious reversal the *ancien régime* and its enemy the 'Enlightenment' became, for Goethe, one and the same.

As for *true* 'Enlightenment' – ah, that was a different matter! Light – not the light passively received by the eye but light emitted by the eye – this was indeed godlike, for Goethe. 'Were there no sunshine in thine eye, how could it perceive the sun?' he wrote, quoting from the neo-Platonist Plotinus but with the authentic accent of the Romantic movement. 'Were God's own power not inherent in ourselves, how could Divinity enchant us?'

In this anecdote we perceive how fertile and perennial, but also how full of paradoxes, is that metaphor by which human thought and vision are considered in terms of 'light'. Goethe, brought up in the eighteenth-century 'Enlightenment', comes to reject it in the name of light.

'Enlightenment', in the eighteenth-century sense, is one of those useful but difficult terms, like 'romantic' or 'classical', which para-doxically are about as indefinable as they are indispensable. A good definition is that of Norman Hampson in *The Enlightenment* (Penguin Books, London 1968), who suggests that there is a cluster of charac-teristic attitudes which, when they occur in a high enough con-centration, we call the Enlightenment. Among such attitudes would be: anticlericalism tending in certain cases to antireligion; a celebration of the pagan classical past as a healthy alternative to Christianity; a stress on the exercise of reason; a growing desire for the systematic, particularly scientific, investigation of nature, and a belief that this would reveal a set both of natural and moral laws; a deep mistrust of excess; and a delight in order brought about by a balance of competing forces. All these attitudes can be found in other countries and in other times, what makes them characteristic of the 'Enlightenment' is that they occurred with greater frequency and with a higher concentration in Europe in the eighteenth century than at any other time. This anthology represents an attempt to assemble a group of writers who display in various combinations, and to various degrees, these attitudes and others generally recognized as characteristically 'enlightened'. Rather than offering a precise definition of the Enlightenment we hope that this work will contribute some useful material to a continuing debate. In order to stir up that debate we have also occasionally included writers who exhibit strong anti-Enlightenment characteristics (such as Whitefield) or whose status as Enlightenment figures is questionable (such as Fielding, Johnson and Rousseau).

The Age of Enlightenment was produced to serve an Open University course, and its shape reflects the particular choices and exigencies of that course. Thus it includes an extract from Fielding, but none from Richardson, Sterne or Smollet for the simple reason that the English novel studied in the course is Fielding's *Tom Jones*. It also includes, and this is more contentious, very little Rousseau, because the course team decided, after some debate, not to designate any work by Rousseau as a central 'text' in the course.

Again, the anthology derives some of its characteristic shape from the inclusion of certain central 'texts' studied in the course, in particular the lengthy extracts from Gibbon, Hume, Buffon, and Adam Smith. The selection of shorter material is designed to put these key texts and others into an illuminating 'context'. In some ways then, *The Age of Enlightenment* attempts to combine the functions of a course reader and a conventional anthology.

We have shown, with a few exceptions, a distinct preference for longer rather than shorter extracts. Inevitably this has meant a smaller number of excerpts than is normal in an anthology of this size. We felt that quotation at length was the only way in which we could offer the student as genuine an experience of reading eighteenth-century texts as possible and, in doing so, do proper justice to the authors of those texts.

The material, as will be seen, has been arranged around certain broad themes. Within each group themes and questions are raised which are then reflected by certain other groups, so that the juxtaposition of two such groups is often illuminating in a variety of ways. We are not claiming that this is the only logical order in which such material could be organized, but we hope it is a stimulating one. We have avoided sectioning off each group with a separate title, for this would give the groups an independent dignity and status which would have been highly misleading. However, to emphasize the interrelationship of documents and writers, in the introduction to each piece we have included references to other pieces which raise similar issues or display similar or dramatically contrasting attitudes. In this way we hope to create a web of cross-references which might go a little way to representing the exciting, rich interchange of ideas which itself was a leading characteristic of the 'Enlightenment'.

The different groups of texts are linked by various means. Sometimes the connection is thematic, e.g. Gibbon followed by Architecture and Interior Design is justified by their common use of Roman civilization as a symbol of balance and order, civil or aesthetic. Sometimes, as in the period itself, texts are linked by the polymaths who wrote them. In Volume One the writer who acts as a link or 'hinge' is Voltaire, who participates in the Providence debate and opens the Politico-Constitutional one. In Volume Two it is Diderot, who rounds off 'Art History' and is involved in the *Encyclopédie* group.

The anthology opens with a group of excerpts (Voltaire, Johnson, Fielding) on the debate about the concept of 'classic' in literature. This juxtaposes English Augustan and French Neoclassical arguments and illustrates the power of this concept, and the problems of its definition, which run right through enlightenment thinking. The difference between English and French attitudes comes out clearly in regard to Shakespeare. Voltaire, brought up in the traditions of the age of Louis XIV, which assume that literature's task is to present a generalized and idealized version of human life, avoiding all reference to the particular and the 'low', is unable to see in Shakespeare's *Hamlet* much more than 'the production of a drunken savage'. Dr Johnson, on the other hand, though a champion of Augustan 'correctness', chooses to publish an edition of Shakespeare. The difference between Johnson and Voltaire comes to a focus especially in regard to 'Nature' (a key word for the eighteenth century in this, as in others of its many senses). Voltaire holds: 'It is not enough to say, as some of your [English] compatriots do, that it [*Hamlet*] is all pure Nature; our reply has to be that it is that very Nature that needs to be carefully veiled'. Johnson's adhesion to 'nature' is altogether more absolute, and it is on Shakespeare's 'adherence to general nature' that he rests the case for his greatness. In his attitude towards Pope's *Homer*, however, Johnson comes closer to Voltaire. Pope, he says, has added many graces and elegances to Homer not present in the original, but 'Elegance is surely to be desired, if it be not gained at the expense of dignity. A hero would wish to be loved as well as to be reverenced.' These are words that Voltaire, who contributed the article on 'Elegance' to the *Encyclopédie*, might well have used. To round up this topic, it is worth noticing in Fielding's Preface to *Joseph Andrews*, the puzzlement of an author, who has, or so he feels, created a new *genre* of writing – the novel –and does not know what to call it, so falls back uncomfortably on the traditional and 'classic' literary categories. He terms it 'a comic epic poem in prose', a term expressive of his problem or challenge in the writing of it, that is to say how to reconcile the 'classical' and elevated with the realistic and 'low'.

This 'classicism' group of extracts is followed by two clusters of texts centred on the contrasting topic of religion, namely, religion and the debate about Providence. The 'Religion' group (Toland, Butler, Whitefield, Hume) runs from the deistic rationalism of Toland to the enthusiasm of Whitefield. Hume's *Of Miracles* which, it might be argued, represents the culmination of reason applied to revelation, closes the religion section, and his *Of a Particular Providence* opens the Providence debate (Hume, Voltaire, Rousseau, Johnson). The debate about the intelligible world order in Providence is paralleled by the similar conviction in the Politico-Constitutional group (Voltaire, Montesquieu, Quesnai, Adam Smith) that there are natural, ordered, reasonable principles behind the apparently chaotic functioning of politics and economics. This group spans some forty years and provides an impression of contemporary debate on political, constitutional and economic matters. In both Voltaire's theoretical comparison between the governments of England and France, and Montesquieu's philosophical study of laws, will be found the admiration with which the philosophes regarded the British constitutional model. The extracts by the French physiocrat Quesnai and by Adam Smith illustrate two influential and systematic approaches to political economy. Classicism as a theme re-emerges in Gibbon's study of what, to the eighteenth century, would have been the greatest of all politico-constitutional systems, the Roman Empire. Gibbon is also linked to the Politico-Constitutional group by the distinct influence Montesquieu's ideas had on his writings.

The classical world as an ordered system and a reservoir of powerful imagery is a theme which is echoed in the Architecture section (Langley, Laugier, Chambers, Stuart and Revett) and re-echoed in the ideas of the French Neoclassical theorists (Le Blanc, Cochin, Blondel). La Font de Saint Yenne's study of painting as interior decor links us into the painting and landscape gardening group (Hogarth, Walpole, Reynolds, Diderot) where the attempt to define stable, classical rules is constantly disturbed by the pressures of actual practice. Diderot, in his role as an enlightenment polymath, provides us with the 'hinge' on which the anthology pivots from Art History to the *Encyclopédie* /Science section which follows it (D'Alembert, Diderot, Buffon). The same desire to discover, through systematic investigation, a coherent world order can be found in the *Encyclopédistes* and Buffon as was displayed by Quesnai, Montesquieu and Adam Smith. D'Alembert's piece on *Men of Letters* brings us round almost full circle back to a literary issue, but this time it is an issue deeply embedded in a wider social question, the problem of patronage and the need for intellectual independence (D'Alembert, Johnson, Beaumarchais). Kant's attempt to answer the question *What is Enlightening?* seems an appropriately provocative end to an anthology one of whose main aims is to fuel the debate on that very question.

Our policy on translation has been to reprint whenever possible the English version published closest to the date of publication of the original, in an attempt to retain as far as possible the 'flavour' of the period. The chief exceptions to this are the twentieth-century American translation of D'Alembert's *Preliminary Discourse* to the *Encyclopédie* and the specially commissioned translation of Diderot's *Salons*.

Our desire to preserve the 'flavour' of the period has led us, wherever possible, to retain the author's original spelling and punctuation, even though this inevitably meant that there would be occasional inconsistencies between texts, and sometimes even within a single text. Most eighteenth-century writers were less particular about such things than we are today.

Our policy on editorial notes, like most editorial policies, has of necessity been flexible. For texts not readily accessible in good modern editions we have provided as full a set of notes as possible. For those texts (such as Gibbon) where reliable editions are available the notes are much less copious. The author's original footnotes are printed at the foot of each page and and are indicated in the text by an italic superior number. Editorial notes are printed at the end of each excerpt and are denoted in the text by the use of an upright superior number. There is a certain amount of duplication in the editorial notes, particularly in the case of short ones where it was as simple to repeat the information as to refer the reader to another note. In the case of longer notes the reader is referred to their first full appearance. This flexible policy has been extended to the author's footnotes. In the case of such writers as Hume, Montesquieu and Buffon we have reproduced a selection of the most relevant of the original footnotes. In the case of Gibbon, where the footnotes are such an integral part of the 'performance', we have reprinted them all. As befits a book based almost exclusively on contemporary material the bibliographic source information is as comprehensive as possible. Full details of the first edition are given and, if we are not reprinting from that, then details of the edition from which our text is taken are also included. The date following the title of each piece normally refers to the year of first publication. In cases where publication was delayed then the date of writing (if known) or of first public performance (in the case of Beaumarchais) is used instead.

VOLTAIRE

On Politeness in Drama (1736)

From F. M. A. de Voltaire, La nouvelle Épître à M. le Chevalier
Fakener [Falkener][1] first printed in *Zayre, tragédie, nouvelle édition
revue... avec une nouvelle Épître dédicatoire*, J-B. Cl. Bauche, Paris,
1736. Translation by P. N. Furbank.

The early eighteenth century was a period in which many familiar
and long-enduring national stereotypes were fixed. It was then
that the opinion became firmly established that France was the
home of the 'polite' arts and similarly of polish or 'politeness' in
social manners; and Voltaire was influential in the promotion of
both these ideas. It is worth remarking, however, that 'politeness'
in these senses was not synonymous with sexual propriety.
Voltaire, who was shocked by the 'indecent' sentiments of
Dryden's Cleopatra (see p. 7), in real life used language so
'indecent' to English ears that, when he visited Alexander Pope in
England, Pope's mother had to leave the room.

[...] Love appears on our [the French] stage with a propriety, a
delicacy, a truthfulness not to be found elsewhere. It is because, among
the nations of the world, the French are the most expert in social
matters.

A continual, lively and polished intercourse between the sexes has
created in France a politeness that is largely unknown elsewhere.

Society depends upon women. All nations that have the misfortune
of shutting women away are unsociable. And among yourselves [the
English] a somewhat austere style of manners, political quarrels, and
wars of religion, which had combined to make you awkward and
unpolished in behaviour, deprived you, until the time of Charles II, of
the joys of society, though in the very home of liberty. Poets have thus
no idea, in all other countries, and even in England, how love was
conducted among truly civilised people.

The true art of comedy was unknown until Molière,[2] as was the art of expressing true and delicate feelings in the theatre until Racine;[3] for the reason that, as you might say, society had not reached its perfection until their time. A poet, in his study, cannot paint manners if he has not observed them; he finds it easier to write a hundred odes or epistles than a single scene where Nature is supposed to speak.

Your Dryden,[4] who by the way was a great genius, makes his heroes, when in love, utter either hyperboles and rhetoric, or indecencies, both of which are equally alien to true tenderness.

If M. Racine makes Titus[5] say:

> Depuis cinq ans entiers chaque jour je la vois,
> Et crois toujours la voir pour la première fois.

Your Dryden makes his Antony say [Voltaire of course gave a French prose translation:]

> How I loved,
> Witness, ye days and nights, and all ye hours,
> That danced away with down upon your feet.
> As all your business were to count my passion!
> One day passed by, and nothing saw but love;
> Another came, and still 'twas only love;
> The suns were wearied out with looking on,
> And I untired with loving.[6]

It is very difficult to imagine that Antony should really have spoken to Cleopatra thus.

In the same play, Cleopatra speaks as follows to Antony:

> Come to me, come, my soldier, to my arms!
> You've been too long away from my embraces;
> But, when I have you fast, and all my own,
> With broken murmurs, and with amorous sighs,
> I'll say, you were unkind, and punish you,
> And mark you red with many an eager kiss.[7]

It is very reasonable to think that Cleopatra did, in fact, often speak in this style, but indecency of this sort is not the kind of thing to enact before a respectable audience.

It is not enough to say, as some of your compatriots do, that is all pure Nature; our reply has to be that it is that very Nature that needs to be carefully veiled.

It does not even show knowledge of the human heart, to imagine that one will please the more by presenting licentious images; on the contrary, all this does is to bar the doors of the soul against true pleasures. If everything is frankly revealed from the start, one soon loses one's appetite; there is nothing more to seek, nothing to desire, and the chase after pleasure ends, before one knows it, in boredom. It is for these reasons that civilised people enjoy pleasures that the vulgar have no conception of.

The audience, in such cases, are like lovers disappointed by too

7

prompt an enjoyment; a hundred veils are needed to conceal ideas that, presented too crudely, would make us blush. It is precisely this veil that is the delight of civilised people; there is no pleasure for them where there is no propriety. [...]

Notes

1   An English friend and well-to-do merchant with whom Voltaire stayed in England.

2   Jean-Baptiste Poquelin, known as Molière (1622–73), the great French comic dramatist, author of *Le Misanthrope*, *Le Bourgeois Gentilhomme*, etc.

3   Jean Racine (1639–99), the great French tragic dramatist, author of *Phèdre*, *Mithridate*, *Athalie*, etc.

4   John Dryden (1631–1700), the great English poet and dramatist. His verse plays, notwithstanding Voltaire's strictures, were to some extent an attempt to import the style of contemporary French drama into Britain. His *All for Love* (1678) was, however, a direct imitation of Shakespeare's *Antony and Cleopatra*.

5   The quotation is from Act II, scene 2 of Racine's *Bérénice* (1670). It may be translated: 'For five whole years I have seen her every day and have the feeling, always, of seeing her for the first time.'

6   Act II scene 1.

7   Act III scene 1.

VOLTAIRE

On Hamlet (1749)

From the Preface to F. M. A. de Voltaire *La Tragédie de Sémiramis et Quelques Autres Pièces de Littérature*, chez P. G. Le Mercier, imprimeur – libraire, rue Saint-Jacques, au livre d'or, et chez Michel Lambert, libraire, à Paris, 1749. Translated by Arthur Murphy in *Shakespeare vindicated, in a letter to Voltaire*, first published in the *Craftsman: or Gray's Inn Journal* No. 12, 15 December 1753; reprinted in Arthur Murphy's *Works*, 1786, 7 vols. Vol V.

Voltaire's criticism of *Hamlet* here resolves itself into two distinct but connected objections. The first is that the events of the play are themselves improbable or 'absurd', and the second is that the characters' actions within those events are often offensive and 'disgusting'. Although both Voltaire and Johnson would have agreed that 'Nature' required generalizing, Voltaire seemed to demand a degree of abstraction from reality in tragedy so extreme that no mixing of the 'sublime' with the 'low' could ever take place. For Johnson, one of Shakespeare's greatest achievements was to mix comedy with tragedy and thus reveal the 'real state of sublunary nature'.

Arthur Murphy (1727–1805), the translator of this piece, was a playwright and friend of Johnson.

I do not mean to justify the tragedy of *Hamlet* in every particular; it is in fact a barbarous piece, abounding with such gross absurdities that it would not be tolerated by the vulgar of *France* and *Italy*. The hero of the play runs mad in the second act, and his mistress meets with the same misfortune in the third. The Prince takes *Ophelia*'s father for a rat, and kills him; in despair she throws herself into a river. Her grave is dug on the stage: the gravedigger, with a skull in his hand, amuses himself with a string of miserable jests, and the Prince answers them in language equally disgusting: *Hamlet*, his mother, and father-in-law drink together on the stage. They divert themselves with bottle songs (*Chansons à boire*), they quarrel, they fight, they kill. One would imagine this play the production of a drunken savage. And yet among these absurdities, which render the *English* drama absolutely barbarous, there are some strokes in *Hamlet* worthy of the most exalted genius. This has always been matter of astonishment to me; it looks as if Nature, in pure sport, diverted herself with mixing in *Shakespeare*'s head every thing sublime and great with all that can be conceived low, mean and detestable.

SAMUEL JOHNSON

On Shakespeare (1765)

From Samuel Johnson, *The Plays of William Shakespeare*. Printed for J. and R. Tonson, C. Corbet..., London 1765. Reprinted from *Samuel Johnson on Shakespeare*, edited W. K. Wimsatt, MacGibbon and Kee, London, 1960.

By the standards of his contemporaries Johnson's edition of Shakespeare was of a very high quality, although today our interest is centred rather on Johnson's critical comments than his editorial scholarship. In the *Preface* to his edition Johnson argues that Shakespeare's greatness lies in his ability to present generalized truth about nature, particularly human nature; that is, his characters are not exaggerated or idiosyncratic, and they do not suffer melodramatic, improbable experiences; rather they enshrine constant human values and undergo trials which, if not common, are at least understandable in the light of common experience. Although this defence of Shakespeare is characteristically eighteenth century in tone, Johnson goes on to transcend his period when, in the final paragraph quoted, he celebrates the extraordinary mingling of tragedy and comedy to be found in Shakespeare's work.

Johnson had voiced some of these ideas nearly twenty years before when, in 1747, he composed a *Prologue* to be spoken by David Garrick in his new production of *The Merchant of Venice* at the Drury Lane Theatre

[. . .] 'Tis yours this night to bid the reign commence,
Of rescued Nature and reviving Sense;
To chase the charms of sound, the pomp of show,
For useful mirth and salutary woe;
Bid scenic Virtue form the rising age
And Truth diffuse her radiance from the stage.

[...] it is proper to inquire by what peculiarities of excellence Shakespeare has gained and kept the favor of his countrymen.

Nothing can please many, and please long, but just representations of general nature. Particular manners can be known to few, and therefore few only can judge how nearly they are copied. The irregular combinations of fanciful invention may delight awhile by that novelty of which the common satiety of life sends us all in quest; but the pleasures of sudden wonder are soon exhausted, and the mind can only repose on the stability of truth.

Shakespeare is, above all writers, at least above all modern writers, the poet of nature, the poet that holds up to his readers a faithful mirror of manners and of life. His characters are not modified by the customs of particular places, unpracticed by the rest of the world; by the peculiarities of studies or professions which can operate but upon small numbers; or by the accidents of transient fashions or temporary opinions: they are the genuine progeny of common humanity, such as the world will always supply, and observation will always find. His persons act and speak by the influence of those general passions and principles by which all minds are agitated and the whole system of life is continued in motion. In the writings of other poets a character is too often an individual; in those of Shakespeare it is commonly a species.

It is from this wide extension of design that so much instruction is derived. It is this which fills the plays of Shakespeare with practical axioms and domestic wisdom. It was said of Euripides that every verse was a precept;[1] and it may be said of Shakespeare that from his works may be collected a system of civil and economical prudence. Yet his real power is not shown in the splendor of particular passages, but by the progress of his fable and the tenor of his dialogue; and he that tries to recommend him by select quotations will succeed like the pedant in Hierocles,[2] who, when he offered his house to sale, carried a brick in his pocket as a specimen.

It will not easily be imagined how much Shakespeare excels in accommodating his sentiments to real life but by comparing him with other authors. It was observed by the ancient schools of declamation that the more diligently they were frequented, the more was the student disqualified for the world, because he found nothing there which he should ever meet in any other place. The same remark may be applied to every stage but that of Shakespeare. The theater, when it is under any other direction, is peopled by such characters as were never seen, conversing in a language which was never heard, upon topics which will never arise in the commerce of mankind. But the dialogue of this author is often so evidently determined by the incident which produces it, and is pursued with so much ease and simplicity, that it seems scarcely to claim the merit of fiction, but to have been gleaned by diligent selection out of common conversation and common occurrences.

Upon every other stage the universal agent is love, by whose power all good and evil is distributed and every action quickened or retarded. To bring a lover, a lady, and a rival into the fable; to entangle them in contradictory obligations, perplex them with oppositions of interest, and harass them with violence of desires inconsistent with each other; to make them meet in rapture and part in agony, to fill their mouths with hyperbolical joy and outrageous sorrow, to distress them as nothing human ever was distressed, to deliver them as nothing human ever was delivered, is the business of a modern dramatist. For this, probability is violated, life is misrepresented, and language is depraved. But love is only one of many passions; and as it has no great influence upon the sum of life, it has little operation in the dramas of a poet who caught his ideas from the living world and exhibited only what he saw before him. He knew that any other passion, as it was regular or exorbitant, was a cause of happiness or calamity.

Characters thus ample and general were not easily discriminated and preserved, yet perhaps no poet ever kept his personages more distinct from each other. I will not say with Pope that every speech may be assigned to the proper speaker,[3] because many speeches there are which have nothing characteristical; but, perhaps, though some may be equally adapted to every person, it will be difficult to find any that can be properly transferred from the present possessor to another claimant. The choice is right, when there is reason for choice.

Other dramatists can only gain attention by hyperbolical or aggravated characters, by fabulous and unexampled excellence or depravity, as the writers of barbarous romances invigorated the reader by a giant and a dwarf; and he that should form his expectations of human affairs from the play, or from the tale, would be equally deceived. Shakespeare has no heroes; his scenes are occupied only by men, who act and speak as the reader thinks that he should himself have spoken or acted on the same occasion. Even where the agency is supernatural, the dialogue is level with life. Other writers disguise the most natural passions and most frequent incidents; so that he who contemplates them in the book will not know them in the world. Shakespeare approximates the remote and familiarizes the wonderful; the event which he represents will not happen, but, if it were possible, its effects would probably be such as he has assigned; and it may be said that he has not only shown human nature as it acts in real exigences, but as it would be found in trials to which it cannot be exposed.

This, therefore, is the praise of Shakespeare, that his drama is the mirror of life; that he who has mazed his imagination in following the phantoms which other writers raise up before him, may here be cured of his delirious ecstasies by reading human sentiments in human language, by scenes from which a hermit may estimate the transactions of the world and a confessor predict the progress of the passions.

His adherence to general nature has exposed him to the censure of critics who form their judgments upon narrower principles. Dennis[4] and Rymer[5] think his Romans not sufficiently Roman; and Voltaire censures his kings as not completely royal. Dennis is offended that Menenius,[6] a senator of Rome, should play the buffoon; and Voltaire perhaps thinks decency violated when the Danish usurper is represented as a drunkard.[7] But Shakespeare always makes nature predominate over accident; and, if he preserves the essential character, is not very careful of distinctions superinduced and adventitious. His story requires Romans or kings, but he thinks only on men. He knew that Rome, like every other city, had men of all dispositions; and wanting a buffoon, he went into the senate house for that which the senate house would certainly have afforded him. He was inclined to show an usurper and a murder not only odious, but despicable; he therefore added drunkenness to his other qualities, knowing that kings love wine like other men, and that wine exerts its natural power upon kings. These are the petty cavils of petty minds; a poet overlooks the casual distinction of country and condition, as a painter, satisfied with the figure, neglects the drapery.

The censure which he has incurred by mixing comic and tragic scenes, as it extends to all his works, deserves more consideration. [. . .]

Shakespeare's plays are not in the rigorous and critical sense either tragedies or comedies, but compositions of a distinct kind; exhibiting the real state of sublunary nature, which partakes of good and evil, joy and sorrow, mingled with endless variety of proportion and innumerable modes of combination; and expressing the course of the world, in which the loss of one is the gain of another; in which, at the same time, the reveller is hasting to his wine, and the mourner burying his friend; in which the malignity of one is sometimes defeated by the frolic of another; and many mischiefs and many benefits are done and hindered without design.

Out of this chaos of mingled purposes and casualties the ancient poets, according to the laws which custom had prescribed, selected some the crimes of men, and some their absurdities; some the momentous vicissitudes of life, and some the lighter occurrences; some the terrors of distress, and some the gaieties of prosperity. Thus rose the two modes of imitation, known by the names of *tragedy* and *comedy*, compositions intended to promote different ends by contrary means, and considered as so little allied that I do not recollect among the Greeks or Romans a single writer who attempted both.

Shakespeare has united the powers of exciting laughter and sorrow not only in one mind but in one composition. Almost all his plays are divided between serious and ludicrous characters, and, in the successive evolutions of the design, sometimes produce seriousness and sorrow, and sometimes levity and laughter.

That this is a practice contrary to the rules of criticism will be readily allowed; but there is always an appeal open from criticism to nature. [. . .]

Notes

1   Euripides (480-406 B.C.) Greek tragic dramatist, author of *Electra, The Bacchae* etc. The comment is from Cicero, *Epistolae ad Familiares*, X VI 8.

2   Fourth century A.D. writer of facetious moral verses. Boswell claimed that Johnson had written 'A free translation of the Jests of Hierocles, with an introduction' which appeared in the *Gentleman's Magazine* in 1741.

14

3   This was claimed by Pope in the Preface to his *Works of Shakespear* (1725). Pope
     considered Shakespeare, though full of terrible faults and 'uncouthnesses', to
     resemble 'an ancient majestick piece of *Gothick* Architecture'. In his *Epistle to
     Augustus* (1737) he wrote:

>   Shakespeare (whom you and ev'ry Play-house bill
>   Style the divine, the matchless, what you will)
>   For gain not glory, wing'd his roving flight
>   And grew immortal in his own despight.
>
>   Late, very late, correctness grew our care
>   When the tir'd nation breath'd from civil war.
>   Exact Racine, and Corneille's noble fire
>   Show'd us that France had something to admire.
>   Not but the Tragic spirit was our own,
>   And full in Shakespear, fair in Otway shone:
>   But Otway fail'd to polish or refine,
>   And fluent Shakespear scarce effac'd a line.
>   Ev'n copious Dryden wanted, or forgot,
>   The last and greatest Art, the Art to blot.
>   (Lines 69-72 and 272-281)

     The best known play of Thomas Otway, mentioned by Pope, is the tragedy
     Venice Preserv'd (1682); it is much influenced by Shakespeare.

4   The poet and critic John Dennis published in 1712 an *Essay on the Genius and Writings
     of Shakespeare*.

5   The playwright and critic Thomas Rymer published in 1693 an influential work, *A
     Short View of Tragedy*, in which he sometimes comments unfavourably on Shake-
     speare.

6   Menenius Agrippa, a character in Shakespeare's *Coriolanus*.

7   See the extract by Voltaire on p. 9.

15

SAMUEL JOHNSON

On Alexander Pope (1781)

From Samuel Johnson, *Life of Pope* in *Prefaces, Biographical and Critical, to the works of the English Poets, volume the seventh*. Printed by J. Nichols; for C. Bathurst, J. Buckland ... London 1781. Reprinted from *Lives of the English Poets*, ed. G. Birckbeck Hill, Oxford, 1905.

Samuel Johnson undertook in 1777 to write a number of prefaces to a collection of the works of English poets which a group of London booksellers planned to publish. The series was to begin with the poems of Abraham Cowley (1618-67) and go on to Johnson's own day. The prefaces were to be both biographical and critical, and Johnson drew material for them from books, conversations and, where appropriate, memory. The first group appeared in 1779 and the second in 1781, the whole occupying ten volumes. Subsequently, the prefaces were printed separately as the *Lives of the most Eminent English Poets*.

The composition of the *Lives of the Poets* was at times wearisome to Johnson but, according to Boswell, he wrote that of Pope *con amore* (with love) because his subject so perfectly embodied in his verse the principles of 'correctness' which Johnson revered. The work frequently reveals indications like this of contemporary taste, and the clear expression of Johnson's views in characteristically vigorous prose is one of its most attractive features.

The first extract is from the beginning of the *Life of Pope*. Johnson conveys a fair quantity of basic biographical information, but even here there are flashes of his distinctively dry and ironic wit. This extract takes the reader up to the start of Pope's career in London and ends just before the publication of the *Pastorals* in 1709.

Alexander Pope was born in London, May 22, 1688, of parents whose rank or station was never ascertained: we are informed that they were of 'gentle blood'; that his father was of a family of which the Earl of Downe was the head, and that his mother was the daughter of William Turner, Esquire, of York, who had likewise three sons, one of whom had the honour of being killed, and the other of dying, in the service of Charles the First; the third was made a general officer in Spain, from whom the sister inherited what sequestrations and forfeitures had left in the family.

This, and this only, is told by Pope; who is more willing, as I have heard observed, to shew what his father was not, than what he was. It is allowed that he grew rich by trade; but whether in a shop or on the Exchange was never discovered, till Mr. Tyers told, on the authority of Mrs. Racket, that he was a linen-draper in the Strand. Both parents were papists.

Pope was from his birth of a constitution tender and delicate; but is said to have shewn remarkable gentleness and sweetness of disposition. The weakness of his body continued through his life, but the mildness of his mind perhaps ended with his childhood. His voice, when he was young, was so pleasing that he was called in fondness the 'little Nightingale.'

Being not sent early to school he was taught to read by an aunt, and when he was seven or eight years old became a lover of books. He first learned to write by imitating printed books; a species of penmanship in which he retained great excellence through his whole life, though his ordinary hand was not elegant.

When he was about eight he was placed in Hampshire under Taverner, a Romish priest, who, by a method very rarely practised, taught him the Greek and Latin rudiments together. He was now first regularly initiated in poetry by the perusal of Ogylby's[1] *Homer*,[2] and Sandys's[3] *Ovid*:[4] Ogylby's assistance he never repaid with any praise; but of Sandys he declared, in his notes to the *Iliad*, that English poetry owed much of its present beauty to his translations. Sandys very rarely attempted original composition.

From the care of Taverner, under whom his proficiency was considerable, he was removed to a school at Twyford near Winchester, and again to another school about Hyde-park Corner; from which he used sometimes to stroll to the playhouse, and was so delighted with theatrical exhibitions that he formed a kind of play from Ogylby's *Iliad*, with some verses of his own intermixed, which he persuaded his schoolfellows to act, with the addition of his master's gardener, who personated Ajax.

At the two last schools he used to represent himself as having lost part of what Taverner had taught him, and on his master at Twyford he had already exercised his poetry in a lampoon. Yet under those masters he translated more than a fourth part of the *Metamorphoses*. If he kept the same proportion in his other exercises it cannot be thought that his loss was great.

He tells of himself in his poems that 'he lisp'd in numbers,' and used to say that he could not remember the time when he began to make verses. In the style of fiction it might have been said of him as of Pindar,[5]

17

that when he lay in his cradle, 'the bees swarmed about his mouth.'

About the time of the Revolution his father, who was undoubtedly disappointed by the sudden blast of popish prosperity, quitted his trade, and retired to Binfield in Windsor Forest, with about twenty thousand pounds, for which, being conscientiously determined not to entrust it to the government, he found no better use than that of locking it up in a chest, and taking from it what his expenses required; and his life was long enough to consume a great part of it, before his son came to the inheritance.

To Binfield Pope was called by his father when he was about twelve years old; and there he had for a few months the assistance of one Deane, another priest, of whom he learned only to construe a little of Tully's[6] *Offices*. How Mr. Deane could spend, with a boy who had translated so much of *Ovid*, some months over a small part of Tully's *Offices*, it is now vain to enquire.

Of a youth so successfully employed, and so conspicuously improved, a minute account must be naturally desired; but curiosity must be contented with confused, imperfect, and sometimes improbable intelligence. Pope, finding little advantage from external help, resolved thenceforward to direct himself, and at twelve formed a plan of study which he completed with little other incitement than the desire of excellence.

His primary and principal purpose was to be a poet, with which his father accidentally concurred, by proposing subjects, and obliging him to correct his performances by many revisals; after which the old gentleman, when he was satisfied, would say, 'these are good rhymes.'

In his perusal of the English poets he soon distinguished the versification of Dryden,[7] which he considered as the model to be studied, and was impressed with such veneration for his instructer that he persuaded some friends to take him to the coffee-house which Dryden frequented, and pleased himself with having seen him.

Dryden died May 1, 1701, some days before Pope was twelve: so early must he therefore have felt the power of harmony, and the zeal of genius. Who does not wish that Dryden could have known the value of the homage that was paid him, and foreseen the greatness of his young admirer?

The earliest of Pope's productions is his *Ode on Solitude*, written before he was twelve, in which there is nothing more than other forward boys have attained, and which is not equal to Cowley's[8] performances at the same age.

His time was now spent wholly in reading and writing. As he read the Classicks he amused himself with translating them; and at fourteen made a version of the first book of the *Thebais*,[9] which, with some revision, he afterwards published. He must have been at this time, if he had no help, a considerable proficient in the Latin tongue.

By Dryden's *Fables*,[10] which had then been not long published, and were much in the hands of poetical readers, he was tempted to try his own skill in giving Chaucer a more fashionable appearance, and put

January and May, and the *Prologue of the Wife of Bath*, into modern English. He translated likewise the *Epistle of Sappho to Phaon* from Ovid, to complete the version, which was before imperfect, and wrote some other small pieces, which he afterwards printed.

He sometimes imitated the English poets, and professed to have written at fourteen his poem upon *Silence*, after Rochester's[11] *Nothing*. He had now formed his versification, and in the smoothness of his numbers surpassed his original; but this is a small part of his praise: he discovers such acquaintance both with human life and public affairs as is not easily conceived to have been attainable by a boy of fourteen in Windsor Forest.

Next year he was desirous of opening to himself new sources of knowledge, by making himself acquainted with modern languages, and removed for a time to London that he might study French and Italian, which, as he desired nothing more than to read them, were by diligent application soon despatched. Of Italian learning he does not appear to have ever made much use in his subsequent studies.

He then returned to Binfield, and delighted himself with his own poetry. He tried all styles, and many subjects. He wrote a comedy, a tragedy, an epick poem, with panegyricks on all the princes of Europe; and, as he confesses, 'thought himself the greatest genius that ever was.' Self-confidence is the first requisite to great undertakings; he, indeed, who forms his opinion of himself in solitude, without knowing the powers of other men, is very liable to error: but it was the felicity of Pope to rate himself at his real value.

Most of his puerile productions were by his maturer judgement afterwards destroyed; *Alcander*, the epick poem, was burnt by the persuasion of Atterbury. The tragedy was founded on the legend of St. Genevieve. Of the comedy there is no account.

Concerning his studies it is related that he translated Tully *On old Age*, and that, besides his books of poetry and criticism, he read Temple's[12] *Essays* and Locke[13] *On human Understanding*. His reading, though his favourite authors are not known, appears to have been sufficiently extensive and multifarious; for his early pieces shew, with sufficient evidence, his knowledge of books.

He that is pleased with himself easily imagines that he shall please others. Sir William Trumbal, who had been ambassador at Constantinople, and secretary of state, when he retired from business fixed his residence in the neighbourhood of Binfield. Pope, not yet sixteen, was introduced to the statesman of sixty, and so distinguished himself that their interviews ended in friendship and correspondence. Pope was through his whole life ambitious of splendid acquaintance, and he seems to have wanted neither diligence nor success in attracting the notice of the great; for from his first entrance into the world, and his entrance was very early, he was admitted to familiarity with those whose rank or station made them most conspicuous.

From the age of sixteen the life of Pope as an author may be properly computed. He now wrote his *Pastorals*, which were shewn to the poets

19

and criticks of that time; as they well deserved they were read with admiration, and many praises were bestowed upon them and upon the Preface, which is both elegant and learned in a high degree: they were, however, not published till five years afterwards.

Cowley, Milton[14] and Pope are distinguished among the English Poets by the early exertion of their powers; but the works of Cowley alone were published in his childhood, and therefore of him only can it be certain that his puerile performances received no improvement from his maturer studies.

At this time began his acquaintance with Wycherley,[15] a man who seems to have had among his contemporaries his full share of reputation, to have been esteemed without virtue, and caressed without good-humour. Pope was proud of his notice; Wycherley wrote verses in his praise, which he was charged by Dennis[16] with writing to himself, and they agreed for a while to flatter one another. It is pleasant to remark how soon Pope learned the cant of an author, and began to treat criticks with contempt, though he had yet suffered nothing from them.

But the fondness of Wycherley was too violent to last. His esteem of Pope was such that he submitted some poems to his revision; and when Pope, perhaps proud of such confidence, was sufficiently bold in his criticisms and liberal in his alterations, the old scribbler was angry to see his pages defaced, and felt more pain from the detection than content from the amendment of his faults. They parted; but Pope always considered him with kindness, and visited him a little time before he died.

Another of his early correspondents was Mr. Cromwell, of whom I have learned nothing particular but that he used to ride a-hunting in a tye-wig. He was fond, and perhaps vain, of amusing himself with poetry and criticism, and sometimes sent his performances to Pope, who did not forbear such remarks as were now and then unwelcome. Pope, in his turn, put the juvenile version of Statius into his hands for correction.

Their correspondence afforded the publick its first knowledge of Pope's epistolary powers; for his letters were given by Cromwell to one Mrs. Thomas, and she many years afterwards sold them to Curll,[17] who inserted them in a volume of his *Miscellanies*.

Walsh, a name yet preserved among the minor poets, was one of his first encouragers. His regard was gained by the *Pastorals*, and from him Pope received the counsel by which he seems to have regulated his studies. Walsh advised him to correctness, which, as he told him, the English poets had hitherto neglected, and which therefore was left to him as a basis of fame; and, being delighted with rural poems, recommended to him to write a pastoral comedy, like those which are read so eagerly in Italy; a design which Pope probably did not approve, as he did not follow it.

Pope had now declared himself a poet; and, thinking himself entitled to poetical conversation, began at seventeen to frequent Will's, a coffee-house on the north side of Russel-street in Covent-garden, where the wits of that time used to assemble, and where Dryden had, when he lived, been accustomed to preside.

During this period of his life he was indefatigably diligent, and insatiably curious; wanting health for violent, and money for expensive pleasures, and having certainly excited in himself very strong desires of intellectual eminence, he spent much of his time over his books: but he read only to store his mind with facts and images, seizing all that his authors presented with undistinguishing voracity, and with an appetite for knowledge too eager to be nice. In a mind like his, however, all the faculties were at once involuntarily improving. Judgement is forced upon us by experience. He that reads many books must compare one opinion or one style with another; and when he compares, must necessarily distinguish, reject, and prefer. But the account given by himself of his studies was that from fourteen to twenty he read only for amusement, from twenty to twenty-seven for improvement and instruction; that in the first part of this time he desired only to know, and in the second he endeavoured to judge.

[Johnson proceeds to describe the writing and publication of Pope's early work, the *Pastorals* of 1709, the *Essay on Criticism* (1711), *The Rape of the Lock* (1712) and *Windsor Forest* (1713), leading up to the poem which finally established Pope as the leading poet of his age, his version of Homer's *Iliad*. Our remaining two extracts deal with this poem.]

The next year (1713) produced a bolder attempt, by which profit was sought as well as praise. The poems which he had hitherto written, however they might have diffused his name, had made very little addition to his fortune. The allowance which his father made him, though, proportioned to what he had, it might be liberal, could not be large; his religion hindered him from the occupation of any civil employment, and he complained that he wanted even money to buy books.

He therefore resolved to try how far the favour of the publick extended, by soliciting a subscription to a version of the *Iliad*, with large notes.

To print by subscription was, for some time, a practice peculiar to the English. The first considerable work for which this expedient was employed is said to have been Dryden's *Virgil*[18] and it had been tried again with great success when *The Tatlers*[19] were collected into volumes.

There was reason to believe that Pope's attempt would be successful. He was in the full bloom of reputation, and was personally known to almost all whom dignity of employment or splendour of reputation had made eminent; he conversed indifferently with both parties, and never disturbed the publick with his political opinions; and it might be naturally expected, as each faction then boasted its literary zeal, that the great men, who on other occasions practised all the violence of opposition, would emulate each other in their encouragement of a poet who had delighted all, and by whom none had been offended.

With those hopes, he offered an English *Iliad* to subscribers, in six volumes in quarto, for six guineas; a sum, according to the value of money at that time, by no means inconsiderable, and greater than I believe to have been ever asked before.

[Our final extract comes much later in Johnson's *Life of Pope*, where he is discussing Pope's works from a critical point of view.]

The train of my disquisition has now conducted me to that poetical wonder, the translation of the *Iliad*; a performance which no age or nation can pretend to equal. To the Greeks translation was almost unknown; it was totally unknown to the inhabitants of Greece. They had no recourse to the Barbarians[20] for poetical beauties, but sought for every thing in Homer, where, indeed, there is but little which they might not find.

The Italians have been very diligent translators; but I can hear of no version, unless perhaps Anguillara's *Ovid* may be excepted, which is read with eagerness. The *Iliad* of Salvini every reader may discover to be punctiliously exact; but it seems to be the work of a linguist skilfully pedantick, and his countrymen, the proper judges of its power to please, reject it with disgust.

Their predecessors the Romans have left some specimens of translation behind them, and that employment must have had some credit in which Tully and Germanicus[21] engaged; but unless we suppose, what is perhaps true, that the plays of Terence[22] were versions of Menander, nothing translated seems ever to have risen to high reputation. The French, in the meridian hour of their learning, were very laudably industrious to enrich their own language with the wisdom of the ancients; but found themselves reduced, by whatever necessity, to turn the Greek and Roman poetry into prose. Whoever could read an author could translate him. From such rivals little can be feared.

The chief help of Pope in this arduous undertaking was drawn from the versions of Dryden. Virgil had borrowed much of his imagery from Homer, and part of the debt was now paid by his translator. Pope searched the pages of Dryden for happy combinations of heroick diction, but it will not be denied that he added much to what he found. He cultivated our language with so much diligence and art that he has left in his *Homer* a treasure of poetical elegances to posterity. His version may be said to have tuned the English tongue, for since its appearance no writer, however deficient in other powers, has wanted melody. Such a series of lines so elaborately corrected and so sweetly modulated took possession of the publick ear; the vulgar was enamoured of the poem, and the learned wondered at the translation.

But in the most general applause discordant voices will always be heard. It has been objected by some, who wish to be numbered among the sons of learning, that Pope's version of Homer is not Homerical; that it exhibits no resemblance of the original and characteristick manner of the Father of Poetry, as it wants his awful simplicity, his artless grandeur, his unaffected majesty. This cannot be totally denied, but it must be remembered that 'necessitas quod cogit defendit,' that may be lawfully done which cannot be forborne. Time and place will always enforce regard. In estimating this translation consideration must be had of the nature of our language, the form of our metre, and, above all, of the change which two thousand years have made in the modes of life and the habits of thought. Virgil wrote in a language of the same general fabrick with that of Homer, in verses of the same measure, and in an age nearer to Homer's time by eighteen hundred years; yet he found even then the state of the world so much altered, and the demand for elegance so much increased, that mere nature would be endured no longer; and perhaps, in the multitude of borrowed passages, very few can be shewn which he has not embellished.

There is a time when nations emerging from barbarity, and falling into regular subordination, gain leisure to grow wise, and feel the shame of ignorance and the craving pain of unsatisfied curiosity. To this hunger of the mind plain sense is grateful; that which fills the void removes uneasiness, and to be free from pain for a while is pleasure; but repletion generates fastidiousness, a saturated intellect soon becomes luxurious, and knowledge finds no willing reception till it is recommended by artificial diction. Thus it will be found in the progress of learning that in all nations the first writers are simple, and that every age improves in elegance. One refinement always makes way for another, and what was expedient to Virgil was necessary to Pope.

I suppose many readers of the English *Iliad*, when they have been touched with some unexpected beauty of the lighter kind, have tried to enjoy it in the original, where, alas! it was not to be found. Homer doubtless owes to his translator many Ovidian graces not exactly suitable to his character; but to have added can be no great crime if nothing be taken away. Elegance is surely to be desired if it be not gained at the expence of dignity. A hero would wish to be loved as well as to be reverenced.

To a thousand cavils one answer is sufficient; the purpose of a writer is to be read, and the criticism which would destroy the power of pleasing must be blown aside. Pope wrote for his own age and his own nation: he knew that it was necessary to colour the images and point the sentiments of his author; he therefore made him graceful, but lost him some of his sublimity.

Notes

1   John Ogilby (1600–76), author and printer, published verse translations of Virgil and Homer.

2   The great Greek epic poet (his date of birth is variously placed between 1050 and 850 B.C.), author of the *Iliad* and the *Odyssey*. The *Iliad* is in 24 books, and concerns the siege of Troy and 'Achilles' Wrath' (see Pope's *Iliad*, Book 1, 1).

3   George Sandys (1578–1644) published a verse translation (1621–6) of Ovid's *Metamorphoses*.

4   Publius Ovidius Naso (43 B.C.–A.D. 18) the Roman poet and author of *Metamorphoses*, a series of mythological tales in verse.

5   Pindar (*c.*522–442 B.C.), the celebrated Greek lyric poet, best known for his *Epinicia* or triumphal odes.

6   'Tully' was the English name for Marcus Tullius Cicero (106–43 B.C.), Roman statesman and student of law and philosophy whose writings included *De Oratore* (on the art of rhetoric) and *De Officiis* (on moral philosophy).

7   John Dryden (see p. 8, note 4) dominated literature in the generation before Pope. He was master of the rhyming couplet which Pope was to develop for his own purposes.

8   Abraham Cowley (1618–67), diplomatist and poet renowned for his precocity (he composed an epical romance *Pyramus and Thisbe*, aged ten, and the epic *Constantia and Philetus*, aged twelve).

9   An epic poem in 12 books by the Roman poet Publius Papinus Statius (*c.* A.D. 40–96) on the war on Thebes.

10   Dryden's *Fables, Ancient and Modern* (1699) was a collection of translations of tales by Chaucer, Boccaccio, Ovid and Homer. They included the first translation into English of the First Book of the *Iliad*.

11   Rochester (John Wilmot, Second Earl of, 1648–80), poet and libertine. His poem 'Upon Nothing' (1679) is a sardonically ironic contemplation of this 'Great Negative' related to philosophical notions about the origin and nature of the world.

12   Sir William Temple (1628–99), diplomat and author whose three volumes of *Miscellanies* (1680, 1692 and 1701) contain essays on various subjects.

13   John Locke (1632–1704) see p. 35, note 1.

14   John Milton (1608–74), the poet and author of *Lycidas*, *Paradise Lost*, *Samson Agonistes*, etc.

15   William Wycherley (1640–1716), comic playwright and friend of Pope who revised many of his works.

16   John Dennis (see p. 15, note 4) was satirized by Pope (with whom he had a literary feud) in his *Essay on Criticism* (iii, 585–8).

17   Edmund Curll (1675–1747), bookseller and pamphleteer, was known for his literary frauds and referred to by Pope in the *Dunciad* (i, 40).

18   Dryden wrote a much-admired verse translation of the whole of the Roman poet Virgil's works. It appeared in its entirety in 1697.

19   This refers to the famous periodical *The Tatler*, edited by Richard Steele and Joseph Addison, which was published (for some time thrice-weekly) between 1709 and 1711.

20   The word 'barbarians' is of Greek origin and for an ancient Greek meant simply 'foreigner'.

21   The Roman general Germanicus Caesar (15 B.C.–A.D. 19), an adopted son of the emperor Tiberius. He conquered most of Germany, and was also an author, leaving fragments of a Latin translation of the *Phaenomena* of Aratus, a Greek poem about astronomy.

22   The Roman comic dramatist Publius Terentius Afer (*c.* 190–159 B.C.) He wrote six plays; most of them are now definitely known to have been based on the comedies of the Greek dramatist Menander (*c.* 342–292 B.C.)

HENRY FIELDING

A Comic Epic Poem in Prose (1742)

From Henry Fielding, *The History of the Adventures of Joseph Andrews and his Friend Mr. Abraham Adams, Written in Imitation of the Manner of Cervantes, Author of Don Quixote*, Printed for A. Millar, Strand, London 1742. Reprinted from *Joseph Andrews*, J. M. Dent and Sons Ltd., London 1960.

The Preface to Fielding's first novel *Joseph Andrews* has particular interest in that Fielding describes himself as the inventor of a new literary *genre* –and this *genre* is, more or less, the Novel as we now understand the term. Not quite, perhaps; for he speaks of this new *genre* as being essentially and exclusively a *comic* form. It is also worth mentioning that his claim to be the inventor of the form is not quite justified, for he had at least one predecessor, in Daniel Defoe, one or two of whose books, for instance *Moll Flanders* (1722), seem indisputably to be novels in our modern sense. One precursor he does mention, though on the title-page rather than in the Preface, is Cervantes, whose *Don Quixote* (1605) has a strong claim to be considered the first novel.

As will be seen, Fielding does not apply the name 'Novel' to his new *genre*, choosing instead a term (comic poem in prose) drawn from traditional literary categories. (In *Tom Jones*, Book V Chapter 1, he speaks of it as the 'prosai-comi-epic' style of writing.) And in *Joseph Andrews*, as in *Tom Jones*, he sometimes, as he says, adopts a *burlesque* (or mock-heroic) diction, a device largely dropped by later novelists. (There is a famous burlesque or mock-heroic episode – the battle in the churchyard – in Book IV, Chapter 8 of *Tom Jones*.)

A further point of interest in the Preface is that it demonstrates the great importance of Hogarth to the birth of the novel.

As it is possible the mere English reader may have a different idea of romance from the author of these little volumes,[1] and may consequently expect a kind of entertainment not to be found, nor which was even intended, in the following pages, it may not be improper to premise a few words concerning this kind of writing, which I do not remember to have seen hitherto attempted in our language.

The EPIC, as well as the DRAMA, is divided into tragedy and comedy. HOMER, who was the father of this species of poetry, gave us a pattern of both these, though that of the latter kind is entirely lost; which Aristotle[2] tells us, bore the same relation to comedy which his Iliad bears to tragedy. And perhaps, that we have no more instances of it among the writers of antiquity, is owing to the loss of this great pattern, which, had it survived, would have found its imitators equally with the other poems of this great original.

And farther, as this poetry may be tragic or comic, I will not scruple to say it may be likewise either in verse or prose: for though it wants one particular, which the critic enumerates in the constituent parts of an epic poem, namely metre; yet, when any kind of writing contains all its other parts, such as fable, action, characters, sentiments, and diction, and is deficient in metre only, it seems, I think, reasonable to refer it to the epic; at least, as no critic hath thought proper to range it under any other head, or to assign it a particular name to itself.

Thus the Telemachus[3] of the archbishop of Cambray appears to me of the epic kind, as well as the Odyssey of Homer; indeed, it is much fairer and more reasonable to give it a name common with that species from which it differs only in a single instance, than to confound it with those which it resembles in no other. Such are those voluminous works, commonly called Romances, namely, Clelia, Cleopatra, Astræa, Cassandra, the Grand Cyrus,[4] and innumerable others, which contain, as I apprehend, very little instruction or entertainment.

Now a comic romance is a comic epic poem in prose; differing from comedy, as the serious epic from tragedy: its action being more extended and comprehensive; containing a much larger circle of incidents, and introducing a greater variety of characters. It differs from the serious romance in its fable and action, in this; that as in the one these are grave and solemn, so in the other they are light and ridiculous: it differs in its characters by introducing persons of inferior rank, and consequently, of inferior manners, whereas the grave romance sets the highest before us: lastly, in its sentiments and diction; by preserving the ludicrous instead of the sublime. In the diction, I think, burlesque itself may be sometimes admitted; of which many instances will occur in this work, as in the description of the battles, and some other places, not necessary to be pointed out to the classical reader, for whose entertainment those parodies or burlesque imitations are chiefly calculated.

But though we have sometimes admitted this in our diction, we have carefully excluded it from our sentiments and characters; for there it is never properly introduced, unless in writings of the burlesque kind, which this is not intended to be. Indeed, no two species of writing can differ more widely than the comic and the burlesque; for as the latter is ever the exhibition of what is monstrous and unnatural, and where our delight, if we examine it, arises from the surprising absurdity, as in appropriating the manners of the highest to the lowest, or *è converso*; so in the former we should ever confine ourselves strictly to nature, from the just imitation of which will flow all the pleasure we can this way convey to a sensible reader. And perhaps there is one reason why a comic writer should of all others be the least excused for deviating from nature, since it may not be always so easy for a serious poet to meet with the great and the admirable; but life everywhere furnishes an accurate observer with the ridiculous.

I have hinted this little concerning burlesque, because I have often heard that name given to performances which have been truly of the comic kind, from the author's having sometimes admitted it in his diction only; which, as it is the dress of poetry, doth, like the dress of men, establish characters (the one of the whole poem, and the other of the whole man), in vulgar opinion, beyond any of their greater excellences: but surely, a certain drollery in stile, where characters and sentiments are perfectly natural, no more constitutes the burlesque, than an empty pomp and dignity of words, where everything else is mean and low, can entitle any performance to the appellation of the true sublime.

And I apprehend my Lord Shaftesbury's opinion[5] of mere burlesque agrees with mine, when he asserts, 'there is no such thing to be found in the writings of the ancients.' But perhaps I have less abhorrence than he professes for it; and that, not because I have had some little success on the stage this way, but rather as it contributes more to exquisite mirth and laughter than any other; and these are probably more wholesome physic for the mind, and conduce better to purge away spleen, melancholy, and ill affections, than is generally imagined. Nay, I will appeal to common observation, whether the same companies are not found more full of good-humour and benevolence, after they have been sweetened for two or three hours with entertainments of this kind, than when soured by a tragedy or a grave lecture.

But to illustrate all this by another science, in which, perhaps, we shall see the distinction more clearly and plainly, let us examine the works of a comic history painter, with those performances which the Italians call Caricatura, where we shall find the true excellence of the former to consist in the exactest copying of nature; insomuch that a judicious eye instantly rejects anything *outré*,[6] any liberty which the painter hath taken with the features of that *alma mater*;[7] whereas in the Caricatura we allow all licence – its aim is to exhibit monsters, not men; and all distortions and exaggerations whatever are within its proper province.

Now, what Caricatura is in painting, Burlesque is in writing; and in the same manner the comic writer and painter correlate to each other. And here I shall observe, that, as in the former the painter seems to have the advantage; so it is in the latter infinitely on the side of the writer; for the Monstrous is much easier to paint than describe, and the Ridiculous to describe than paint.

And though perhaps this latter species doth not in either science so strongly affect and agitate the muscles as the other; yet it will be owned, I believe, that a more rational and useful pleasure arises to us from it. He who should call the ingenious Hogarth a burlesque painter, would, in my opinion, do him very little honour; for sure it is much easier, much less the subject of admiration, to paint a man with a nose, or any other feature, of a preposterous size, or to expose him in some absurd or monstrous attitude, than to express the affections of men on canvas. It hath been thought a vast commendation of a painter to say his figures seem to breathe; but surely it is a much greater and nobler applause, that they appear to think.

But to return. The Ridiculous only, as I have before said, falls within my province in the present work. Nor will some explanation of this word be thought impertinent by the reader, if he considers how wonderfully it hath been mistaken, even by writers who have professed it: for to what but such a mistake can we attribute the many attempts to ridicule the blackest villanies, and, what is yet worse, the most dreadful calamities? What could exceed the absurdity of an author, who should write the comedy of Nero,[8] with the merry incident of ripping up his mother's belly? or what would give a greater shock to humanity than an attempt to expose the miseries of poverty and distress to ridicule? And yet the reader will not want much learning to suggest such instances to himself.

Besides, it may seem remarkable, that Aristotle, who is so fond and free of definitions, hath not thought proper to define the Ridiculous. Indeed, where he tells us it is proper to comedy, he hath remarked that villany is not its object: but he hath not, as I remember, positively asserted what is. Nor doth the Abbé Bellegarde,[9] who hath written a treatise on this subject, though he shows us many species of it, once trace it to its fountain.

The only source of the true Ridiculous (as it appears to me) is affectation. But though it arises from one spring only, when we consider the infinite streams into which this one branches, we shall presently cease to admire at the copious field it affords to an observer. Now, affectation proceeds from one of these two causes, vanity or hypocrisy: for as vanity puts us on affecting false characters, in order to purchase applause; so hypocrisy sets us on an endeavour to avoid censure, by concealing our vices under an appearance of their opposite virtues. And though these two causes are often confounded (for there is some difficulty in distinguishing them), yet, as they proceed from very different motives, so they are as clearly distinct in their operations: for indeed, the affectation which arises from vanity is nearer to truth than the other, as it hath not that violent repugnancy of nature to struggle with, which that of the hypocrite hath. It may be likewise noted, that affectation doth not imply an absolute negation of those qualities which are affected; and, therefore, though, when it proceeds from hypocrisy, it be nearly allied to deceit; yet when it comes from vanity only, it partakes of the nature of ostentation: for instance, the affectation of liberality in a vain man differs visibly from the same affectation in the avaricious; for though the vain man is not what he would appear, or hath not the virtue he affects, to the degree he would be thought to have it; yet it sits less awkwardly on him than on the avaricious man, who is the very reverse of what he would seem to be.

From the discovery of this affectation arises the Ridiculous, which always strikes the reader with surprise and pleasure; and that in a higher and stronger degree when the affectation arises from hypocrisy than when from vanity; for to discover any one to be the exact reverse of what he affects, is more surprising, and consequently more ridiculous, than to find him a little deficient in the quality he desires the reputation of. I might observe that our Ben Jonson,[10] who of all men understood the Ridiculous the best, hath chiefly used the hypocritical affectation.

Now, from affectation only, the misfortunes and calamities of life, or the imperfections of nature, may become the objects of ridicule. Surely he hath a very ill-framed mind who can look on ugliness, infirmity, or poverty, as ridiculous in themselves: nor do I believe any man living, who meets a dirty fellow riding through the streets in a cart, is struck with an idea of the Ridiculous from it; but if he should see the same figure descend from his coach and six, or bolt from his chair with his hat under his arm, he would then begin to laugh, and with justice. In the same manner, were we to enter a poor house and behold a wretched family shivering with cold and languishing with hunger, it would not incline us to laughter (at least we must have very diabolical natures if it would); but should we discover there a grate, instead of coals, adorned with flowers, empty plate or china dishes on the sideboard, or any other affectation of riches and finery, either on their persons or in their furniture, we might then indeed be excused for ridiculing so fantastical an appearance. Much less are natural imperfections the object of derision; but when ugliness aims at the applause of beauty, or lameness endeavours to display agility, it is then that these unfortunate circumstances, which at first moved our compassion, tend only to raise our mirth.

The poet[11] carries this very far:

> None are for being what they are in fault,
> But for not begin what they would be thought.

Where if the metre would suffer the word Ridiculous to close the first line, the thought would be rather more proper. Great vices are the proper objects of our detestation, smaller faults, of our pity; but affectation appears to me the only true source of the Ridiculous.

But perhaps it may be objected to me, that I have against my own rules introduced vices, and of a very black kind, into this work. To which I shall answer: first, that it is very difficult to pursue a series of human actions, and keep clear from them. Secondly, that the vices to be found here are rather the accidental consequences of some human frailty or foible, than causes habitually existing in the mind. Thirdly, that they are never set forth as the objects of ridicule, but detestation. Fourthly, that they are never the principal figure at that time on the scene: and lastly, they never produce the intended evil.

Having thus distinguished Joseph Andrews from the productions of romance writers on the one hand and burlesque writers on the other, and given some few very short hints (for I intended no more) of this species of writing, which I have affirmed to be hitherto unattempted in our language; I shall leave to my good-natured reader to apply my piece to my observations, and will detain him no longer than with a word concerning the characters in this work.

And here I solemnly protest I have no intention to vilify or asperse any one; for though everything is copied from the book of nature, and scarce a character or action produced which I have not taken from my own observations and experience; yet I have used the utmost care to obscure the persons by such different circumstances, degrees, and colours, that it will be impossible to guess at them with any degree of certainty; and if it ever happens otherwise, it is only where the failure characterised is so minute, that it is a foible only which the party himself may laugh at as well as any other.

As to the character of Adams,[12] as it is the most glaring in the whole, so I conceive it is not to be found in any book now extant. It is designed a character of perfect simplicity; and as the goodness of his heart will recommend him to the good-natured, so I hope it will excuse me to the gentlemen of his cloth; for whom, while they are worthy of their sacred order, no man can possibly have a greater respect. They will therefore excuse me, notwithstanding the low adventures in which he is engaged, that I have made him a clergyman; since no other office could have given him so many opportunities of displaying his worthy inclinations.

Notes

1 *Joseph Andrews* was originally published in two volumes.
2 A reference to the *Poetics* of the Greek philosopher Aristotle (384–322B.C.).
3 i.e. *Télémaque* (1699) a didactic romance by Fénélon, Archibishop of Cambrai, about Telemachus, son of Odysseus the hero of Homer's epic *The Odyssey*.
4 High-flown prose romances by Mme. de Scudéry (1607–1701), Honoré D'Urfé (1567–1625), etc.
5 A reference to *Sensus Communis: An Essay on the Freedom of Wit and Humour* (1709) by Anthony Ashley Cooper, 3rd Earl of Shaftesbury (1671–1713).
6 (French) exceptional or abnormal.
7 (Latin) dear mother; a traditional phrase for 'mother' nature.
8 The dissolute Roman emperor Nero (A.D.37–68) had his mother Agrippina murdered to please his mistress.
9 Jean Baptiste Morvan de Bellegarde, known as L'Abbé de Bellegarde, published *Réflexions sur le ridicule* in 1696. It was translated into English in 1706.
10 The great comic dramatist and contemporary of Shakespeare, author of *Volpone* (1607), *The Alchemist* (1610), etc.
11 William Congreve (1670–1729). The quotation comes from *Of Pleasing; An Epistle to Sir Richard Temple*, II, 63–4.
12 For much of *Joseph Andrews* the hero travels in the company of the generous, quixotic and gullible Anglican parson Abraham Adams, the most celebrated character in the book.

JOHN TOLAND

Christianity Not Mysterious (1696)

From John Toland, *Christianity Not Mysterious: Or, a treatise showing, that there is nothing in the Gospel contrary to reason, nor above it: and that no Christian Doctrine can be properly called a mystery*, London, 1696.

John Toland (1670–1722) was born in Ireland of Roman Catholic parents but was converted to Protestantism in youth. He was sent to school by some 'eminent dissenters', attended the University of Leyden and came under the influence of John Locke.[1] His *Christianity Not Mysterious*, published when he was still a very young man, argued that the superiority of Christianity is precisely that it makes plain and comprehensible what is mysterious in other religions, and it called for a return to the simplicity of primitive Christianity as against the mysteries and quackeries with which priests had later loaded it (in which he seems tacitly to have included the doctrine of the Trinity). His book created much scandal and was condemned to be burned by the common hangman, but it began a fashion in Britain for deistical writings which lasted for several decades.

The argument presented in the following extract, viz. that it is absurd to speak of believing in propositions to which the human mind can give no clear meaning, is central to his book.

That the Doctrines of the Gospel are not contrary to Reason.

After having said so much of *Reason*, I need not operosely[2] shew what it is to be contrary to it; for I take it to be very intelligible from the precedent Section, that *what is evidently repugnant to clear and distinct Idea's, or to our common Notions, is contrary to Reason*: I go on therefore to prove, that *the Doctrines of the Gospel*, if it be the Word of God, *cannot be so*. But if it be objected, that very few maintain they are: I reply, that no *Christian* I know of now (for we shall not disturb the Ashes of the Dead) expresly says *Reason* and the *Gospel* are contrary to one another. But, which returns to the same, very many affirm, that though the Doctrines of the latter cannot in themselves be contradictory to the Principles of the former, as proceeding both from God; yet, that according to our Conceptions of them, *they may seem directly to clash*: And that though we cannot reconcile them by reason of our corrupt and limited Understandings; yet that from the Authority of *Divine Revelation*, we are bound to believe and acquiesce in them; or, as the *Fathers* taught 'em to speak, *to adore what we cannot comprehend*.

The Absurdity and Effects of admitting any real or seeming Contradictions in Religion.

This famous and admirable Doctrine is the undoubted Source of all the *Absurdities* that ever were seriously vented among *Christians*. Without the Pretence of it, we should never hear of the *Transubstantiation*,[3] and other ridiculous Fables of the Church of *Rome*; nor of any of the *Eastern Ordures*,[4] almost all receiv'd into this *Western Sink*:[5] Nor should we be ever banter'd[6] with the *Lutheran Impanation*,[7] or the *Ubiquity*[8] it has produc'd, as one Monster ordinarily begets another. And tho the *Socinians*[9] disown this Practice, I am mistaken if either they or the *Arians*[10] can make their Notions of a *dignifi'd and Creature-God capable of Divine Worship*, appear more reasonable than the Extravagancies of other Sects touching the Article of the *Trinity*.

In short, this Doctrine is the known Refuge of some Men, when they are at a loss in explaining any Passage of the Word of God. Lest they should appear to others less knowing than they would be thought, they make nothing of fathering that upon the secret Counsels of the Almighty, or the Nature of the Thing, which is indeed the Effect of Inaccurate Reasoning, Unskilfulness in the Tongues, or Ignorance of History. But more commonly it is the Consequence of *early Impressions*, which they dare seldom afterwards correct by more free and riper Thoughts: *So desiring to be Teachers of the Law, and understanding neither what they say, nor those things which they affirm*, they obtrude upon us for *Doctrines the Commandments of Men*. And truly well they may; for if we once admit this Principle, I know not what we can deny that is told us in the Name of the Lord. This Doctrine, I must remark it too, does highly concern us of the *Laity*; for however it came to be first establish'd, the *Clergy* (always excepting such as deserve it) have not been since wanting to themselves, but improv'd it so far as not only to make the plainest, but the most trifling things in the World *mysterious*, that we might constantly depend upon them for the Explication. And, nevertheless they must not, if they could, explain them to us without ruining their own Design, let them never so fairly pretend it. But, overlooking all Observations proper for this Place, let us enter upon the immediate Examen of the Opinion it self.

I Tim. 1:7.[11]
Matt. 15:9.

32

The first thing I shall insist upon is, that if any Doctrine of the *New Testament* be contrary to Reason, we have no manner of Idea of it. To say, for instance, that *a Ball is white and black at once*, is to say just nothing; for these Colours are so incompatible in the same Subject, as to exclude all Possibility of a real positive Idea or Conception. So to say, as the *Papists*, that *Children dying before Baptism are damn'd without Pain*, signifies nothing at all: For if they be intelligent Creatures in the other World, to be eternally excluded God's Presence, and the Society of the Blessed, must prove ineffable Torment to them: But if they think they have no Understanding, then they are not capable of Damnation in their Sense; and so they should not say they are in *Limbo*-Dungeon;[12] but that either they had no Souls, or were annihilated; which (had it been true, as they can never shew) would be reasonable enough, and easily conceiv'd. Now if we have no Idea's of a thing, it is certainly but lost Labour for us to trouble our selves about it: For what I don't conceive, can no more give me right Notions of God, or influence my Actions, than a Prayer deliver'd in an unknown Tongue can excite my Devotion: *If the Trumpet gives an uncertain Sound, who shall prepare himself to the Battel? And except Words easy to be understood be utter'd, how shall it be known what is spoken?* Syllables, though never so well put together, if they have not Idea's fix'd to them, are but *Words spoken in the Air*; and cannot be the Ground of a *reasonable Service*, or Worship.

I Cor. 14: 8, 9.
Ver. 9.
Rom. 12:1.

If any should think to evade the Difficulty by saying, that the Idea's of certain Doctrines may be contrary indeed to common Notions, yet consistent with themselves, and I know not what supra-intellectual Truths, he's but just where he was. But supposing a little that the thing were so; it still follows, that none can understand these Doctrines except their Perceptions be communicated to him in an extraordinary manner, as by new Powers and Organs. And then too, others cannot be edifi'd by what is discours'd of 'em, unless they enjoy the same Favour. So that if I would go preach the Gospel to the *Wild Indians*, I must expect the Idea's of my Words should be, I know not how infus'd into their Souls in order to apprehend me: And according to this Hypothesis, they could no more, without a Miracle, understand my Speech than the chirping of Birds; and *if they knew not the Meaning of my Voice, I should even to them be a Barbarian*, notwithstanding I *spoke Mysteries in the Spirit*. But what do they mean by consisting with themselves, yet not with our common Notions? *Four* may be call'd *Five* in Heaven; but so the Name only is chang'd, the Thing remains still the same. And since we cannot in this World know any thing but by our common Notions, how shall we be sure of this pretended Consistency between our present seeming Contradictions, and the Theology of the World to come? For as 'tis by *Reason* we arrive at the Certainty of God's own Existence, so we cannot otherwise discern his *Revelations* but by their Conformity with our natural Notices of him, which is in so many words, to agree with our common Notions.

I Cor.14:11.
Ver. 2

The next thing I shall remark is, That those, who stick not to say *they could believe a downright Contradiction to Reason, did they find it contain'd in the*

33

Scripture, do justify all Absurdities whatsoever; and by opposing one Light to another, undeniably make God the Author of all Incertitude. The very Supposition, that Reason might authorize one thing, and the Spirit of God another, throws us into inevitable *Scepticism*; for we shall be at a perpetual Uncertainty which to obey: Nay we can never be sure which is which. For the Proof of the Divinity of *Scripture* depending upon Reason, if the clear Light of the one might be any way contradicted, how shall we be convinc'd of the Infallibility of the other? Reason may err in this Point as well as in any thing else; and we have no particular Promise it shall not, no more than the *Papists* that their Senses may not deceive them in every thing as well as in *Transubstantiation*. To say it bears witness to it self, is equally to establish the *Alcoran*[13] or the *Poran*.[14] And 'twere a notable Argument to tell a *Heathen*, that the Church has declared it, when all Societies will say as much for themselves, if we take their word for it. Besides, it may be, he would ask whence the *Church* had Authority to decide this Matter? And if it should be answer'd from the *Scripture*, a thousand to one but he would divert himself[15] with this Circle. You must believe that the *Scripture* is Divine, because the *Church* has so determined it, and the *Church* has this deciding Authority from the *Scripture*. 'Tis doubted if this Power of the *Church* can be prov'd from the Passages alleged to that Purpose; but the *Church* it self (a Party concern'd) affirms it. Hey-day! are not these eternal Rounds very exquisite Inventions to giddy and entangle the Unthinking and the Weak?

But if we believe the *Scripture* to be Divine, not upon its own bare Assertion, but from a real Testimony consisting in the Evidence of the things contain'd therein; from undoubted Effects, and not from Words and Letters; what is this but to prove it by *Reason?* It has in it self, I grant, the brightest Characters of *Divinity*: but 'tis *Reason* finds them out, examines them, and by its Principles approves and pronounces them sufficient; which orderly begets in us an Acquiescence of *Faith* or Perswasion. Now if Particulars be thus severely sifted; if not only the Doctrine of *Christ* and his *Apostles* be consider'd, but also their Lives, Predictions, Miracles and Deaths; surely all this Labour would be in vain, might we upon any account dispense with Contradictions. O! blessed and commodious System, that dischargest at one stroak those troublesome Remarks about History, Language, figurative and literal Senses, Scope of the Writer, Circumstances, and other Helps of Interpretation! We judge of a Man's Wisdom and Learning by his Actions, and his Discourses; but God, who we are assur'd *has not left himself without a Witness*, must have no Privileges above the maddest Enthusiast, or the *Devil* himself, at this rate.

Acts 14:17.

But a Veneration for the very Words of God will be pretended: This we are pleas'd with; for we *Know that God is not a Man that he should lie*. But the Question is not about the Words, but their Sense, which must be always worthy of their Author, and therefore according to the Genius of all Speech, figuratively interpreted, when occasion requires it. Otherwise, under pretence of *Faith in the Word of God*, the highest Follies and

Num. 23:19.

34

Blasphemies may be deduc'd from the Letter of *Scripture*; as, that God is subject to Passions, is the Author of Sin, that *Christ* is a Rock, was actually guilty of and defil'd with our Transgressions, that we are Worms or Sheep, and no Men. And if a Figure[16] be admitted in these Passages, why not, I pray, in all Expressions of the like Nature, when there appears an equal Necessity for it?

It may be demanded why I have so long insisted upon this Article, since that none expressly makes *Scripture* and *Reason* contradictory, was acknowledg'd before. But in the same place mention is made of some who hold, *that they may seem directly to clash*; and that though we cannot reconcile them together, yet that we are bound to acquiesce in the Decisions of the former. A seeming Contradiction is to us as good as a real one: and our Respect for the *Scripture* does not require us to grant any such in it, but rather to conclude, that we are ignorant of the right Meaning when a Difficulty occurs; and so to suspend our Judgments concerning it, till with suitable Helps and Industry we discover the Truth. As for acquiescing in what a Man understands not, or cannot reconcile to his Reason, they know best the fruits of it that practise it. For my part, I'm a Stranger to it, and cannot reconcile my self to such a Principle. On the contrary, I am pretty sure he pretends in vain to convince the Judgment, who explains not the Nature of the Thing. A Man may give his verbal Assent to he knows not what, out of Fear, Superstition, Indifference, Interest, and the like feeble and unfair Motives: but as long as he conceives not what he believes, he cannot sincerely acquiesce in it, and remains depriv'd of all solid Satisfaction. He is constantly perplex'd with Scruples not to be remov'd by his *implicit Faith*; and so is ready to be shaken, and *carried away with every wind of Doctrine*. I will believe because I will believe, that is, *because I'm in the Humour so to do*, is the top of his Apology. Such are unreasonable Men, *walking after the Vanity of their Minds, having their Understandings darkened, being Strangers to the Life of God through the Ignorance that is in them, because of the Hardness of their Hearts.* But he that comprehends a thing, is as sure of it as if he were himself the Author. He can never be brought to suspect his Profession; and, if he be honest, will always render a pertinent account of it to others. Ephes. 4:14. Ephes. 4:17, 18.

The natural Result of what has been said is, That to believe the Divinity of *Scripture*, or the Sense of any Passage thereof, without rational Proofs, and an evident Consistency, is a blameable Credulity, and a temerarious[17] Opinion, ordinarily grounded upon an ignorant and wilful Disposition; but more generally maintain'd out of a gainful Prospect. For we frequently embrace certain Doctrines not from any convincing Evidence in them, but because they serve our Designs better than the Truth; and because other Contradictions we are not willing to quit, are better defended by their means.

Notes
1   John Locke (1632–1704) wrote, among other works, *Essay concerning Human*

Understanding (1690), *Treatises on Government* (1690) and *Reasonableness of Christianity* (1695). He opposed the arguments of Hobbes (see p. 43, note 1) and supported the rights of the individual and his property against those of government. He is often thought of as laying the foundations of Whig political philosophy, a cluster of ideas which became very important in eighteenth-century English politics. (See also p. 142, note 22.)

2   Laboriously.
3   The conversion in the Eucharist of the substance of the bread into the body and of the wine into the blood of Christ, only the appearances of bread and wine remaining.
4   Presumably Toland means the doctrinal mysteries of the Greek Orthodox Church.
5   Cesspool.
6   Cheated or imposed upon.
7   Lutheran modification of the doctrine of the 'Real presence' of Christ's body in the eucharistic bread after consecration. (*Panis* is Latin for bread.)
8   The doctrine of the omnipresence of Christ or of his body.
9   Followers of the sixteenth century Italian theologians Laelius and Socinus, who denied the divinity of Christ. Socinianism, of which Toland himself was accused, was a penal offence in many European countries.
10 Followers of the fourth century Alexandrian theologian Arius, who denied that Christ was consubstantial with God.
11 *I Tim. 1:7,* etc., Toland's Biblical quotations are not exact.
12 It was the doctrine of the Roman Catholic Church that the souls of unbaptized children and of virtuous pagans went at death to a region known as 'Limbo', on the borders of hell, where they were not made to suffer.
13 i.e. The Koran.
14 The Puranas: mythological works written in Sanskrit and sacred to the Hindu.
15 Would be provoked to laughter.
16 Metaphor or allegory.
17 Rash or reckless.

JOSEPH BUTLER

On Compassion (1726)

From Joseph Butler, *Fifteen Sermons Preached at the Rolls' Chapel*. Printed for W. Botham, London, 1726. Reprinted from edition by W. R. Mathews, G. Bell & Sons Ltd., London, 1914.

This is the fifth of *Fifteen Sermons* preached at the Rolls' Chapel by Bishop Joseph Butler (1692–1752), a leading Anglican divine, who was successively Bishop of Bristol and of Durham. His argument that the appetites and the affections are not the enemy of Reason (as they are often represented as being by the more austere schools of religion and philosophy) but its ally, figures also in Pope's *Essay on Man*, and indeed it was one of the main tenets of eighteenth-century optimism. Butler's mode of attack on the theory of Thomas Hobbes[1] (and others) that any apparently altruistic feeling for others is really only disguised self-interest has affinities with that of Hume in his *Enquiry Concerning Morals*.

The Rolls' Chapel was attached to the Rolls' Office in Chancery Lane and was originally the chapel of a house built by Henry III for converted Jews. The Rolls' Office contained the records (mostly in the form of manuscript rolls) of the Court of Chancery.

"Rejoice with them that do rejoice, and weep with them that weep." – Rom. xii. 15.

Every man is to be considered in two capacities, the private and public; as designed to pursue his own interest, and likewise to contribute to the good of others. Whoever will consider, may see, that in general there is no contrariety between these; but that from the original constitution of man, and the circumstances he is placed in, they perfectly coincide, and mutually carry on each other. But, amongst the great variety of affections or principles of action in our nature, some in their primary intention and design seem to belong to the single or private, others to the public or social capacity. The affections required in the text are of the latter sort. When we rejoice in the prosperity of

37

others, and compassionate their distresses, we, as it were, substitute them for ourselves, their interest for our own; and have the same kind of pleasure in their prosperity and sorrow in their distress, as we have from reflection upon our own. Now there is nothing strange or unaccountable in our being thus carried out, and affected towards the interests of others. For, if there be any appetite, or any inward principle besides self-love; why may there not be an affection to the good of our fellow-creatures, and delight from that affection's being gratified, and uneasiness from things going contrary to it?[2]

Of these two, delight in the prosperity of others and compassion for their distresses, the last is felt much more generally than the former. Though men do not universally rejoice with all whom they see rejoice, yet, accidental obstacles removed, they naturally compassionate all in some degree whom they see in distress: so far as they have any real perception or sense of that distress; insomuch that words expressing this latter, pity, compassion, frequently occur; whereas we have scarce any single one, by which the former is distinctly expressed. Congratulation indeed answers condolence: but both these words are intended to signify certain forms of civility, rather than any inward sensation or feeling. This difference or inequality is so remarkable, that we plainly consider compassion as itself an original, distinct, particular affection in human nature; whereas to rejoice in the good of others, is only a consequence of the general affection of love and good-will to them. The reason and account of which matter is this: when a man has obtained any particular advantage or felicity, his end is gained; and he does not in that particular want the assistance of another: there was therefore no need of a distinct affection towards that felicity of another already obtained; neither would such affection directly carry him on to do good to that person: whereas men in distress want assistance; and compassion leads us directly to assist them. The object of the former is the present felicity of another; the object of the latter is the present misery of another. It is easy to see that the latter wants a particular affection for its relief, and that the former does not want one, because it does not want assistance. And upon supposition of a distinct affection in both cases, the one must rest in the exercise of itself, having nothing further to gain; the other does not rest in itself, but carries us on to assist the distressed.

But, supposing these affections natural to the mind, particularly the last; "Has not each man troubles enough of his own? must he indulge an affection which appropriates to himself those of others? which leads him to contract the least desirable of all friendships, friendships with the unfortunate? Must we invert the known rule of prudence, and choose to associate ourselves with the distressed? or, allowing that we ought, so far as it is in our power, to relieve them, yet is it not better to do this from reason and duty? Does not passion and affection of every kind perpetually mislead us? Nay, is not passion and affection itself a weakness, and what a perfect being must be entirely free from?" Perhaps so: but it is mankind I am speaking of; imperfect creatures, and who naturally, and from the condition we are placed in, necessarily depend upon each other. With respect to such creatures, it would be found of as bad consequence to eradicate all natural affections, as to be entirely governed by them. This would almost sink us to the condition of brutes; and that would leave us without a sufficient principle of action. Reason alone, whatever any one may wish, is not in reality a sufficient motive of virtue in such a creature as man; but this reason joined with those affections which God has impressed upon his heart: and when these are allowed scope to exercise themselves, but under strict government and direction of reason; then it is we act suitably to our nature, and to the circumstances God has placed us in. Neither is affection itself at all a weakness; nor does it argue defect, any otherwise than as our senses and appetites do; they belong to our condition of nature, and are what we cannot do without. God Almighty is, to be sure, unmoved by passion or appetite, unchanged by affection; but then it is to be added, that he neither sees, nor hears, nor perceives things by any senses like ours; but in a manner infinitely more perfect. Now, as it is an absurdity almost too gross to be mentioned, for a man to endeavour to get rid of his senses, because the Supreme Being discerns things more perfectly without them; it is as real, though not so obvious an absurdity, to endeavour to eradicate the passions he has given us, because he is without them. For, since our passions are as really a part of our constitution as our senses; since the former as really belong to our condition of nature as the latter; to get rid of either is equally a violation of and breaking in upon that nature and constitution He has given us. Both our senses and our passions are a supply to the imperfection of our nature: thus they show that we are such sort of creatures, as to stand in need of those helps which higher orders of creatures do not. But it is not the supply, but the deficiency; as it is not a remedy, but a disease, which is the imperfection. However, our appetites, passions, senses no way imply disease: nor indeed do they imply deficiency or imperfection of any sort; but only this, that the constitution of nature, according to which God has made us, is such as to require them. And it is far from being true, that a wise man must entirely suppress compassion, and all fellow feeling for others, as a weakness; and trust to reason alone to teach and enforce upon him the practice of the several charities we owe to our kind; that on the contrary, even the bare exercise of such affections would itself be for the good and happiness of the world; and the imperfection of the higher principles of reason and religion in man, the little influence they have upon our practice, and the strength and prevalency of contrary ones, plainly require these affections to be a restraint upon these latter and a supply to the deficiencies of the former.

First, the very exercise itself of these affections in a just and reasonable manner and degree, would upon the whole increase the satisfactions, and lessen the miseries of life.

It is the tendency and business of virtue and religion to procure, as much as may be, universal good-will, trust and friendship amongst mankind. If this could be brought to obtain; and each man enjoyed the happiness of others, as every one does that of a friend; and looked upon the success and prosperity of his neighbour, as every one does upon that of his children and family; it is too manifest to be insisted upon, how much the enjoyments of life would be increased. There would be so much happiness introduced into the world, without any deduction or inconvenience from it, in proportion as the precept of *rejoicing with those who rejoice* was universally obeyed. Our Saviour has owned this good affection as belonging to our nature, in the parable of the *lost sheep*; and does not think it to the disadvantage of a perfect state, to represent its happiness as capable of increase, from reflection upon that of others.

But since in such a creature as man, compassion or sorrow for the distress of others seems so far necessarily connected with joy in their prosperity, as that whoever rejoices in one must unavoidably compassionate the other; there cannot be that delight or satisfaction, which appears to be so considerable, without the inconveniences, whatever they are, of compassion.

However, without considering this connection, there is no doubt but that more good than evil, more delight than sorrow, arises from compassion itself; there being so many things which balance the sorrow of it. There is first the relief which the distressed feel from this affection in others towards them. There is likewise the additional misery which they would feel from the reflection that no one commiserated their case. It is indeed true, that any disposition, prevailing beyond a certain degree, becomes somewhat wrong; and we have ways of speaking, which, though they do not directly express that excess, yet always lead our thoughts to it, and give us the notion of it. Thus, when mention is made of delight in being pitied, this always conveys to our mind the notion of somewhat which is really a weakness: the manner of speaking, I say, implies a certain weakness and feebleness of mind, which is and ought to be disapproved. But men of the greatest fortitude would in distress feel uneasiness, from knowing that no person in the world had any sort of compassion or real concern for them; and in some cases, especially when the temper is enfeebled by sickness or any long and great distress, doubtless would feel a kind of relief even from the helpless good-will and ineffectual assistances of those about them. Over against the sorrow of compassion is likewise to be set a peculiar calm kind of satisfaction, which accompanies it, unless in cases where the distress of another is by some means so brought home to ourselves, as to become in a manner our own; or when from weakness of mind the affection rises too high, which ought to be corrected. This tranquillity or calm satisfaction proceeds, partly from consciousness of a right affection and temper of mind, and partly from a sense of our own freedom from the misery we compassionate. This last may possibly appear to some at first sight faulty; but it really is not so. It is the same with that positive enjoyment, which sudden ease from pain for the present affords, arising from a real sense of misery, joined with a sense of our freedom from it; which in all cases must afford some degree of satisfaction.

To these things must be added the observation, which respects both the affections we are considering; that they who have got over all fellow feeling for others, have withal contracted a certain callousness of heart, which renders them insensible to most other satisfactions, but those of the grossest kind.

Secondly, Without the exercise of these affections, men would certainly be much more wanting in the offices of charity they owe to each other, and likewise more cruel and injurious, than they are at present.

The private interest of the individual would not be sufficiently provided for by reasonable and cool self-love alone; therefore the appetites and passions are placed within as a guard and further security, without which it would not be taken due care of. It is manifest our life would be neglected, were it not for the calls of hunger, and thirst, and weariness; notwithstanding that without them reason would assure us, that the recruits of food and sleep are the necessary means of our preservation. It is therefore absurd to imagine, that, without affection, the same reason alone would be more effectual to engage us to perform the duties we owe to our fellow-creatures. One of this make would be as defective, as much wanting, considered with respect to society, as one of the former make would be defective, or wanting, considered as an individual, or in his private capacity. Is it possible any can in earnest think, that a public spirit, *i.e.* a settled reasonable principle of benevolence to mankind, is so prevalent and strong in the species, as that we may venture to throw off the under affections, which are its assistants, carry it forward and mark out particular courses for it; family, friends, neighbourhood, the distressed, our country? The common joys and the common sorrows, which belong to these relations and circumstances, are as plainly useful to society, as the pain and pleasure belonging to hunger, thirst and weariness are of service to the individual. In defect of that higher principle of reason, compassion is often the only way by which the indigent can have access to us: and therefore to eradicate this, though it is not indeed formally to deny them that assistance which is their due; yet it is to cut them off from that which is too frequently their only way of obtaining it. And as for those who have shut up this door against the complaints of the miserable, and conquered this affection in themselves; even these persons will be under great restraints from the same affection in others. Thus a man who has himself no sense of injustice, cruelty, oppression, will be kept from running the utmost lengths of wickedness, by fear of that detestation, and even resentment of inhumanity, in many particular instances of it, which compassion for the object, towards whom such humanity is exercised, excites in the bulk of mankind. And this is frequently the chief danger, and the chief restraint, which tyrants and the great oppressors of the world feel.

In general, experience will show, that as want of natural appetite to food supposes and proceeds from some bodily disease; so the apathy the Stoics talk of as much supposes, or is accompanied with, somewhat amiss in the moral character, in that which is the health of the mind. Those who formerly aimed at this upon the foot of philosophy, appear to have had better success in eradicating the affections of tenderness and compassion, than they had with the passions of envy, pride and resentment: these latter, at best, were but concealed, and that imperfectly too. How far this observation may be extended to such as endeavour to suppress the natural impulses of their affections, in order to form themselves for business and the world, I shall not determine. But there does not appear any capacity or relation to be named, in which men ought to be entirely deaf to the calls of affection, unless the judicial one is to be excepted.

And as to those who are commonly called the men of pleasure, it is manifest that the reason they set up for hardness of heart, is to avoid being interrupted in their course, by the ruin and misery they are the authors of: neither are persons of this character always the most free from the impotencies of envy and resentment. What may men at last bring themselves to, by suppressing their passions and affections of one kind, and leaving those of the other in their full strength? But surely it might be expected that persons who make pleasure their study and business, if they understood what they profess, would reflect, how many of the entertainments of life, how many of those kind of amusements which seem peculiarly to belong to men of leisure and education, they become insensible to by this acquired hardness of heart.

I shall close these reflections with barely mentioning the behaviour of that divine Person, Who was the example of all perfection in human nature, as represented in the Gospels mourning, and even, in a literal sense, weeping over the distresses of His creatures.

The observation already made, that, of the two affections mentioned in the text, the latter exerts itself much more than the former; that, from the original constitution of human nature, we much more generally and sensibly compassionate the distressed, than rejoice with the prosperous, requires to be particularly considered. This observation therefore, with the reflections which arise out of it, and which it leads our thoughts to, shall be the subject of another Discourse.

For the conclusion of this, let me just take notice of the danger of over-great refinements; of going besides or beyond the plain, obvious, first appearances of things, upon the subject of morals and religion. The least observation will show, how little the generality of men are capable of speculations. Therefore morality and religion must be somewhat plain and easy to be understood: it must appeal to what we call plain common sense, as distinguished from superior capacity and improvement; because it appeals to mankind. Persons of superior capacity and improvement[3] have often fallen into errors, which no one of mere common understanding could. Is it possible that one of this latter character could ever of himself have thought that there was absolutely no such thing in mankind as affection to the good of others; suppose of parents to their children; or that what he felt upon seeing a friend in distress was only fear for himself; or, upon supposition of the affections of kindness and compassion, that it was the business of wisdom and virtue to set him about extirpating them as fast as he could? And yet each of these manifest contradictions to nature has been laid down by men of speculation, as a discovery in moral philosophy; which they, it seems, have found out through all the specious appearances to the contrary. This reflection may be extended further. The extravagances of enthusiasm[4] and superstition do not at all lie in the road of common sense; and therefore so far as they are *original mistakes*, must be owing to going beside or beyond it. Now, since inquiry and examination can relate only to things so obscure and uncertain as to stand in need of it, and to persons who are capable of it; the proper advice to be given to plain honest men, to secure them from the extremes both of superstition and irreligion, is that of the son of *Sirach: In every good work trust thy own soul; for this is the keeping of the commandment.*[5]

Notes
1 Thomas Hobbes (1588–1679). In *Leviathan* (1651) and other works he argued that individual men are ruthlessly selfish and must be curbed by a powerful, authoritarian state. His radically pessimistic view of man was strongly opposed by many philosophers (e.g. Locke, see p. 35, note 1) while the atheistical tendencies in his philosophy provoked a powerful reaction from the Church.
2 Butler here appends a long footnote attacking the Hobbesian position.
3 A fairly direct reference to Thomas Hobbes.
4 This refers to the sort of religious experience offered by the predecessors of Whitefield in the seventeenth and early eighteenth century.
5 Ecclesiasticus 32: 23.

GEORGE WHITEFIELD

Beseeching Sinners (c. 1750–70)

From Robert Philip, *The Life and Times of the Reverend George Whitefield MA*, George Virtue, London, 1838, pp. 579–81.

George Whitefield (1714–70) was the founder of the Calvinistic branch of the Methodists and in 1739, with John Wesley, he set the example of open-air preaching, his field-meetings, with their appeal to instant conversion. Quite often these meetings produced extraordinary scenes of religious 'enthusiasm'. His power as an orator, which can be felt from the following extract from one of his sermons, was heightened by great personal magnetism and histrionic abilities. (The actor Garrick once said of him, admiringly, that 'he could make men weep or tremble by his varied utterances of the word "Mesopotamia" '.)

The many attacks and satires upon religious 'enthusiasm' by rationalistic writers in the mid-eighteenth century were aimed, above all, at Whitefield and his followers.

O my brethren, my heart is enlarged towards you. I trust I feel something of that hidden, but powerful presence of Christ, whilst I am preaching to you. Indeed, it is sweet, it is exceedingly comfortable.[1] All the harm I wish you, who without cause are my enemies, is, that you felt the like. Believe me, though it would be hell to my soul, to return to a natural state[2] again, yet I would willingly change states with you for a little while, that you might know what it is to have Christ dwelling in your hearts by faith. Do not turn your backs; do not let the devil hurry you away; be not afraid of convictions; do not think worse of the doctrine, because preached without the church walls. Our Lord, in the days of his flesh, preached on a mount, in a ship, and a field; and I am persuaded, many have felt his gracious presence here. Indeed, we speak what we know. Do not reject the kingdom of God against yourselves; be so wise as to receive our witness. I *cannot, I will not* let you go; stay a *little*, let us reason together. However lightly you may esteem your souls, I know our Lord has set an unspeakable value on them. He thought them

44

worthy of his most precious blood. I beseech you, therefore, O sinners, be ye reconciled to God. I hope you do not fear being accepted in the Beloved. Behold, he calleth you; behold, he prevents and follows you with his mercy, and hath sent forth his servants into the highways and hedges to compel you to come in. Remember, then, that at such an hour of such a day, in such a year, in this place, you were all told what you ought to think concerning Jesus Christ. If you now perish, it will not be for lack of knowledge: I am free from the blood of you all. You cannot say I have, like legal preachers,[3] been requiring you to make brick without straw. I have not bidden you to make yourselves saints, and then come to God; but I have offered you salvation on as cheap terms as you can desire.[4] I have offered you Christ's whole wisdom, Christ's whole righteousness, Christ's whole sanctification and eternal redemption, if you will but believe on him. If you say, you cannot believe, you say right; for faith, as well as every other blessing, is the gift of God: but then wait upon God, and who knows but he may have mercy on thee? Why do we not entertain more loving thoughts of Christ? Or do you think he will have mercy on others, and not on you? But are you not sinners? And did not Jesus Christ come into the world to save sinners? If you say you are the chief of sinners, I answer, that will be no hinderance to your salvation; indeed it will not, if you lay hold on him by faith. Read the evangelists, and see how kindly he behaved to his disciples who fled from and denied him; 'Go tell my brethren,' says he. He did not say, Go tell those traitors; but, 'Go tell my brethren, and *Peter*;' as though he had said, Go tell my brethren in general, and poor *Peter* in particular, 'that I am risen:' O comfort his poor drooping heart, tell him I am reconciled to him; bid him weep no more so bitterly: for though with oaths and curses he thrice denied me, yet I have died for his sins, I am risen again for his justification;[5] I freely forgive him all. Thus slow to anger, and of great kindness, was our all-merciful High Priest. And do you think he has changed his nature, and forgets poor sinners, now he is exalted to the right hand of God? No, he is the same yesterday, to-day, and for ever, and sitteth there only to make intercession for us. Come then, ye harlots; come, ye publicans; come, ye most abandoned of sinners, come and believe on Jesus Christ. Though the whole world despise you and cast you out, yet he will not disdain to take you up. O amazing, O infinitely condescending love! even you he will not be ashamed to call his brethren. How will you escape, if you neglect such a glorious offer of salvation? What would the damned spirits, now in the prison of hell, give, if Christ was so freely offered to their souls! And why are not we lifting up our eyes in torments? Does any one out of this great multitude dare say, he does not deserve damnation? If not, why are we left, and others taken away by death? What is this but an instance of God's free grace, and a sign of his good will towards us? Let God's goodness lead us to repentance! O let there be joy in heaven over some of you repenting! Though we are in a *field*, I am persuaded the blessed angels are hovering now around us, and do long, 'as the hart panteth after the water-brooks,' to sing an anthem at your conversion. Blessed be God, I hope their joy will be fulfilled. An *awful silence* appears amongst us. I have good hope that the words which the Lord has enabled me to speak in your ears this day, have not altogether fallen to the ground. Your tears and deep attention, are an evidence that the Lord God is amongst us of a truth. Come, ye Pharisees, come and see, in spite of your fanatical rage and fury, the Lord Jesus is getting himself the victory. And, brethren, I speak the truth in Christ, I lie not; if one soul of you, by the blessing of God, be brought to think savingly of Jesus Christ this day, I care not if my enemies were permitted to carry me to prison and put my feet fast in the stocks, as soon as I have delivered this sermon. Brethren, my heart's desire and prayer to God is, that you may be saved. For this cause I follow my Master without the camp. I care not how much of his sacred reproach I bear, so that some of you be converted from the errors of your ways. I rejoice, yea, and I will rejoice. Ye men, ye devils, do your *worst*: the Lord who sent will support me. And when Christ, who is our life, and whom I have now been preaching, shall appear, I also, together with his despised little ones, shall appear with him in glory. And then, what will you think of Christ? I know what you will think of him. You will think him to be the fairest among ten thousand: you will then think and feel him to be a just and sin-avenging Judge. Be ye then persuaded to kiss him lest he be angry, and so you be banished for ever from the presence of the Lord. Behold, I come to you as the angel did to Lot. Flee, flee for your lives; haste, linger no longer in your spiritual Sodom, for otherwise you will be eternally destroyed. Numbers, no doubt, there are amongst you, that may regard me no more than Lot's sons-in-law regarded him. I am persuaded I seem to some of you as one that mocketh: but I speak the truth in Christ, I lie not; as sure as fire and brimstone was rained from the Lord out of heaven, to destroy Sodom and Gomorrah, so surely, at the great day, shall the vials of God's wrath be poured on you, if you do not think seriously of, and act agreeably to, the gospel of the Lord's Christ. Behold, I have told you before; and I pray God, all you that forget him may seriously think of what has been said, before he pluck you away, and there be none to deliver you.

Notes
1 This, like many of Whitefield's favourite phrases, was taken from the language of the Puritans of the previous century.
2 That is, the sinful state of 'fallen' nature into which all are born and from which they can only be rescued by acceptance of Christ's freely-offered grace.
3 Those who, like most orthodox divines in Whitefield's view, only taught the 'works of the law', i.e. obedience to the Ten Commandments, etc.
4 Dissenting preachers, and later Evangelicals, often used commercial phraseology in referring to Salvation; they would speak of 'an interest maturing in Heaven' and of 'closing with Christ's offer', etc.
5 A technical term in theology, meaning 'freeing from the penalty of sin and rendering righteous in God's eyes'.

DAVID HUME

Of Miracles (1748)

David Hume, Section X, *Of Miracles*, first published in *Philosophical Essays Concerning Human Understanding*. Printed for A. Millar, opposite Katherine Street in the Strand, London 1748. Reprinted from *An Enquiry Concerning Human Understanding*, from the posthumous edition of 1777, ed. L. A. Selby-Bigge; revised by P. H. Nidditch, Collier-Macmillan, 1975. Section X.

This is the earliest of Hume's essays on religion. He originally intended to include it in his *Treatise of Human Nature* (1739). Writing to his friend Henry Home in 1737, however, he intimated his intention to omit it: 'I am at present castrating my work, that is, cutting off its noble Parts, that is, endeavouring it shall give as little Offence as possible . . .'.[1] Hume seems to have engaged in this piece of self-censorship out of a fear that the controversy which his essay *Of Miracles* would provoke might divert attention from the merits of the rest of the *Treatise*.

Hume was bitterly disappointed with the response to the *Treatise*, which he described as having fallen 'dead-born from the press'. (See *My Own Life*, p. 78.) Some years later he set about revising the way in which he had stated his position so as to make it more accessible and more closely related to the interests of his potential readers. The essay *Of Miracles* was included in the 1748 work to which Hume subsequently gave the title by which it is now known – *An Enquiry Concerning Human Understanding*.

Hume proved to have been entirely right in his judgment of the controversial character of this essay. It is a barely concealed attack on revealed religion and, as such, drew as much adverse attention in his own time as anything else which Hume wrote.

PART I.

There is, in Dr. Tillotson's[2] writings, an argument against the *real presence*, which is as concise, and elegant, and strong as any argument can

47

possibly be supposed against a doctrine, so little worthy of a serious refutation. It is acknowledged on all hands, says that learned prelate, that the authority, either of the scripture or of tradition, is founded merely in the testimony of the apostles, who were eye-witnesses to those miracles of our Saviour, by which he proved his divine mission. Our evidence, then, for the truth of the Christian religion is less than the evidence for the truth of our senses; because, even in the first authors of our religion, it was no greater; and it is evident it must diminish in passing from them to their disciples; nor can any one rest such confidence in their testimony, as in the immediate object of his senses. But a weaker evidence can never destroy a stronger; and therefore, were the doctrine of the real presence ever so clearly revealed in scripture, it were directly contrary to the rules of just reasoning to give our assent to it. It contradicts sense,[3] though both the scripture and tradition, on which it is supposed to be built, carry not such evidence with them as sense; when they are considered merely as external evidences, and are not brought home to every one's breast, by the immediate operation of the Holy Spirit.

Nothing is so convenient as a decisive argument of this kind, which must at least *silence* the most arrogant bigotry and superstition, and free us from their impertinent solicitations. I flatter myself, that I have discovered an argument of a like nature, which, if just, will, with the wise and learned, be an everlasting check to all kinds of superstitious delusion, and consequently, will be useful as long as the world endures. For so long, I presume, will the accounts of miracles and prodigies be found in all history, sacred and profane.

Though experience be our only guide in reasoning concerning matters of fact; it must be acknowledged, that this guide is not altogether infallible, but in some cases is apt to lead us into errors. One, who in our climate, should expect better weather in any week of June than in one of December, would reason justly, and conformably to experience; but it is certain, that he may happen, in the event, to find himself mistaken. However, we may observe, that, in such a case, he would have no cause to complain of experience; because it commonly informs us beforehand of the uncertainty, by that contrariety of events, which we may learn from a diligent observation. All effects follow not with like certainty from their supposed causes. Some events are found, in all countries and all ages, to have been constantly conjoined together: Others are found to have been more variable, and sometimes to disappoint our expectations; so that, in our reasonings concerning matter of fact, there are all imaginable degrees of assurance, from the highest certainty to the lowest species of moral evidence.[4]

A wise man, therefore, proportions his belief to the evidence. In such conclusions as are founded on an infallible experience, he expects the event with the last[5] degree of assurance, and regards his past experience as a full *proof* of the future existence of that event. In other cases, he proceeds with more caution: He weighs the opposite experiments: He considers which side is supported by the greater number of experiments:[6] to that side he inclines, with doubt and hesitation; and when at last he fixes his judgement, the evidence exceeds not what we properly call *probability*. All probability, then, supposes an opposition of experiments and observations, where the one side is found to overbalance the other, and to produce a degree of evidence, proportioned to the superiority. A hundred instances or experiments on one side, and fifty on another, afford a doubtful expectation of any event; though a hundred uniform experiments, with only one that is contradictory, reasonably beget a pretty strong degree of assurance. In all cases, we must balance the opposite experiments, where they are opposite, and deduct the smaller number from the greater, in order to know the exact force of the superior evidence.

To apply these principles to a particular instance; we may observe, that there is no species of reasoning more common, more useful, and even necessary to human life, than that which is derived from the testimony of men, and the reports of eye-witnesses and spectators. This species of reasoning, perhaps, one may deny to be founded on the relation of cause and effect. I shall not dispute about a word. It will be sufficient to observe that our assurance in any argument of this kind is derived from no other principle than our observation of the veracity of human testimony, and of the usual conformity of facts to the reports of witnesses. It being a general maxim, that no objects have any discoverable connexion together, and that all the inferences, which we can draw from one to another, are founded merely on our experience of their constant and regular conjunction; it is evident, that we ought not to make an exception to this maxim in favour of human testimony, whose connexion with any event seems, in itself, as little necessary as any other. Were not the memory tenacious to a certain degree; had not men commonly an inclination to truth and a principle of probity; were they not sensible to shame, when detected in a falsehood: Were not these, I say, discovered by *experience* to be qualities, inherent in human nature, we should never repose the least confidence in human testimony. A man delirious, or noted for falsehood and villany, has no manner of authority with us.

And as the evidence, derived from witnesses and human testimony, is founded on past experience, so it varies with the experience, and is regarded either as a *proof* or a *probability*, according as the conjunction between any particular kind of report and any kind of object has been found to be constant or variable. There are a number of circumstances to be taken into consideration in all judgements of this kind; and the ultimate standard, by which we determine all disputes, that may arise concerning them, is always derived from experience and observation. Where this experience is not entirely uniform on any side, it is attended with an unavoidable contrariety in our judgements, and with the same opposition and mutual destruction of argument as in every other kind of evidence. We frequently hesitate concerning the reports of others. We balance the opposite circumstances, which cause any doubt or uncertainty; and when we discover a superiority on any side, we incline to it; but still with a diminution of assurance, in proportion to the force of its antagonist.

This contrariety of evidence, in the present case, may be derived from several different causes; from the opposition of contrary testimony; from the character or number of the witnesses; from the manner of their delivering their testimony; or from the union of all these circumstances. We entertain a suspicion concerning any matter of fact, when the witnesses contradict each other; when they are but few, or of a doubtful character; when they have an interest in what they affirm; when they deliver their testimony with hesitation, or on the contrary, with too violent asseverations. There are many other particulars of the same kind, which may diminish or destroy the force of any argument, derived from human testimony.

Suppose, for instance, that the fact, which the testimony endeavours to establish, partakes of the extraordinary and the marvellous; in that case, the evidence, resulting from the testimony, admits of a diminution, greater or less, in proportion as the fact is more or less unusual. The reason why we place any credit in witnesses and historians, is not derived from any *connexion*, which we perceive *a priori*,[7] between testimony and reality, but because we are accustomed to find a conformity between them. But when the fact attested is such a one as has seldom fallen under our observation, here is a contest of two opposite experiences; of which the one destroys the other, as far as its force goes, and the superior can only operate on the mind by the force, which remains. The very same principle of experience, which gives us a certain degree of assurance in the testimony of witnesses, gives us also, in this case, another degree of assurance against the fact, which they endeavour to establish; from which contradiction there necessarily arises a counterpoize, and mutual destruction of belief and authority.

I should not believe such a story were it told me by Cato,[8] was a proverbial saying in Rome, even during the lifetime of that philosophical patriot. The incredibility of a fact, it was allowed, might invalidate so great an authority.

The Indian prince, who refused to believe the first relations concerning the effects of frost, reasoned justly; and it naturally required very strong testimony to engage his assent to facts, that arose from a state of nature, with which he was unacquainted, and which bore so little analogy to those events, of which he had had constant and uniform experience. Though they were not contrary to his experience, they were not conformable to it.[1]

But in order to encrease the probability against the testimony of

---

1 No Indian, it is evident, could have experience that water did not freeze in cold climates. This is placing nature in a situation quite unknown to him; and it is impossible for him to tell *a priori* what will result from it. It is making a new experiment, the consequence of which is always uncertain. One may sometimes conjecture from analogy what will follow; but still this is but conjecture. And it must be confessed, that, in the present case of freezing, the event follows contrary to the rules of analogy, and is such as a rational Indian would not look for. The operations of cold upon water are not gradual, according to the degrees of cold; but whenever it comes to the freezing point, the water

witnesses, let us suppose, that the fact, which they affirm, instead of being only marvellous, is really miraculous; and suppose also, that the testimony considered apart and in itself, amounts to an entire proof; in that case, there is proof against proof, of which the strongest must prevail, but still with a diminution of its force, in proportion to that of its antagonist.

A miracle is a violation of the laws of nature; and as a firm and unalterable experience has established these laws, the proof against a miracle, from the very nature of the fact, is as entire as any argument from experience can possibly be imagined. Why is it more than probable, that all men must die; that lead cannot, of itself, remain suspended in the air; that fire consumes wood, and is extinguished by water; unless it be, that these events are found agreeable to the laws of nature, and there is required a violation of these laws, or in other words, a miracle to prevent them? Nothing is esteemed a miracle, if it ever happen in the common course of nature. It is no miracle that a man, seemingly in good health, should die on a sudden: because such a kind of death, though more unusual than any other, has yet been frequently observed to happen. But it is a miracle, that a dead man should come to life; because that has never been observed in any age or country. There must, therefore, be a uniform experience against every miraculous event, otherwise the event would not merit that appellation. And as a uniform experience amounts to a proof, there is here a direct and full *proof*, from the nature of the fact, against the existence of any miracle; nor can such a proof be destroyed, or the miracle rendered credible, but by an opposite proof, which is superior.[2]

The plain consequence is (and it is a general maxim worthy of our

passes in a moment, from the utmost liquidity to perfect hardness. Such an event, therefore, may be denominated *extraordinary*, and requires a pretty strong testimony, to render it credible to people in a warm climate: But still it is not *miraculous*, nor contrary to uniform experience of the course of nature in cases where all the circumstances are the same. The inhabitants of Sumatra have always seen water fluid in their own climate, and the freezing of their rivers ought to be deemed a prodigy: But they never saw water in Muscovy[9] during the winter; and therefore they cannot reasonably be positive what would there be the consequence.

2 Sometimes an event may not, *in itself, seem* to be contrary to the laws of nature, and yet, if it were real, it might, by reason of some circumstance, be denominated a miracle; because, in *fact*, it is contrary to these laws. Thus if a person, claiming a divine authority, should command a sick person to be well, a healthful man to fall down dead, the clouds to pour rain, the winds to blow, in short, should order many natural events, which immediately follow upon his command; these might justly be esteemed miracles, because they are really, in this case, contrary to the laws of nature. For if any suspicion remain, that the event and command concurred by accident, there is no miracle and no transgression of the laws of nature. If this suspicion be removed, there is evidently a miracle, and a transgression of these laws; because nothing can be more contrary to nature than that the voice of command of a man should have such an influence. A miracle may be accurately defined, *a transgression of a law of nature by a particular volition of the Deity or, by the interposition of some invisible agent.* A miracle may either be discoverable by men or not. This alters not its nature and essence. The raising of a house or ship into the air is a visible miracle. The raising of a feather, when the wind wants ever so little of a force requisite for that purpose, is as real a miracle, though not so sensible with regard to us.

attention), 'That no testimony is sufficient to establish a miracle, unless the testimony be of such a kind, that its falsehood would be more miraculous, than the fact, which it endeavours to establish; and even in that case there is a mutual destruction of arguments, and the superior only gives us an assurance suitable to that degree of force, which remains, after deducting the inferior.' When anyone tells me, that he saw a dead man restored to life, I immediately consider with myself, whether it be more probable, that this person should either deceive or be deceived, or that the fact, which he relates, should really have happened. I weigh the one miracle against the other; and according to the superiority, which I discover, I pronounce my decision, and always reject the greater miracle. If the falsehood of his testimony would be more miraculous, than the event which he relates; then, and not till then, can he pretend to command my belief or opinion.

Part II.

In the foregoing reasoning we have supposed, that the testimony, upon which a miracle is founded, may possibly amount to an entire proof, and that the falsehood of that testimony would be a real prodigy: But it is easy to shew, that we have been a great deal too liberal in our concession, and that there never was a miraculous event established on so full an evidence.

For *first*, there is not to be found, in all history, any miracle attested by a sufficient number of men, of such unquestioned good-sense, education, and learning, as to secure us against all delusion in themselves; of such undoubted integrity, as to place them beyond all suspicion of any design to deceive others; of such credit and reputation in the eyes of mankind, as to have a great deal to lose in case of their being detected in any falsehood; and at the same time, attesting facts performed in such a public manner and in so celebrated a part of the world, as to render the detection unavoidable: All which circumstances are requisite to give us a full assurance in the testimony of men.

Secondly. We may observe in human nature a principle which, if strictly examined, will be found to diminish extremely the assurance, which we might, from human testimony, have, in any kind of prodigy. The maxim, by which we commonly conduct ourselves in our reasonings, is, that the objects, of which we have no experience, resemble those, of which we have; that what we have found to be most usual is always most probable; and that where there is an opposition of arguments, we ought to give the preference to such as are founded on the greatest number of past observations. But though, in proceeding by this rule, we readily reject any fact which is unusual and incredible in an ordinary degree; yet in advancing farther, the mind observes not always the same rule; but when anything is affirmed utterly absurd and miraculous, it rather the more readily admits of such a fact, upon account of that very circumstance, which ought to destroy all its authority. The passion of *surprise* and *wonder*, arising from miracles, being an agreeable emotion, gives a sensible tendency towards the belief of those events, from which it is derived. And this goes so far, that even those who cannot enjoy this pleasure immediately, nor can believe those miraculous events, of which they are informed, yet love to partake of the satisfaction at second-hand or by rebound, and place a pride and delight in exciting the admiration of others.

With what greediness are the miraculous accounts of travellers received, their descriptions of sea and land monsters, their relations of wonderful adventures, strange men, and uncouth manners? But if the spirit of religion join itself to the love of wonder, there is an end of common sense; and human testimony, in these circumstances, loses all pretensions to authority. A religionist may be an enthusiast, and imagine he sees what has no reality: he may know his narrative to be false, and yet persevere in it, with the best intentions in the world, for the sake of promoting so holy a cause: or even where this delusion has not place, vanity, excited by so strong a temptation, operates on him more powerfully than on the rest of mankind in any other circumstances; and self-interest with equal force. His auditors may not have, and commonly have not, sufficient judgement to canvass his evidence: what judgement they have, they renounce by principle, in these sublime and mysterious subjects: or if they were ever so willing to employ it, passion and a heated imagination disturb the regularity of its operations. Their credulity increases his impudence; and his impudence overpowers their credulity.

Eloquence, when at its highest pitch, leaves little room for reason or reflection; but addressing itself entirely to the fancy or the affections, captivates the willing hearers, and subdues their understanding. Happily, this pitch it seldom attains. But what a Tully[10] or a Demosthenes[11] could scarcely effect over a Roman or Athenian audience, every *Capuchin*,[12] every itinerant or stationary teacher can perform over the generality of mankind, and in a higher degree, by touching such gross and vulgar passions.

The many instances of forged miracles, and prophecies, and supernatural events, which, in all ages, have either been detected by contrary evidence, or which detect themselves by their absurdity, prove sufficiently the strong propensity of mankind to the extraordinary and the marvellous, and ought reasonably to beget a suspicion against all relations of this kind. This is our natural way of thinking, even with regard to the most common and most credible events. For instance: There is no kind of report which arises so easily, and spreads so quickly, especially in country places and provincial towns, as those concerning marriages; insomuch that two young persons of equal condition never see each other twice, but the whole neighbourhood immediately join them together. The pleasure of telling a piece of news so interesting, of propagating it, and of being the first reporters of it, spreads the intelligence. And this is so well known, that no man of sense gives attention to these reports, till he find them confirmed by some greater evidence. Do not the same passions, and others still stronger, incline the generality of mankind to believe and report, with the greatest vehemence and assurance, all religious miracles?

Thirdly. It forms a strong presumption against all supernatural and miraculous relations, that they are observed chiefly to abound among ignorant and barbarous nations; or if a civilized people has ever given admission to any of them, that people will be found to have received them from ignorant and barbarous ancestors, who transmitted them with that inviolable sanction and authority, which always attend received opinions. When we peruse the first histories of all nations, we are apt to imagine ourselves transported into some new world; where the whole frame of nature is disjointed, and every element performs its operations in a different manner, from what it does at present. Battles, revolutions, pestilence, famine and death, are never the effect of those natural causes, which we experience. Prodigies, omens, oracles, judgements, quite obscure the few natural events, that are intermingled with them. But as the former grow thinner every page, in proportion as we advance nearer the enlightened ages, we soon learn, that there is nothing mysterious or supernatural in the case, but that all proceeds from the usual propensity of mankind towards the marvellous, and that, though this inclination may at intervals receive a check from sense and learning, it can never be thoroughly extirpated from human nature.

It is strange, a judicious reader is apt to say, upon the perusal of these wonderful historians, *that such prodigious events never happen in our days*. But it is nothing strange, I hope, that men should lie in all ages. You must surely have seen instances enough of that frailty. You have yourself heard many such marvellous relations started, which, being treated with scorn by all the wise and judicious, have at last been abandoned even by the vulgar. Be assured, that those renowned lies, which have spread and flourished to such a monstrous height, arose from like beginnings; but being sown in a more proper soil, shot up at last into prodigies almost equal to those which they relate.

It was a wise policy in that false prophet, Alexander,[13] who though now forgotten, was once so famous, to lay the first scene of his impostures in Paphlagonia, where, as Lucian tells us, the people were extremely ignorant and stupid, and ready to swallow even the grossest delusion. People at a distance, who are weak enough to think the matter at all worth enquiry, have no opportunity of receiving better information. The stories come magnified to them by a hundred circumstances. Fools are industrious in propagating the imposture; while the wise and learned are contented, in general, to deride its absurdity, without informing themselves of the particular facts, by which it may be distinctly refuted. And thus the impostor above mentioned was enabled to proceed, from his ignorant Paphlagonians, to the enlisting of votaries, even among the Grecian philosophers, and men of the most eminent rank and distinction in Rome: nay, could engage the attention of that sage emperor Marcus Aurelius;[14] so far as to make him trust the success of a military expedition to his delusive prophecies.

The advantages are so great, of starting an imposture among an ignorant people, that, even though the delusion should be too gross to impose on the generality of them (*which, though seldom, is sometimes the case*) it has a much better chance for succeeding in remote countries, than if the first scene had been laid in a city renowned for arts and knowledge. The most ignorant and barbarous of these barbarians carry the report abroad. None of their countrymen have a large correspondence, or sufficient credit and authority to contradict and beat down the delusion. Men's inclination to the marvellous has full opportunity to display itself. And thus a story, which is universally exploded in the place where it was first started, shall pass for certain at a thousand miles distance. But had Alexander fixed his residence at Athens, the philosophers of that renowned mart of learning had immediately spread, throughout the whole Roman empire, their sense of the matter; which, being supported by so great authority, and displayed by all the force of reason and eloquence, had entirely opened the eyes of mankind. It is true; Lucian, passing by chance through Paphlagonia, had an opportunity of performing this good office. But, though much to be wished, it does not always happen, that every Alexander meets with a Lucian, ready to expose and detect his impostures.

I may add as a *fourth* reason, which diminishes the authority of prodigies, that there is no testimony for any, even those which have not been expressly detected, that is not opposed by an infinite number of witnesses; so that not only the miracle destroys the credit of testimony, but the testimony destroys itself. To make this the better understood, let us consider, that, in matters of religion, whatever is different is contrary; and that it is impossible the religions of ancient Rome, of Turkey, of Siam, and of China should, all of them, be established on any solid foundation. Every miracle, therefore, pretended to have been wrought in any of these religions (and all of them abound in miracles), as its direct scope is to establish the particular system to which it is attributed; so has it the same force, though more indirectly, to overthrow every other system. In destroying a rival system, it likewise destroys the credit of those miracles, on which that system was established; so that all the prodigies of different religions are to be regarded as contrary facts, and the evidences of these prodigies, whether weak or strong, as opposite to each other. According to this method of reasoning, when we believe any miracle of Mahomet or his successors, we have for our warrant the testimony of a few barbarous Arabians: And on the other hand, we are to regard the authority of Titus Livius,[15] Plutarch, Tacitus,[16] and, in short, of all the authors and witnesses, Grecian, Chinese, and Roman Catholic, who have related any miracle in their particular religion; I say, we are to regard their testimony in the same light as if they had mentioned that Mahometan miracle, and had in express terms contradicted it, with the same certainty as they have for the miracle they relate. This argument may appear over subtile and refined; but is not in reality different from the reasoning of a judge, who supposes, that the credit of two witnesses, maintaining a crime against any one, is destroyed by the testimony of two others, who affirm him to have been two hundred leagues distant, at the same instant when the crime is said to have been committed.

One of the best attested miracles in all profane history, is that which Tacitus reports of Vespasian,[17] who cured a blind man in Alexandria,[18] by means of his spittle, and a lame man by the mere touch of his foot; in obedience to a vision of the god Serapis,[19] who had enjoined them to have recourse to the Emperor, for these miraculous cures. The story may be seen in that fine historian; where every circumstance seems to add weight to the testimony, and might be displayed at large with all the force of argument and eloquence, if any one were now concerned to enforce the evidence of that exploded and idolatrous superstition. The gravity, solidity, age, and probity of so great an emperor, who, through the whole course of his life, conversed in a familiar manner with his friends and courtiers, and never affected those extraordinary airs of divinity assumed by Alexander [20]and Demetrius.[21]The historian, a cotemporary writer, noted for candour and veracity, and withal, the greatest and most penetrating genius, perhaps, of all antiquity; and so free from any tendency to credulity, that he even lies under the contrary imputation, of atheism and profaneness: The persons, from whose authority he related the miracle, of established character for judgement and veracity, as we may well presume; eye-witnesses of the fact, and confirming their testimony, after the Flavian family[22] was despoiled of the empire, and could no longer give any reward, as the price of a lie. *Utrumque, qui interfuere, nunc quoque memorant, postquam nullum mendacio pretium.*[23] To which if we add the public nature of the facts, as related, it will appear, that no evidence can well be supposed stronger for so gross and so palpable a falsehood.

There is also a memorable story related by Cardinal de Retz,[24] which may well deserve our consideration. When that intriguing politician fled into Spain, to avoid the persecution of his enemies, he passed through Saragossa, the capital of Aragon,[25] where he was shewn, in the cathedral, a man, who had served seven years as a door-keeper, and was well known to every body in town, that had ever paid his devotions at that church. He had been seen, for so long a time, wanting a leg; but recovered that limb by the rubbing of holy oil upon the stump; and the cardinal assures us that he saw him with two legs. This miracle was vouched by all the canons of the church; and the whole company in town were appealed to for a confirmation of the fact; whom the cardinal found, by their zealous devotion, to be thorough believers of the miracle. Here the relater was also cotemporary to the supposed prodigy, of an incredulous and libertine character, as well as of great genius; the miracle of so *singular* a nature as could scarcely admit of a counterfeit, and the witnesses very numerous, and all of them, in a manner, spectators of the fact, to which they gave their testimony. And what adds mightily to the force of the evidence, and may double our surprise on this occasion is that the cardinal himself, who relates the story, seems not to give any credit to it, and consequently cannot be suspected of any concurrence in the holy fraud. He considered justly, that it was not requisite, in order to reject a fact of this nature, to be able accurately to disprove the testimony, and to trace its falsehood, through all the circumstances of knavery and credulity which produced it. He knew, that, as this was commonly altogether impossible at any small distance of time and place; so was it extremely difficult, even where one was immediately present, by reason of the bigotry, ignorance, cunning, and roguery of a great part of mankind. He therefore concluded, like a just reasoner, that such an evidence carried falsehood upon the very face of it, and that a miracle, supported by any human testimony, was more properly a subject of derision than of argument.

There surely never was a greater number of miracles ascribed to one person, than those, which were lately said to have been wrought in France upon the tomb of Abbé·Paris, the famous Jansenist,[26] with whose sanctity the people were so long deluded. The curing of the sick, giving hearing to the deaf, and sight to the blind, were every where talked of as the usual effects of that holy sepulchre. But what is more extraordinary; many of the miracles were immediately proved upon the spot, before judges of unquestioned integrity, attested by witnesses of credit and distinction, in a learned age, and on the most eminent theatre that is now in the world. Nor is this all: a relation of them was published and dispersed everywhere; nor were the *Jesuits*, though a learned body, supported by the civil magistrate, and determined enemies to those opinions, in whose favour the miracles were said to have been wrought, ever able distinctly to refute or detect them. Where shall we find such a number of circumstances, agreeing to the corroboration of one fact? And what have we to oppose to such a cloud of witnesses, but the absolute impossibility or miraculous nature of the events, which they relate? And this surely, in the eyes of all reasonable people, will alone be regarded as a sufficient refutation.

Is the consequence just, because some human testimony has the utmost force and authority in some cases, when it relates the battle of Philippi[27] or Pharsalia[28] for instance; that therefore all kinds of testimony must, in all cases, have equal force and authority? Suppose that the Caesarean and Pompeian factions had, each of them, claimed the victory in these battles, and that the historians of each party had uniformly ascribed the advantage to their own side; how could mankind, at this distance, have been able to determine between them? The contrariety is equally strong between the miracles related by Herodotus[29] or Plutarch, and those delivered by Mariana,[30] Bede,[31] or any monkish historian.

The wise lend a very academic faith to every report which favours the passion of the reporter; whether it magnifies his country, his family, or himself, or in any other way strikes in with his natural inclinations and propensities. But what greater temptation than to appear a missionary, a prophet, an ambassador from heaven? Who would not encounter many dangers and difficulties, in order to attain so sublime a character?

Or if, by the help of vanity and a heated imagination, a man has first made a convert of himself, and entered seriously into the delusion; who ever scruples to make use of pious frauds, in support of so holy and meritorious a cause?

The smallest spark may here kindle into the greatest flame; because the materials are always prepared for it. The *avidum genus auricularum*,[32] the gazing populace, receive greedily, without examination, whatever sooths superstition, and promotes wonder.

How many stories of this nature have, in all ages, been detected and exploded in their infancy? How many more have been celebrated for a time, and have afterwards sunk into neglect and oblivion? Where such reports, therefore, fly about, the solution of the phenomenon is obvious; and we judge in conformity to regular experience and observation, when we account for it by the known and natural principles of credulity and delusion. And shall we, rather than have a recourse to so natural a solution, allow of a miraculous violation of the most established laws of nature?

I need not mention the difficulty of detecting a falsehood in any private or even public history, at the place, where it is said to happen; much more when the scene is removed to ever so small a distance. Even a court of judicature, with all the authority, accuracy, and judgement, which they can employ, find themselves often at a loss to distinguish between truth and falsehood in the most recent actions. But the matter never comes to any issue, if trusted to the common method of altercations and debate and flying rumours; especially when men's passions have taken part on either side.

In the infancy of new religions, the wise and learned commonly esteem the matter too inconsiderable to deserve their attention or regard. And when afterwards they would willingly detect the cheat, in order to undeceive the deluded multitude, the season is now past, and the records and witnesses, which might clear up the matter, have perished beyond recovery.

No means of detection remain, but those which must be drawn from the very testimony itself of the reporters: and these, though always sufficient with the judicious and knowing, are commonly too fine to fall under the comprehension of the vulgar.

Upon the whole, then, it appears, that no testimony for any kind of miracle has ever amounted to a probability, much less to a proof; and that, even supposing it amounted to a proof, it would be opposed by another proof; derived from the very nature of the fact, which it would endeavour to establish. It is experience only, which gives authority to human testimony; and it is the same experience, which assures us of the laws of nature. When, therefore, these two kinds of experience are contrary, we have nothing to do but substract the one from the other, and embrace an opinion, either on one side or the other, with that assurance which arises from the remainder. But according to the principle here explained, this substraction, with regard to all popular religions, amounts to an entire annihilation; and therefore we may establish it as a maxim, that no human testimony can have such force as to prove a miracle, and make it a just foundation for any such system of religion.

I beg the limitations here made may be remarked, when I say, that a miracle can never be proved, so as to be the foundation of a system of religion. For I own, that otherwise, there may possibly be miracles, or violations of the usual course of nature, of such a kind as to admit of proof from human testimony; though, perhaps, it will be impossible to find any such in all the records of history. Thus, suppose, all authors, in all languages, agree, that, from the first of January 1600, there was a total darkness over the whole earth for eight days: suppose that the tradition of this extraordinary event is still strong and lively among the people: that all travellers, who return from foreign countries, bring us accounts of the same tradition, without the least variation on contradiction: it is evident, that our present philosophers, instead of doubting the fact, ought to receive it as certain, and ought to search for the causes whence it might be derived. The decay, corruption, and dissolution of nature, is an event rendered probable by so many analogies, that any phenomenon, which seems to have a tendency towards that catastrophe, comes within the reach of human testimony, if that testimony be very extensive and uniform.

But suppose, that all the historians who treat of England, should agree, that, on the first of January 1600, Queen Elizabeth died; that both before and after her death she was seen by her physicians and the whole court, as is usual with persons of her rank; that her successor was acknowledged and proclaimed by the parliament; and that, after being interred a month, she again appeared, resumed the throne, and governed England for three years: I must confess that I should be surprised at the concurrence of so many odd circumstances, but should not have the least inclination to believe so miraculous an event. I should not doubt of her pretended death, and of those other public circumstances that followed it: I should only assert it to have been pretended, and that it neither was, nor possibly could be real. You would in vain object to me the difficulty, and almost impossibility of deceiving the world in an affair of such consequence; the wisdom and solid judgement of that renowned queen; with the little or no advantage which she could reap from so poor an artifice: All this might astonish me; but I would still reply, that the knavery and folly of men are such common phenomena, that I should rather believe the most extraordinary events to arise from their concurrence, than admit of so signal a violation of the laws of nature.

But should this miracle be ascribed to any new system of religion; men, in all ages, have been so much imposed on by ridiculous stories of that kind, that this very circumstance would be a full proof of a cheat, and sufficient, with all men of sense, not only to make them reject the fact, but even reject it without farther examination. Though the Being to whom the miracle is ascribed, be, in this case, Almighty, it does not, upon that account, become a whit more probable; since it is impossible for us to know the attributes or actions of such a Being, otherwise than from the experience which we have of his productions, in the usual course of nature. This still reduces us to past observation, and obliges us to compare the instances of the violation of truth in the testimony of men, with those of the violation of the laws of nature by miracles, in order to judge which of them is most likely and probable. As the violations of truth are more common in the testimony concerning religious miracles, than in that concerning any other matter of fact; this must diminish very much the authority of the former testimony, and make us form a general resolution, never to lend any attention to it, with whatever specious pretence it may be covered.

Lord Bacon[33] seems to have embraced the same principles of reasoning. 'We ought,' says he, 'to make a collection or particular history of all monsters and prodigious births or productions, and in a word of every thing new, rare, and extraordinary in nature. But this must be done with the most severe scrutiny, lest we depart from truth. Above all, every relation must be considered as suspicious, which depends in any degree upon religion, as the prodigies of Livy: And no less so, every thing that is to be found in the writers of natural magic or alchimy, or such authors, who seem, all of them, to have an unconquerable appetite for falsehood and fable.'

I am the better pleased with the method of reasoning here delivered, as I think it may serve to confound those dangerous friends or disguised enemies to the *Christian Religion*, who have undertaken to defend it by the principles of human reason. Our most holy religion is founded on *Faith*, not on reason; and it is a sure method of exposing it to put it to such a trial as it is, by no means, fitted to endure. To make this more evident, let us examine those miracles, related in scripture; and not to lose ourselves in too wide a field, let us confine ourselves to such as we find in the *Pentateuch*, which we shall examine, according to the principles of these pretended Christians, not as the word or testimony of God himself, but as the production of a mere human writer and historian. Here then we are first to consider a book, presented to us by a barbarous and ignorant people, written in an age when they were still more barbarous, and in all probability long after the facts which it relates, corroborated by no concurring testimony, and resembling those fabulous accounts, which every nation gives of its origin. Upon reading this book, we find it full of prodigies and miracles. It gives an account of a state of the world and of human nature entirely different from the present: Of our fall from that state: Of the age of man, extended to near a thousand years: Of the destruction of the world by a deluge: Of the arbitrary choice of one people, as the favourites of heaven; and that people the countrymen of the author: Of their deliverance from bondage by prodigies the most astonishing imaginable: I desire any one to lay his hand upon his heart, and after a serious consideration declare, whether he thinks that the falsehood of such a book, supported by such a testimony, would be more extraordinary and miraculous than all the miracles it relates; which is, however, necessary to make it be received, according to the measures of probability above established.

What we have said of miracles may be applied, without any variation, to prophecies; and indeed, all prophecies are real miracles, and as such only, can be admitted as proofs of any revelation. If it did not exceed the capacity of human nature to foretell future events, it would be absurd to employ any prophecy as an argument for a divine mission or authority from heaven. So that, upon the whole, we may conclude, that the *Christian Religion* not only was at first attended with miracles, but even at this day cannot be believed by any reasonable person without one. Mere reason is insufficient to convince us of its veracity: And whoever is moved by *Faith* to assent to it, is conscious of a continued miracle in his own person, which subverts all the principles of his understanding, and gives him a determination to believe what is most contrary to custom and experience.

ADDITIONAL NOTE TO p. 57

This book was writ by Mons. Montgeron, counsellor or judge of the parliament of Paris, a man of figure and character, who was also a martyr to the cause, and is now said to be somewhere in a dungeon on account of his book.

There is another book in three volumes (called *Recueil des Miracles de l'Abbé* Paris) giving an account of many of these miracles, and accompanied with prefatory discourses, which are very well written. There runs, however, through the whole of these a ridiculous comparison between the miracles of our Saviour and those of the Abbé; wherein it is asserted, that the evidence for the latter is equal to that for the former: As if the testimony of men could ever be put in the balance with that of God himself, who conducted the pen of the inspired writers. If these writers, indeed, were to be considered merely as human testimony, the French author is very moderate in his comparison; since he might, with some appearance of reason, pretend, that the Jansenist miracles much surpass the other in evidence and authority. The following circumstances are drawn from authentic papers, inserted in the abovementioned book.

Many of the miracles of Abbé Paris were proved immediately by witnesses before the officiality or bishop's court at Paris, under the eye of cardinal Noailles, whose character for integrity and capacity was never contested even by his enemies.

His successor in the archbishopric was an enemy to the Jansenists, and for that reason promoted to the see by the court. Yet 22 rectors or *curés* of Paris, with infinite earnestness, press him to examine those miracles, which they assert to be known to the whole world, and undisputably certain: But he wisely forbore.

The Molinist party[34] had tried to discredit these miracles in one instance, that of Mademoiselle le Franc. But, besides that their proceedings were in many respects the most irregular in the world, particularly in citing only a few of the Jansenist witnesses, whom they tampered with: Besides this, I say, they soon found themselves overwhelmed by a cloud of new witnesses, one hundred and twenty in number, most of them persons of credit and substance in Paris, who gave oath for the miracle. This was accompanied with a solemn and earnest appeal to the parliament. But the parliament were forbidden by authority to meddle in the affair. It was at last observed, that where men are heated by zeal and enthusiasm, there is no degree of human testimony so strong as may not be procured for the greatest absurdity: And those who will be so silly as to examine the affair by that medium, and seek particular flaws in the testimony, are almost sure to be confounded. It must be a miserable imposture, indeed, that does not prevail in that contest.

All who have been in France about that time have heard of the reputation of Mons. Heraut, the *lieutenant de Police*, whose vigilance, penetration, activity, and extensive intelligence have been much talked of. This magistrate, who by the nature of his office is almost absolute, was invested with full powers, on purpose to suppress or discredit these miracles; and he frequently seized immediately, and examined the witnesses and subjects of them: But never could reach any thing satisfactory against them.

In the case of Mademoiselle Thibaut he sent the famous De Sylva to examine her; whose evidence is very curious. The physician declares, that it was impossible she could have been so ill as was proved by witnesses; because it was impossible she could, in so short a time, have recovered so perfectly as he found her. He reasoned, like a man of sense, from natural causes; but the opposite party told him, that the whole was a miracle, and that his evidence was the very best proof of it.

The Molinists were in a sad dilemma. They durst not assert the absolute insufficiency of human evidence, to prove a miracle. They were obliged to say, that these miracles were wrought by witchcraft and the devil. But they were told, that this was the resource of the Jews of old.

No Jansenist was ever embarrassed to account for the cessation of the miracles, when the church-yard was shut up by the king's edict. It was the touch of the tomb, which produced these extraordinary effects; and when no one could approach the tomb, no effects could be expected. God, indeed, could have thrown down the walls in a moment; but he is master of his own graces and works, and it belongs not to us to account for them. He did not throw down the walls of every city like those of Jericho, on the sounding of the rams horns, nor break up the prison of every apostle, like that of St. Paul.

No less a man, than the Duc de Chatillon, a duke and peer of France, of the highest rank and family, gives evidence of a miraculous cure, performed upon a servant of his, who had lived several years in his house with a visible and palpable infirmity.

I shall conclude with observing, that no clergy are more celebrated for strictness of life and manners than the secular clergy of France, particularly the rectors or curés of Paris, who bear testimony to these impostures.

The learning, genius, and probity of the gentlemen, and the austerity of the nuns of Port-Royal,[35] have been much celebrated all over Europe. Yet they all give evidence for a miracle, wrought on the niece of the famous Pascal,[36] whose sanctity of life, as well as extraordinary capacity, is well known. The famous Racine gives an account of this miracle in his famous history of Port-Royal, and fortifies it with all the proofs, which a multitude of nuns, priests, physicians, and men of the world, all of them of undoubted credit, could bestow upon it. Several men of letters, particularly the bishop of Tournay, thought this miracle so certain, as to employ it in the refutation of atheists and free-thinkers. The queen-regent of France, who was extremely prejudiced against the Port-Royal, sent her own physician to examine the miracle, who returned an absolute convert. In short, the supernatural cure was so uncontestable, that it saved, for a time, that famous monastery from the ruin with which it was threatened by the Jesuits. Had it been a cheat, it had certainly been detected by such sagacious and powerful antagonists, and must have hastened the ruin of the contrivers. Our divines, who can build up a formidable castle from such despicable materials; what a prodigious fabric could they have reared from these and many other circumstances, which I have not mentioned! How often would the great names of Pascal, Racine, Arnaud, Nicole,[37] have resounded in our ears? But if they be wise, they had better adopt the miracle, as being more worth, a thousand times, than all the rest of their collection. Besides, it may serve very much to their purpose. For that miracle was really performed by the touch of an authentic holy prickle of the holy thorn, which composed the holy crown, which, etc.

Notes

1   *Letters of David Hume*, ed. J. Y. T. Greig, Oxford 1969, Vol. 1.
2   John Tillotson (1630–94) was an Anglican divine who, at the end of his life, became Archbishop of Canterbury. His polemic against Roman Catholicism, *Rule of Faith* (1666), contains the arguments against 'the real presence' (see p. 36, notes 3 and 5) to which Hume refers.
3   Sense-experience.
4   That is, having, at best, a probable conclusion.
5   Utmost.
6   Experiences.
7   A latin phrase widely used as a piece of philosophical terminology to mean 'in advance of, or independently of, experience'.
8   Cato the Younger (95–46B.C.), Roman politician and moral philosopher. Hume is quoting here from the life of Cato by the Greek writer Plutarch (A.D.46–120).
9   Russia.
10   Marcus Tullius Cicero (106–43B.C.), Roman politician, rhetorician and philosopher. He was famed for his oratory and his defence of Republican ideals. His prose style became a model for many sixteenth- and seventeenth-century writers.
11   (384–322B.C.) Orator in Athens.
12   A Franciscan friar (from Italian *cappuccio*, meaning a hood).

13   Leader of a religious cult in the second century A.D. He claimed to have a new manifestation of Asclepius, the god of healing, in the form of a serpent. The Greek writer Lucian of Samosata (c.A.D.115–200) wrote 'Alexander, or the False Prophet' denouncing him as an impostor.

14   Marcus Aurelius (A.D.121–80), Roman emperor and philosopher.

15   The Roman historian Livy (59B.C.–A.D.17).

16   Roman historian (A.D.55–117).

17   The Roman emperor Vespasian (A.D.9–79).

18   City on the coast of Egypt, founded by Alexander the Great.

19   Egyptian god whose cult was at Alexandria.

20   Alexander the Great of Macedonia (356–323B.C.), whose armies conquered Greece and lands in the Near and Middle East.

21   King of Macedonia (336–283B.C.).

22   The Roman Emperors Vespasian and his sons Titus and Domitian.

23   'Both facts are told by eye-witnesses even now when falsehood brings no reward.' This sentence appears in Tacitus's *Histories*, Book Four, Chapter 81.

24   Paul de Gondi, Cardinal de Retz (1614–79) author of *Memoirs of his age*, and remarkable for his libertinism. He was instrumental in the civil wars in France known as *La fronde* (1648–52) and became Archbishop of Paris in 1653.

25   A region of north-eastern Spain.

26   Jansenism was a revivalist movement which originated in the seventeenth century and is named after Cornelius Jansen (1585–1638). In eighteenth-century France there was considerable rivalry between the Jansenists and another very influential Roman Catholic movement, the Jesuits. The Abbé Paris (1690–1727) was a young Jansenist cleric noted for his piety. The miracles performed on his tomb at St. Médard had been the talk of Paris a few years before Hume made the visit to France during which he wrote the essay *Of Miracles*. Such had been the commotion surrounding the 'miracles' that the French government felt it necessary, in 1732, to close the cemetery. Hume added a lengthy additional note on the miracles of the Abbé Paris which is included here.

27   A city in Macedonia; where in 42B.C. Octavian (later Augustus) and Antony defeated Brutus and Cassius, the assassins of Julius Caesar.

28   A city in Thessaly, Greece; near where in 48B.C. Julius Caesar defeated his rival Pompey.

29   Greek historian of fifth centuryB.C.

30   Juan de Mariana (1532–1624), a Jesuit, author of a history of Spain.

31   'The Venerable Bede', a monk at Jarrow (A.D.673–735); known as the 'father of English history' for his *Ecclesiastical History of the English People*.

32   'Eagerness for hearsay'; from the Roman poet Lucretius's work *Concerning the Nature of Things*.

33   The experimental philosopher, Francis Bacon (1561–1626), author of the essays, the *Advancement of Learning*, and a philosophical treatise in Latin, the *Novum Organum* from which Hume quotes here. (See also Vol. 2, p. 140, note 13.)

34   Followers of the Spanish mystic Miguel de Molinos (1640–97), otherwise known as 'Quietists'.

35   The convent of Port-Royal-des-Champs, near Versailles, which formed the headquarters of the Jansenist movement.

36   Blaise Pascal (1623–62), the great French philosopher and mathematician, closely associated with Port-Royal.

37   Antoine Arnauld (1612–94) was religious director of the nuns of Port-Royal and author of an important work on logic. Pierre Nicole (1625–95) was a leading figure in the Jansenist movement and a close associate of Arnauld.

DAVID HUME

Of a Particular Providence (1748)

David Hume, ibid. Section IX, *Of a Particular Providence and of a Future State*.

Hume originally entitled this essay *Of the Practical Consequences of Natural Religion*. One of its two main themes is a discussion of whether freedom of opinion and debate about religion could have subversive consequences for the prevailing social order. Hume and his fictional friend both agree that it does not, though their reasons are different.

By 'natural religion' Hume means religion as established and practised without reference to revelation. One of the main arguments in discussion of natural religion is that which seeks to establish that the universe provides evidence of a divine purpose. Those who believed in a 'particular providence' believed that men receive rewards or punishments according as they behave virtuously or viciously. Some believed that the evils suffered in this life were evidence of an underlying moral purpose to be discovered in the course of events. Others believed that reward and retribution belonged primarily to a future state. Hume and his friend again agree that the course of nature does not provide evidence of a 'particular providence' which determines it.

I was lately engaged in conversation with a friend who loves sceptical paradoxes; where, though he advanced many principles, of which I can by no means approve, yet as they seem to be curious, and to bear some relation to the chain of reasoning carried on throughout this enquiry, I shall here copy them from my memory as accurately as I can, in order to submit them to the judgement of the reader.

Our conversation began with my admiring the singular good fortune of philosophy, which, as it requires entire liberty above all other privileges, and chiefly flourishes from the free opposition of sentiments and argumentation, received its first birth in an age and country of freedom and toleration,[1] and was never cramped, even in its most extravagant principles, by any creeds, concessions, or penal statutes. For, except the banishment of Protagoras,[2] and the death of Socrates,[3] which last event proceeded partly from other motives, there are scarcely any instances to be met with, in ancient history, of this bigotted jealousy, with which the present age is so much infested. Epicurus[4] lived at Athens to an advanced age, in peace and tranquillity: Epicureans were even admitted to receive the sacerdotal character,[5] and to officiate at the altar, in the most sacred rites of the established religion: And the public encouragement of pensions and salaries was afforded equally, by the wisest of all the Roman emperors,[6] to the professors of every sect of philosophy. How requisite such kind of treatment was to philosophy, in her early youth, will easily be conceived, if we reflect, that, even at present, when she may be supposed more hardy and robust, she bears with much difficulty the inclemency of the seasons, and those harsh winds of calumny and persecution, which blow upon her.

You admire, says my friend, as the singular good fortune of philosophy, what seems to result from the natural course of things, and to be unavoidable in every age and nation. This pertinacious bigotry, of which you complain, as so fatal to philosophy, is really her offspring, who, after allying with superstition, separates himself entirely from the interest of his parent, and becomes her most inveterate enemy and persecutor. Speculative dogmas of religion, the present occasions of such furious dispute, could not possibly be conceived or admitted in the early ages of the world; when mankind, being wholly illiterate, formed an idea of religion more suitable to their weak apprehension, and composed their sacred tenets of such tales chiefly as were the objects of traditional belief, more than of argument or disputation. After the first alarm, therefore, was over, which arose from the new paradoxes and principles of the philosophers; these teachers seem ever after, during the ages of antiquity, to have lived in great harmony with the established superstition, and to have made a fair partition of mankind between them; the former claiming all the learned and wise, the latter possessing all the vulgar and illiterate.

It seems then, say I, that you leave politics entirely out of the question, and never suppose, that a wise magistrate can justly be jealous of certain tenets of philosophy, such as those of Epicurus, which, denying a divine existence, and consequently a providence and a future state, seem to loosen, in a great measure, the ties of morality, and may be supposed, for that reason, pernicious to the peace of civil society.

I know, replied he, that in fact these persecutions never, in any age, proceeded from calm reason, or from experience of the pernicious consequences of philosophy; but arose entirely from passion and prejudice. But what if I should advance farther, and assert, that if Epicurus had been accused before the people, by any of the *sycophants* or informers of those days, he could easily have defended his cause, and proved his principles of philosophy to be as salutary as those of his adversaries, who endeavoured, with such zeal, to expose him to the public hatred and jealousy?

I wish, said I, you would try your eloquence upon so extraordinary a topic, and make a speech for Epicurus, which might satisfy, not the mob of Athens, if you will allow that ancient and polite city to have contained any mob, but the more philosophical part of his audience, such as might be supposed capable of comprehending his arguments.

The matter would not be difficult, upon such conditions, replied he: And if you please, I shall suppose myself Epicurus for a moment, and make you stand for the Athenian people, and shall deliver you such an harangue as will fill all the urn with white beans,[7] and leave not a black one to gratify the malice of my adversaries.

Very well: Pray proceed upon these suppositions.

I come hither, O ye Athenians, to justify in your assembly what I maintained in my school, and I find myself impeached by furious antagonists, instead of reasoning with calm and dispassionate enquirers. Your deliberations, which of right should be directed to questions of public good, and the interest of the commonwealth, are diverted to the disquisitions of speculative philosophy; and these magnificent, but perhaps fruitless enquiries, take place of your more familiar but more useful occupations. But so far as in me lies, I will prevent this abuse. We shall not here dispute concerning the origin and government of worlds. We shall only enquire how far such questions concern the public interest. And if I can persuade you, that they are entirely indifferent to the peace of society and security of government, I hope that you will presently send us back to our schools, there to examine, at leisure, the question the most sublime, but at the same time, the most speculative of all philosophy.

The religious philosophers, not satisfied with the tradition of your forefathers, and doctrine of your priests (in which I willingly acquiesce), indulge a rash curiosity, in trying how far they can establish religion upon the principles of reason; and they thereby excite, instead of satisfying, the doubts, which naturally arise from a diligent and scrutinous enquiry. They paint, in the most magnificent colours, the order, beauty, and wise arrangement of the universe; and then ask, if such a glorious display of intelligence could proceed from the fortuitous concourse of atoms, or if chance could produce what the greatest genius can never sufficiently admire. I shall not examine the justness of this argument. I shall allow it to be as solid as my antagonists and accusers can desire. It is sufficient, if I can prove, from this very reasoning, that the question is entirely speculative, and that, when, in my philosophical disquisitions, I deny a providence and a future state, I undermine not the foundations of society, but advance principles, which they themselves, upon their own topics, if they argue consistently, must allow to be solid and satisfactory.

You then, who are my accusers, have acknowledged, that the chief or sole argument for a divine existence (which I never questioned) is derived from the order of nature; where there appear such marks of intelligence and design, that you think it extravagant to assign for its cause, either chance, or the blind and unguided force of matter. You allow, that this is an argument drawn from effects to causes. From the order of the work, you infer, that there must have been project and forethought in the workman. If you cannot make out this point, you allow, that your conclusion fails; and you pretend not to establish the conclusion in a greater latitude than the phenomena of nature will justify. These are your concessions. I desire you to mark the consequences.

When we infer any particular cause from an effect, we must proportion the one to the other, and can never be allowed to ascribe to the cause any qualities, but what are exactly sufficient to produce the effect. A body of ten ounces raised in any scale may serve as a proof, that the counterbalancing weight exceeds ten ounces; but can never afford a reason that it exceeds a hundred. If the cause, assigned for any effect, be not sufficient to produce it, we must either reject that cause, or add to it such qualities as will give it a just proportion to the effect. But if we ascribe to it farther qualities, or affirm it capable of producing other effects, we can only indulge the licence of conjecture, and arbitrarily suppose the existence of qualities and energies, without reason or authority.

The same rule holds, whether the cause assigned be brute unconscious matter, or a rational intelligent being. If the cause be known only by the effect, we never ought to ascribe to it any qualities, beyond what are precisely requisite to produce the effect: Nor can we, by any rules of just reasoning, return back from the cause, and infer other effects from it, beyond those by which alone it is known to us. No one, merely from the sight of one of Zeuxis's[8] pictures, could know, that he was also a statuary or architect, and was an artist no less skilful in stone and marble than in colours. The talents and taste, displayed in the particular work before us; these we may safely conclude the workman to be possessed of. The cause must be proportioned to the effect; and if we exactly and precisely proportion it, we shall never find in it any qualities, that point farther, or afford an inference concerning any other design or performance. Such qualities must be somewhat beyond what is merely requisite for producing the effect, which we examine.

Allowing, therefore, the gods to be the authors of the existence or order of the universe; it follows, that they possess that precise degree of power, intelligence, and benevolence, which appears in their workmanship; but nothing farther can ever be proved, except we call in the assistance of exaggeration and flattery to supply the defects of argument and reasoning. So far as the traces of any attributes, at present, appear, so far may we conclude these attributes to exist. The supposition of farther attributes is mere hypothesis; much more the supposition, that, in distant regions of space or periods of time, there has been, or will be, a more magnificent display of these attributes, and a scheme of administration more suitable to such imaginary virtues. We can never be allowed to mount up from the universe, the effect, to Jupiter,[9] the cause; and then descend downwards, to infer any new effect from that cause; as if the present effects alone were not entirely worthy of the glorious attributes, which we ascribe to that deity. The knowledge of the cause being derived solely from the effect, they must be exactly adjusted to each other; and the one can never refer to anything farther, or be the foundation of any new inference and conclusion.

You find certain phenomena in nature. You seek a cause or author. You imagine that you have found him. You afterwards become so enamoured of this offspring of your brain, that you imagine it impossible, but he must produce something greater and more perfect than the present scene of things, which is so full of ill and disorder. You forget, that this superlative intelligence and benevolence are entirely imaginary, or, at least, without any foundation in reason; and that you have no ground to ascribe to him any qualities, but what you see he has actually exerted and displayed in his productions. Let your gods, therefore, O philosophers, be suited to the present appearances of nature: and presume not to alter these appearances by arbitrary suppositions, in order to suit them to the attributes, which you so fondly ascribe to your deities.

When priests and poets, supported by your authority, O Athenians, talk of a golden or silver age,[10] which preceded the present state of vice and misery, I hear them with attention and with reverence. But when philosophers, who pretend to neglect authority, and to cultivate reason, hold the same discourse, I pay them not, I own, the same obsequious submission and pious deference. I ask; who carried them into the celestial regions, who admitted them into the councils of the gods, who opened to them the book of fate, that they thus rashly affirm, that their deities have executed, or will execute, any purpose beyond what has actually appeared? If they tell me, that they have mounted on the steps or by the gradual ascent of reason, and by drawing inferences from effects to causes, I still insist, that they have aided the ascent of reason by the wings of imagination; otherwise they could not thus change their manner of inference, and argue from causes to effects; presuming, that a more perfect production than the present world would be more suitable to such perfect beings as the gods, and forgetting that they have no reason to ascribe to these celestial beings any perfection or any attribute, but what can be found in the present world.

Hence all the fruitless industry to account for the ill appearances of nature, and save the honour of the gods; while we must acknowledge the reality of that evil and disorder, with which the world so much abounds. The obstinate and intractable qualities of matter, we are told, or the observance of general laws, or some such reason, is the sole cause, which controlled the power and benevolence of Jupiter, and obliged him to create mankind and every sensible creature so imperfect and so unhappy. These attributes then, are, it seems, beforehand, taken for granted, in their greatest latitude. And upon that supposition, I own that such conjectures may, perhaps, be admitted as plausible solutions of the ill phenomena. But still I ask; Why take these attributes for granted, or why ascribe to the cause any qualities but what actually appear in the effect? Why torture your brain to justify the course of nature upon suppositions, which, for aught you know, may be entirely imaginary, and of which there are to be found no traces in the course of nature?

The religious hypothesis, therefore, must be considered only as a particular method of accounting for the visible phenomena of the universe: but no just reasoner will ever presume to infer from it any single fact, and alter or add to the phenomena, in any single particular. If you think, that the appearances of things prove such causes, it is allowable for you to draw an inference concerning the existence of these causes. In such complicated and sublime subjects, every one should be indulged in the liberty of conjecture and argument. But here you ought to rest. If you come backward, and arguing from your inferred causes, conclude, that any other fact has existed, or will exist, in the course of nature, which may serve as a fuller display of particular attributes; I must admonish you, that you have departed from the method of reasoning, attached to the present subject, and have certainly added something to the attributes of the cause, beyond what appears in the effect; otherwise you could never, with tolerable sense or propriety, add anything to the effect, in order to render it more worthy of the cause.

Where, then, is the odiousness of that doctrine, which I teach in my school, or rather, which I examine in my gardens? Or what do you find in this whole question, wherein the security of good morals, or the peace and order of society, is in the least concerned?

I deny a providence, you say, and supreme governor of the world, who guides the course of events, and punishes the vicious with infamy and disappointment, and rewards the virtuous with honour and success, in all their undertakings. But surely, I deny not the course itself of events, which lies open to every one's inquiry and examination. I acknowledge, that, in the present order of things, virtue is attended with more peace of mind than vice, and meets with a more favourable reception from the world. I am sensible, that, according to the past experience of mankind, friendship is the chief joy of human life, and moderation the only source of tranquillity and happiness. I never balance[11] between the virtuous and the vicious course of life; but am sensible, that, to a well-disposed mind, every advantage is on the side of the former. And what can you say more, allowing all your suppositions and reasonings? You tell me, indeed, that this disposition of things proceeds from intelligence and design. But whatever it proceeds from, the disposition itself, on which depends our happiness or misery, and consequently our conduct and deportment in life is still the same. It is still open for me, as well as you, to regulate my behaviour, by my experience of past events. And if you affirm, that, while a divine providence is allowed, and a supreme distributive justice in the universe, I ought to expect some more particular reward of the good, and punishment of the bad, beyond the ordinary course of events; I here find the same fallacy, which I have before endeavoured to detect.

You persist in imagining, that, if we grant that divine existence, for which you so earnestly contend, you may safely infer consequences from it, and add something to the experienced order of nature, by arguing from the attributes which you ascribe to your gods. You seem not to remember, that all your reasonings on this subject can only be drawn from effects to causes; and that every argument, deducted from causes to effects, must of necessity be a gross sophism; since it is impossible for you to know anything of the cause, but what you have antecedently, not inferred, but discovered to the full, in the effect.

But what must a philosopher think of those vain reasoners, who, instead of regarding the present scene of things as the sole object of their contemplation, so far reverse the whole course of nature, as to render this life merely a passage to something farther; a porch, which leads to a greater, and vastly different building; a prologue, which serves only to introduce the piece, and give it more grace and propriety? Whence, do you think, can such philosophers derive their idea of the gods? From their own conceit and imagination surely. For if they derived it from the present phenomena, it would never point to anything farther, but must be exactly adjusted to them. That the divinity may *possibly* be endowed with attributes, which we have never seen exerted; may be governed by principles of action, which we cannot discover to be satisfied: all this will freely be allowed. But still this is mere *possibility* and hypothesis. We never can have reason to *infer* any attributes, or any principles of action in him, but so far as we know them to have been exerted and satisfied.

Are there any marks of a distributive justice in the world? If you answer in the affirmative, I conclude, that, since justice here exerts itself, it is satisfied. If you reply in the negative, I conclude, that you have then no reason to ascribe justice, in our sense of it, to the gods. If you hold a medium between affirmation and negation, by saying, that the justice of the gods, at present, exerts itself in part, but not in its full extent; I answer, that you have no reason to give it any particular extent, but only so far as you see it, *at present*, exert itself.

Thus I bring the dispute, O Athenians, to a short issue with my antagonists. The course of nature lies open to my contemplation as well as to theirs. The experienced train of events is the great standard, by which we all regulate our conduct. Nothing else can be appealed to in the field, or in the senate. Nothing else ought ever to be heard of in the school, or in the closet. In vain would our limited understanding break through those boundaries, which are too narrow for our fond imagination. While we argue from the course of nature, and infer a particular intelligent cause, which first bestowed, and still preserves order in the universe, we embrace a principle, which is both uncertain and useless. It is uncertain; because the subject lies entirely beyond the reach of human experience. It is useless; because our knowledge of this cause being derived entirely from the course of nature, we can never, according to the rules of just reasoning, return back from the cause with any new inference, or making additions to the common and experi-

71

enced course of nature, establish any new principles of conduct and behaviour.

I observe (said I, finding he had finished his harangue) that you neglect not the artifice of the demagogues of old; and as you were pleased to make me stand for the people, you insinuate yourself into my favour by embracing those principles, to which, you know, I have always expressed a particular attachment. But allowing you to make experience (as indeed I think you ought) the only standard of our judgement concerning this, and all other questions of fact; I doubt not but, from the very same experience, to which you appeal, it may be possible to refute this reasoning, which you have put into the mouth of Epicurus. If you saw, for instance, a half-finished building, surrounded with heaps of brick and stone and mortar, and all the instruments of masonry; could you not *infer* from the effect, that it was a work of design and contrivance? And could you not return again, from this inferred cause, to infer new additions to the effect, and conclude, that the building would soon be finished, and receive all the further improvements, which art could bestow upon it? If you saw upon the sea-shore the print of one human foot, you would conclude, that a man had passed that way, and that he had also left the traces of the other foot, though effaced by the rolling of the sands or inundation of the waters. Why then do you refuse to admit the same method of reasoning with regard to the order of nature? Consider the world and the present life only as an imperfect building, from which you can infer a superior intelligence; and arguing from that superior intelligence, which can leave nothing imperfect; why may you not infer a more finished scheme or plan, which will receive its completion in some distant point of space or time? Are not these methods of reasoning exactly similar? And under what pretence can you embrace the one, while you reject the other?

The infinite difference of the subjects, replied he, is a sufficient foundation for this difference in my conclusions. In works of *human* art and contrivance, it is allowable to advance from the effect to the cause, and returning back from the cause, to form new inferences concerning the effect, and examine the alterations, which it has probably undergone, or may still undergo. But what is the foundation of this method of reasoning? Plainly this; that man is a being, whom we know by experience, whose motives and designs we are acquainted with, and whose projects and inclinations have a certain connexion and coherence, according to the laws which nature has established for the government of such a creature. When, therefore, we find, that any work has proceeded from the skill and industry of man; as we are otherwise acquainted with the nature of the animal, we can draw a hundred inferences concerning what may be expected from him; and these inferences will all be founded in experience and observation. But did we know man only from the single work or production which we examine, it were impossible for us to argue in this manner; because our knowledge of all the qualities, which we ascribe to him, being in that case derived from the production, it is impossible they could point to anything farther, or be the foundation of any new inference. The print of a foot in the sand can only prove, when considered alone, that there was some figure adapted to it, by which it was produced: but the print of a human foot proves likewise, from our other experience, that there was probably another foot, which also left its impression, though effaced by time or other accidents. Here we mount from the effect to the cause; and descending again from the cause, infer alterations in the effect; but this is not a continuation of the same simple chain of reasoning. We comprehend in this case a hundred other experiences and observations, concerning the *usual* figure and members of that species of animal, without which this method of argument must be considered as fallacious and sophistical.

The case is not the same with our reasonings from the works of nature. The Deity is known to us only by his productions, and is a single being in the universe, not comprehended under any species or genus, from whose experienced attributes or qualities, we can, by analogy, infer any attribute or quality in him. As the universe shews wisdom and goodness, we infer wisdom and goodness. As it shews a particular degree of these perfections, we infer a particular degree of them, precisely adapted to the effect which we examine. But farther attributes or farther degrees of the same attributes, we can never be authorised to infer or suppose, by any rules of just reasoning. Now, without some such licence of supposition, it is impossible for us to argue from the cause, or infer any alteration in the effect, beyond what has immediately fallen under our observation. Greater good produced by this Being must still prove a greater degree of goodness: a more impartial distribution of rewards and punishments must proceed from a greater regard to justice and equity. Every supposed addition to the works of nature makes an addition to the attributes of the Author of nature; and consequently, being entirely unsupported by any reason or argument, can never be admitted but as mere conjecture and hypothesis.[1]

The great source of our mistake in this subject, and of the unbounded licence of conjecture, which we indulge, is, that we tacitly consider ourselves, as in the place of the Supreme Being, and conclude, that he will, on every occasion, observe the same conduct, which we ourselves,

---

1 In general, it may, I think, be established as a maxim, that where any cause is known only by its particular effects, it must be impossible to infer any new effects from that cause; since the qualities, which are requisite to produce these new effects along with the former, must either be different, or superior, or of more extensive operation, than those which simply produced the effect, whence alone the cause is supposed to be known to us. We can never, therefore, have any reason to suppose the existence of these qualities. To say, that the new effects proceed only from a continuation of the same energy, which is already known from the first effects, will not remove the difficulty. For even granting this to be the case (which can seldom be supposed), the very continuation and exertion of a like energy (for it is impossible it can be absolutely the same), I say, this exertion of a like energy, in a different period of space and time, is a very arbitrary supposition, and what there cannot possibly be any traces of in the effects, from which all our knowledge of the cause is originally derived. Let the *inferred* cause be exactly proportioned (as it should be) to the known effect; and it is impossible that it can possess any qualities, from which new or different effects can be *inferred*.

in his situation, would have embraced as reasonable and eligible. But, besides that the ordinary course of nature may convince us, that almost everything is regulated by principles and maxims very different from ours; besides this, I say, it must evidently appear contrary to all rules of analogy to reason, from the intentions and projects of men, to those of a Being so different, and so much superior. In human nature, there is a certain experienced coherence of designs and inclinations; so that when, from any fact, we have discovered one intention of any man, it may often be reasonable, from experience, to infer another, and draw a long chain of conclusions concerning his past or future conduct. But this method of reasoning can never have place with regard to a Being, so remote and incomprehensible, who bears much less analogy to any other being in the universe than the sun to a waxen taper, and who discovers himself[12] only by some faint traces or outlines, beyond which we have no authority to ascribe to him any attribute or perfection. What we imagine to be a superior perfection, may really be a defect. Or were it ever so much a perfection, the ascribing of it to the Supreme Being, where it appears not to have been really exerted, to the full, in his works, savours more of flattery and panegyric, than of just reasoning and sound philosophy. All the philosophy, therefore, in the world, and all the religion, which is nothing but a species of philosophy, will never be able to carry us beyond the usual course of experience, or give us measures of conduct and behaviour different from those which are furnished by reflections on common life. No new fact can ever be inferred from the religious hypothesis; no event foreseen or foretold; no reward or punishment expected or dreaded, beyond what is already known by practice and observation. So that my apology for Epicurus will still appear solid and satisfactory; nor have the political interests of society any connexion with the philosophical disputes concerning metaphysics and religion.

There is still one circumstance, replied I, which you seem to have overlooked. Though I should allow your premises, I must deny your conclusion. You conclude, that religious doctrines and reasonings *can* have no influence on life, because they *ought* to have no influence; never considering, that men reason not in the same manner you do, but draw many consequences from the belief of a divine Existence, and suppose that the Deity will inflict punishments on vice, and bestow rewards on virtue, beyond what appear in the ordinary course of nature. Whether this reasoning of theirs be just or not, is no matter. Its influence on their life and conduct must still be the same. And, those, who attempt to disabuse them of such prejudices, may, for aught I know, be good reasoners, but I cannot allow them to be good citizens and politicians; since they free men from one restraint upon their passions, and make the infringement of the laws of society, in one respect, more easy and secure.

After all, I may, perhaps, agree to your general conclusion in favour of liberty, though upon different premises from those, on which you endeavour to found it. I think, that the state ought to tolerate every principle of philosophy; nor is there an instance, that any government has suffered in its political interests by such indulgence. There is no enthusiasm among philosophers; their doctrines are not very alluring to the people; and no restraint can be put upon their reasonings, but what must be of dangerous consequence to the sciences, and even to the state, by paving the way for persecution and oppression in points, where the generality of mankind are more deeply interested and concerned.

But there occurs to me (continued I) with regard to your main topic, a difficulty, which I shall just propose to you without insisting on it; lest it lead into reasonings of too nice[13] and delicate a nature. In a word, I much doubt whether it be possible for a cause to be known only by its effect (as you have all along supposed) or to be of so singular and particular a nature as to have no parallel and no similarity with any other cause or object, that has ever fallen under our observation. It is only when two *species* of objects are found to be constantly conjoined, that we can infer the one from the other; and were an effect presented, which was entirely singular, and could not be comprehended under any known *species*, I do not see, that we could form any conjecture or inference at all concerning its cause. If experience and observation and analogy be, indeed, the only guides which we can reasonably follow in inferences of this nature; both the effect and cause must bear a similarity and resemblance to other effects and causes, which we know, and which we have found, in many instances, to be conjoined with each other. I leave it to your own reflection to pursue the consequences of this principle. I shall just observe, that, as the antagonists of Epicurus always suppose the universe, an effect quite singular and unparalleled, to be the proof of a Deity, a cause no less singular and unparalleled; your reasonings, upon that supposition, seem, at least, to merit our attention. There is, I own, some difficulty, how we can ever return from the cause to the effect, and, reasoning from our ideas of the former, infer any alteration on the latter, or any addition to it.

Notes

1 Ancient Greece, especially Athens, in the period *c.* 600–250B.C.

2 One of the Sophists, a group of philosophers in Athens in fifth centuryB.C.

3 Philosopher in Athens (469–399B.C.); in 399B.C. he was tried by a jury and condemned on charges of introducing strange gods and corrupting the youth of the city.

4 Greek philosopher (*c.* 340–270B.C.) who advocated a materialist view of the world as consisting of atoms and void. Contrary to popular misunderstanding, Epicurus did not give a high value to sensual pleasures. Hume shows himself aware, in paragraph 19, of Epicurus's actual view – namely, that moderation is the only source of tranquility and happiness. Epicurus's philosophy was, nonetheless, an irreligious one.

5 The status of priest.

6 Marcus Aurelius.

7 In Athens beans were used in ballots, white ones for election or agreement; and black ones for rejection or opposition.

8 Greek painter of the fifth century B.C.

9   Supreme Deity of the Ancient Romans, Epicurus himself would have referred to Jupiter's Greek counterpart, Zeus, had he made any such speech.
10   According to the Greek and Roman poets there was a Golden Age during the reign of Saturn followed by a Silver Age, and these were the two first and best ages of the world.
11   Waver.
12   Reveals himself.
13   Difficult to determine or distinguish; minutely or delicately precise.

DAVID HUME

My Own Life (1777)

From David Hume, *The Life of David Hume Esq.* and *Letter from Adam Smith, LL.D., to William Strahan Esq.* Printed for W. Strahan, and T. Cadell, in the Strand, London 1777. Reprinted from *The Philosophical Works of David Hume*, ed. T. H. Green and T. H. Grose, Longmans, Green and Co., London, 1875.

Hume wrote this brief autobiography during the last year of his life and it was published in the following year, together with the Letter by Adam Smith to William Strahan (also printed here) describing Hume's last days. Smith's letter, depicting Hume's serene and stoical death-bed, caused much scandal among the orthodox, who refused to believe that an atheist could make a good death and accused Smith of insidious anti-religious propaganda.

It is difficult for a man to speak long of himself without vanity; therefore, I shall be short. It may be thought an instance of vanity that I pretend at all to write my life; but this Narrative shall contain little more than the History of my Writings; as, indeed, almost all my life has been spent in literary pursuits and occupations. The first success of most of my writings was not such as to be an object of vanity.

I was born the 26th of April 1711, old style,[1] at Edinburgh. I was of a good family, both by father and mother: my father's family is a branch of the Earl of Home's, or Hume's; and my ancestors had been proprietors of the estate, which my brother possesses, for several generations. My mother was daughter of Sir David Falconer, President of the College of Justice: the title of Lord Halkerton came by succession to her brother.

My family, however, was not rich, and being myself a younger brother, my patrimony, according to the mode of my country, was of course very slender. My father, who passed for a man of parts, died when I was an infant, leaving me, with an elder brother and a sister, under the care of our mother, a woman of singular merit, who, though young and handsome, devoted herself entirely to the rearing and educating of her children. I passed through the ordinary course of education with success, and was seized very early with a passion for literature, which has been the ruling passion of my life, and the great source of my enjoyments. My studious disposition, my sobriety, and my industry, gave my family a notion that the law was a proper profession for me; but I found an unsurmountable aversion to every thing but the pursuits of philosophy and general learning; and while they fancied I was poring upon Voet and Vinnius,[2] Cicero and Virgil were the authors which I was secretly devouring.

My very slender fortune, however, being unsuitable to this plan of life, and my health being a little broken by my ardent application, I was tempted, or rather forced, to make a very feeble trial for entering into a more active scene of life. In 1734, I went to Bristol, with some recommendations to eminent merchants, but in a few months found that scene totally unsuitable to me. I went over to France, with a view of prosecuting my studies in a country retreat; and I there laid that plan of life, which I have steadily and successfully pursued. I resolved to make a very rigid frugality supply my deficiency of fortune, to maintain unimpaired my independency, and to regard every object as contempt-ible, except the improvement of my talents in literature.

During my retreat in France, first at Reims, but chiefly at La Fleche, in Anjou, I composed my *Treatise of Human Nature*. After passing three years very agreeably in that country, I came over to London in 1737. In the end of 1738, I published my Treatise, and immediately went down to my mother and my brother, who lived at his country house and was employing himself very judiciously and successfully in the improve-ment of his fortune.

Never literary attempt was more unfortunate than my Treatise of Human Nature. It fell *dead-born from the press*, without reaching such distinction, as even to excite a murmur among the zealots. But being naturally of a cheerful and sanguine temper, I very soon recovered the blow, and prosecuted with great ardour my studies in the country. In 1742 I printed at Edinburgh the first part of my Essays: the work was favourably received, and soon made me entirely forget my former disappointment. I continued with my mother and brother in the country, and in that time recovered the knowledge of the Greek language, which I had too much neglected in my early youth.

In 1745, I received a letter from the Marquis of Annandale, inviting me to come and live with him in England; I found also, that the friends and family of that young nobleman were desirous of putting him under my care and direction, for the state of his mind and health required it. I lived with him a twelvemonth. My appointments during that time made a considerable accession to my small fortune. I then received an invitation from General St. Clair[3] to attend him as a secretary to his expedition, which was at first meant against Canada, but ended in an incursion on the coast of France. Next year, to wit, 1747, I received an invitation from the General to attend him in the same station in his military embassy to the courts of Vienna and Turin. I then wore the uniform of an officer, and was introduced at these courts as aide-de-camp to the general, along with Sir Harry Erskine and Captain Grant, now General Grant. These two years were almost the only interruptions which my studies have received during the course of my life: I passed them agreeably and in good company; and my appointments, with my frugality, had made me reach a fortune, which I called independent, though most of my friends were inclined to smile when I said so; in short, I was now master of near a thousand pounds.

I had always entertained a notion, that my want of success in publishing the Treatise of Human Nature, had proceeded more from the manner than the matter, and that I had been guilty of a very usual indiscretion, in going to the press too early. I, therefore, cast the first part of that work anew in the Enquiry concerning Human Understanding, which was published while I was at Turin. But this piece was at first little more successful than the Treatise of Human Nature. On my return from Italy, I had the mortification to find all England in a ferment, on account of Dr. Middleton's Free Enquiry,[4] while my performance was entirely overlooked and neglected. A new edition, which had been published at London, of my Essays, moral and political, met not with a much better reception.

Such is the force of natural temper, that these disappointments made little or no impression on me. I went down in 1749, and lived two years with my brother at his country house, for my mother was now dead. I there composed the second part of my Essays, which I called Political Discourses, and also my Enquiry concerning the Principles of Morals, which is another part of my treatise that I cast anew. Meanwhile, my bookseller, A. Millar, informed me, that my former publications (all but the unfortunate Treatise) were beginning to be the subject of conversation; that the sale of them was gradually increasing, and that new editions were demanded. Answers by Reverends, and Right Reverends,[5] came out two or three in a year; and I found, by Dr. Warburton's railing,[6] that the books were beginning to be esteemed in good company. However, I had fixed a resolution, which I inflexibly maintained, never to reply to anybody; and not being very irascible in my temper, I have easily kept myself clear of all literary squabbles. These symptoms of a rising reputation gave me encouragement, as I was ever more disposed to see the favourable than unfavourable side of things; a turn of mind which it is more happy to possess, than to be born to an estate of ten thousand a year.

In 1751, I removed from the country to the town, the true scene for a man of letters. In 1752, were published at Edinburgh, where I then lived, my Political Discourses, the only work of mine that was successful on the first publication. It was well received abroad and at home. In the same year was published at London, my Enquiry concerning the Principles of Morals: which, in my own opinion (who ought not to judge on that subject), is of all my writings, historical, philosophical, or literary, incomparably the best. It came unnoticed and unobserved into the world.

In 1752, the Faculty of Advocates chose me their Librarian, an office from which I received little or no emolument, but which gave me the command of a large library. I then formed the plan of writing the History of England; but being frightened with the notion of continuing a narrative through a period of 1700 years, I commenced with the accession of the House of Stuart, an epoch when, I thought, the misrepresentations of faction began chiefly to take place. I was, I own, sanguine in my expectations of the success of this work. I thought that I was the only historian, that had at once neglected present power, interest, and authority, and the cry of popular prejudices; and as the subject was suited to every capacity, I expected proportional applause. But miserable was my disappointment: I was assailed by one cry of reproach, disapprobation, and even detestation; English, Scotch, and Irish, Whig and Tory, churchman and sectary, free-thinker and re-ligionist, patriot and courtier, united in their rage against the man, who had presumed to shed a generous tear for the fate of Charles I[7] and the Earl of Strafford; and after the first ebullitions of their fury were over, what was still more mortifying, the book seemed to sink into oblivion. Mr. Millar told me, that in a twelvemonth he sold only forty-five copies of it. I scarcely, indeed, heard of one man in the three kingdoms, considerable for rank or letters, that could endure the book. I must only except the primate of England, Dr. Herring, and the primate of Ireland, Dr. Stone, which seem two odd exceptions. These dignified prelates separately sent me messages not to be discouraged.

I was, however, I confess, discouraged; and had not the war been at that time breaking out between France and England, I had certainly retired to some provincial town of the former kingdom, have changed my name, and never more have returned to my native country. But as this scheme was not now practicable, and the subsequent volume was considerably advanced, I resolved to pick up courage and to persevere.

In this interval, I published at London my Natural History of Religion, along with some other small pieces: its public entry was rather obscure, except only that Dr. Hurd[8] wrote a pamphlet against it, with all the illiberal petulance, arrogance, and scurrility which distinguish the Warburtonian school. This pamphlet gave me some consolation for the otherwise indifferent reception of my performance.

In 1756, two years after the fall of the first volume, was published the second volume of my History, containing the period from the death of Charles I. till the Revolution. This performance happened to give less displeasure to the Whigs, and was better received. It not only rose itself, but helped to buoy up its unfortunate brother.

But though I had been taught by experience, that the Whig party were in possession of bestowing all places, both in the state and in literature, I was so little inclined to yield to their senseless clamour, that in about a hundred alterations, which farther study, reading, or reflection engaged me to make in the reigns of the first two Stuarts, I have made all of them invariably to the Tory side. It is ridiculous to consider the English constitution before that period as a regular plan of liberty.

In 1759, I published my History of the House of Tudor. The clamour against this performance was almost equal to that against the History of the two first Stuarts. The reign of Elizabeth was particularly obnoxious. But I was now callous against the impressions of public folly, and continued very peaceably and contentedly in my retreat at Edinburgh, to finish, in two volumes, the more early part of the English History, which I gave to the public in 1761, with tolerable, and but tolerable success.

But, notwithstanding this variety of winds and seasons, to which my writings had been exposed, they had still been making such advances, that the copy-money[9] given me by the booksellers, much exceeded any thing formerly known in England; I was become not only independent, but opulent. I retired to my native country of Scotland, determined never more to set my foot out of it; and retaining the satisfaction of never having preferred a request to one great man, or even making advances of friendship to any of them. As I was now turned of fifty, I thought of passing all the rest of my life in this philosophical manner, when I received, in 1763, an invitation from the Earl of Hertford,[10] with whom I was not in the least acquainted, to attend him on his embassy to Paris, with a near prospect of being appointed secretary to the embassy; and, in the meanwhile, of performing the functions of that office. This offer, however inviting, I at first declined, both because I was reluctant to begin connexions with the great, and because I was afraid that the civilities and gay company of Paris, would prove disagreeable to a person of my age and humour: but on his lordship's repeating the invitation, I accepted of it. I have every reason, both of pleasure and interest, to think myself happy in my connexions with that nobleman, as well as afterwards with his brother, General Conway.[11]

Those who have not seen the strange effects of modes, will never imagine the reception I met with at Paris, from men and women of all ranks and stations. The more I resiled[12] from their excessive civilities, the more I was loaded with them. There is, however, a real satisfaction in living at Paris, from the great number of sensible, knowing, and polite company with which that city abounds above all places in the universe. I thought once of settling there for life.

I was appointed secretary to the embassy; and in summer 1765, Lord Hertford left me, being appointed Lord Lieutenant of Ireland. I was chargé d'affaires till the arrival of the Duke of Richmond, towards the end of the year. In the beginning of 1766, I left Paris, and next summer went to Edinburgh, with the same view as formerly, of burying myself in a philosophical retreat. I returned to that place, not richer, but with much more money, and a much larger income, by means of Lord Hertford's friendship, than I left it; and I was desirous of trying what superfluity could produce, as I had formerly made an experiment of a competency. But in 1767, I received from Mr. Conway an invitation to be Under-secretary; and this invitation, both the character of the person, and my connexions with Lord Hertford, prevented me from declining. I returned to Edinburgh in 1769, very opulent (for I possessed a revenue of 1,000*l*. a year), healthy, and though somewhat stricken in years, with the prospect of enjoying long my ease, and of seeing the increase of my reputation.

In spring 1775, I was struck with a disorder in my bowels, which at first gave me no alarm, but has since, as I apprehend it, become mortal and incurable. I now reckon upon a speedy dissolution. I have suffered very little pain from my disorder; and what is more strange, have, notwithstanding the great decline of my person, never suffered a moment's abatement of my spirits; insomuch, that were I to name the period of my life, which I should most choose to pass over again, I might be tempted to point to this latter period. I possess the same ardour as ever in study, and the same gaiety in company. I consider, besides, that a man of sixty-five, by dying, cuts off only a few years of infirmities; and though I see many symptoms of my literary reputation's breaking out at last with additional lustre, I knew that I could have but few years to enjoy it. It is difficult to be more detached from life than I am at present.

To conclude historically with my own character. I am, or rather was (for that is the style I must now use in speaking of myself, which emboldens me the more to speak my sentiments); I was, I say, a man of mild dispositions, of command of temper, of an open, social, and cheerful humour, capable of attachment, but little susceptible of enmity, and of great moderation in all my passions. Even my love of literary fame, my ruling passion, never soured my temper, notwithstanding many frequent disappointments. My company was not unacceptable to the young and careless, as well as to the studious and literary; and as I took a particular pleasure in the company of modest women, I had no reason to be displeased with the reception I met with from them. In a word, though most men anywise eminent, have found reason to complain of calumny, I never was touched, or even attacked by her baleful tooth: and though, I wantonly exposed myself to the rage of both civil and religious factions, they seemed to be disarmed in my behalf of their wonted fury. My friends never had occasion to vindicate any one circumstance of my character and conduct: not but that the zealots, we may well suppose, would have been glad to invent and propagate any story to my disadvantage, but they could never find any which they thought would wear the face of probability. I cannot say there is no vanity in making this funeral oration of myself, but I hope it is not a misplaced one; and this is a matter of fact which is easily cleared and ascertained.

April 18, 1776.

LETTER FROM ADAM SMITH, LL.D.,

TO

WILLIAM STRAHAN,[13] ESQ.

Kirkaldy, Fifeshire, Nov. 9, 1776.

Dear Sir, – It is with a real, though a very melancholy pleasure, that I sit down to give you some account of the behaviour of our late excellent friend, Mr. Hume, during his last illness.

Though, in his own judgment, his disease was mortal and incurable, yet he allowed himself to be prevailed upon, by the entreaty of his friends, to try what might be the effects of a long journey. A few days before he set out, he wrote that account of his own life, which, together with his other papers, he has left to your care. My account, therefore, shall begin where his ends.

He set out for London towards the end of April, and at Morpeth met with Mr. John Home[14] and myself, who had both come down from London on purpose to see him, expecting to have found him at Edinburgh. Mr. Home returned with him, and attended him during the whole of his stay in England, with that care and attention which might be expected from a temper so perfectly friendly and affectionate. As I had written to my mother that she might expect me in Scotland, I was under the necessity of continuing my journey. His disease seemed to yield to exercise and change of air, and when he arrived in London, he was apparently in much better health than when he left Edinburgh. He was advised to go to Bath to drink the waters, which appeared for some time to have so good an effect upon him, that even he himself began to entertain, what he was not apt to do, a better opinion of his own health. His symptoms, however, soon returned with their usual violence, and from that moment he gave up all thoughts of recovery, but submitted with the utmost cheerfulness, and the most perfect complacency and resignation. Upon his return to Edinburgh, though he found himself much weaker, yet his cheerfulness never abated, and he continued to divert himself, as usual, with correcting his own works for a new edition, with reading books of amusement, with the conversation of his friends; and, sometimes in the evening, with a party at his favourite game of whist. His cheerfulness was so great, his conversation and amusements run so much in their usual strain, that, notwithstanding all bad symptoms, many people could not believe he was dying. 'I shall tell your friend, Colonel Edmondstone,' said Doctor Dundas to him one day, 'that I left you much better, and in a fair way of recovery.' 'Doctor,' said he, 'as I believe you would not chuse to tell any thing but the truth, you had better tell him, that I am dying as fast as my enemies, if I have any, could wish, and as easily and cheerfully as my best friends could desire.' Colonel Edmondstone soon afterwards came to see him, and take leave of him; and on his way home, he could not forbear writing him a letter bidding him once more an eternal adieu, and applying to him, as to a dying man, the beautiful French verses in which the Abbé Chaulieu,[15] in expectation of his own death, laments his approaching separation from his friend, the Marquis de la Fare. Mr. Hume's magnanimity and firmness were such, that his most affectionate friends knew, that they hazarded nothing in talking or writing to him as to a dying man, and that so far from being hurt by this frankness, he was rather pleased and flattered by it. I happened to come into his room while he was reading this letter, which he had just received, and which he immediately showed me. I told him, that though I was sensible how very much he was weakened, and that appearances were in many respects very bad, yet his cheerfulness was still so great, the spirit of life seemed still to be so very strong in him, that I could not help entertaining some faint hopes. He answered, 'Your hopes are groundless. An habitual diarrhoea of more than a year's standing, would be a very bad disease at any age: at my age it is a mortal one. When I lie down in the evening, I feel myself weaker than when I rose in the morning; and when I rise in the morning, weaker than when I lay down in the evening. I am sensible, besides, that some of my vital parts are affected, so that I must soon die.' 'Well,' said I, 'if it must be so, you have at least the satisfaction of leaving all your friends, your brother's family in particular, in great prosperity.' He said that he felt that satisfaction so sensibly, that when he was reading, a few days before, Lucian's Dialogues of the Dead,[16] among all the excuses which are alleged to Charon[17] for not entering readily into his boat, he could not find one that fitted him; he had no house to finish, he had no daughter to provide for, he had no enemies upon whom he wished to revenge himself. 'I could not well imagine,' said he, 'what excuse I could make to Charon in order to obtain a little delay. I have done every thing of consequence which I ever meant to do; and I could at no time expect to leave my relations and friends in a better situation than that in which I am now likely to leave them; I, therefore, have all reason to die contented.' He then diverted himself with inventing several jocular excuses, which he supposed he might make to Charon, and with imagining the very surly answers which it might suit the character of Charon to return to them. 'Upon further consideration,' said he, 'I thought I might say to him, Good Charon, I have been correcting my works for a new edition. Allow me a little time, that I may see how the Public receives the alterations.' But Charon would answer, 'When you have seen the effect of these, you will be for making other alterations. There will be no end of such excuses; so, honest friend, please step into the boat.' But I might still urge, 'Have a little patience, good Charon; I have been endeavouring to open the eyes of the Public. If I live a few years longer, I may have the satisfaction of seeing the downfall of some of the prevailing systems of superstition.' But Charon would then lose all temper and decency. 'You loitering rogue, that will not happen these many hundred years. Do you fancy I will grant you a lease for so long a term? Get into the boat this instant, you lazy loitering rogue.'

But, though Mr. Hume always talked of his approaching dissolution with great cheerfulness, he never affected to make any parade of his magnanimity. He never mentioned the subject but when the conversation naturally lead to it, and never dwelt longer upon it than the course of the conversation happened to require: it was a subject indeed which occurred pretty frequently, in consequence of the inquiries which his friends, who came to see him, naturally made concerning the state of his health. The conversation which I mentioned above, and which passed on Thursday the 8th of August, was the last, except one, that I ever had with him. He had now become so very weak, that the company of his most intimate friends fatigued him; for his cheerfulness was still so great, his complaisance and social disposition were still so entire, that when any friend was with him, he could not help talking more, and with greater exertion, than suited the weakness of his body. At his own desire, therefore, I agreed to leave Edinburgh, where I was staying partly upon his account, and returned to my mother's house here, at Kirkaldy, upon condition that he would send for me whenever he wished to see me; the physician who saw him most frequently, Dr. Black, undertaking, in the mean time, to write me occasionally an account of the state of his health.

On the 22nd of August, the Doctor wrote me the following letter:

'Since my last, Mr. Hume has passed his time pretty easily, but is much weaker. He sits up, goes down stairs once a day, and amuses himself with reading, but seldom sees anybody. He finds that even the conversation of his most intimate friends fatigues and oppresses him; and it is happy that he does not need it, for he is quite free from anxiety, impatience, or low spirits, and passes his time very well with the assistance of amusing books.' I received the day after a letter from Mr. Hume himself, of which the following is an extract.

'Edinburgh, 23 August, 1776.

'MY DEAREST FRIEND, – I am obliged to make use of my nephew's hand in writing to you, as I do not rise to-day.

* * * * * * * * *

I go very fast to decline, and last night had a small fever, which I hoped might put a quicker period to this tedious illness, but unluckily it has, in a great measure, gone off. I cannot submit to your coming over here on my account, as it is possible for me to see you so small a part of the day, but Doctor Black can better inform you concerning the degree of strength which may from time to time remain with me. Adieu,' etc.

Three days after I received the following letter from Doctor Black.

'Edinburgh, Monday, 26th August, 1776.

85

'DEAR SIR, – Yesterday, about four o'clock afternoon, Mr. Hume expired. The near approach of his death became evident in the night between Thursday and Friday, when his disease became excessive, and soon weakened him so much, that he could no longer rise out of his bed. He continued to the last perfectly sensible, and free from much pain or feelings of distress. He never dropped the smallest expression of impatience; but when he had occasion to speak to the people about him, always did it with affection and tenderness. I thought it improper to write to bring you over, especially as I heard that he had dictated a letter to you desiring you not to come. When he became very weak, it cost him an effort to speak, and he died in such a happy composure of mind, that nothing could exceed it.'

Thus died our most excellent, and never to be forgotten friend; concerning whose philosophical opinions men will, no doubt, judge variously, every one approving, or condemning them, according as they happen to coincide or disagree with his own; but concerning whose character and conduct there can scarce be a difference of opinion. His temper, indeed, seemed to be more happily balanced, if I may be allowed such an expression, than that perhaps of any other man I have every known. Even in the lowest state of his fortune, his great and necessary frugality never hindered him from exercising, upon proper occasions, acts both of charity and generosity. It was a frugality, founded, not upon avarice, but upon the love of independency. The extreme gentleness of his nature never weakened either the firmness of his mind or the steadiness of his resolutions. His constant pleasantry was the genuine effusion of good-nature and good-humour, tempered with delicacy and modesty, and without even the slightest tincture of malignity, so frequently the disagreeable source of what is called wit in other men. It never was the meaning of his raillery to mortify; and therefore, far from offending, it seldom failed to please and delight, even those who were the objects of it. To his friends, who were frequently the objects of it, there was not perhaps any one of all his great and amiable qualities, which contributed more to endear his conversation. And that gaiety of temper, so agreeable in society, but which is so often accompanied with frivolous and superficial qualities, was in him certainly attended with the most severe application, the most extensive learning, the greatest depth of thought, and a capacity in every respect the most comprehensive. Upon the whole, I have always considered him, both in his lifetime and since his death, as approaching as nearly to the idea of a perfectly wise and virtuous man, as perhaps the nature of human frailty will permit.

I ever am, dear Sir,

Most affectionately your's,

ADAM SMITH.

Notes

1   That is, according to the calendar as it was before the Act of 1751 by which the

Julian or 'old style' calendar was replaced by the Gregorian or 'new style' calendar, involving a readjustment of eleven days, and the year was declared to begin henceforth on 1 January rather than on 25 March.

2   The seventeenth-century Dutch jurists John Voetius and Arnoldus Vinnius.

3   General James Sinclair, (d. 1762). In 1746 he was appointed to lead a force of 6,000 men in an attack on Quebec, but the expedition was delayed till too late in the season, and it was diverted into a descent upon Brittany, with the aim of surprising Port L'Orient, where the French East India Company had its depot.

4   *The Free Enquiry into the Miraculous Powers* (1748) by Conyers Middleton argues against the credibility of miracles later than those of the first age of the church.

5   Bishops have the courtesy title of 'Right Reverend'.

6   William Warburton (1698–1779), who became Bishop of Gloucester, was a contentious and bullying writer and divine who made frequent attacks on Hume and of whom Hume, in turn, made a butt.

7   One of the best-known attacks on Hume for his indulgence towards King Charles I and hostility to the Puritans in his *History* was the pamphlet *Letters on Mr. Hume's History of Great Britain* (1756) by the presbyterian minister Daniel Macqueen.

8   Richard Hurd (1720–1808) was Bishop of Worcester. He edited Warburton's '*Remarks*' on Hume's *Natural History of Religion* in 1757; the pamphlet appeared without either author's or editor's name, but Hume at once attributed it to Hurd.

9   Copyright payments.

10 Francis Seymour Conway, Marquis of Hertford (1719–94).

11 Henry Seymour Conway (1721–95); field marshal and politician.

12 Shrank.

13 William Strahan (1715–85), well-known printer and publisher, associated with the publication of Johnson, Gibbon etc.

14 Brother of David Hume. (The surname was sometimes spelt as 'Hume' and sometimes as 'Home'.)

15 The Abbé Guillaume Amfrye Chaulieu (1639–1720) was a friend of the Marquis de la Fare and associate of his in the free-thinking literary circle of the *Temple*; but the particular verses referred to by Smith have not been definitely identified.

16 A fanciful satire by the Greek writer Lucian.

17 The boatman in Greek mythology, who ferried the souls of the dead over the rivers Styx and Acheron, to the infernal regions.

VOLTAIRE

Poem on the Lisbon Disaster (1756)

F. M. A. de Voltaire, *Poèmes sur le Désastre de Lisbonne et sur La Loi Naturelle avec des Préfaces, des Notes etc.*, Genève, n.d. [1756]. Reprinted from *Selected Works of Voltaire*, edited and translated by Joseph McCabe, Watts and Co., London, 1911.

On the morning of Saturday 1 November 1755 there was a violent earthquake at Lisbon, destroying innumerable buildings at the first shock and even more when the city caught on fire and the river Tagus overflowed in three enormous waves. In all, some 10,000 to 15,000 people were killed, and the city was left in ruins.

The whole of Europe was stirred by the news of the disaster. There was an outpouring of scientific and religious controversy over it (mixed with prophecies of general doom). And in the weeks following the earthquake Voltaire was fired to write his famous *Poem on the Lisbon Disaster or an Examination of the Axiom 'All is well'* (his 'sermon', as he called it to friends) in which he used the disaster as conclusive argument against what he saw as the shallow optimism of Pope's 'Whatever is, is right'. In his Preface he writes:

> The author of the poem on *The Disaster of Lisbon* is not an adversary of the illustrious Pope, whom he has always admired and loved: he thinks like him on practically all matters; but, pierced to the heart by the misfortunes of mankind, he wishes to attack the abuse that can be made of that ancient axiom 'All is for the best'. He adopts in its place that sad and more ancient truth, recognised by all men, that 'There is evil upon the earth'; he declares that the phrase 'All is for the best', taken in a strict sense and without hope of a future life, is merely an insult to the miseries of our existence.

And in the same Preface he teases his orthodox readers by pretending to condemn the inference which people had drawn from Pope's theories, viz. that if 'Whatever is, is right' and all is for the best in the best of all possible worlds, then there is no reason to believe that Man is 'fallen' or that there is any need for a Redeemer. To take such a view would mean that you were a Deist, and Voltaire implies that this is what Pope must really have been – as he is himself, though for different reasons.

That the Lisbon earthquake genuinely was a decisive event in the development of Voltaire's pessimism (or at any rate of his 'anti-optimism') may be seen from the fact that it figures again as one of the major incidents in his *Candide*, written two or three years later; and in the novel it leads to discussion of much the same arguments about optimism and Deism.

Voltaire's poem occasioned a controversy between him and Jean-Jacques Rousseau, who, in a long 'Reply to M. de Voltaire', explained pessimism such as Voltaire's as being the product of the unnatural and unhealthy life of the pampered and privileged intellectual. Ask a humble craftsman or a Swiss peasant whether evil predominated over good in human life, as Voltaire suggests, and you would get a very different answer.

UNHAPPY mortals! Dark and mourning earth!
Affrighted gathering of human kind!
Eternal lingering of useless pain!
Come, ye philosophers, who cry, "All's well,"[1]
And contemplate this ruin of a world.
Behold these shreds and cinders of your race,
This child and mother heaped in common wreck,
These scattered limbs beneath the marble shafts–
A hundred thousand whom the earth devours,
Who, torn and bloody, palpitating yet,
Entombed beneath their hospitable roofs,
In racking torment end their stricken lives.
To those expiring murmurs of distress,
To that appalling spectacle of woe,
Will ye reply: "You do but illustrate
The iron laws that chain the will of God"?[2]
Say ye, o'er that yet quivering mass of flesh:
"God is avenged: the wage of sin is death"?
What crime, what sin, had those young hearts
  conceived
That lie, bleeding and torn, on mother's breast?
Did fallen Lisbon deeper drink of vice
Than London, Paris, or sunlit Madrid?
In these men dance; at Lisbon yawns the abyss.
Tranquil spectators of your brothers' wreck,
Unmoved by this repellent dance of death,
Who calmly seek the reason of such storms,
Let them but lash your own security;
Your tears will mingle freely with the flood.

When earth its horrid jaws half open shows,
My plaint is innocent, my cries are just.
Surrounded by such cruelties of fate,
By rage of evil and by snares of death,
Fronting the fierceness of the elements,
Sharing our ills, indulge me my lament.
"'Tis pride," ye say– "the pride of rebel heart,
To think we might fare better than we do."
Go, tell it to the Tagus' stricken banks;
Search in the ruins of that bloody shock;
Ask of the dying in that house of grief,
Whether 'tis pride that calls on heaven for help
And pity for the sufferings of men.
"All's well," ye say, "and all is necessary."
Think ye this universe had been the worse
Without this hellish gulf in Portugal?
Are ye so sure the great eternal cause,
That knows all things, and for itself creates,
Could not have placed us in this dreary clime
Without volcanoes seething 'neath our feet?
Set you this limit to the power supreme?
Would you forbid it use its clemency?
Are not the means of the great artisan
Unlimited for shaping his designs?
The master I would not offend, yet wish
This gulf of fire and sulphur had outpoured
Its baleful flood amid the desert wastes.
God I respect, yet love the universe.
Not pride, alas, it is, but love of man,[3]
To mourn so terrible a stroke as this.

Would it console the sad inhabitants
Of these aflame and desolated shores
To say to them: "Lay down your lives in peace;
For the world's good your homes are sacrificed;
Your ruined palaces shall others build,
For other peoples shall your walls arise;
The North grows rich on your unhappy loss;
Your ills are but a link in general law;
To God you are as those low creeping worms
That wait for you in your predestined tombs"?
What speech to hold to victims of such ruth!
Add not such cruel outrage to their pain.

Nay, press not on my agitated heart
These iron and irrevocable laws,
This rigid chain of bodies, minds, and worlds.
Dreams of the bloodless thinker are such thoughts.

God holds the chain: is not himself enchained;
By his indulgent choice is all arranged;
Implacable he's not, but free and just.
Why suffer we, then, under one so just?[1]
There is the knot your thinkers should undo.
Think ye to cure our ills denying them?
All peoples, trembling at the hand of God,
Have sought the source of evil in the world.
When the eternal law that all things moves
Doth hurl the rock by impact of the winds,
With lightning rends and fires the sturdy oak,
They have no feeling of the crashing blows;
But I, I live and feel, my wounded heart
Appeals for aid to him who fashioned it.

Children of that Almighty Power, we stretch
Our hands in grief towards our common sire.
The vessel, truly, is not heard to say:
"Why should I be so vile, so coarse, so frail?"
Nor speech nor thought is given unto it.
The urn that, from the potter's forming hand,
Slips and is shattered has no living heart
That yearns for bliss and shrinks from misery.
"This misery," ye say, "is others' good."
Yes; from my mouldering body shall be born
A thousand worms, when death has closed my pain.
Fine consolation this in my distress!
Grim speculators on the woes of men,
Ye double, not assuage, my misery.
In you I mark the nerveless boast of pride
That hides its ill with pretext of content.

I am a puny part of the great whole.
Yes; but all animals condemned to live,
All sentient things, born by the same stern law,
Suffer like me, and like me also die.

The vulture fastens on his timid prey,
And stabs with bloody beak the quivering limbs:
All's well, it seems, for it. But in a while
An eagle tears the vulture into shreds;
The eagle is transfixed by shaft of man;
The man, prone in the dust of battlefield,
Mingling his blood with dying fellow men,
Becomes in turn the food of ravenous birds.

---

1 "Sub Deo justo nemo miser nisi mereatur. [Under a just God no one is miserable who has not deserved misery.]" – *St. Augustine.*

Thus the whole world in every member groans:
All born for torment and for mutual death.
And o'er this ghastly chaos you would say
The ills of each make up the good of all!
What blessedness! And as, with quaking voice,
Mortal and pitiful, ye cry, "All's well,"
The universe belies you, and your heart
Refutes a hundred times your mind's conceit.

All dead and living things are locked in strife.
Confess it freely – evil stalks the land
Its secret principle unknown to us.
Can it be from the author of all good?
Are we condemned to weep by tyrant law
Of black Typhon or barbarous Ahriman?[2]
These odious monsters, whom a trembling world
Made gods, my spirit utterly rejects.

But how conceive a God supremely good,
Who heaps his favours on the sons he loves,
Yet scatters evil with as large a hand?
What eye can pierce the depth of his designs?
From that all-perfect Being came not ill:
And came it from no other, for he's lord:
Yet it exists. O stern and numbing truth!
O wondrous mingling of diversities!
A God came down to lift our stricken race:
He visited the earth, and changed it not!
One sophist says he had not power to change;
"He had," another cries, "but willed it not:
In time he will, no doubt." And, while they prate,
The hidden thunders, belched from underground,
Fling wide the ruins of a hundred towns
Across the smiling face of Portugal.
God either smites the inborn guilt of man,
Or, arbitrary lord of space and time,
Devoid alike of pity and of wrath,
Pursues the cold designs he has conceived.
Or else this formless stuff, recalcitrant,
Bears in itself inalienable faults;
Or else God tries us, and this mortal life
Is but the passage to eternal spheres.[4]
'Tis transitory pain we suffer here,
And death its merciful deliverance.
Yet, when this dreadful passage has been made,
Who will contend he has deserved the crown?

2 The Egyptian and Persian principles of evil.

Whatever side we take we needs must groan;
We nothing know, and everything must fear.
Nature is dumb, in vain appeal to it,
The human race demands a word of God.
'Tis his alone to illustrate his work,
Console the weary, and illume the wise.
Without him man, to doubt and error doomed,
Finds not a reed that he may lean upon.

From Leibnitz learn we not by what unseen
Bonds, in this best of all imagined worlds,
Endless disorder, chaos of distress,
Must mix our little pleasures thus with pain;
Nor why the guiltless suffer all this woe
In common with the most abhorrent guilt.
'Tis mockery to tell me all is well.
Like learned doctors, nothing do I know.

Plato has said that men did once have wings[5]
And bodies proof against all mortal ill;
That pain and death were strangers to their world.
How have we fallen from that high estate!
Man crawls and dies: all is but born to die:
The world's the empire of destructiveness.
This frail construction of quick nerves and bones
Cannot sustain the shock of elements;
This temporary blend of blood and dust
Was put together only to dissolve;
This prompt and vivid sentiment of nerve
Was made for pain, the minister of death:
Thus in my ear does nature's message run.
Plato and Epicurus I reject,[6]
And turn more hopefully to learned Bayle.[7]
With even poised scale Bayle bids me doubt.
He, wise enough and great to need no creed,
Has slain all systems[8] – combats even himself:
Like that blind conqueror of Philistines,[9]
He sinks beneath the ruin he has wrought.
What is the verdict of the vastest mind?
Silence: the book of fate is closed to us.
Man is a stranger to his own research;
He knows not whence he comes, nor whither goes.
Tormented atoms in a bed of mud,
Devoured by death, a mockery of fate.
But thinking atoms, whose far-seeing eyes,
Guided by thought, have measured the faint stars,
Our being mingles with the infinite;
Ourselves we never see, or come to know.

This world, this theatre of pride and wrong,
Swarms with sick fools who talk of happiness.
With plaints and groans they follow up the quest,
To die reluctant, or be born again.
At fitful moments in our pain-racked life
The hand of pleasure wipes away our tears;
But pleasure passes like a fleeting shade,
And leaves a legacy of pain and loss.
The past for us is but a fond regret,
The present grim, unless the future's clear.
If thought must end in darkness of the tomb,
All will be well one day – so runs our hope.
All *now* is well, is but an ideal dream.
The wise deceive me: God alone is right.
With lowly sighing, subject in my pain,
I do not fling myself 'gainst Providence.
Once did I sing, in less lugubrious tone,
The sunny ways of pleasure's genial rule;[10]
The times have changed, and, taught by growing
  age,
And sharing of the frailty of mankind,
Seeking a light amid the deepening gloom,
I can but suffer, and will not repine.

A caliph once, when his last hour had come,
This prayer addressed to him he reverenced:
"To thee, sole and all-powerful king, I bear
What thou dost lack in thy immensity–
Evil and ignorance, distress and sin."
He might have added one thing further – hope.[11]

Notes

1   Voltaire has Leibniz and Pope particularly in mind.

2   Voltaire appends a long note in which he equates the Great Chain of Being (i.e. the theory that there is a continuous chain or ladder of creatures, extending without break from the worm to the angel) with the notion that every event in the history of the universe is necessarily connected with every other. He attacks both theories; the first, on much the same grounds as Dr Johnson (see p. 111) and the second on the grounds that, though every event must inevitably have a *cause* in some preceding event, not every event has an *effect*. If Caesar's mother had not had a 'caesarian' operation, Caesar would not have destroyed the Roman Republic; but whether Caesar spat to his left side or to his right would have changed nothing in future history.

3   Voltaire is evidently alluding to Epistle 1 of Pope's *Essay on Man*, in which Pope repeatedly argues that it is pride and presumption on Man's part to question the benevolence of Providence.

4   Voltaire has a note on these eight lines: 'Here, when you add the theory of the "two principles" (i.e. Manicheism) you have all the solutions available to the human mind in this great problem; and only Revelation can instruct us rightly on what is incomprehensible to the human intelligence.'

5   See Socrates's discourse on Love in the *Phaedrus*, in which he says that a soul that has lost its feathers falls to earth and takes on an earthly body, thereby becoming what is known as an 'animal' or a 'mortal' (*Phaedrus*, 246).

6   That is as the exponents of, respectively, the attaching of *all* importance or of *no* importance to the afterlife and to divine as opposed to human existence.

7   Pierre Bayle (1647–1706) sceptical French philosopher and lexicographer revered by Voltaire and the *philosophes* generally and whose *Critical and Historical Dictionary* (1697) was in some ways the forerunner of the *Encyclopédie*.

8   This word had a special and pejorative sense for Voltaire and his fellow-*philosophes*, as signifying elaborate philosophical constructions built upon a hypothesis (or hypotheses) rather than upon experiment and observation.

9   Samson.

10   In his youth Voltaire wrote a number of cheerful and libertine poems praising wordly pleasures, for instance *Le mondain* [The Man of the World] (1736).

11   The point of this is ironical, for the hope of which Voltaire speaks is the hope that there is a better life to come after this on earth; which is to say, more or less, the hope that God exists, or that there is anyone in the universe to hear the caliph's prayer – thus a hope that is even less appropriate to God's situation than 'evil and ignorance, distress and sin'. (You can hardly hope that you yourself exist.)

ROUSSEAU

On Providence (1756)

From Jean-Jacques Rousseau, *Lettre de J. J. Rousseau à Monsieur de Voltaire Le 18 Aout 1756*. [Berlin] 1759. Reprinted from *The Miscellaneous Works of M. J. J. Rousseau* [translation by W. Kenrick], 5 vols, 1767. Printed for T. Becket and P. A. DeHondt, in the Strand, Volume II.

Jean-Jacques Rousseau (1712–78), was the author of *Emile*, *Of the Social Contract* and the *Confessions*. His Letter to Voltaire on Providence, dated 18 August 1756, published some time after, became renowned. The passages commenting on Pope and Leibniz were frequently included in later anthologies of Rousseau's 'Thoughts' or 'Philosophy'. Voltaire had sent copies of his poems *On Natural Law* and *On the Lisbon Disaster* to Diderot, D'Alembert and Rousseau. This is Rousseau's reply, and it combines incisive logic with personal testimony. If Voltaire viewed the Lisbon earthquake as a frightening challenge to his faith in providence, Rousseau held his beliefs intact, and used the occasion to set out the issues with lucidity.

He begins by considering whether the earthquake was truly an evil. He attacks man's attachment to property and possessions and argues (as Swift had done in *Gulliver's Travels*) that death need not be an evil; men forget the 'delightful consciousness of existence', and 'the vanity of despising death' induces philosphers 'to under-value life'. This line of thought leads later in the letter to the distinction between evil in the physical order of things, and evil in the moral order.

Rousseau replies to Voltaire in another way, by explaining the basis of beliefs in providence such as that expressed in Pope's *Essay on Man*. Occasional disasters and personal misfortunes do not disprove the power of providence: 'it is very likely that in the order of human things Providence is neither right nor wrong; because everything depends on a certain general law, that makes no exception of persons'.

Thirdly, Rousseau shows that belief in providence is not a rational assumption, but a religious one: 'The true principles of optimism cannot be *deduced* either from the properties of matter, or the mechanism of the universe; but only by *induction* from the perfections of the Deity, who presides over the whole: so that we cannot prove the existence of God, from the system of Pope, but the system of Pope, from the existence of God.'

Rousseau has used his intellectual powers to lay bare the foundation of Voltaire's (and his own) faith. In the last analysis, he confesses, 'a state of doubt is a state too violent for my soul, but when my reason is afloat, my faith cannot remain in suspense, but determines without its direction'.

---

18 August 1756

Your two last poems,[1] Sir, reached me in this solitude; but, though all my friends are acquainted with the passion I have for your writings, I know not from whom these pieces could come, unless from yourself. I have found in them both pleasure and instruction, and discovered the hand of a master; thinking myself indebted to you, at once, for the copy and the work. I cannot say that every part appears to me equally good; but the things which displease me, serve only to make me place greater confidence in those which give me delight. It is not without pain I sometimes arm my reason against the charms of your poesy: but it is with a view to render my admiration more worthy of your works, that I thus endeavour not to admire them indiscriminately.

I will do more, Sir, I will tell you ingenuously, not the beauties which I think I perceive in your two poems; the task is too great for my indolence; nor even the faults, which it is possible persons of greater judgment than I, may find in them: but the displeasure which at present affects the taste I have for your lessons; and I will tell it you, while I am still moved by a first perusal, in which my heart listened attentively to yours; loving you as a brother, honouring you as my master, flattering myself, in fine, that you will discover in my intentions the frankness of an ingenuous mind, and in my discourse, the voice of a friend to truth who is speaking to a philosopher. Besides, the more your second poem enchants me, the more freely can I take part against the first. For if you have not been afraid to oppose yourself, why should I be afraid of being of your opinion? I ought not to think you can make any great dependence on sentiments you have so well refuted.

The whole cause of my complaint is in your poem on the fatal disaster which hath befallen Lisbon; because I expected from it effects more worthy of that humanity with which you seem to have been inspired. You reproach Pope and Leibnitz with insulting mankind under their misfortunes, by maintaining that every thing is good, and expatiate so amply on the picture of our miseries, that you aggravate the sense of them. Instead of the consolation I hoped for; you have only given me affliction. One would think you were afraid I should not sufficiently feel my own unhappiness; and seem to think you give me much tranquillity in proving that every thing is evil.

Be not mistaken, Sir, the very contrary happened to what you seem to have proposed. That optimism, which appears to you so cruel, consoles me, under the very miseries which you describe as insupportable.

Mr. Pope's poem alleviates my evils, and induces me to patience; yours embitters my sorrows, excites my complaints, and, depriving me of every thing but a doubtful hope, reduces me to despair.

Amidst this strange opposition which subsists between what you lay down and what I experience, calm the perplexity with which I am agitated, and tell me who is misled either by sentiment or reason. "Man, have patience," say Pope and Leibnitz: "The evils you experience are the necessary effect of your nature, and the constitution of the universe. That benevolent and eternal Being which governs, will protect you. Of all possible systems, he hath chosen that which contains the least evil with the greatest good; or (to say the same thing more crudely, if it be necessary) if he hath not done better, it was because it was out of his power."

Now what says your poem? "Continue, unhappy wretch, to suffer. If there be a God, who hath created you, he is, without doubt, omnipotent; he could have prevented all the evils you suffer. You must not hope, therefore, they will have an end; for we cannot see why you exist, except to suffer and to die." I do not know what such a doctrine can contain more consolatory than optimism, or even fatality itself. For my own part, I confess it appears still more cruel than Manicheism.[2] If the difficulty attending the origin of evil obliges you to alter any of the perfections of the Deity, why would you justify his power at the expense of his goodness? Were I to chuse between the two errours, I should certainly prefer the former.

You would not have your work looked upon as a poem against Providence; and I shall beware of calling it such, although you have called a performance,[3] in which I pleaded the cause of mankind against themselves, a book written against mankind. I am not to learn that a distinction is necessary to be made between the intentions of an author, and the consequences which may be deduced from his doctrines. The just defence of myself, obliges me only to observe to you, that my end, in describing the miseries of mankind, was, in my opinion, excusable and even commendable: for I shewed in what manner men brought their own misfortunes on themselves, and consequently how they might avoid them.

I see not where we must look for the source of moral evil, except in man, a free, improved and yet corrupted Being; and as to physical evils, if matter cannot be at once susceptible and impenetrable, as it appears to me it cannot, they must be unavoidable in every system of which man constitutes a part: and then the question is not, "Why is not man perfectly happy?" but, "Why does he exist?" Again, I think I have shewn that, death excepted, which can be called an evil only from its preceding preparatives, the greater part of our physical evils are our own work. Without quitting the subject of Lisbon, you must agree, for example, that nature never assembled there twenty thousand houses of six or seven stories high; and that, if the inhabitants of that great city had been more equally dispersed, and more lightly lodged, the damage would have been much less, and perhaps none at all. Every body would have taken flight at the first shock, and would have been seen the next day twenty leagues off, as gay as if nothing had happened. But as it was, every one was obliged to stay, obstinately determined to remain near the ruins, exposed to new shocks, because what they must leave was worth more than what they could take away. How many unhappy persons must have perished in that disaster, merely from persisting, some to take their cloaths, some their papers, and others their money! Is it not well known that the person of a man is become the least part of him, and that there is hardly any trouble in saving that, when he has lost everything else?

You could have wished (and who would not have wished the same?) that the earthquake had happened rather in the middle of a desart than in Lisbon. Can it be doubted that earthquakes happen also in desarts? But no notice is taken of them, because they do no harm to the gentry of the cities, the only persons of whom any account is made. Not that they do much even to the animals and savages dispersed throughout those solitary wilds, who are neither afraid of the falling of tiles, nor the tottering of houses. But what signifies such a privilege? Will it therefore be said, that the order of things ought to be changed agreeably to our caprices; that nature ought to be submitted to our laws; and that, we have nothing more to do than to build a city on a certain spot, to secure it for ever from earthquakes?

There are many events which strike us more or less, according to the light in which they are seen; and which become much less horrible than they at first appeared, when they are examined more nearly. I have learned from Zadig,[4] and nature daily confirms the truth of it, that an untimely death is not always a real evil, and may sometimes pass for a relative good. Among the number of those who perished under the ruins of Lisbon, many of them, doubtless, avoided greater misfortunes; and notwithstanding the occasion which such a subject affords for pathetic and poetic description, it is not certain that any one individual of those unfortunate persons actually suffered more than he might have done, if, according to the ordinary course of things, he had received the stroke of death through the lingering anguish of disease. In a word, could their end be more lamentable than that of a dying man, tormented by fruitless solicitudes; whom his heirs and their lawyers will hardly permit to breathe; whom the physicians murder in his bed at their ease; and to whom the barbarous priests administer the bitterest potion of death, and artfully make the patient taste it drop by drop, even to the very dregs? For my part, look which way I will, I see the evils, to which we are exposed by nature, are much less cruel than those which unnecessarily add to them.

But how ingenious soever we may be in fomenting our miseries by dint of curious institutions, we have not been able as yet to improve ourselves to such a degree, as to make life a burthen, and to cause us generally to prefer annihilation to existence: which if we did not do, discouragement and despair would soon take off the greater part of mankind, and the human race could not long subsist. Now, if it be better for us to be than not to be, this would be sufficient to justify our existence, even if we had no indemnification to expect for the evils we are to endure, and if those evils were as great as you describe them. But it is difficult to find men sincere, or philosophers good calculators, on this subject. Because the one, in making an estimate of the good and ill of human life, always forget the delightful consciousness of existence, which is independent of every other sensation; and because the vanity of despising death, induces the others to undervalue life; just as those sluttish women, who having dirty gowns and a pair of scissars at hand, pretend to loves holes better than spots.

You think, with Erasmus,[5] that there are very few people in the world who would wish to live their lives over again; but a man may set an high price upon a commodity, and yet be glad to bate a good deal, on a fair prospect of concluding the bargain. Besides, Sir, whom am I to suppose you have consulted on this head? The rich, perhaps, sated with false pleasures, but ignorant of the true; always weary of life, yet always fearing to lose it? Or men of letters perhaps, who of all ranks of men are the most sedentary, unhealthful, thoughtful, and of course unhappy. Would you find men of better constitution, or at least generally more sincere, and who forming the majority of the people, ought to be heard in preference to the former? Consult an honest tradesman who hath passed his life in obscurity and tranquillity, free from projects or ambition; a good artizan who lives well by his business; or even a peasant; not indeed in France, where it is pretended necessary to starve the peasants in order to enable us to live; but in the country where you now reside, and almost in every other free country. I will venture to lay it down as a fact, that there is not in the higher Valais,[6] a single mountaineer discontent with his almost mechanical existence, and who would not readily accept, even in exchange for the raptures of paradise, a perpetual regeneration in this life: fully satisfied to vegetate thus for ever. It is this palpable difference which makes me believe that it is often the abuse we make of life, which makes it burthensome to us; and I have a much less good opinion of those who regret their having been born, than of him who should say, with Cato, 'Nec me vixisse poenitet, quoniam ita vixi, ut frustra me natum non existimem'.[7] This does not prevent the sage, however, from rushing voluntarily on death, when nature or fortune bring him a very distinct order for his departure. But, according to the ordinary course of things, whatever evils are interspersed throughout human life, it is not, on the whole, a bad present; and if it be not always an evil to die, it is very seldom one to live.

Our different manner of thinking upon all these articles, sufficiently informs me why so many of your arguments appear to me inconclusive. For I am not ignorant that human reason takes more easily the form of our opinions than that of truth, and that when two people are of contrary notions, what appears demonstrated to the one is often mere sophistry to the other. Thus for example, when you attack the chain of beings, so well described by Pope, you say it is not true, that if a single atom were taken from the universe, the world would not subsist. On this head, you quote M. de Crouzas;[8] to whose authority you add that nature is not confined to any precise measure or form; that none of the planets moves in orbits absolutely regular; that no known created being is of any precise mathematical figure; that no precise quantity is required for any physical operation; that nature never acts rigorously exact; so that we have no reason to affirm that the loss of an atom would be the destruction of the whole earth. I must confess, Sir, that I am much more struck with the force of the assertion than with that of the proofs, and that on this occasion I should sooner concede to your authority than your argument.

With regard to M. de Crouzas, I never read his performance against Pope, nor am I capable perhaps of understanding it; but this is very certain, that I shall not give up to him what I dispute with you, and that I place as little confidence in his arguments as in his authority. I am indeed so far from thinking that nature is not confined to precision in regard to figure and quantity, that I believe, on the contrary, nature alone follows that rigorous precision; because nature alone is capable of making an exact comparison between the end and the means, and of adjusting the proportion between force and resistance. As to those pretended irregularities you speak of, can it be doubted that they have all their physical cause, and are we authorized to deny the existence of such cause, merely because we cannot perceive it? Those apparent irregularities arise, without doubt, from some laws, of which we are ignorant, and which nature follows as constantly as she does those we are acquainted with; from some agent which we do not perceive, the measures of whose opposition or concurrence are fixed in all its operations; otherwise we must flatly assert that there are actions that have no principle, and effects that have no cause, which is repugnant to all philosophy. [...]

As for the rest, you have certainly made a just correction of the system of Pope, in observing that there can be no proportional gradation between the creatures and their Creator; and that if the chain of created beings reaches up to God, it is because he holds that chain, not because he terminates it. With regard to the good of the whole, in preference to that of a part, you make man say, "I ought surely to be as dear to my master; I, who am a sensible thinking being, as the planets, which probably do not think." Doubtless the material universe ought not to be more dear to its author, than a sensible thinking being. But the system of that universe, which produces, preserves and perpetuates, all sensible and thinking beings, ought surely to be more dear to him than any single individual of those beings: he may, therefore,

101

notwithstanding his goodness, sacrifice something of the happiness of individuals to the preservation of the whole. I believe, and hope, that I am more estimable in the eyes of God than the earth, or mere material substance of a planet; but if the planets are all inhabited, as is very probable, why should I be more estimable in his eyes, than all the inhabitants of Saturn? These notions, it is true, may be turned into ridicule; but it is certain, that such population is supported by analogy, and that nothing but human pride is against it. Now this population supposed, the preservation of the universe seems, even with regard to the Deity, to be a moral object, which is multiplied by the number of habitable worlds.

That the dead body of a man affords nourishment for worms, for wolves, or plants, is not, I confess, an indemnification for the death of that man; but if, in the general system of the universe, it be necessary to the preservation of the human species, that there should be a circulation of substance between men, animals, and vegetables, the particular inconvenience to the individual, contributes to the good of the whole. I die, I am eaten by worms; but my children, my brothers live as I have lived; and I only do that by the order of nature, for all mankind, what Codrus, Curtius, Decius,[9] and a thousand others have done voluntarily, for a small part of it.

To return, Sir, to the system you have attacked; I conceive it cannot be conveniently examined, without carefully distinguishing that particular evil, the existence of which no philosopher ever denied, from that general evil which is denied by the optimist. The question is not whether individuals suffer; but whether the existence of the universe be, on the whole, good or not, and whether our particular sufferings are not unavoidable in the constitution of that universe. Thus it appears to me, that the addition of a single particle will render the proposition exact; that is instead of saying *Tout est bien* (all is good) we should say *Le tout est bien* (the whole is good) or *Tout est bien pour le tout* (all is good for the whole). It is thus very evident, that no body can bring a direct proof, either for or against it: for these proofs depend on a perfect knowledge of the constitution of the world, and the design of its Author; which knowledge is incontestibly above the reach of the human understanding.

The true principles of optimism cannot be deduced either from the properties of matter, or the mechanism of the universe; but only by induction from the perfections of the Deity, who presides over the whole: so that we cannot prove the existence of God, from the system of Pope, but the system of Pope, from the existence of God: and without contradiction, the question about the origin of evil, is derived from that of Providence. If one of these questions also hath been treated no better than the other, it is because we have always reasoned so badly about Providence, that the absurdities of the argument have confused all the corollaries that might be deduced from this important and consolatory tenet.

The first of those who hurt the cause of God were the priests and devotees, who will not admit, that any thing happens according to the established order of things; but always suppose an intervention of Divine Justice, in events that are purely natural; and, to be certain of being right, punish the wicked and reward the good, exactly according to the event. For my part, I know not but it may be good divinity; but I think it a very bad way of reasoning, to conclude for or against individuals, on those pretended proofs of Providence; and to impute to design that which would have happened equally without it.

Again, the philosophers, on their side, do not appear to me a jot more reasonable, when we hear them complaining against Heaven, because they are not insensible; and crying out that all is wrong, when they have got the toothach, are indigent, or are robbed; and charging the Deity, as Seneca[10] says, with the care of their portmantua. Had any tragical accident put an end to Cartouche[11] or Caesar in their infancy, it had been asked, what crimes have they committed?

Those two robbers have lived, and we cry, Why were they suffered to exist? A devotee, on the contrary, would say, in the first case, that God designed to punish the father in depriving him of his child; and in the second, that God preserved the child for the punishment of the people. Thus let nature act as it will, Providence is always in the right in the opinion of the devotees, and always wrong in the opinion of the philosophers. Whereas it is very likely that in the order of human things, Providence is neither right nor wrong; because everything depends on a certain general law, that makes no exception of persons. It is probable that the particular events which happen here below, are nothing in the sight of the Creator and Governor of the universe; that he contents himself with the preservation of the genus and species, and with presiding over the whole, without troubling himself about the manner in which each individual passes this short and transitory life. Doth a prudent monarch, who nevertheless would have every body live happy under his government, give himself any concern whether or not the inns are good on the roads through his kingdom? The traveller, indeed, grumbles for a night, when he finds them bad, and laughs all the rest of his life at the absurdity of his impatience.

Commemorandi enim natura diversorium nobis, non habitandi dedit.[12] To enable us to form just conceptions on this subject, it seems that things should be considered as relative in the *physical* order, and as absolute in the *moral*; so that the greatest idea I can form of Providence, is that every material Being is disposed in the best manner possible with regard to the whole universe; and every sensible and intelligent Being in the best manner possible with regard to himself: that is in other terms, it must be better for every Being, conscious of his existence, to exist than not to exist. But this rule must be applied to the total duration of every sensible Being, and not to some particular moments of his duration, such as is that of human life: a circumstance, that shews how closely the subject of providence is connected with that of the immortality of the soul; which I have the happiness to believe, without being ignorant that it may be reasonably doubted; and with that of the eternity of Hell-torments, which neither you nor I, nor any thinking Being that believes in God, ever can believe.

If we apply these several questions to their common principle, it appears to me that they all relate to that of the existence of God. If God exists, he is perfect; if he is perfect, he is wise, powerful and just; if he is wise and powerful, all is good; if he is just and powerful my soul is immortal; if my soul is immortal, thirty years of life are nothing to me, and are necessary perhaps to the preservation of the universe. If the first proposition is granted me, the following cannot be affected: if it be denied, we have no business to dispute about the following.

We are, neither of us, in the latter case. So far at least am I from presuming any thing like it on your part, from the perusal of your works, that the greater part of them present the greatest, most merciful and most consolatory ideas of the Deity; and I love a Christian of your order much better than one of the Sorbonne.[13] As to my own part, I will confess to you ingenuously, that I think neither the pro nor contrary are demonstrable merely by the light of reason; and that if the Theist[14] founds his sentiments only on probabilities, the Atheist, still less exact, appears to found his only on opposite possibilities. Add to this, that the objections which arise, both on one side and the other, are insoluble; because they relate to things, of which mankind have no true idea. I agree to all this, and yet I believe in God as firmly as in any other truth whatever; because to believe and not to believe, depend less than any thing else on myself: a state of doubt is a state too violent for my soul, but when my reason is afloat, my faith cannot remain long in suspense, but determines without its direction. In short, a thousand motives draw me to the most consolatary side, and add the weight of hope to the equilibrium of reason.

This then is a truth at which we both set out, and on the support of which you perceive how easy it is to defend optimism, and to justify providence, and it is not necessary to repeat to you those hackneyed but solid arguments, which have so often been made use of on the subject. With regard to such philosophers as do not agree to the first principle, it is in vain to dispute with them on these matters; because that which is only a sentimental proof to us, cannot be a demonstrative one to them; and it is by no means reasonable to say to any man, "You ought to believe so or so, because I believe it." They, on their side, also ought to dispute with us as little on these matters; because they are only corollaries of a principal proposition, which a candid opponent would hardly oppose them with; while, on their part, they would be wrong to insist on our proving the corollary independent of the proposition on which it is founded. I think also they ought not for another reason. And that is, it is inhuman to disturb the peace of mind, and make men unhappy; when what we teach them is neither certain nor useful. In a word, I think, after your example, that we cannot too strongly attack superstition which is the disturber of society, nor too highly respect religion which is the support of it.

But I am incensed, as well as you, that every man's faith should not be left at perfect liberty; and that man should dare to lay a restraint on conscience, which it is impossible for him to penetrate; as if it depended on ourselves to believe or not to believe respecting things incapable of demonstration, or as if reason could be ever subjected to authority. Have the kings of this world any inspection into the next? And have they a right to torture their subjects here below, in order to force them into paradise? No. Every human government is limited by its nature to civil obligations; and, whatever that sophist Hobbes[15] may say about the matter, if a man discharges his duty toward the state, he owes no account to any one, in what manner he serves God. I know not if that just Being will not one day punish every instance of tyranny exercised in his name: at least, I am very sure, he will never justify them, nor refuse eternal happiness to any sincere and virtuous believer. Can I doubt, without offending his goodness and even his justice, that an upright heart will be excused an involuntary errour, or that irreproachable morals are not more estimable than a thousand whimsical modes of worship prescribed by authority and rejected by reason? I will go farther; if it were in my power to chuse, to purchase good works at the expence of faith, and to make up for my supposed infidelity, I should not hesitate a moment; but had rather have to say to the Deity; "I have done, without thinking of you, the good which is agreeable to you; my heart hath been inclined to your will without knowing it;" than have to say to him, as I must one day do; "Alas, I love and yet have never ceased to offend you; I have known your will, and yet have done nothing conformable to it."

I confess there is a sort of profession of faith which the laws may impose; but if the principles of morality and natural right be excepted, it ought to be purely negative; because there may exist religions that attack the foundation of society, and it is necessary to begin by exterminating those religions, to secure the tranquillity of the state. Of such tenets as ought to be proscribed, intolerance is without doubt the most odious: but it must be checked in its sources; for the most sanguinary fanatics change their language with their fortune; preaching up patience and candour only when they are not the strongest. Thus I call every man intolerant from principle, who conceives no man can be a man of virtue and probity, who does not believe exactly what he does, and unmercifully consigns to perdition all those who do not think like himself. In a word, the faithful are very seldom in a humour to leave the reprobate at peace in this world; while a saint who imagines he lives among the damned, readily anticipates the task of playing the devil with them. Again, if there should be any such thing as intolerant Infidels, who would compel other people to believe nothing, I would banish them no less severely than I would those who would compel people to believe just what they pleased.

I would have therefore, in every state a moral code, or a kind of civil profession of faith; containing positively the several social maxims which every one should be bound to admit, and negatively the fanatical maxims he should be bound to reject; not as impious, but as seditious.

In which case, every religion reconcileable to the code, should be admitted; and every religion irreconcileable to it, rejected; while individuals should be at liberty to have no other religion than the code itself. A work of this kind, carefully drawn up, would, in my opinion, be the most useful book that ever was composed, and perhaps the only one necessary for mankind. Here, Sir, is a subject worthy of your genius; and I passionately wish you would undertake such a work, and embellish it with your poetry, so that, being easily learned, it might inspire into all hearts, even in infancy, those sentiments of candour and humanity which are so conspicuous in your writings, and are always wanting in those of devotees. I advise you to meditate on this project, which ought at least to give pleasure to your soul. You have given us in your poem on natural religion, the Catachism of Man; give us in that which I propose to you the Catechism of a Citizen. It is a subject that requires long contemplation, and to be reserved perhaps for the last of your works, in order that you may finish, by an act of benevolence to mankind, the most brilliant career that ever was run by a man of letters.

I cannot help remarking, Sir, on this head, a very singular contrast between you and me with regard to the subject of this letter. Sated with glory, and undeceived with regard to the inanity of wordly grandeur, you live at freedom in the midst of plenty; certain of immortality, you peaceably philosophise on the nature of the soul; and if the body or the heart are indisposed, you have Tronchin[16] for your physician and friend: yet with all this you find nothing but evil on the face of the earth. I, on the other hand, obscure, indigent, tormented with an incurable disorder, meditate with pleasure in my solitude, and find everything to be good. Whence arise these apparent contradictions? You have yourself explained them; you live in a state of enjoyment; I in a state of hope; and hope gives charms to every thing.

It is with as much difficulty I close this tedious letter as you will have to go through it. Forgive me, Sir, a zeal which, however it may be indiscreet, would not have displayed itself before you, if I had esteemed you less. God forbid I should offend him, whose talents I honour above those of all my contemporaries, and whose writings speak the most forcibly to my heart; but the cause of Providence is at stake, on which all my expectations depend. After having so long deduced courage and consolation from your lessons, it is hard for you to deprive me of them now; to give me only a vague and uncertain hope, rather by way of a present palliative, than as a future indemnity. No. I have suffered too much in this life not to expect another. Not all the subtilties of metaphysics can make me doubt a moment of the immortality of the soul, and of a beneficent providence. I feel it, I believe it, I desire it, I hope it, and will defend it to my last breath: and this, of all the disputes in which I have been engaged, is the only one in which my own interest will not be forgotten.

I am, Sir, etc.

Notes

1   Voltaire's poems *On Natural Law* and *On the Lisbon Disaster*.
2   A doctrine originating in Persia in third century A.D. according to which the universe is controlled by two antagonistic powers, light or goodness (identified with God), and darkness, chaos or evil.
3   Rousseau's *Discourse on Inequality* (1755).
4   Oriental tale by Voltaire (1748).
5   Desiderius Erasmus (1469–1536), Dutch humanist and scholar.
6   Valais: a mountainous 'canton' in the South-west of Switzerland Voltaire was living in the neighbouring region, in Geneva, at this time.
7   From Cicero, *Concerning Old Age*; 'Nor do I regret having lived, since I have so lived that I think I was not born to no purpose'. Rousseau took the quotation from Erasmus, however, not directly from Cicero.
8   Crouzas or, more commonly, J. P. de Crousaz, Swiss professor of philosophy and theologian; author of two commentaries on Pope's *Essay on Man*, both attacking the poem on religious grounds. Crousaz accused Pope of being a disciple of Leibniz.
9   Heroes who sacrificed themselves for others. Codrus was the last king of Athens; after it had been prophesied that only a king's death could ensure the Athenians' victory, he entered the enemies' camp and was killed. Marcus Curtius threw himself into the gulf which opened in the Forum in 362B.C. The seers had said that it would never close until Rome's most valuable treasure (a brave citizen) was cast into it. Publius Decius Mus and his son sacrificed themselves in battle to ensure victory for their side.
10   Lucius Annaeus Seneca (4B.C.–A.D.65), Roman writer, tutor to Nero; author of philosophical dialogues, treatises and tragedies.
11   Louis Dominique Cartouche (1693–1721), leader of a band of thieves.
12   From Cicero (see note 7 above); 'for it is as an hostelry for tarrying in, not as a place for dwelling in, that nature has assigned life to us'.
13   The Faculty of Theology at the University of Paris; it was a centre of Roman Catholic Orthodoxy.
14   'Deist'.
15   Thomas Hobbes (1588–1679) (see p. 43, note 1).
16   Théodore Tronchin (1709–81), a famous Swiss doctor; honorary professor of medicine at Geneva 1755–66.

SAMUEL JOHNSON

On Optimism (1757)

From Samuel Johnson, Review of Soame Jenyns's *A Free Inquiry into the Nature and Origin of Evil*, first published in the Literary Magazine: or Universal Review in May, June and July 1757. Reprinted from *The Works of Samuel Johnson LLD*. Edited by Robert Lynam, George Cowie and Co., London 1825 in six vols., Vol. 5.

This attack by Johnson on Soame Jenyns, a writer otherwise forgotten, is widely regarded as a classic of irony and satire. In its ridicule of facile and unfeeling optimism (based in Jenyn's case on the doctrines of Pope in his *Essay on Man*) it can be regarded as a small-scale English equivalent to Voltaire's *Candide*. The force of Johnson's attack, as of Voltaire's, lies to a considerable extent in the appeal to experience – i.e. to what we all, but especially such widely-experienced men as themselves, know to be the actual conditions of human life. As Johnson remarks (p. 113) 'Life must be seen before it can be known. This author and Pope perhaps never saw the miseries which they imagine thus easy to be borne.'

An important part of Johnson's satire is that directed against the notion of the Great Chain of Being – the theory, which dates back to ancient Greece but in particular favour in the early eighteenth century, that the universe presents the spectacle of a continuous chain or ladder of creatures, extending without break from the worm to the angel. Johnson's remark (p. 111) that he had 'often considered' this theory, but he always 'left the inquiry in doubt and uncertainty' may be taken as ironical understatement, since in a later paragraph (omitted here) he says of the theory, that 'no system can be more hypothetical than this, and perhaps no hypothesis more absurd'.

This is a treatise consisting of Six Letters upon a very difficult and important question, which I am afraid this author's endeavours will not free from the perplexity which has entangled the speculatists of all ages, and which must always continue while *we see* but *in part*. He calls it a *Free*

Inquiry, and indeed his *freedom* is, I think, greater than his modesty. Though he is far from the contemptible arrogance, or the impious licentiousness of Bolingbroke,[1] yet he decides too easily upon questions out of reach of human determination, with too little consideration of mortal weakness and with too much vivacity for the necessary caution.

In the first letter *on Evil in general*, he observes, that, "it is the solution of this important question, *whence came Evil*, alone, that can ascertain the moral characteristick of God, without which there is an end of all distinction between Good and Evil." Yet he begins this Inquiry by this declaration: "That there is a Supreme Being, infinitely powerful, wise, and benevolent, the great Creator and Preserver of all things, is a truth so clearly demonstrated, that it shall be here taken for granted." What is this but to say, that we have already reason to grant the existence of those attributes of God, which the present Inquiry is designed to prove? The present Inquiry is then surely made to no purpose. The attributes, to the demonstration of which the solution of this great question is necessary, have been demonstrated without any solution, or by means of the solution of some former writer.

He rejects the Manichean system,[2] but imputes to it an absurdity, from which, amidst all its absurdities, it seems to be free, and adopts the system of Mr. Pope.[3] "That pain is no evil, if asserted with regard to the individuals who suffer it, is downright nonsense; but if considered as it affects the universal system, is an undoubted truth, and means only that there is no more pain in it than what is necessary to the production of happiness. How many soever of these evils then force themselves into the creation, so long as the good preponderates, it is a work well worthy of infinite wisdom and benevolence; and notwithstanding the imperfections of its parts, the whole is most undoubtedly perfect." And in the former part of the Letter he gives the principle of his system in these words: "Omnipotence cannot work contradictions, it can only effect all possible things. But so little are we acquainted with the whole system of nature, that we know not what are possible, and what are not: but if we may judge from that constant mixture of pain with pleasure, and inconveniency with advantage, which we must observe in every thing round us, we have reason to conclude, that to endue created beings with perfection, that is, to produce Good exclusive of Evil, is one of those impossibilities which even infinite power cannot accomplish."

This is elegant and acute, but will by no means calm discontent, or silence curiosity; for whether Evil can be wholly separated from Good or not, it is plain that they may be mixed in various degrees, and as far as human eyes can judge, the degree of Evil might have been less without any impediment to Good.

The second Letter *on the evils of imperfection*, is little more than a paraphrase of Pope's Epistles, or yet less than a paraphrase, a mere translation of poetry into prose. This is surely to attack difficulty with very disproportionate abilities, to cut the Gordian knot with very blunt instruments. When we are told of the insufficiency of former solutions, why is one of the latest, which no man can have forgotten, given us again? I am told, that this pamphlet is not the effort of hunger: what can it be then but the product of vanity? and yet how can vanity be gratified by plagiarism or transcription? When this speculatist finds himself prompted to another performance, let him consider whether he is about to disburthen his mind, or employ his fingers; and if I might venture to offer him a subject, I should wish that he would solve this question, Why he that has nothing to write, should desire to be a writer?

Yet is not this Letter without some sentiments, which, though not new, are of great importance, and may be read with pleasure in the thousandth repetition.

"Whatever we enjoy is purely a free gift from our Creator; but that we enjoy no more, can never sure be deemed an injury, or a just reason to question his infinite benevolence. All our happiness is owing to his goodness; but that it is no greater, is owing only to ourselves; that is, to our not having any inherent right to any happiness, or even to any existence at all. This is no more to be imputed to God, than the wants of a beggar to the person who has relieved him: that he had something, was owing to his benefactor; but that he had no more, only to his own original poverty."

Thus far he speaks what every man must approve, and what every wise man has said before him. He then gives us the system of subordination, not invented, for it was known I think to the Arabian metaphysicians,[4] but adopted by Pope; and from him borrowed by the diligent researches of this great investigator.

"No system can possibly be formed, even in imagination, without a subordination of parts. Every animal body must have different members subservient to each other: every picture must be composed of various colours, and of light and shade; all harmony must be formed of trebles, tenors, and basses; every beautiful and useful edifice must consist of higher and lower, more and less magnificent apartments. This is in the very essence of all created things, and therefore cannot be prevented by any means whatever, unless by not creating them at all."

These instances are used instead of Pope's *Oak* and *Weeds*, or *Jupiter* and his *Satellites*;[5] but neither Pope, nor this writer, have much contributed to solve the difficulty. Perfection or imperfection of unconscious beings has no meaning as referred to themselves; the *bass* and the *treble* are equally perfect: the mean and magnificent apartments feel no pleasure or pain from the comparison. Pope might ask the *weed*, why it was less than the *oak*, but the *weed* would never ask the question for itself. The *bass* and *treble* differ only to the hearer, meanness and magnificence only to the inhabitant. There is no evil but must inhere in a conscious being, or be referred to it; that is, evil must be felt before it is evil. Yet even on this subject many questions might be offered, which human understanding has not yet answered, and which the present haste of this extract will not suffer me to dilate.

He proceeds to an humble detail of Pope's opinion: "The universe is a system whose very essence consists in subordination; a scale of beings descending by insensible degrees from infinite perfection to absolute nothing; in which, though we may justly expect to find perfection in the whole, could we possibly comprehend it; yet would it be the highest absurdity to hope for it in all its parts, because the beauty and happiness of the whole depend altogether on the just inferiority of its parts, that is, on the comparative imperfection of the several beings of which it is composed."

"It would have been no more an instance of God's wisdom to have created no beings but of the highest and most perfect order, than it would be of a painter's art to cover his whole piece with one single colour, the most beautiful he could compose. Had he confined himself to such, nothing could have existed but demi-gods, or arch-angels, and then all inferiour orders must have been void and uninhabited: but as it is surely more agreeable to infinite benevolence, that all these should be filled up with beings capable of enjoying happiness themselves, and contributing to that of others, they must necessarily be filled with inferior beings, that is, with such as are less perfect, but from whose existence, notwithstanding that less perfection, more felicity upon the whole accrues to the universe, than if no such had been created. It is moreover highly probable, that there is such a connexion between all ranks and orders by subordinate degrees, that they mutually support each other's existence, and every one in its place is absolutely necessary towards sustaining the whole vast and magnificent fabrick."

"Our pretences for complaint could be of this only, that we are not so high in the scale of existence as our ignorant ambition may desire; a pretence which must eternally subsist; because, were we ever so much higher, there would be still room for infinite power to exalt us; and since no link in the chain can be broke, the same reason for disquiet must remain to those who succeed to that chasm, which must be occasioned by our preferment. A man can have no reason to repine that he is not an angel; nor a horse that he is not a man; much less, that in their several stations they possess not the faculties of another; for this would be an insufferable misfortune."

This doctrine of the regular subordination of beings, the scale of existence, and the chain of nature, I have often considered, but always left the inquiry in doubt and uncertainty.

That every being not infinite, compared with infinity, must be imperfect, is evident to intuition; that whatever is imperfect must have a certain line which it cannot pass, is equally certain. But the reason which determined this limit, and for which such being was suffered to advance thus far and no farther, we shall never be able to discern. Our discoveries tell us, the Creator has made beings of all orders, and that therefore one of them must be such as man. But this system seems to be established on a concession, which, if it be refused, cannot be extorted.

Every reason which can be brought to prove, that there are beings of every possible sort, will prove that there is the greatest number possible of every sort of beings; but this with respect to man we know, if we know anything, not to be true.

It does not appear even to the imagination, that of three orders of being, the first and the third receive any advantage from the imperfection of the second, or that indeed they may not equally exist, though the second had never been, or should cease to be; and why should that be concluded necessary, which cannot be proved even to be useful?

The scale of existence from infinity to nothing, cannot possibly have being. The highest being not infinite must be, as has been often observed, at an infinite distance below infinity. Cheyne,[6] who, with the desire inherent in mathematicians to reduce every thing to mathematical images, considers all existence as a *cone*, allows that the basis is at an infinite distance from the body. And in this distance between finite and infinite, there will be room for ever for an infinite series of indefinable existence.

Between the lowest positive existence and nothing, wherever we suppose positive existence to cease, is another chasm infinitely deep; where there is room again for endless orders of subordinate nature, continued for ever and for ever, and yet infinitely superiour to non-existence.

To these meditations humanity is unequal. But yet we may ask, not of our Maker, but of each other, since on the one side creation, wherever it stops, must stop infinitely below infinity, and on the other infinitely above nothing, what necessity there is that it should proceed so far either way, that beings so high or so low should ever have existed? We may ask; but I believe no created wisdom can give an adequate answer.

Nor is this all. In the scale,[7] wherever it begins or ends, are infinite vacuities. At whatever distance we suppose the next order of beings to be above man, there is room for an intermediate order of beings between them; and if for one order, then for infinite orders: since every thing that admits of more or less, and consequently all the parts of that which admits them, may be infinitely divided. So that, as far as we can judge, there may be room in the vacuity between any two steps of the scale, or between any two points of the cone of being, for infinite exertion of infinite power.

Thus it appears how little reason those who repose their reason upon the scale of being have to triumph over them who recur to any other expedient of solution, and what difficulties arise on every side to repress the rebellions of presumptuous decision. *Qui pauca considerat, facile pronunciat.*[8] In our passage through the boundless ocean of disquisition we often take fogs for land, and after having long toiled to approach them, find, instead of repose and harbours, new storms of objection, and fluctuations of uncertainty.

We are next entertained with Pope's alleviations of those evils which we are doomed to suffer.

"Poverty, or the want of riches, is generally compensated by having more hopes, and fewer fears, by a greater share of health, and a more exquisite relish of the smallest enjoyments, than those who possess them are usually blessed with. The want of taste and genius, with all the pleasures that arise from them, are commonly recompensed by a more useful kind of common sense, together with a wonderful delight, as well as success, in the busy pursuits of a scrambling world. The sufferings of the sick are greatly relieved by many trifling gratifications imperceptible to others, and sometimes almost repaid by the inconceivable transports occasioned by the return of health and vigour. Folly cannot be very grievous, because imperceptible; and I doubt not but there is some truth in that rant of a mad poet, that there is a pleasure in being mad, which none but madmen know. Ignorance, or the want of knowledge and literature, the appointed lot of all born to poverty, and the drudgeries of life, is the only opiate capable of infusing that insensibility which can enable them to endure the miseries of the one and the fatigues of the other. It is a cordial administered by the gracious hand of Providence; of which they ought never to be deprived by an ill-judged and improper education. It is the basis of all subordination, the support of society, and the privilege of individuals: and I have ever thought it a most remarkable instance of the divine wisdom, that whereas in all animals, whose individuals rise little above the rest of their species, knowledge is instinctive: in man, whose individuals are so widely different, it is acquired by education; by which means the prince and the labourer, the philosopher and the peasant, are in some measure fitted for their respective situations."

Much of these positions is perhaps true, and the whole paragraph might well pass without censure, were not objections necessary to the establishment of knowledge. *Poverty* is very gently paraphrased by *want of riches*. In that sense almost every man may in his own opinion be poor. But there is another poverty, which is *want of competence*,[9] of all that can soften the miseries of life, of all that can diversify attention, or delight imagination. There is yet another poverty, which is *want of necessaries*, a species of poverty which no care of the publick, no charity of particulars, can preserve many from feeling openly, and many secretly.

That hope and fear are inseparably or very frequently connected with poverty, and riches, my surveys of life have not informed me. The milder degrees of poverty are sometimes supported by hope, but the more severe often sink down in motionless despondence. Life must be seen before it can be known. This authour and Pope perhaps never saw the miseries which they imagine thus easy to be borne. The poor indeed are insensible of many little vexations which sometimes imbitter the possessions and pollute the enjoyments of the rich. They are not pained by casual incivility, or mortified by the mutilation of a compliment;[10] but this happiness is like that of a malefactor, who ceases to feel the cords that bind him when the pincers are tearing his flesh.

That want of taste for one enjoyment is supplied by the pleasures of some other, may be fairly allowed. But the compensations of sickness I have never found near to equivalence, and the transports of recovery only prove the intenseness of the pain.

With folly no man is willing to confess himself very intimately acquainted, and therefore its pains and pleasures are kept secret. But

113

what the authour says of its happiness seems applicable only to fatuity, or gross dulness; for that inferiority of understanding which makes one man without any other reason the slave, or tool, or property of another, which makes him sometimes useless, and sometimes ridiculous, is often felt with very quick sensibility. On the happiness of madmen, as the case is not very frequent, it is not necessary to raise a disquisition, but I cannot forbear to observe, that I never yet knew disorders of mind increase felicity; every madman is either arrogant and irascible, or gloomy and suspicious, or possessed by some passion or notion destructive to his quiet. He has always discontent in his look, and malignity in his bosom. And, if he had the power of choice, he would soon repent who should resign his reason to secure his peace.

Concerning the portion of ignorance necessary to make the condition of the lower classes of mankind safe to the publick and tolerable to themselves, both morals and policy exact a nicer inquiry than will be very soon or very easily made. There is undoubtedly a degree of knowledge which will direct a man to refer all to Providence, and to acquiesce in the condition with which omniscient Goodness has determined to allot him; to consider this world as a phantom that must soon glide from before his eyes, and the distresses and vexations that encompass him, as dust scattered in his path, as a blast that chills him for a moment, and passes off for ever.

Such wisdom, arising from the comparison of a part with the whole of our existence, those that want it most cannot possibly obtain from philosophy, nor unless the method of education, and the general tenour of life are changed, will very easily receive it from religion. The bulk of mankind is not likely to be very wise or very good: and I know not whether there are not many states of life, in which all knowledge, less than the highest wisdom, will produce discontent and danger. I believe it may be sometimes found, that a *little learning* is to a poor man a *dangerous thing*.[11] But such is the condition of humanity, that we easily see, or quickly feel the wrong, but cannot always distinguish the right. Whatever knowledge is superfluous, in irremediable poverty, is hurtful, but the difficulty is to determine when poverty is irremediable, and at what point superfluity begins. Gross ignorance every man has found equally dangerous with perverted knowledge. Men left wholly to their appetites and their instincts, with little sense of moral or religious obligation, and with very faint distinctions of right and wrong, can never be safely employed, or confidently trusted: they can be honest only by obstinacy, and diligent only by compulsion or caprice. Some instruction, therefore, is necessary, and much perhaps may be dangerous.

Though it should be granted that those who are *born to poverty and drudgery* should not be *deprived* by an *improper education* of the *opiate* of *ignorance*; even this concession will not be of much use to direct our practice, unless it be determined who are those that are *born to poverty*. To entail irreversible poverty upon generation after generation, only because the ancestor happened to be poor, is in itself cruel, if not unjust, and is wholly contrary to the maxims of a commercial nation,[12] which always suppose and promote a rotation of property, and offer every individual a chance of mending his condition by his diligence. Those who communicate literature to the son of a poor man, consider him as one not born to poverty, but to the necessity of deriving a better fortune from himself. In this attempt, as in others, many fail, and many succeed. Those that fail will feel their misery more acutely; but since poverty is now confessed to be such a calamity as cannot be borne without the opiate of insensibility, I hope the happiness of those whom education enables to escape from it, may turn the balance against that exacerbation which the others suffer.

I am always afraid of determining on the side of envy or cruelty. The privileges of education may sometimes be improperly bestowed, but I shall always fear to withhold them, lest I should be yielding to the suggestions of pride, while I persuade myself that I am following the maxims of policy,[13] and under the appearance of salutary restraints, should be indulging the lust of dominion, and that malevolence which delights in seeing others depressed.

Pope's doctrine is at last exhibited in a comparison, which, like other proofs of the same kind, is better adapted to delight the fancy than convince the reason.

"Thus the universe resembles a large and well-regulated family, in which all the officers and servants, and even the domestick animals are subservient to each other in a proper subordination: each enjoys the privileges and perquisites peculiar to his place, and at the same time contributes by that just subordination to the magnificence and happiness of the whole."

The magnificence of a house is of use or pleasure always to the master, and sometimes to the domesticks. But the magnificence of the universe adds nothing to the Supreme Being; for any part of its inhabitants with which human knowledge is acquainted, an universe much less spacious or splendid would have been sufficient; and of happiness it does not appear that any is communicated from the beings of a lower world to those of a higher.

The inquiry after the cause of *natural evil* is continued in the third Letter, in which, as in the former, there is mixture of borrowed truth, and native folly, of some notions just and trite, with others uncommon and ridiculous.

His opinion of the value and importance of happiness is certainly just, and I shall insert it, not that it will give any information to any reader, but it may serve to shew how the most common notion may be swelled in sound, and diffused in bulk, till it shall perhaps astonish the authour himself.

"Happiness is the only thing of real value in existence, neither riches, nor power, nor wisdom, nor learning, nor strength, nor beauty, nor virtue, nor religion, nor even life itself, being of any importance, but as they contribute to its production. All these are in themselves neither good nor evil: happiness alone is their great end, and they are desirable only as they tend to promote it."

Success produces confidence. After this discovery of the value of happiness, he proceeds, without any distrust of himself, to tell us what has been hid from all former inquirers.

"The true solution of this important question, so long and so vainly searched for by the philosophers of all ages and all countries, I take to be at last no more than this, that these real evils proceed from the same source as those imaginary ones of imperfection, before treated of, namely, from that subordination, without which no created system can subsist; all subordination implying imperfection, all imperfection evil, and all evil some kind of inconveniency or suffering: so that there must be particular inconveniencies and sufferings annexed to every particular rank of created beings by the circumstances of things, and their modes of existence."

"God indeed might have made us quite other creatures, and placed us in the world quite differently constituted; but then we had been no longer men, and whatever beings had occupied our stations in the universal system, they must have been liable to the same inconveniencies."

In all this there is nothing that can silence the inquiries of curiosity, or calm the perturbations of doubt. Whether subordination implies imperfection may be disputed. The means respecting themselves may be as perfect as the end. The weed as a weed is no less perfect than the oak as an oak. That *imperfection implies evil, and evil suffering*, is by no means evident. Imperfection may imply privative evil, or the absence of some good, but this privation produces no suffering, but by the help of knowledge. An infant at the breast is yet an imperfect man, but there is no reason for belief that he is unhappy by his immaturity, unless some positive pain be superadded.

When this authour presumes to speak of the universe, I would advise him a little to distrust his own faculties, however large and comprehensive. Many words easily understood on common occasion, become uncertain and figurative when applied to the works of Omnipotence. Subordination in human affairs is well understood; but when it is attributed to the universal system, its meaning grows less certain, like the petty distinctions of locality, which are of good use upon our own globe, but have no meaning with regard to infinite space, in which nothing is *high* or *low*.

That if man, by exaltation to a higher nature, were exempted from the evils which he now suffers, some other being must suffer them; that if man were not man, some other being must be man, is a position arising from his established notion of the scale of being. A notion to which Pope has given some importance by adopting it, and of which I have therefore endeavoured to shew the uncertainty and inconsistency. This scale of being I have demonstrated to be raised by presumptuous imagination, to rest on nothing at the bottom, to lean on nothing at the top, and to have vacuities from step to step through which any order of being may sink into nihility without any inconvenience, so far as we can judge, to the next rank above or below it. We are therefore little enlightened by a writer who tells us, that any being in the state of man must suffer what man suffers, when the only question that requires to be resolved is, Why any being is in this state?

Of poverty and labour he gives just and elegant representations, which yet do not remove the difficulty of the first and fundamental question, though supposing the present state of man necessary, they may supply some motives to content.

"Poverty is what all could not possibly have been exempted from, not only by reason of the fluctuating nature of human possessions, but because the world could not subsist without it; for had all been rich, none could have submitted to the commands of another, or the necessary drudgeries of life; thence all governments must have been dissolved, arts neglected, and lands uncultivated, and so an universal penury have overwhelmed all, instead of now and then pinching a few. Hence, by the by, appears the great excellence of charity, by which men are enabled, by a particular distribution of the blessings and enjoyments of life, on proper occasions, to prevent that poverty which by a general one Omnipotence itself could never have prevented? so that, by inforcing this duty, God as it were demands our assistance to promote universal happiness, and to shut out misery at every door, where it strives to intrude itself."

"Labour, indeed, God might easily have excused us from, since at his command the earth would readily have poured forth all her treasures without our inconsiderable assistance: but if the severest labour cannot sufficiently subdue the malignity of human nature, what plots and machinations, what wars, rapine, and devastation, what profligacy and licentiousness, must have been the consequences of universal idleness! so that labour ought only to be looked upon as a task kindly imposed upon us by our indulgent creator, necessary to preserve our health, our safety, and our innocence."

I am afraid that *the latter end of his commonwealth forgets the beginning*. If God *could easily have excused us from labour*; I do not comprehend why *he could not possibly have exempted all from poverty*. For poverty, in its easier and more tolerable degree, is little more than necessity of labour; and in its more severe and deplorable state, little more than inability for labour. To be poor is to work for others, or to want the succour of others without work. And the same exuberant fertility which would make work unnecessary, might make poverty impossible.

Surely a man who seems not completely master of his own opinion, should have spoken more cautiously of Omnipotence, nor have presumed to say what it could perform, or what it could prevent. I am in doubt whether those who stand highest in *the scale of being* speak thus confidently of the dispensations of their Maker:

For fools rush in, where angels fear to tread.[14]

Of our inquietudes of mind his account is still less reasonable. "Whilst

117

men are injured, they must be inflamed with anger; and whilst they see cruelties, they must be melted with pity; whilst they perceive danger, they must be sensible of fear." This is to give a reason for all evil, by shewing that one evil produces another. If there is danger there ought to be fear; but if fear is an evil, why should there be danger? His vindication of pain is of the same kind: pain is useful to alarm us, that we may shun greater evils, but those greater evils must be presupposed, that the fitness of pain may appear.[. . .]

Having thus dispatched the consideration of particular evils, he comes at last to a general reason for which *evil* may be said to be *our good*. He is of opinion that there is some inconceivable benefit in pain abstractedly considered; that pain, however inflicted, or wherever felt, communicates some good to the general system of being, and that every animal is some way or other the better for the pain of every other animal. This opinion he carries so far as to suppose that there passes some principle of union through all animal life, as attraction is communicated to all corporeal nature; and that the evils suffered on this globe, may by some inconceivable means contribute to the felicity of the inhabitants of the remotest planet.

How the origin of evil is brought nearer to human conception by any *inconceivable* means, I am not able to discover. We believed that the present system of creation was right, though we could not explain the adaptation of one part to the other, or for the whole succession of causes and consequences. Where has this inquirer added to the little knowledge that we had before? He has told us of the benefits of evil, which no man feels, and relations between distant parts of the universe, which he cannot himself conceive. There was enough in this question inconceivable before, and we have little advantage from a new inconceivable solution.

I do not mean to reproach this authour for not knowing what is equally hidden from learning and from ignorance. The shame is to impose words for ideas upon ourselves or others. To imagine that we are going forward when we are only turning round. To think that there is any difference between him that gives no reason, and him that gives a reason, which by his own confession cannot be conceived.

But that he may not be thought to conceive nothing but things inconceivable, he has at last thought on a way by which human sufferings may produce good effects. He imagines that as we have not only animals for food, but choose some for our diversion, the same privilege may be allowed to some beings above us, *who may deceive, torment, or destroy us for the ends only of their own pleasure or utility*. This he again finds impossible to be conceived, *but that impossibility lessens not the probability of the conjecture, which by analogy is so strongly confirmed*.

I cannot resist the temptation of contemplating this analogy, which, I think, he might have carried further, very much to the advantage of his argument. He might have shewn that these *hunters, whose game is man*, have many sports analogous to our own. As we drown whelps and kittens, they amuse themselves now and then with sinking a ship, and stand round the fields of Blenheim[15] or the walls of Prague,[16] as we encircle a cock-pit. As we shoot a bird flying, they take a man in the midst of his business or pleasure, and knock him down with an apoplexy. Some of them, perhaps, are virtuosi, and delight in the operations of an asthma, as a human philosopher[17] in the effects of the air-pump. To swell a man with a tympany[18] is as good sport as to blow a frog. Many a merry bout have these frolick beings at the vicissitudes of an ague, and good sport it is to see a man tumble with an epilepsy, and revive and tumble again, and all this he knows not why. As they are wiser and more powerful than we, they have more exquisite diversions, for we have no way of procuring any sport so brisk and so lasting, as the paroxysms of the gout and stone, which undoubtedly must make high mirth, especially if the play be a little diversified with the blunders and puzzles of the blind and deaf. We know not how far their sphere of observation may extend. Perhaps now and then a merry being may place himself in such a situation as to enjoy at once all the varieties of epidemical disease, or amuse his leisure with the tossings and contortions of every possible pain exhibited together.

One sport the merry malice of these beings has found means of enjoying, to which we have nothing equal or similar. They now and then catch a mortal proud of his parts, and flattered either by the submission of those who court his kindness, or the notice of those who suffer him to court theirs. A head thus prepared for the reception of false opinions, and the projection of vain designs, they easily fill with idle notions, till in time they make their plaything an authour: their first diversion commonly begins with an ode or an epistle, then rises perhaps to a political irony, and is at last brought to its height, by a treatise of philosophy. Then begins the poor animal to entangle himself in sophisms, and flounder in absurdity, to talk confidently of the scale of being, and to give solutions which himself confesses impossible to be understood. Sometimes, however, it happens that their pleasure is without much mischief. The authour feels no pain, but while they are wondering at the extravagance of his opinion, and pointing him out to one another as a new example of human folly, he is enjoying his own applause, and that of his companions, and perhaps is elevated with the hope of standing at the head of a new sect.

Many of the books which now crowd the world, may be justly suspected to be written for the sake of some invisible order of beings, for surely they are of no use to any of the corporeal inhabitants of the world. Of the productions of the last bounteous year, how many can be said to serve any purpose of use or pleasure? The only end of writing is to enable the readers better to enjoy life, or better to endure it: and how will either of those be put more in our power by him who tells us that we are puppets, of which some creature not much wiser than ourselves manages the wires? That a set of beings unseen and unheard, are hovering about us, trying experiments upon our sensibility, putting us in agonies to see our limbs quiver, torturing us to madness, that they may laugh at our vagaries, sometimes obstructing the bile, that they may see how a man looks when he is yellow; sometimes breaking a traveller's bones, to try how he will get home; sometimes wasting a man to a skeleton, and sometimes killing him fat for the greater elegance of his hide. [...]

Notes

1 Henry St. John, first Viscount Bolingbroke (1678–1751). Celebrated politician and philosopher of extreme Tory views and Deistical opinions, at one time attainted by his political opponents and forced to take refuge in France. He is the 'St. John' addressed by Pope in the *Essay on Man*.

2 See p. 107, note 2.

3 Johnson is referring to the doctrine expressed by Pope in Epistle I, lines 290–4 of *An Essay on Man* (and in other places also in that poem) that all 'partial Evil' is 'universal Good'.

4 Johnson is referring to the theory, originally proposed by Aristotle, of the Great Chain of Being. The 'Arabian metaphysicians' would have included Avicenna (Ibn-Sina 980–1036), Persian physician and commentator on Aristotle, and Averroës (Ibn-Ruoshd 1126–98), philosopher and commentator on Aristotle.

5 An allusion to lines 39–42 of Epistle I of the *Essay on Man*:

> Ask of thy mother earth, why oaks are made
> Taller or stronger than the weeds they shade?
> Or ask of younder argent fields above,
> Why JOVE's Satellites are less than JOVE?

6 Presumably the Scottish mathematician and philosopher James Cheyne (*d.* 1602).

7 Scale here means 'ladder'.

8 (Latin) 'those who take little thought find it easy to pronounce an opinion'.

9 Sufficiency of income.

10 Johnson presumably means 'a compliment bestowed in an ungraceful fashion'.

11 An allusion to Pope's famous couplet in his *Essay on Criticism*:

> A little learning is a dangerous thing:
> Drink deep, or taste not the Pierian spring.

12 Johnson's allusion to Britain as 'a commercial nation' is of some historical interest. It reveals that, though he was a devout Christian and a high Tory, he took a very matter-of-fact and eighteenth-century view of society. And it seems probably true that Britain at this period, though in retrospect it seems rigidly socially-stratified and largely run by patronage and family interest, was (by comparison with, say, France) a place of free opportunity and of the 'career open to talent'.

13 Social and political wisdom.

14 Pope's *Essay on Criticism*, line 66.

15 Scene of Marlborough's victory over the French in 1704: a village in Bavaria on the left bank of the Danube.

16 Scene of a Prussian victory during the Seven Years' War, in 1757, the year in which Johnson is writing.

17 That is, 'natural philosopher' or scientist.

18 Tumour.

VOLTAIRE

On Parliament; On Government; On Trade (1733)

From F. M. A. de Voltaire, Letters VIII, IX, X of *Letters Concerning the English Nation*. Printed for C. Davis and A. Lyon, London 1733. [Translation by John Lockman.] First edition published in France: *Lettres Philosophiques, par M. de V . . .* , à Amsterdam [actually Rouen], chez E. Lucas, au livre d'or, 1734. Reprinted from *Letters on England*, ed. H. Morley, Cassell's National Library, 1889.

When Voltaire visited England for the first time in 1726 he had already suffered two brief terms of arbitrary imprisonment in the Bastille – the first for some impolitic verses, the second for 'insulting' a nobleman by challenging him to a duel. He stayed in England for some three years. He was impressed by what he saw as its freedom from the arbitrariness and intolerance which he hated in France.

His *Letters Concerning the English Nation* was published first in English in 1733 and only in the following year appeared in French, though still published in London. The first edition to be published in France (in 1734) carried the title *Lettres Philosophiques*. A panegyric on English history, thought and government, the book invited its readers to contrast England's enviable state with that of France. Shortly after publication in France the *Letters* were condemned in June and were publicly burned. A warrant was issued for Voltaire's arrest, but he escaped to the independent duchy of Lorraine.

Extravagant claims have been made for the impact of the *Letters* on France. But whether or not they can truly be considered as 'the first bomb' thrown at the old régime, they undoubtedly popularized English ideas among a wide audience and encouraged many to see 'English liberty' as an alternative to the *status quo* in France.

ON PARLIAMENT

The members of the English Parliament are fond of comparing themselves to the old Romans.[1]

Not long since Mr. Shippen[2] opened a speech in the House of Commons with these words, "The majesty of the people of England would be wounded." The singularity of the expression occasioned a loud laugh; but this gentleman, so far from being disconcerted, repeated the same words with a resolute tone of voice, and the laugh ceased. In my opinion, the majesty of the people of England has nothing in common with that of the people of Rome, much less is there any affinity between their Governments. There is in London a senate, some of the members whereof are accused (doubtless very unjustly) of selling their voices on certain occasions, as was done in Rome; this is the only resemblance. Besides, the two nations appear to me quite opposite in character, with regard both to good and evil. The Romans never knew the dreadful folly of religious wars, an abomination reserved for devout preachers of patience and humility. Marius and Sylla, Caesar and Pompey, Anthony and Augustus,[3] did not draw their swords and set the world in a blaze merely to determine whether the flamen[4] should wear his shirt over his robe, or his robe over his shirt, or whether the sacred chickens should eat and drink, or eat only, in order to take the augury. The English have hanged one another by law, and cut one another to pieces in pitched battles, for quarrels of as trifling a nature. The sects of the Episcopalians and Presbyterians quite distracted these very serious heads for a time. But I fancy they will hardly ever be so silly again, they seeming to be grown wiser at their own expense; and I do not perceive the least inclination in them to murder one another merely about syllogisms, as some zealots among them once did.

But here follows a more essential difference between Rome and England, which gives the advantage entirely to the latter – viz., that the civil wars of Rome ended in slavery, and those of the English in liberty. The English are the only people upon earth who have been able to prescribe limits to the power of kings by resisting them; and who, by a series of struggles, have at last established that wise Government where the Prince is all-powerful to do good, and, at the same, is restrained from committing evil; where the nobles are great without insolence, though there are no vassals; and where the people share in the Government without confusion.

The House of Lords and that of the Commons divide the legislative power under the king, but the Romans had no such balance. The patricians and plebeians in Rome were perpetually at variance, and there was no intermediate power to reconcile them. The Roman senate, who were so unjustly, so criminally proud as not to suffer the plebeians to share with them in anything, could find no other artifice to keep the latter out of the administration than by employing them in foreign wars. They considered the plebeians as a wild beast, whom it behoved them to let loose upon their neighbours, for fear they should devour their masters. Thus the greatest defect in the Government of the Romans raised them to be conquerors. By being unhappy at home, they triumphed over and possessed themselves of the world, till at last their divisions sunk them to slavery.

The Government of England will never rise to so exalted a pitch of glory, nor will its end be so fatal. The English are not fired with the splendid folly of making conquests, but would only prevent their neighbours from conquering. They are not only jealous of their own liberty, but even of that of other nations. The English were exasperated against Louis XIV for no other reason but because he was ambitious, and declared war against him merely out of levity, not from any interested motives.

The English have doubtless purchased their liberties at a very high price, and waded through seas of blood to drown the idol of arbitrary power. Other nations have been involved in as great calamities, and have shed as much blood; but then the blood they spilt in defence of their liberties only enslaved them the more.

That which rises to a revolution in England is no more than a sedition in other countries. A city in Spain, in Barbary, or in Turkey, takes up arms in defence of its privileges, when immediately it is stormed by mercenary troops, it is punished by executioners, and the rest of the nation kiss the chains they are loaded with. The French are of opinion that the government of this island is more tempestuous than the sea which surrounds it, which indeed is true; but then it is never so but when the king raises the storm – when he attempts to seize the ship of which he is only the chief pilot. The civil wars of France lasted longer, were more cruel, and productive of greater evils than those of England; but none of these civil wars had a wise and prudent liberty for their object.

In the detestable reigns of Charles IX. and Henry III. the whole affair was only whether the people should be slaves to the Guises.[5] With regard to the last war of Paris,[6] it deserves only to be hooted at. Methinks I see a crowd of schoolboys rising up in arms against their master, and afterwards whipped for it. Cardinal de Retz, who was witty and brave (but to no purpose), rebellious without a cause, factious without design, and head of a defenceless party, caballed for caballing sake, and seemed to foment the civil war merely out of diversion. The Parliament did not know what he intended, nor what he did not intend. He levied troops by Act of Parliament, and the next moment cashiered them. He threatened, he begged pardon; he set a price upon Cardinal Mazarin's head, and afterwards congratulated him in a public manner. Our civil wars under Charles VI.[7] were bloody and cruel, those of the League[8] execrable, and that of the Frondeurs ridiculous.

That for which the French chiefly reproach the English nation is the murder of King Charles I., whom his subjects treated exactly as he would have treated them had his reign been prosperous. After all, consider on one side Charles I., defeated in a pitched battle, imprisoned, tried, sentenced to die in Westminster Hall, and then beheaded. And on the other, the Emperor Henry VII., poisoned by his chaplain at his receiving the Sacrament; Henry III. stabbed by a monk; thirty assassinations projected against Henry IV.,[9] several of them put in execution, and the last bereaving that great monarch of his life. Weigh, I say, all these wicked attempts, and then judge.

Notes

1   That is, the free citizens of ancient Rome.

2   William Shippen (1673–1743) was a principal Tory spokesman in the House of Commons in the early years of the Hanoverian succession. He was notable for invoking the democratic sanction in politics. In 1718 his outspoken criticism of the King's speech led to a brief spell of imprisonment in the Tower.

3   Gaius Marius (157–86B.C.), Roman general, seven times consul; Lucius Cornelius Sulla (138–78B.C.), Roman general and statesman; Gaius Julius Caesar (c.101–44B.C.), the great Roman general and conqueror of Gaul, assassinated in the Senate; Gnaeus Pompeius (106–48B.C.), defeated opponent of Julius Caesar; Marcus Antonius (c.82–30B.C.), defeated rival of the future emperor Augustus; Caius Julius Caesar Octavianus, known as Augustus (63B.C.–A.D.14) founder of the Roman Empire.

4   An ancient Roman priest.

5   The Dukes of Guise played a prominent role in the politics and the religious wars of sixteenth-century France. Henry, the third Duke, played a central part in organizing the massacre of Protestants on St. Bartholemew's Day 1572.

6   Cardinal Jean François de Retz (see p. 64, note 24) aspired to become the principal minister of France in place of Cardinal Jules Mazarin (1602–61). Mazarin was the protégé of Cardinal Richelieu, and was principal minister in France for twenty years following Richelieu's death in 1642.

7   Those between the dukes of Orleans and Burgundy at the end of the fourteenth century in France, during the reign of the mad king Charles VI.

8   The League (Fr. 'la Ligue') was an extreme Catholic and anti-Protestant association of the 1570s and 1580s in France led by Henry of Guise.

9   Henry VII (1269?–1313), King of the Romans and Holy Roman Emperor; Henry III (1551–89), assassinated by Jacques Clément, a Dominican friar; Henry IV (1553–1610), responsible for the Edict of Nantes (1598) which granted toleration to French Protestants. He too was assassinated.

ON GOVERNMENT

That mixture in the English Government, that harmony between King, Lords, and Commons, did not always subsist. England was enslaved for a long series of years by the Romans, the Saxons, the Danes, and the French successively. William the Conqueror particularly, ruled them with a rod of iron. He disposed as absolutely of the lives and fortunes of his conquered subjects as an eastern monarch; and forbade, upon pain of death, the English either fire or candle in their houses after eight o'clock; whether was this to prevent their nocturnal meetings, or only to try, by an odd and whimsical prohibition, how far it was possible for one man to extend his power over his fellow-creatures. It is true, indeed, that the English had Parliaments before and after William the Conqueror, and they boast of them, as though these assemblies then called Parliaments, composed of ecclesiastical tyrants and of plunderers entitled barons, had been the guardians of the public liberty and happiness.

The barbarians who came from the shores of the Baltic, and settled in the rest of Europe, brought with them the form of government called States or Parliaments, about which so much noise is made, and which are so little understood. Kings, indeed, were not absolute in those days; but then the people were more wretched upon that very account, and more completely enslaved. The chiefs of these savages, who had laid waste France, Italy, Spain, and England, made themselves monarchs. Their generals divided among themselves the several countries they had conquered, whence sprung those margraves,[1] those peers, those barons, those petty tyrants, who often contested with their sovereigns for the spoils of whole nations. These were birds of prey fighting with an eagle for doves whose blood the victorious was to suck. Every nation, instead of being governed by one master, was trampled upon by a hundred tyrants. The priests soon played a part among them. Before this it had been the fate of the Gauls, the Germans, and the Britons, to be always governed by their Druids and the chiefs of their villages, an ancient kind of barons, not so tyrannical as their successors. These Druids pretended to be mediators between God and man. They enacted laws, they fulminated their excommunications, and sentenced to death. The bishops succeeded, by insensible degrees, to their temporal authority in the Goth and Vandal government. The popes set themselves at their head, and armed with their briefs, their bulls, and reinforced by monks, they made even kings tremble, deposed and assassinated them at pleasure, and employed every artifice to draw into their own purses moneys from all parts of Europe. The weak Ina, one of the tyrants of the Saxon Heptarchy in England, was the first monarch who submitted, in his pilgrimage to Rome, to pay St. Peter's penny (equivalent very near to a French crown) for every house in his dominions. The whole island soon followed his example; England became insensibly one of the Pope's provinces, and the Holy Father used to send from time to time his legates thither to levy exorbitant taxes. At last King John delivered up by a public instrument[2] the kingdom of England to the Pope, who had excommunicated him; but the barons, not finding their account in this resignation, dethroned the wretched King John and seated Louis, father to St. Louis, King of France, in his place. However, they were soon weary of their new monarch, and accordingly obliged him to return to France.

Whilst that the barons, the bishops, and the popes, all laid waste England, where all were for ruling the most numerous, the most useful, even the most virtuous, and consequently the most venerable part of mankind, consisting of those who study the laws and the sciences, of traders, of artificers, in a word, of all who were not tyrants – that is, those who are called the people: these, I say, were by them looked upon as so many animals beneath the dignity of the human species. The Commons in those ages were far from sharing in the government, they being villains or peasants, whose labour, whose blood, were the property of their masters who entitled themselves the nobility. The major part of men in Europe were at that time what they are to this day in several parts of the world – they were villains or bondsmen of lords – that is, a kind of cattle bought and sold with the land. Many ages passed away before justice could be done to human nature – before mankind were conscious that it was abominable for many to sow, and but few reap. And was not France very happy, when the power and authority of those petty robbers was abolished by the lawful authority of kings and of the people?

Happily, in the violent shocks which the divisions between kings and nobles gave to empires, the chains of nations were more or less heavy. Liberty in England sprang from the quarrels of tyrants. The barons forced King John and King Henry III to grant the famous Magna Charta, the chief design of which was indeed to make kings dependent on the Lords; but then the rest of the nation were a little favoured in it, in order that they might join on proper occasions with their pretended masters. This great Charter, which is considered as the sacred origin of the English liberties, shows itself how little liberty was known.

The title alone proves that the king thought he had a just right to be absolute; and that the barons, and even the clergy, forced him to give up the pretended right, for no other reason but becase they were most powerful.

Magna Charta begins in this style: "We grant, of our own free will, the following privileges to the archbishops, bishops, priors, and barons of our kingdom," etc.

The House of Commons is not once mentioned in the articles of this Charter – a proof that it did not yet exist, or that it existed without power. Mention is therein made, by name, of the freemen of England – a melancholy proof that some were not so. It appears, by Article XXXII, that these pretended freemen owed service to their lords. Such a liberty as this was not many removes from slavery.

By Article XXI, the king ordains that his officers shall not henceforward seize upon, unless they pay for them, the horses and carts of freemen. The people considered this ordinance as a real liberty, though it was a greater tyranny. Henry VII, that happy usurper and great politician, who pretended to love the barons, though he in reality hated and feared them, got their lands alienated. By this means the villains, afterwards acquiring riches by their industry, purchased the estates and country seats of the illustrious peers who had ruined themselves by their folly and extravagance, and all the lands got by insensible degrees into other hands.

The power of the House of Commons increased every day. The families of the ancient peers were at last extinct; and as peers only are properly noble in England, there would be no such thing in strictness of law as nobility in that island, had not the kings created new barons from time to time, and preserved the body of peers, once a terror to them, to oppose them to the Commons, since become so formidable.

All these new peers who compose the Higher House receive nothing but their titles from the king, and very few of them have estates in those places whence they take their titles. One shall be Duke of D_____, though he has not a foot of land in Dorsetshire; and another is Earl of a village, though he scarce knows where it is situated. The peers have power, but it is only in the Parliament House.

There is no such thing here as *haute, moyenne*, and *basse justice*[3] – that is, a power to judge in all matters civil and criminal; nor a right or privilege of hunting in the grounds of a citizen, who at the same time is not permitted to fire a gun in his own field.

No one is exempted in this country from paying certain taxes because he is a nobleman or a priest. All duties and taxes are settled by the House of Commons, whose power is greater than that of the Peers, though inferior to it in dignity. The spiritual as well as temporal Lords have the liberty to reject a Money Bill brought in by the Commons; but they are not allowed to alter anything in it, and must either pass or throw it out without restriction. When the Bill has passed the Lords and is signed by the king, then the whole nation pays, every man in proportion to his revenue or estate, not according to his title, which would be absurd. There is no such thing as an arbitrary subsidy or poll-tax, but a real tax on the lands, of all which an estimate was made in the reign of the famous King William III.

The land-tax continues still upon the same foot, though the revenue of the lands is increased. Thus no one is tyrannised over, and every one is easy. The feet of the peasants are not bruised by wooden shoes; they eat white bread, are well clothed, and are not afraid of increasing their stock of cattle, nor of tiling their houses, from any apprehension that their taxes will be raised the year following. The annual income of the estates of a great many commoners in England amounts to two hundred thousand livres, and yet these do not think it beneath them to plough the lands which enrich them, and on which they enjoy their liberty.

Notes

1 A German title, originally given to the military governor of a border province; subsequently, the hereditary title of the princes of certain states of the Holy Roman Empire.

2 On 15 May 1213 King John surrendered his Kingdom to the papal nuncio at Ewell, near Dover, receiving it back as a vassal.

3 *Haute, moyenne* and *basse justice* were the differing powers of administering justice which were held by seigneurs. The privilege of *haute justice* (high justice) enabled the man who held it to pass judgment on major criminal and civil cases. *Basse justice* (increasingly called *moyenne justice* from the late sixteenth century) dealt with less serious matters, particularly those where there was no death penalty involved.

ON TRADE

As trade enriched the citizens in England, so it contributed to their freedom, and this freedom on the other side extended their commerce, whence arose the grandeur of the State. Trade raised by insensible degrees the naval power, which gives the English a superiority over the seas, and they now are masters of very near two hundred ships of war. Posterity will very probably be surprised to hear that an island whose only produce is a little lead, tin, fuller's-earth, and coarse wool, should become so powerful by its commerce, as to be able to send, in 1723, three fleets at the same time to three different and far distanced parts of the globe. One before Gibraltar, conquered and still possessed by the English; a second to Portobello, to dispossess the King of Spain of the treasures of the West Indies; and a third into the Baltic, to prevent the Northern Powers from coming to an engagement.

At the same time when Louis XIV. made all Italy tremble, and that his armies, which had already possessed themselves of Savoy and Piedmont, were upon the point of taking Turin; Prince Eugene was obliged to march from the middle of Germany in order to succour Savoy. Having no money, without which cities cannot be either taken or defended, he addressed himself to some English merchants.[1] These, at an hour and half's warning, lent him five millions, whereby he was enabled to deliver Turin, and to beat the French; after which he wrote the following short letter to the persons who had disbursed him the above-mentioned sums: "Gentlemen, I have received your money, and flatter myself that I have laid it out to your satisfaction." Such a circumstance as this raises a just pride in an English merchant, and makes him presume (not without some reason) to compare himself to a Roman citizen; and, indeed, a peer's brother does not think traffic beneath him. When the Lord Townshend was Minister of State,[2] a brother of his was content to be a City merchant; and at the time that the Earl of Oxford[3] governed Great Britain, a younger brother was no more than a factor in Aleppo, where he chose to live, and where he died. This custom, which begins, however, to be laid aside, appears monstrous to Germans, vainly puffed up with their extraction. These think it morally impossible that the son of an English peer should be no more than a rich and powerful citizen, for all are princes in Germany. There have been thirty highnesses of the same name, all whose patrimony consisted only in their escutcheons and their pride.

In France the title of marquis is given gratis to any one who will accept of it; and whosoever arrives at Paris from the midst of the most remote provinces with money in his purse, and a name terminating in *ac* or *ille*, may strut about, and cry, "Such a man as I! A man of my rank and figure!" and may look down upon a trader with sovereign contempt; whilst the trader on the other side, by thus often hearing his profession treated so disdainfully, is fool enough to blush at it. However, I need not say which is most useful to a nation; a lord, powdered in the tip of the mode, who knows exactly at what o'clock the king rises and goes to bed, and who gives himself airs of grandeur and state, at the same time that he is acting the slave in the ante-chamber of a prime minister; or a merchant, who enriches his country, despatches orders from his counting-house to Surat and Grand Cairo, and contributes to the well-being of the world.

Notes

1 In January 1706 the ministers of the Holy Roman Emperor, pressed by Prince Eugene – Marlborough's comrade-in-arms against Louis XIV – proposed to raise a loan at 8% interest in London. The loan was raised by subscription over six days, and it was not confined simply to merchants, for example Marlborough subscribed £5,000.

2 Charles Townshend, second Viscount (1676–1739), secretary of state for foreign affairs in the 1720s. He later devoted himself to agricultural experiments, earning the nickname 'Turnip' Townshend.

3 Charles Townshend's brother was Robert Harley, first Earl of Oxford (1661–1724), lord high treasurer under Queen Anne, being later dismissed and impeached. His brother Nathaniel (1665–1720) was a merchant.

MONTESQUIEU

On Political Liberty; Of Laws in Relation to Climate; On Commerce (1748)

From Charles Louis de Secondat Baron de Montesquieu, *De l'esprit des Loix*, n.d. [1748], chez Barrillot et Fils, à Genève. First translation: *The Spirit of Laws* [translation by T. Nugent]. Printed for J. Nourse and P. Vaillant, in the Strand, London, 1750. Reprinted from the 'New Edition', revised by J. V. Prichard, Bohn's Standard Library 1914. 2 vols.

Charles Louis de Secondat, Baron de la Brède et de Montesquieu (1689–1755) was born in Bordeaux of a family noble on both sides and partly of English origin. He was trained in the law and first achieved notice with his *Persian Letters* of 1721, a gay and free-thinking satire in which, in the form of a collection of imaginary letters written and received by two Persians in Paris, he makes fun of various aspects of French life and institutions. His permanent fame, however, rests on his monumental *Spirit of the Laws* (1748), a pioneering work in the comparative study of political and legal institutions. The implication of the title is that he is not merely describing the various forms of legal and constitutional system but analysing them as an expression of the physical, moral, historical and geographical character of the nations possessing them. He divides government into three broad categories, republic, monarchy and despotism, attributing to each an animating principle: in the case of a republic, *virtue*; of a monarchy, *honour*; and of a despotism, *fear*. He considers a republic as the ideal but as being in practice unstable and therefore is in favour of limited monarchy, with a clear separation of the legislative, the executive and the judicial powers – a form of government of which he considered Great Britain to be, in theory at least, the most perfect example.

Montesquieu was greatly revered by the later French *philosophes* and the influence of his work can be traced in the American Declaration of Independence of 1776, the political experiments of the French Revolution and the French parliamentary constitutions which followed 1815.

Of the three extracts given here, the first represents the opening five chapters of his famous eleventh book, in which he praises the British Constitution as a model of political liberty; the second, from Book XIV gives a sample of his view, very important to him though appearing to us somewhat naive, about the influence of climate upon national character and institutions; and the third, from Book XX, gives a clear résumé of economic beliefs current in France in the period before economics had become a systematic science.

ON POLITICAL LIBERTY

---

ibid. Book XI, Of the Laws which Establish Political Liberty with Regard to the Constitution.

---

1 *A general Idea.*

I make a distinction between the laws that establish political liberty, as it relates to the constitution, and those by which it is established, as it relates to the citizen. The former shall be the subject of this book; the latter I shall examine in the next.

2 *Different Significations of the word Liberty.*

There is no word that admits of more various significations, and has made more varied impressions on the human mind, than that of Liberty. Some have taken it as a means of deposing a person on whom they had conferred a tyrannical authority; others for the power of choosing a superior whom they are obliged to obey; others for the right of bearing arms, and of being thereby enabled to use violence; others, in fine, for the privilege of being governed by a native of their own country, or by their own laws.[1] A certain nation for a long item thought liberty consisted in the privilege of wearing a long beard.[2] Some have annexed this name to one form of government exclusive of others: those who had a republican taste applied it to this species of polity;[1] those who liked a monarchical state gave it to monarchy.[3] Thus they

---

1 "I have copied," says Cicero, "Scævola's edict, which permits the Greeks to terminate their difference among themselves according to their own laws; this makes them consider themselves a free people."

2 The Russians could not bear that Czar Peter should make them cut it off.

3 The Cappadocians refused the condition of a republican state which was offered them by the Romans.

have all applied the name of *liberty* to the government most suitable to their own customs and inclinations: and as in republics the people have not so constant and so present a view of the causes of their misery, and as the magistrates seem to act only in conformity to the laws, hence liberty is generally said to reside in republics, and to be banished from monarchies. In fine, as in democracies, the people seem to act almost as they please, this sort of government has been deemed the most free, and the power of the people has been confounded with their liberty.

3 *In what Liberty consists.*

It is true that in democracies the people seem to act as they please; but political liberty does not consist in an unlimited freedom. In governments, that is, in societies directed by laws, liberty can consist only in the power of doing what we ought to will, and in not being constrained to do what we ought not to will.

We must have continually present to our minds the difference between independence and liberty. Liberty is a right of doing whatever the laws permit, and if a citizen could do what they forbid he would be no longer possessed of liberty, because all his fellow-citizens would have the same power.

4 *The same Subject continued.*

Democratic and aristocratic states are not in their own nature free. Political liberty is to be found only in moderate governments; and even in these it is not always found. It is there only when there is no abuse of power. But constant experience shows us that every man invested with power is apt to abuse it, and to carry his authority as far as it will go. Is it not strange, though true, to say that virtue itself has need of limits?

To prevent this abuse, it is necessary from the very nature of things that power should be a check to power. A government may be so constituted, as no man shall be compelled to do things to which the law does not oblige him, nor forced to abstain from things which the law permits.

5 *Of the End or View of different Governments.*

Though all governments have the same general end, which is that of preservation, yet each has another particular object. Increase of dominion was the object of Rome; war, that of Sparta; religion, that of the Jewish laws; commerce, that of Marseilles; public tranquillity, that of the laws of China;[4] navigation, that of the laws of Rhodes; natural liberty, that of the policy of the Savages; in general, the pleasures of the prince, that of despotic states; that of monarchies, the prince's and the

4 The natural end of a state that has no foreign enemies, or that thinks itself secured against them by barriers.

kingdom's glory; the independence of individuals is the end aimed at by the laws of Poland, thence results the oppression of the whole.

One nation there is also in the world[2] that has for the direct end of its constitution political liberty. We shall presently examine the principles on which this liberty is founded; if they are sound, liberty will appear in its highest perfecion.

To discover political liberty in a constitution, no great labour is requisite. If we are capable of seeing it where it exists, it is soon found, and we need not go far in search of it.

Notes
1   Form of government.
2   Montesquieu means Britain.

OF LAWS IN RELATION TO CLIMATE

ibid., Book XIV, Of Laws in Relation to the Nature of the Climate.

1 *General Idea.*

If it be true that the temper of the mind and the passions of the heart are extremely different in different climates, the laws ought to be in relation both to the variety of those passions and to the variety of those tempers.

2 *Of the Difference of Men in different Climates.*

Cold air constringes the extremities of the external fibres of the body;[1] this increases their elasticity, and favours the return of the blood from the extreme parts to the heart. It contracts[2] those very fibres; consequently it increases also their force. On the contrary, warm air relaxes and lengthens the extremes of the fibres; of course it diminishes their force and elasticity.

People are therefore more vigorous in cold climates. Here the action of the heart and the reaction of the extremities of the fibres are better performed, the temperature of the humours is greater, the blood moves more freely towards the heart, and reciprocally the heart has more power. This superiority of strength must produce various effects; for instance, a greater boldness, that is, more courage; a greater sense of superiority, that is, less desire of revenge; a greater opinion of security, that is, more frankness, less suspicion, policy, and cunning. In short, this must be productive of very different tempers. Put a man into a close, warm place, and for the reasons above given he will feel a great faintness. If under this circumstance you propose a bold enterprise to him, I believe you will find him very little disposed towards it; his present weakness will throw him into despondency; he will be afraid of everything, being in a state of total incapacity. The inhabitants of warm countries are, like old men, timorous; the people in cold countries are, like young men, brave. If we reflect on the late wars,[3] which are more recent in our memory, and in which we can better distinguish some particular effects that escape us at a greater distance of time, we shall find that the northern people, transplanted into southern regions,[4] did

1 This appears even in the countenance; in cold weather people look thinner.
2 We know that it shortens iron.
3 .Those for the succession to the Spanish monarchy.
4 For instance, in Spain.

not perform such exploits as their countrymen, who, fighting in their own climate, possessed their full vigour and courage.

This strength of the fibres in northern nations is the cause that the coarser juices are extracted from their aliments.[1] Hence two things result: one, that the parts of the chyle or lymph are more proper, by reason of their large surface, to be applied to and to nourish the fibres; the other, that they are less proper, from their coarseness, to give a certain subtilty to the nervous juice. Those people have therefore large bodies and but little vivacity.

The nerves that terminate from all parts in the cutis form each a nervous bundle; generally speaking, the whole nerve is not moved, but a very minute part. In warm climates, where the cutis is relaxed, the ends of the nerves are expanded and laid open to the weakest action of the smallest objects. In cold countries the cutis is constringed and the papillæ compressed: the miliary glands are in some measure paralytic; and the sensation does not reach the brain, except when it is very strong and proceeds from the whole nerve at once. Now, imagination, taste, sensibility, and vivacity depend on an infinite number of small sensations.

I have observed the outermost part of a sheep's tongue, where, to the naked eye, it seems covered with papillæ. On these papillæ I have discerned through a microscope small hairs, or a kind of down; between the papillæ were pyramids shaped towards the ends like pincers. Very likely these pyramids are the principal organ of taste.

I caused the half of this tongue to be frozen, and observing it with the naked eye I found the papillæ considerably diminished: even some rows of them were sunk into their sheath. The outermost part I examined with the microscope, and perceived no pyramids. In proportion as the frost went off, the papillæ seemed to the naked eye to rise, and with the microscope the miliary glands began to appear.

This observation confirms what I have been saying, that in cold countries the nervous glands are less expanded: they sink deeper into their sheaths, or they are sheltered from the action of external objects; consequently they have not such lively sensations.

In cold countries they have very little sensibility for pleasure; in temperate countries, they have more; in warm countries, their sensibility is exquisite. As climates are distinguished by degrees of latitude, we might distinguish them also in some measure by those of sensibility. I have been at the opera in England and in Italy, where I have seen the same pieces and the same performers: and yet the same music produces such different effects on the two nations: one is so cold and phlegmatic, and the other so lively and enraptured, that it seems almost inconceivable.

It is the same with regard to pain, which is excited by the laceration of some fibre of the body. The Author of nature has made it an established rule that this pain should be more acute in proportion as the laceration is greater: now it is evident that the large bodies and coarse fibres of the people of the north are less capable of laceration than the delicate fibres of the inhabitants of warm countries; consequently the soul is there less sensible of pain. You must flay a Muscovite[2] alive to make him feel.

From this delicacy of organs peculiar to warm climates it follows that the soul is most sensibly moved by whatever relates to the union of the two sexes: here everything leads to this object.

In northern climates scarcely has the animal part of love a power of making itself felt. In temperate climates, love, attended by a thousand appendages, endeavours to please by things that have at first the appearance, though not the reality, of this passion. In warmer climates it is liked for its own sake, it is the only cause of happiness, it is life itself.

In southern countries a machine[3] of a delicate frame but strong sensibility resigns itself either to a love which rises and is incessantly laid in a seraglio, or to a passion which leaves women in a greater independence, and is consequently exposed to a thousand inquietudes. In northern regions a machine robust and heavy finds pleasure in whatever is apt to throw the spirits into motion, such as hunting, travelling, war, and wine. If we travel towards the north, we meet with people who have few vices, many virtues, and a great share of frankness and sincerity. If we draw near the south, we fancy ourselves entirely removed from the verge of morality; here the strongest passions are productive of all manner of crimes, each man endeavouring, let the means be what they will, to indulge his inordinate desires. In temperate climates we find the inhabitants inconstant in their manners, as well as in their vices and virtues: the climate has not a quality determinate enough to fix them.   The heat of the climate may be so excessive as to deprive the body of all vigour and strength. Then the faintness is communicated to the mind; there is no curiosity, no enterprise, no generosity of sentiment; the inclinations are all passive; indolence constitutes the utmost happiness; scarcely any punishment is so severe as mental employment; and slavery is more supportable than the force and vigour of mind necessary for human conduct.

3 Contradiction in the Tempers of some Southern Nations.

The Indians[5] are naturally a pusillanimous people; even the children[6] of Europeans born in India lose the courage peculiar to their own climate. But how shall we reconcile this with their customs and penances so full of barbarity? The men voluntarily undergo the greatest hardships,[4] and the women burn themselves[5]; here we find a very odd compound of fortitude and weakness.

Nature, having framed those people of a texture so weak as to fill them with timidity, has formed them at the same time of an imagination so lively that every object makes the strongest impression upon them. That delicacy of organs which renders them apprehensive of death

5 "One hundred European soldiers," says Tavernier, "would without any great difficulty beat a thousand Indian soldiers."
6 Even the Persians who settle in the Indies contract in the third generation the indolence and cowardice of the Indians. See Bernier on the Mogul, tom. i. p. 182.

contributes likewise to make them dread a thousand things more than death: the very same sensibility induces them to fly and dare all dangers.

As a good education is more necessary to children than to such as have arrived at maturity of understanding, so the inhabitants of those countries have much greater need than the European nations of a wiser legislator. The greater their sensibility, the more it behoves them to receive proper impressions, to imbibe no prejudices, and to let themselves be directed by reason.

At the time of the Romans the inhabitants of the north of Europe were destitute of arts, education, and almost of laws; and yet the good sense annexed to the gross fibres of those climates enabled them to make an admirable stand against the power of Rome, till the memorable period[6] in which they quitted their woods to subvert that great empire.

4 *Cause of the Immutability of Religion, Manners, Customs, and Laws in the Eastern Countries.*

If to that delicacy of organs which renders the eastern nations so susceptible of every impression you add likewise a sort of indolence of mind, naturally connected with that of the body, by means of which they grow incapable of any exertion or effort, it is easy to comprehend that when once the soul has received an impression it cannot change it. This is the reason that the laws, manners, and customs,[7] even those which seem quite indifferent, such as their mode of dress, are the same to this very day in eastern countries as they were a thousand years ago.

5 *That those are bad Legislators who favour the Vices of the Climate, and good Legislators who oppose those Vices.*

The Indians believe that repose and non-existence are the foundation of all things, and the end in which they terminate. Hence they consider entire inaction as the most perfect of all states, and the object of their desires. To the Supreme Being they give the title of immovable. The inhabitants of Siam believe that their utmost happiness consists in not being obliged to animate a machine, or to give motion to a body.

In those countries where the excess of heat enervates and exhausts the body, rest is so delicious, and motion so painful, that this system of metaphysics seems natural; and Foe,[8] the legislator of the Indies, was directed by his own sensations when he placed mankind in a state extremely passive; but his doctrine arising from the laziness of the

---

7 We find by a fragment of Nicolaus Damascenus, collected by constantine Porphyrogenitus, that it was an ancient custom in the East to send to strangle a governor who had given any displeasure; it was in the time of the Medes.

8 Foe[7] endeavoured to reduce the heart to a mere vacuum: "We have eyes and ears, but perfection consists in neither seeing nor hearing; a mouth, hands, &c., but perfection requires that these members should be inactive." This is taken from the dialogue of a Chinese philosopher, quoted by Father Du Halde, tom. iii.

climate favoured it also in its turn; which has been the source of an infinite deal of mischief.

The legislators of China were more rational when, considering men not in the peaceful state which they are to enjoy hereafter, but in the situation proper for discharging the several duties of life, they made their religion, philosophy, and laws all practical.[8] The more the physical causes incline mankind to inaction, the more the moral causes should estrange them from it.

6 Of Agriculture in warm Climates.

Agriculture is the principal labour of man. The more the climate inclines him to shun this labour, the more the religion and laws of the country ought to incite him to it. Thus the Indian laws, which give the lands to the prince, and destroy the spirit of property among the subjects, increase the bad effects of the climate, that is, their natural indolence.

7 Of Monkery.[9]

The very same mischiefs result from monkery: it had its rise in the warm countries of the East, where they are less inclined to action than to speculation.

In Asia the number of dervishes or monks seems to increase together with the warmth of the climate. The Indies, where the heat is excessive, are full of them; and the same difference is found in Europe.

In order to surmount the laziness of the climate, the laws ought to endeavour to remove all means of subsisting without labour: but in the southern parts of Europe they act quite the reverse. To those who want to live in a state of indolence, they afford retreats the most proper for a speculative life, and endow them with immense revenues. These men, who live in the midst of plenty which they know not how to enjoy, are in the right to give their superfluities away to the common people. The poor are bereft of property; and these men indemnify them by supporting them in idleness, so as to make them even grow fond of their misery.[. . .]

Notes

1   Food.
2   Russian.
3   That is, the human body.
4   Montesquieu is referring to the ascetic practices of Indian 'holy men', like daubing their bodies with ashes or lying upon beds of nails.
5   That is, in *suttee*.
6   The time of the barbarian invasions of the Roman Empire. Gibbon (see p. 250 *et seq.*) displays a much more qualified admiration for northern barbarians.
7   'Fo' is the Chinese name for the Buddha. Montesquieu is referring, however, to the fact that there were Buddhist Kingdoms in India.
8   Montesquieu is referring to the Confucian system, which was a philosophy much

concerned with everyday conduct and civil government.

9   One of the leading characteristics of eighteenth-century *philosophes* and their British counterparts was intense hostility towards monasticism.

ON COMMERCE

ibid. Book XX, Of Laws in Relation to Commerce Considered in its Nature and Distinctions.

The following subjects deserve to be treated in a more extensive manner than the nature of this work will permit. Fain would I glide down a gentle river, but I am carried away by a torrent.

Commerce is a cure for the most destructive prejudices; for it is almost a general rule, that wherever we find agreeable manners, there commerce flourishes; and that wherever there is commerce, there we meet with agreeable manners.

Let us not be astonished, then, if our manners are now less savage than formerly. Commerce has everywhere diffused a knowledge of the manners of all nations: these are compared one with another, and from this comparison arise the greatest advantages.

Commercial laws, it may be said, improve manners for the same reason that they destroy them. They corrupt the purest morals.[1] This was the subject of Plato's complaints;[1] and we every day see that they polish and refine the most barbarous.

2 Of the Spirit of Commerce.

Peace is the natural effect of trade. Two nations who traffic with each other become reciprocally dependent; for if one has an interest in buying, the other has an interest in selling; and thus their union is founded on their mutual necessities.

But if the spirit of commerce unites nations, it does not in the same manner unite individuals. We see that in countries where the people move only by the spirit of commerce,[2] they make a traffic of all the humane, all the moral virtues; the most trifling things, those which humanity would demand, are there done, or there given, only for money.

The spirit of trade produces in the mind of a man a certain sense of exact justice, opposite, on the one hand, to robbery, and on the other to those moral virtues which forbid our always adhering rigidly to the rules of private interest, and suffer us to neglect this for the advantage of others.

The total privation of trade, on the contrary, produces robbery,

1 Caesar said of the Gauls that they were spoiled by the neighbourhood and commerce of Marseilles; insomuch that they who formerly always conquered the Germans had now become inferior to them. −War of the Gauls, lib. VI.

which Aristotle ranks in the number of means of acquiring,[3] yet it is not at all inconsistent with certain moral virtues. Hospitality, for instance, is most rare in trading countries, while it is found in the most admirable pefection among nations of vagabonds.

It is a sacrilege, says Tacitus[4] for a German to shut his door against any man whomsoever, whether known or unknown. He who has behaved with hospitality to a stranger goes to show him another house where this hospitality is also practised; and he is there received with the same humanity. But when the Germans had founded kingdoms, hospitality had become burdensome. This appears by two laws of the code of the Burgundians; one of which inflicted a penalty on every barbarian who presumed to show a stranger the house of a Roman; and the other decreed, that whoever received a stranger should be indemnified by the inhabitants, every one being obliged to pay his proper proportion.

3 *Of the Poverty of the People.*

There are two sorts of poor; those who are rendered such by the severity of government: these are, indeed, incapable of performing almost any great action, because their indigence is a consequence of their slavery. Others are poor, only because they either despise or know not the conveniences of life; and these are capable of accomplishing great things, because their poverty constitutes a part of their liberty.

4 *Of Commerce in different Governments.*

Trade has some relation to forms of government. In a monarchy, it is generally founded on luxury; and though it be also founded on real wants, yet the principal view with which it is carried on is to procure everything that can contribute to the pride, the pleasure, and the capricious whims of the nation. In republics, it is commonly founded on economy.[5] Their merchants, having an eye to all the nations of the earth, bring from one what is wanted by another. It is thus that the republics of Tyre, Carthage, Athens, Marseilles, Florence, Venice, and Holland engaged in commerce.

This kind of traffic has a natural relation to a republican government: to monarchies it is only occasional. For as it is founded on the practice of gaining little, and even less than other nations, and of remedying this by gaining incessantly, it can hardly be carried on by a people swallowed up in luxury[6] who spend much, and see nothing but objects of grandeur.

Cicero was of this opinion, when he so justly said, *that he did not like that the same people should be at once both the lords and factors[7] of the whole earth.* For this would, indeed, be to suppose that every individual in the state, and the whole state collectively had their heads constantly filled with grand views, and at the same time with small ones; which is a contradiction.

Not but that the most noble enterprises are completed also in those states which subsist by economical commerce: they have even an intrepidity not to be found in monarchies. And the reason is this:–

One branch of commerce leads to another, the small to the moderate, the moderate to the great; thus he who has gratified his desire of gaining a little raises himself to a situation in which he is not less desirous of gaining a great deal.

Besides, the grand enterprises of merchants are always necessarily connected with the affairs of the public. But, in monarchies, these public affairs give as much distrust to the merchants as in free states they appear to give safety. Great enterprises, therefore, in commerce are not for monarchical, but for republican, governments.

In short, an opinion of greater certainty, as to the possession of property in these states, makes them undertake everything. They flatter themselves with the hopes of receiving great advantages from the smiles of fortune; and thinking themselves sure of what they have already acquired, they boldly expose it in order to acquire more; risking nothing, but as the means of obtaining.

I do not pretend to say that any monarchy is entirely excluded from an economical commerce; but of its own nature it has less tendency towards it: neither do I mean that the republics with which we are acquainted are absolutely deprived of the commerce of luxury; but it is less connected with their constitution.

With regard to a despotic state, there is no occasion to mention it. A general rule: A nation in slavery labours more to preserve than to acquire; a free nation, more to acquire than to preserve.

5 *Of Nations that have entered into an economical Commerce.*

Marseilles,[8] a necessary retreat in the midst of a tempestuous sea; Marseilles, a harbour which all the winds, the shelves of the sea, the disposition of the coasts, point out for a landing-place, became frequented by mariners; while the sterility of the adjacent country determined the citizens to an economical commerce. It was necessary that they should be laborious to supply what nature had refused; that they should be just, in order to live among barbarous nations, from whom they were to derive their prosperity; that they should be moderate, to the end that they might always taste the sweets of a tranquil government; in fine, that they should be frugal in their manners, to enable them to subsist by trade – a trade the more certain as it was less advantageous.

We everywhere see violence and oppression give birth to a commerce founded on economy, while men are constrained to take refuge in marshes, in isles, in the shallows of the sea, and even on rocks themselves. Thus it was that Tyre, Venice, and the cities of Holland were founded. Fugitives found there a place of safety. It was necessary that they should subsist; they drew, therefore, their subsistence from all parts of the world.

143

6 *Some Effects of an extensive Navigation.*

It sometimes happens that a nation, when engaged in an economical commerce, having need of the merchandise of one country, which serves as a capital or stock for procuring the commodities of another, is satisfied with making very little profit, and frequently none at all, in trading with the former, in expectation of gaining greatly by the latter. Thus, when the Dutch were almost the only nation that carried on the trade from the south to the north of Europe, the French wines which they imported to the north were in some measure only a capital or stock for conducting their commerce in that part of the world.

It is a known fact that there are some kinds of merchandise in Holland which, though imported from afar, sell for very little more than they cost upon the spot. They account for it thus: a captain who has occasion to ballast his ship will load it with marble; if he wants wood for stowage, he will buy it; and, provided he loses nothing by the bargain, he will think himself a gainer. Thus it is that Holland has its quarries and its forests.[9]

Further, it may happen so that not only a commerce which brings in nothing shall be useful, but even a losing trade shall be beneficial. I have heard it affirmed in Holland that the whale fishery in general does not answer the expense; but it must be observed that the persons employed in building the ships, as also those who furnish the rigging and provisions, are jointly concerned in the fishery. Should they happen to lose in the voyage, they have had a profit in fitting out the vessel. This commerce, in short, is a kind of lottery, and every one is allured with the hopes of a prize. Mankind are generally fond of gaming; and even the most prudent have no aversion to it, when the disagreeable circumstances attending it, such as dissipation, anxiety, passion, loss of time, and even of life and fortune, are concealed from their view.

7 *The Spirit of England with respect to Commerce.*

The tariff or customs of England are very unsettled with respect to other nations; they are changed, in some measure, with every parliament, either by taking off particular duties, or by imposing new ones. They endeavour by these means still to preserve their independence. Supremely jealous with respect to trade, they bind themselves but little by treaties, and depend only on their own laws.

Other nations have made the interests of commerce yield to those of politics: the English, on the contrary, have ever made their political interests give way to those of commerce.

They know better than any other people upon earth how to value, at the same time, these three great advantages – religion, commerce, and liberty.

8 *In what Manner economical Commerce has been sometimes restrained.*

In several kingdoms laws have been made extremely proper to humble the states that have entered into economical commerce. They have forbidden their importing any merchandise except the product of their respective countries; and have permitted them to traffic only in vessels built in the kingdom to which they brought their commodities.

It is necessary that the kingdom which imposes these laws should itself be able easily to engage in commerce; otherwise it will, at least, be an equal sufferer. It is much more advantageous to trade with a commercial nation, whose profits are moderate, and who are rendered in some sort dependent by the affairs of commerce; with a nation whose larger views and whose extended trade enables them to dispose of their superfluous merchandise; with a wealthy nation, who can take off many of their commodities, and make them a quicker return in specie;[10] with a nation under a kind of necessity to be faithful, pacific from principle, and that seeks to gain, and not to conquer: it is much better, I say, to trade with such a nation than with others, their constant rivals, who will never grant such great advantages. [. . .]

Notes
1   Plato makes repeated complaints of the corrupting effect of trade upon morals, and in the *Laws* (742 a,c) he lays it down that in his ideal community citizens shall use a currency which is valueless outside their own country.
2   Montesquieu has in mind Holland, especially.
3   Aristotle in his *Politics*, Bk. 1, 1256b, compares robbery to farming, fishing, hunting and nomadic life as a direct means of obtaining food 'without recourse to exchange or retail trade'.
4   The Roman historian, author of an account of Germany written *circa* A.D.100.
5   Prudent management of material resources.
6   Montesquieu no doubt has in mind his own country, among others.
7   Agents; i.e. those who buy and sell or fetch and carry, etc., on behalf of their superiors.
8   Marseilles was a major port and trading state as far back as the time of ancient Rome.
9   That is, it has what is just as good as actual quarries and forests.
10   In coin.

QUESNAI

General Maxims for Economic Government (1768)

From François Quesnai, *General Maxims for the Economic Government of an Agricultural Kingdom*. The idea first appeared in his *Tableau oeconomique*, Versailles, 1758. Revised and expanded in *Physiocratie, ou Constitution Naturelle Du Gouvernement*, recueil publié par Du Pont; Pékin: chez Merlin, Paris 1767. Reprinted from the translation by R. L. Meek in *The Economics of Physiocracy*, Allen & Unwin 1962.

These maxims form a fairly complete statement of the physiocratic principles of political economy. Quesnai was a leading advocate of what Adam Smith referred to in *The Wealth of Nations* as the 'Agricultural System', which Smith (see pp. 154–171) held to be 'the nearest approximation to the truth that has yet been published upon the subject of political economy'. Smith could not have been referring to this work but he may have been familiar with the similar maxims which Quesnai had included in his article on *Grains* in the *Encyclopédie* some ten years earlier.

The maxims are included here without the long notes attached to them by Quesnai himself.

I

That there should be a single sovereign authority, standing above all the individuals in the society and all the unjust undertakings of private interests; for the object of dominion and allegiance is the security of all and the lawful interest of all. The view that there should be a balance of forces in goverment is a disastrous one, leaving scope for nothing but dissension among the great and the oppression of the small.[1] The division of societies into different orders of citizens, some of whom exercise sovereign authority over the others, destroys the general interest of the nation and ushers in the conflict of private interests between the different classes of citizens.

Such a division would play havoc with the order of government in an agricultural kingdom which ought to reconcile all interests for one main purpose – that of securing the prosperity of agriculture, which is the source of all the wealth of the state and that of all its citizens.

II

That the nation should be given instruction in the general laws of the natural order, which constitute the form of government which is self-evidently the most perfect. The study of human jurisprudence is not sufficient to make a statesman; it is necessary that those who are destined for administrative positions should be obliged to make a study of the natural order which is most advantageous to men combined together in society. It is also necessary that the practical knowledge and insight which the nation acquires through experience and reflection should be brought together in the general science of government, so that the sovereign authority, always guided by what is self-evident, should institute the best laws and cause them to be scrupulously observed, in order to provide for the security of all and to attain to the greatest degree of prosperity possible for the society.

III

That the sovereign and the nation should never lose sight of the fact that the land is the unique source of wealth, and that it is agriculture which causes wealth to increase. For the growth of wealth ensures the growth of the population; men and wealth cause agriculture to prosper, expand trade, stimulate industry, and increase and perpetuate wealth. Upon this abundant source depends the success of all branches of the administration of the kingdom.

IV

That the ownership of landed property and movable wealth should be guaranteed to those who are their lawful possessors; for SECURITY OF OWNERSHIP IS THE ESSENTIAL FOUNDATION OF THE ECONOMIC ORDER OF SOCIETY. In the absence of surety of ownership the territory would remain uncultivated. It would have neither proprietors nor farmers to make the expenditure necessary to improve and cultivate it, if protection of funds and products were not guaranteed to those who make the advances of this expenditure. It is the security of permanent possession which stimulates labour and the employment of wealth in the improvement and cultivation of the land and in commercial and industrial enterprises. It is only the sovereign power which guarantees the property of its subjects which has a right to the first share of the fruits of the land, the unique source of wealth.

V

That taxes should not be destructive or disproportionate to the mass of the nation's revenue; that their increase should follow the increase of the revenue; and that they should be laid directly on the net product of landed property, and not on men's wages, or on produce where they would increase the costs of collection, operate to the detriment of trade, and destroy every year a portion of the nation's wealth. That they should also not be taken from the wealth of the farmers of landed property; for the ADVANCES[2] OF A KING-DOM'S AGRICULTURE OUGHT TO BE REGARDED AS IF THEY WERE FIXED PROPERTY REQUIRING TO BE PRESERVED WITH GREAT CARE IN ORDER TO ENSURE THE PRODUCTION OF TAXES, REVENUE AND SUBSISTENCE FOR ALL CLASSES OF CITIZENS. Otherwise taxation degenerates into spoliation,[3] and brings about a state of decline which very soon ruins the state.

VI

That the advances of the cultivators should be sufficient to enable the greatest possible product to be annually regenerated by expenditure on the cultivation of the land; for if the advances are not sufficient, the expenses of cultivation are proportionately higher and yield a smaller net product.

VII

That the whole of the sum of revenue should come back into the annual circulation, and run through it to the full extent of its course; and that it should never be formed into monetary fortunes, or at least that those which are formed should be counterbalanced by those which come back into circulation. For otherwise these monetary fortunes would check the distribution of a part of the annual revenue of the nation, and hold back the money stock of the kingdom to the detriment of the return of the advances of cultivation, the payment of the artisans' wages and the consumption which ought to be carried on by the different classes of men who follow remunerative occupations. Such an interception of the money stock would reduce the reproduction[4] of revenue and taxes.

VIII

That the government's economic policy should be concerned only with encouraging productive expenditure and trade in raw produce, and that it should refrain from interfering with sterile[5] expenditure.

IX

That the nation which has a large territory to cultivate, and the means of carrying on a large trade in raw produce, should not extend too far the employment of money and men in manufacturing and trading in luxury goods, to the detriment of the work and expenditure involved in agriculture; for more than anything else THE KINGDOM OUGHT TO BE WELL FURNISHED WITH WEALTHY CULTIVATORS.

X

That no part of the sum of revenue should pass into the hands of foreign countries without return in money or commodities.

XI

That the desertion of inhabitants who would take their wealth out of the kingdom should be avoided.

XII

That the children of rich farmers should settle down in the countryside, so that there are always husbandmen[6] there; for if they are harassed into abandoning the countryside and settling in the towns, they take their fathers' wealth which used to be employed in cultivation. IT IS NOT SO MUCH MEN AS WEALTH WHICH OUGHT TO BE ATTRACTED TO THE COUNTRYSIDE; for the more wealth is employed in cultivation, the fewer men it requires, the more it prospers, and the more revenue it yields. Such, for example, in the case of corn is the large-scale cultivation carried on by rich farmers in comparison with the small-scale cultivation carried on by poor métayers[7] who plough with the aid of oxen or cows.

XIII

That each person should be free to cultivate in his fields such produce as his interests, his means, and the nature of the land suggest to him, in order that he may extract from them the greatest possible product. Monopoly in the cultivation of landed property should never be encouraged, for it is detrimental to the general revenue of the nation. The prejudice which leads to the encouragement of an abundance of produce of primary necessity in preference to other produce, to the detriment of the market value of one or the other, is inspired by short-sighted views which do not extend as far as the effects of mutual external trade, which makes provision for

149

everything and determines the price of the produce which each nation can cultivate with the most profit. AFTER THE WEALTH EMPLOY-ED IN CULTIVATION, IT IS REVENUE AND TAXES WHICH ARE THE WEALTH OF PRIMARY NECESSITY in a state, in order to defend subjects against scarcity and against the enemy, and to maintain the glory and power of the monarch and the prosperity of the nation.

XIV

That the breeding of live-stock should be encouraged, for it is live-stock which provides the land with the manure which procures abundant crops.

XV

That the land employed in the cultivation of corn should be brought together, as far as possible, into large farms worked by rich husbandmen; for in large agricultural enterprises there is less expenditure required for the upkeep and repair of buildings, and proportionately much less cost and much more net product, than in small ones. A multiplicity of small farmers is detrimental to the population. The population whose position is most assured, and which is most readily available for the different occupations and different kinds of work which divide men into different classes, is that maintained by the net product. All economies profitably made use of in work which can be done with the aid of animals, machines, rivers, etc., bring benefit to the population and the state, because the greater net product procures men a greater reward for other services or other kinds of work.

XVI

That no barriers at all should be raised to external trade in raw produce; for AS THE MARKET IS, SO IS THE REPRODUCTION.

XVII

That the marketing and transport of produce and manufactured commodities should be facilitated, through the repair of roads and the navigation of canals, rivers, and the sea; for the more that is saved on trading costs, the more the territory's revenue increases.

XVIII

That the prices of produce and commodities in the kingdom should never be made to fall; for then mutual foreign trade would become disadvantageous to the nation. AS THE MARKET VALUE IS, SO IS THE REVENUE: *Abundance plus valuelessness does not equal wealth. Scarcity plus dearness equals poverty. Abundance plus dearness equals opulence.*

XIX

That it should not be believed that cheapness of produce is profitable to the lower classes, for a low price of produce causes a fall in the wages of the lower orders of people, reduces their well-being, makes less work and remunerative occupations available for them, and destroys the nation's revenue.

XX

That the well-being of the latter classes of citizens should not be reduced; for then they would not be able to contribute sufficiently to the consumption of the produce which can be consumed only within the country, which would bring about a reduction in the reproduction and revenue of the nation.

XXI

That the proprietors and those engaged in remunerative occupations should not give themselves over to sterile savings, which would deduct from circulation and distribution a portion of their revenue or gains.

XXII

That no encouragement at all should be given to luxury in the way of ornamentation to the detriment of the expenditure involved in the operations and improvement of agriculture, and of expenditure on the consumption of subsistence goods, which sustains the market for raw produce, its proper price, and the reproduction of the nation's revenue.

XXIII

That the nation should not suffer any loss in its mutual trade with foreign countries, even if this trade were profitable to the merchants who make gains out of their fellow-citizens on the sale of commodities which were imported. For then the increase in the fortunes of these merchants would bring about a deduction from the circulation of the revenue, which would be detrimental to distribution and reproduction.

151

XXIV

That people should not be taken in by a seeming advantage in mutual trade with foreign countries, through judging it simply with reference to the balance of the sums of money involved and not examining the greater or lesser profit which results from the particular commodities which are sold and purchased. For the loss often falls on the nation which receives a surplus in money, and this loss works to the detriment of the distribution and reproduction of the revenue.

XXV

That complete freedom of trade should be maintained; for THE POLICY FOR INTERNAL AND EXTERNAL TRADE WHICH IS THE MOST SECURE, THE MOST CORRECT, AND THE MOST PROFITABLE FOR THE NATION AND THE STATE, CONSISTS IN FULL FREEDOM OF COMPETITION.

XXVI

That less attention should be paid to augmenting the population than to increasing the revenue; for the greater well-being which a high revenue brings about is preferable to the greater pressure of subsistence needs which a population in excess of the revenue entails; and when the people are in a state of well-being there are more resources to meet the needs of the state and also more means to enable agriculture to prosper.

XXVII

That the government should trouble itself less with economizing than with the operations necessary for the prosperity of the kingdom; for very high expenditure may cease to be excessive by virtue of the increase of wealth. But abuses must not be confused with simple expenditure, for abuses could swallow up all the wealth of the nation and the sovereign.

XXVIII

That the administration of finance, whether in the collection of taxes or in the expenditure of government, should not bring about the formation of monetary fortunes, which steal a portion of the revenue away from circulation, distribution, and reproduction.

XXIX

That means to meet the extraordinary needs of a state should be expected to be found in the prosperity of the nation and not in the credit of financiers; for MONETARY FORTUNES ARE A CLANDESTINE FORM OF WEALTH WHICH KNOWS NEITHER KING NOR COUNTRY.

XXX

That the state should avoid contracting loans which create rentier incomes,[8] which burden it with devouring debts, and which bring about a trade or traffic in finance, through the medium of negotiable bills, the discount on which causes a greater and greater increase in sterile monetary fortunes. These fortunes separate finance from agriculture, and deprive the countryside of the wealth necessary for the improvement of landed property and for the operations involved in the cultivation of the land.

Notes

1 A clear attack on Montesquieu's ideas.
2 That is, capital-appreciation.
3 Robbery.
4 That is re-creation or renewal.
5 Unproductive.
6 A man who tills and cultivates the soil; a farmer.
7 A *métayer* is a farmer who pays a proportion (usually half) of the produce as rent to the landowner, who furnishes the stock or a part of it.
8 Incomes derived from investment.

ADAM SMITH

Of the Agricultural Systems (1776)

From Adam Smith, *An Inquiry into the Nature and Causes of the Wealth of Nations*, W. Strahan and T. Cadell, London 1776. Reprinted from edition by R. H. Campbell, A. S. Skinner and W. B. Todd, 2 vols. Oxford 1976. Vol. 2.

Book IV, Chapter IX, of the Agricultural Systems, or of those Systems of political Oeconomy, which represent the produce of land as either the sole or the principal source of the Revenue and Wealth of every country.

The Wealth of Nations (1776), by the Scottish philosopher Adam Smith (1723–90), was the first great classic of economics, or 'political economy' as it was then called, and is still an influential statement of the theory of economic *laissez-faire*. In Book IV, having at some length attacked the 'mercantile system', which he thought was biased in favour of merchants and manufacturers, Smith turns in this chapter to a consideration of the system which reflects the contrary bias in favour of the produce of the country.

The agricultural system is the one advocated by the French philosophers known as 'The Physiocrats' (these are the 'few men of great learning and ingenuity in France' mentioned in the second paragraph of Adam Smith's text).

The agriculture systems of political œconomy will not require so long an explanation as that which I have thought it necessary to bestow upon the mercantile or commercial system.

That system which represents the produce of land as the sole source of the revenue and wealth of every country, has, so far as I know, never been adopted by any nation, and it at present exists only in the speculations of a few men of great learning and ingenuity in France. It would not, surely, be worth while to examine at great length the errors of a system which never has done, and probably never will do any harm in any part of the world. I shall endeavour to explain, however, as distinctly as I can, the great outlines of this very ingenious system.

Mr. Colbert,[1] the famous minister of Lewis XIV was a man of probity, of great industry and knowledge of detail; of great experience and acuteness in the examination of publick accounts, and of abilities, in short, every way fitted for introducing method and good order into the collection and expenditure of the publick revenue. That minister had unfortunately embraced all the prejudices of the mercantile system, in its nature and essence a system of restraint and regulation, and such as could scarce fail to be agreeable to a laborious and plodding man of business, who had been accustomed to regulate the different departments of publick offices, and to establish the necessary checks and controuls for confining each to its proper sphere. The industry and commerce of a great country he endeavoured to regulate upon the same model as the departments of a publick office; and instead of allowing every man to pursue his own interest his own way, upon the liberal plan of equality, liberty and justice, he bestowed upon certain branches of industry extraordinary privileges, while he laid others under as extraordinary restraints. He was not only disposed, like other European ministers, to encourage more the industry of the towns than that of the country; but, in order to support the industry of the towns, he was willing even to depress and keep down that of the country. In order to render provisions cheap to the inhabitants of the towns, and thereby to encourage manufactures and foreign commerce, he prohibited altogether the exportation of corn, and thus excluded the inhabitants of the country from every foreign market for by far the most important part of the produce of their industry. This prohibition, joined to the restraints imposed by the ancient provincial laws of France upon the transportation of corn from one province to another, and to the arbitrary and degrading taxes which are levied upon the cultivators in almost all the provinces, discouraged and kept down the agriculture of that country very much below the state to which it would naturally have risen in so very fertile a soil and so very happy a climate. This state of discouragement and depression was felt more or less in every different part of the country, and many different enquiries were set on foot concerning the causes of it. One of those causes appeared to be the preference given, by the institutions of Mr. Colbert, to the industry of the towns above that of the country.

If the rod be bent too much one way, says the proverb, in order to make it straight you must bend it as much the other. The French philosophers, who have proposed the system which represents agriculture as the sole source of the revenue and wealth of every country, seem to have adopted this proverbial maxim; and as in the plan of Mr. Colbert the industry of the towns was certainly over-valued in comparison with that of the country; so in their system it seems to be as certainly under-valued.

The different orders of people who have ever been supposed to contribute in any respect towards the annual produce of the land and labour of the country, they divide into three classes. The first is the class of the proprietors of land. The second is the class of the cultivators, of farmers and country labourers, whom they honour with the peculiar appellation of the productive class. The third is the class of artificers, manufacturers and merchants, whom they endeavour to degrade by the humiliating appellation of the barren or unproductive class.

The class of proprietors contributes to the annual produce by the expence which they may occasionally lay out upon the improvement of the land, upon the buildings, drains, enclosures and other ameliorations, which they may either make or maintain upon it, and by means of which the cultivators are enabled, with the same capital, to raise a greater produce, and consequently to pay a greater rent. This advanced rent may be considered as the interest or profit due to the proprietor upon the expence or capital which he thus employs in the improvement of his land. Such expences are in this system called ground expences (dépenses foncières).

The cultivators or farmers contribute to the annual produce by what are in this system called the original and annual expences (dépenses primitives et dépenses annuelles) which they lay out upon the cultivation of the land. The original expences consist in the instruments of husbandry, in the stock of cattle, in the seed, and in the maintenance of the farmer's family, servants and cattle, during at least a great part of the first year of his occupancy, or till he can receive some return from the land. The annual expences consist in the seed, in the wear and tear of the instruments of husbandry, and in the annual maintenance of the farmer's servants and cattle, and of his family too, so far as any part of them can be considered as servants employed in cultivation. That part of the produce of the land which remains to him after paying the rent, ought to be sufficient, first, to replace to him within a reasonable time, at least during the term of his occupancy, the whole of his original expences, together with the ordinary profits of stock; and, secondly, to replace to him annually the whole of his annual expences, together likewise with the ordinary profits of stock. Those two sorts of expences are two capitals which the farmer employs in cultivation; and unless they are regularly restored to him, together with a reasonable profit, he cannot carry on his employment upon a level with other employments; but, from a regard to his own interest, must desert it as soon as possible, and seek some other. That part of the produce of the land which is thus necessary for enabling the farmer to continue his business, ought to be considered as a fund sacred to cultivation, which if the landlord violates, he necessarily reduces the produce of his own land, and in a few years not only disables the farmer from paying this racked rent, but from paying the reasonable rent which he might otherwise have got for his land. The rent which properly belongs to the landlord, is no more than the neat[2] produce which remains after paying in the compleatest manner all the necessary expences which must be previously laid out in order to raise the gross, or the whole produce. It is because the labour of the cultivators, over and above paying completely all those necessary expences, affords a neat produce of this kind, that this class of people are in this system peculiarly distinguished by the honourable appellation of the productive class. Their original and annual expences are for the same reason called, in this system, productive expences, because, over and above replacing their own value, they occasion the annual reproduction of this neat produce.

The ground expences, as they are called, or what the landlord lays out upon the improvement of his land, are in this system too honoured with the appellation of productive expences. Till the whole of those expences, together with the ordinary profits of stock, have been compleatly repaid to him by the advanced rent which he gets from his land, that advanced rent ought to be regarded as sacred and inviolable, both by the church and by the king; ought to be subject neither to tithe nor to taxation. If it is otherwise, by discouraging the improvement of land, the church discourages the future increase of her own tithes, and the king the future increase of his own taxes. As in a well-ordered state of things, therefore, those 'ground expences, over and above repro-ducing in the compleatest manner their own value, occasion likewise after a certain time a reproduction of a neat produce, they are in this system considered as productive expences.

The ground expences of the landlord, however, together with the original and the annual expences of the farmer, are the only three sorts of expences which in this system are considered as productive. All other expences and all other orders of people, even those who in the common apprehensions of men are regarded as the most productive, are in this account of things represented as altogether barren and unproductive.

Artificers and manufacturers, in particular, whose industry, in the common apprehensions of men, increases so much the value of the rude produce of land, are in this system represented as a class of people altogether barren and unproductive. Their labour, it is said, replaces only the stock which employs them, together with its ordinary profits. That stock consists in the materials, tools, and wages, advanced to them by their employer; and is the fund destined for their employment and maintenance. Its profits are the fund destined for the maintenance of their employer. Their employer, as he advances to them the stock of materials, tools and wages necessary for their employment, so he advances to himself what is necessary for his own maintenance, and this maintenance he generally proportions to the profit which he expects to make by the price of their work. Unless its price repays to him the maintenance which he advances to himself, as well as the materials, tools and wages which he advances to his workmen, it evidently does not repay to him the whole expence which he lays out upon it. The profits of manufacturing stock, therefore, are not, like the rent of land, a neat produce which remains after compleatly repaying the whole expence which must be laid out in order to obtain them. The stock of the farmer yields him a profit as well as that of the master manufacturer; and it yields a rent likewise to another person, which that of the master manufacturer does not. The expence, therefore, laid out in employing and maintaining artificers and manufacturers, does no more than continue, if one may say so, the existence of its own value, and does not

157

produce any new value. It is therefore altogether a barren and unproductive expence. The expence, on the contrary, laid out in employing farmers and country labourers, over and above continuing the existence of its own value, produces a new value, the rent of the landlord. It is therefore a productive expence.

Mercantile stock is equally barren and unproductive with manufacturing stock. It only continues the existence of its own value, without producing any new value. Its profits are only the repayment of the maintenance which its employer advances to himself during the time that he employs it, or till he receives the returns of it. They are only the repayment of a part of the expence which must be laid out in employing it.

The labour of artificers and manufacturers never adds any thing to the value of the whole annual amount of the rude produce of the land. It adds indeed greatly to the value of some particular parts of it. But the consumption which in the mean time it occasions of other parts, is precisely equal to the value which it adds to those parts; so that the value of the whole amount is not, at any one moment of time, in the least augmented by it. The person who works the lace of a pair of fine ruffles, for example, will sometimes raise the value of perhaps a pennyworth of flax to thirty pounds sterling. But though at first sight he appears thereby to multiply the value of a part of the rude produce about seven thousand and two hundred times, he in reality adds nothing to the value of the whole annual amount of the rude produce. The working of that lace costs him perhaps two years labour. The thirty pounds which he gets for it when it is finished, is no more than the repayment of the subsistence which he advances to himself during the two years that he is employed about it. The value which, by every day's, month's, or year's labour, he adds to the flax, does no more than replace the value of his own consumption during that day, month, or year. At no moment of time, therefore, does he add any thing to the value of the whole annual amount of the rude produce of the land: the portion of that produce which he is continually consuming, being always equal to the value which he is continually producing. The extreme poverty of the greater part of the persons employed in this expensive, though trifling manufacture, may satisfy us that the price of their work does not in ordinary cases exceed the value of their subsistence. It is otherwise with the work of farmers and country labourers. The rent of the landlord is a value, which, in ordinary cases, it is continually producing, over and above replacing, in the most compleat manner, the whole consumption, the whole expence laid out upon the employment and maintenance both of the workmen and of their employer.

Artificers, manufacturers and merchants, can augment the revenue and wealth of their society, by parsimony[3] only; or, as it is expressed in this system, by privation, that is, by depriving themselves of a part of the funds destined for their own subsistence. They annually reproduce nothing but those funds. Unless, therefore, they annually save some part of them, unless they annually deprive themselves of the enjoyment of some part of them, the revenue and wealth of their society can never be in the smallest degree augmented by means of their industry. Farmers and country labourers, on the contrary, may enjoy completely the whole funds destined for their own subsistence, and yet augment at the same time the revenue and wealth of their society. Over and above what is destined for their own subsistence, their industry annually affords a neat produce, of which the augmentation necessarily augments the revenue and wealth of their society. Nations, therefore, which, like France or England, consist in a great measure of proprietors and cultivators, can be enriched by industry and enjoyment. Nations, on the contrary, which, like Holland and Hamburgh, are composed chiefly of merchants, artificers and manufacturers, can grow rich only through parsimony and privation. As the interest of nations so differently circumstanced, is very different, so is likewise the common character of the people. In those of the former kind, liberality, frankness, and good fellowship, naturally make a part of that common character. In the latter, narrowness, meanness, and a selfish disposition, averse to all social pleasure and enjoyment.

The unproductive class, that of merchants, artificers, and manufacturers, is maintained and employed altogether at the expence of the two other classes, of that of proprietors, and of that of cultivators. They furnish it both with the materials of its work and with the fund of its subsistence, with the corn and cattle which it consumes while it is employed about that work. The proprietors and cultivators finally pay both the wages of all the workmen of the unproductive class, and the profits of all their employers. Those workmen and their employers are properly the servants of the proprietors and cultivators. They are only servants who work without doors, as menial servants work within. Both the one and the other, however, are equally maintained at the expence of the same masters. The labour of both is equally unproductive. It adds nothing to the value of the sum total of the rude produce of the land. Instead of increasing the value of that sum total, it is a charge and expence which must be paid out of it.

The unproductive class, however, is not only useful, but greatly useful to the other two classes. By means of the industry of merchants, artificers and manufacturers, the proprietors and cultivators can purchase both the foreign goods and the manufactured produce of their own country which they have occasion for, with the produce of a much smaller quantity of their own labour, than what they would be obliged to employ, if they were to attempt, in an aukward and unskilful manner, either to import the one, or to make the other for their own use. By means of the unproductive class, the cultivators are delivered from many cases which would otherwise distract their attention from the cultivation of land. The superiority of produce, which, in consequence of this undivided attention, they are enabled to raise, is fully sufficient to pay the whole expence which the maintenance and employment of the unproductive class costs either the proprietors, or themselves. The industry of merchants, artificers, and manufacturers, though in its own nature altogether unproductive, yet contributes in this manner indirectly to increase the produce of the land. It increases the productive powers of productive labour, by leaving it at liberty to confine itself to its proper employment, the cultivation of land; and the plough goes frequently the easier and the better by means of the labour of the man whose business is most remote from the plough.

It can never be the interest of the proprietors and cultivators to restrain or to discourage in any respect the industry of merchants, artificers and manufacturers. The greater the liberty which this unproductive class enjoys, the greater will be the competition in all the different trades which compose it, and the cheaper will the other two classes be supplied, both with foreign goods and with the manufactured produce of their own country.

It can never be the interest of the unproductive class to oppress the other two classes. It is the surplus produce of the land, or what remains after deducting the maintenance, first, of the cultivators, and afterwards, of the proprietors, that maintains and employs the unproductive class. The greater this surplus, the greater must likewise be the maintenance and employment of that class. The establishment of perfect justice, of perfect liberty, and of perfect equality, is the very simple secret which most effectually secures the highest degree of prosperity to all the three classes.

The merchants, artificers, and manufacturers of those mercantile states which, like Holland and Hamburgh, consist chiefly of this unproductive class, are in the same manner maintained and employed altogether at the expence of the proprietors and cultivators of land. The only difference is, that those proprietors and cultivators are, the greater part of them, placed at a most inconvenient distance from the merchants, artificers, and manufacturers whom they supply with the materials of their work and the fund of their subsistence, are the inhabitants of other countries, and the subjects of other governments.

Such mercantile states, however, are not only useful, but greatly useful to the inhabitants of those other countries. They fill up, in some measure, a very important void, and supply the place of the merchants, artificers and manufacturers, whom the inhabitants of those countries ought to find at home, but whom, from some defect in their policy, they do not find at home.

It can never be the interest of those landed nations, if I may call them so, to discourage or distress the industry of such mercantile states, by imposing high duties upon their trade, or upon the commodities which they furnish. Such duties, by rendering those commodities dear, could serve only to sink the real value of the surplus produce of their own land, with which, or, what comes to the same thing, with the price of which those commodities are purchased. Such duties could serve only to discourage the increase of that surplus produce, and consequently the improvement and cultivation of their own land. The most effectual expedient, on the contrary, for raising the value of that surplus produce, for encouraging its increase, and consequently the improvement and cultivation of their own land, would be to allow the most perfect freedom to the trade of all such mercantile nations.

This perfect freedom of trade would even be the most effectual expedient for supplying them, in due time, with all the artificers, manufacturers and merchants, whom they wanted at home, and for filling up in the properest and most advantageous manner that very important void which they felt there.

The continual increase of the surplus produce of theiould be employed with the ordinary rate of profit in the improvement and cultivation of land; and the surplus part of it would naturally turn itself to the employment of artificers and manufacturers at home. But those artificers and manufacturers, finding at home both the materials of their work and the fund of their subsistence, might immediately, even with much less art and skill, be able to work as cheap as the like artificers and manufacturers of such mercantiles states, who had both to bring from a great distance. Even though from want of art and skill, they might not for some time be able to work as cheap, yet, finding a market at home, they might be able to sell their work there a cheap as that of the artificers and manufacturers of such mercantile states, which could not be brought to that market but from so great a distance; and as their art and skill improved, they would soon be able to sell it cheaper. The artificers and manufacturers of such mercantile states, therefore, would immediately be rivalled in the market of those landed nations, and soon after undersold and justled out of it altogether. The cheapness f the manufactures of those landed nations, in consequence of the gradual improvements of art and skill, would, in due time, extend their sale beyond the home market, and carry them to many foreign markets, from which they would in the same manner gradually justle out many of the manufacturers of such mercantile nations.

This continual increase both of the rude and manufactured produce of those landed nations would in due time create a greater capital than could, with the ordinary rate of profit, be employed either in agri-culture or in manufactures. The surplus of this capital would naturally turn itself to foreign trade, and be employed in exporting, to foreign countries, such parts of the rude and manufactured produce of its own country, as exceeded the demand of the home market. In the export-ation of the produce of their own country, the merchants of a landed nation would have an advantage of the same kind over those of mercantile nations, which its artificers and manufacturers had over the artificers and manufacturers of such nations; the advantage of finding at home that cargo, and those stores and provisions, which the others were obliged to seek for at a distance. With inferior art and skill in navigation, therefore, they would be able to sell that cargo as cheap in foreign markets as the merchants of such mercantile nations; and with equal art and skill they would be able to sell it cheaper. They would soon, therefore, rival those mercantile nations in this branch of foreign trade, and in due time would justle them out of it altogether.

According to this liberal and generous system, therefore, the most advantageous method in which a landed nation can raise up artificers, manufacturers and merchants of its own, is to grant the most perfect freedom of trade to the artificers, manufacturers and merchants of all other nations. It thereby raises the value of the surplus produce of its own land, of which the continual increase gradually establishes a fund which in due time necessarily raises up all the artificers, manufacturers and merchants whom it has occasion for.

When a landed nation, on the contrary, oppresses either by high duties or by prohibitions the trade of foreign nations, it necessarily hurts its own interest in two different ways. First, by raising the price of all foreign goods and of all sorts of manufactures, it necessarily sinks the real value of the surplus produce of its own land, with which, or, what comes to the same thing, with the price of which, it purchases those foreign goods and manufactures. Secondly, by giving a sort of monopoly of the home market to its own merchants, artificers and manufacturers, it raises the rate of mercantile and manufacturing profit in proportion to that of agricultural profit, and consequently either draws from agriculture a part of the capital which had before been employed in it, or hinders from going to it a part of what would otherwise have gone to it. This policy, therefore, discourages agriculture in two different ways; first, by sinking the real value of its produce, and thereby lowering the rate of its profit; and, secondly, by raising the rate of profit in all other employments. Agriculture is rendered less advantageous, and trade and manufactures more advantageous than they otherwise would be; and every man is tempted by his own interest to turn, as much as he can, both his capital and his industry from the former to the latter employments.

Though, by this oppressive policy, a landed nation should be able to raise up artificers, manufacturers and merchants of its own, somewhat sooner than it could do by the freedom of trade; a matter, however, which is not a little doubtful; yet it would raise them up, if one may say so, prematurely, and before it was perfectly ripe for them. By raising up too hastily one species of industry, it would depress another more valuable species of industry. By raising up too hastily a species of industry which only replaces the stock which employs it, together with the ordinary profit, it would depress a species of industry which, over and above replacing that stock with its profit, affords likewise a neat produce, a free rent to the landlord. It would depress productive labour, by encouraging too hastily that labour which is altogether barren and unproductive.

In what manner, according to this system, the sum total of the annual produce of the land is distributed among the three classes above mentioned, and in what manner the labour of the unproductive class, does no more than replace the value of its own consumption, without increasing in any respect the value of that sum total, is represented by Mr. Quesnai, the very ingenious and profound author of this system, in some arithmetical formularies. The first of these formularies, which by way of eminence he peculiarly distinguishes by the name of the

Oeconomical Table,[4] represents the manner in which he supposes this distribution takes place, in a state of the most perfect liberty, and therefore of the highest prosperity; in a state where the annual produce is such as to afford the greatest possible neat produce, and where each class enjoys its proper share of the whole annual produce. Some subsequent formularies represent the manner in which, he supposes, this distribution is made in different states of restraint and regulation; in which, either the class of proprietors, or the barren and unproductive class, is more favoured than the class of cultivators, and in which, either the one or the other encroaches more or less upon the share which ought properly to belong to this productive class. Every such encroachment, every violation of that natural distribution, which the most perfect liberty would establish, must, according to this system, necessarily degrade more or less, from one year to another, the value and sum total of the annual produce, and must necessarily occasion a gradual declension in the real wealth and revenue of the society; a declension of which the progress must be quicker or slower, according to the degree of this encroachment, according as that natural distribution, which the most perfect liberty would establish, is more or less violated. Those subsequent formularies represent the different degrees of declension, which, according to this system correspond to the different degrees in which this natural distribution of things is violated.

Some speculative physicians seem to have imagined that the health of the human body could be preserved only by a certain precise regimen of diet and exercise, of which every, the smallest, violation necessarily occasioned some degree of disease or disorder proportioned to the degree of the violation. Experience, however, would seem to show that the human body frequently preserves, to all appearance at least, the most perfect state of health under a vast variety of different regimens; even under some which are generally believed to be very far from being perfectly wholesome. But the healthful state of the human body, it would seem, contains in itself some unknown principle of preservation, capable either of preventing or of correcting, in many respects, the bad effects even of a very faulty regimen. Mr. Quesnai, who was himself a physician, and a very speculative physician, seems to have entertained a notion of the same kind concerning the political body, and to have imagined that it would thrive and prosper only under a certain precise regimen, the exact regimen of perfect liberty and perfect justice. He seems not to have considered that in the political body, the natural effort which every man is continually making to better his own condition, is a principle of preservation capable of preventing and correcting, in many respects, the bad effects of a political œconomy, in some degree, both partial and oppressive. Such a political œconomy, though it no doubt retards more or less, is not always capable of stopping altogether the natural progress of a nation towards wealth and prosperity, and still less of making it go backwards. If a nation could not prosper without the enjoyment of perfect liberty and perfect justice, there is not in the world a nation which could ever have prospered. In the political body, however, the wisdom of nature has fortunately made ample provision for remedying many of the bad effects of the folly and injustice of man; in the same manner as it has done in the natural body, for remedying those of his sloth and intemperance.

The capital error of this system, however, seems to lie in its representing the class of artificers, manufacturers and merchants, as altogether barren and unproductive. The following observations may serve to show the impropriety of this representation.

First, this class, it is acknowledged, reproduces annually the value of its own annual consumption, and continues, at least, the existence of the stock or capital which maintains and employs it. But upon this account alone the denomination of barren or unproductive should seem to be very improperly applied to it. We should not call a marriage barren or unproductive, though it produced only a son and a daughter, to replace the father and mother, and though it did not increase the number of the human species, but only continued it as it was before. Farmers and country labourers, indeed, over and above the stock which maintains and employs them, reproduce annually a neat produce, a free rent to the landlord. As a marriage which affords three children is certainly more productive than one which affords only two; so the labour of farmers and country labourers is certainly more productive than that of merchants, artificers and manufacturers. The superior produce of the one class, however, does not render the other barren or unproductive.

Secondly, it seems, upon this account, altogether improper to consider artificers, manufacturers and merchants, in the same light as menial servants. The labour of menial servants does not continue the existence of the fund which maintains and employs them. Their maintenance and employment is altogether at the expence of their masters, and the work which they perform is not of a nature to repay that expence. That work consists in services which perish generally in the very instant of their performance, and does not fix or realize itself in any vendible[5] commodity which can replace the value of their wages and maintenance. The labour, on the contrary, of artificers, manufacturers and merchants, naturally does fix and realize itself in some such vendible commodity. It is upon this account that, in the chapter in which I treat of productive and unproductive labour, I have classed artificers, manufacturers and merchants, among the productive labourers, and menial servants among the barren or unproductive.

Thirdly, it seems, upon every supposition, improper to say, that the labour of artificers, manufacturers and merchants, does not increase the real revenue of the society. Though we should suppose, for example, as it seems to be supposed in this system, that the value of the daily, monthly, and yearly consumption of this class was exactly equal to that of its daily, monthly, and yearly production, yet it would not from thence follow that its labour added nothing to the real revenue, to the real value of the annual produce of the land and labour of the society. An artificer, for example, who in the first six months after harvest, executes ten pounds worth of work, though he should in the same time consume ten pounds worth of corn and other necessaries, yet really adds the value of ten pounds to the annual produce of the land and labour of the society. While he has been consuming a half yearly revenue of ten pounds worth of corn and other necessaries, he has produced an equal value of work capable of purchasing, either to himself or to some other person, an equal half yearly revenue. The value, therefore, of what has been consumed and produced during these six months is equal, not to ten, but to twenty pounds. It is possible, indeed, that no more than ten pounds worth of this value, may even have existed at any one moment of time. But if the ten pounds worth of corn and other necessaries, which were consumed by the artificer, had been consumed by a soldier or by a menial servant, the value of that part of the annual produce which existed at the end of the six months, would have been ten pounds less than it actually is in consequence of the labour of the artificer. Though the value of what the artificer produces, therefore, should not at any one moment of time be supposed greater than the value he consumes, yet at every moment of time the actually existing value of goods in the market is, in consequence of what he produces, greater than it otherwise would be.

When the patrons of this system assert that the consumption of artificers, manufacturers and merchants, is equal to the value of what they produce, they probably mean no more than that their revenue, or the fund destined for their consumption, is equal to it. But if they had expressed themselves more accurately, and only asserted that the revenue of this class was equal to the value of what they produced, it might readily have occurred to the reader, that what would naturally be saved out of this revenue, must necessarily increase more or less the real wealth of the society. In order, therefore, to make out something like an argument, it was necessary that they should express themselves as they have done; and this argument, even supposing things actually were as it seems to presume them to be, turns out to be a very inconclusive one.

Fourthly, farmers and country labourers can no more augment, without parsimony, the real revenue, the annual produce of the land and labour of their society, than artificers, manufacturers and merchants. The annual produce of the land and labour of any society can be augmented only in two ways; either, first, by some improvement in the productive powers of the useful labour actually maintained within it; or, secondly, by some increase in the quantity of that labour.

The improvement in the productive powers of useful labour depends, first, upon the improvement in the ability of the workman; and, secondly, upon that of the machinery with which he works. But the labour of artificers and manufacturers, as it is capable of being more subdivided, and the labour of each workman reduced to a greater simplicity of operation, than that of farmers and country labourers, so it is likewise capable of both these sorts of improvement in a much higher degree. In this respect, therefore, the class of cultivators can

165

have no sort of advantage over that of artificers and manufacturers.

The increase in the quantity of useful labour actually employed within any society, must depend altogether upon the increase of the capital which employs it; and the increase of that capital again must be exactly equal to the amount of the savings from the revenue, either of the particular persons who manage and direct the employment of that capital, or of some other persons who lend it to them. If merchants, artificers and manufacturers are, as this system seems to suppose, naturally more inclined to parsimony and saving than proprietors and cultivators, they are, so far, more likely to augment the quantity of useful labour employed within their society, and consequently to increase its real revenue, the annual produce of its land and labour.

Fifthly and lastly, though the revenue of the inhabitants of every country was supposed to consist altogether, as this system seems to suppose, in the quantity of subsistence which their industry could procure to them; yet, even upon this supposition the revenue of a trading and manufacturing country must, other things being equal, always be much greater than that of one without trade or manufactures. By means of trade and manufactures, a greater quantity of subsistence can be annually imported into a particular country than what its own lands, in the actual state of their cultivation, could afford. The inhabitants of a town, though they frequently possess no lands of their own, yet draw to themselves by their industry such a quantity of the rude produce of the lands of other people as supplies them, not only with the materials of their work, but with the fund of their subsistence. What a town always is with regard to the country in its neighbourhood, one independent state or country may frequently be with regard to other independent states or countries. It is thus that Holland draws a great part of its subsistence from other countries; live cattle from Holstein and Jutland, and corn from almost all the different countries of Europe. A small quantity of manufactured produce purchases a great quantity of rude produce. A trading and manufacturing country, therefore, naturally purchases with a small part of its manufactured produce a great part of the rude produce of other countries; while, on the contrary, a country without trade and manufactures is generally obliged to purchase, at the expence of a great part of its rude produce, a very small part of the manufactured produce of other countries. The one exports what can subsist and accommodate but a very few, and imports the subsistence and accommodation of a great number. The other exports the accommodation and subsistence of a great number, and imports that of a very few only. The inhabitants of the one must always enjoy a much greater quantity of subsistence than what their own lands, in the actual state of their cultivation, could afford. The inhabitants of the other must always enjoy a much smaller quantity.

This system, however, with all its imperfections is, perhaps, the nearest approximation to the truth that has yet been published upon the subject of political oeconomy, and is upon that account well worth the consideration of every man who wishes to examine with attention the principles of that very important science. Though in representing the labour which is employed upon land as the only productive labour, the notions which it inculcates are perhaps too narrow and confined; yet in representing the wealth of nations as consisting, not in the unconsumable riches of money, but in the consumable goods annually reproduced by the labour of the society; and in representing perfect liberty as the only effectual expedient for rendering this annual reproduction the greatest possible, its doctrine seems to be in every respect as just as it is generous and liberal. Its followers are very numerous; and as men are fond of paradoxes, and of appearing to understand what surpasses the comprehension of ordinary people, the paradox which it maintains, concerning the unproductive nature of manufaturing labour, has not perhaps contributed a little to increase the number of its admirers. They have for some years past made a pretty considerable sect, distinguished in the French republick of letters by the name of, The Oeconomists.[6] Their works have certainly been of some service to their country; not only by bringing into general discussion, many subjects which had never been well examined before, but by influencing in some measure the publick administration in favour of agriculture. It has been in consequence of their represent-ations, accordingly, that the agriculture of France has been delivered from several of the oppressions which it before laboured under. The term during which such a lease can be granted, as will be valid against every future purchaser or proprietor of the land, has been prolonged from nine to twenty-seven years. The antient provincial restraints upon the transportation of corn from one province of the kingdom to another, have been entirely taken away, and the liberty of exporting it to all foreign countries, has been established as the common law of the kingdom in all ordinary cases. This sect, in their works, which are very numerous, and which treat not only of what is properly called Political Oeconomy, or of the nature and causes of the wealth of nations, but of every other branch of the system of civil government, all follow implicitly, and without any sensible variation, the doctrine of Mr. Quesnai. There is upon this account little variety in the greater part of their works. The most distinct and best connected account of this doctrine is to be found in a little book written by Mr. Mercier de la Rivière[7], sometime Intendant of Martinico, intitled, The natural and essential Order of Political Societies. The admiration of this whole sect for their master, who was himself a man of the greatest modesty and simplicity, is not inferior to that of any of the antient philosophers for the founders of their respective systems. "There have been, since the world began," says a very diligent and respectable author, the Marquis de Mirabeau,[8] "three great inventions which have principally given stability to political societies, independent of many other inventions which have enriched and adorned them. The first, is the invention of writing, which alone gives human nature the power of transmitting, without alteration, its laws, its contracts, its annals, and its discoveries. The second, is the invention of money, which binds together all the relations between civilized societies. The third, is the Oeconomical Table, the result of the other two, which completes them both by perfecting their object; the great discovery of our age, but of which our posterity will reap the benefit."

As the political oeconomy of the nations of modern Europe, has been more favourable to manufactures and foreign trade, the industry of the towns, than to agriculture, the industry of the country; so that of other nations has followed a different plan, and has been more favourable to agriculture than to manufactures and foreign trade.

The policy of China favours agriculture more than all other employments. In China, the condition of a labourer is said to be as much superior to that of an artificer; as in most parts of Europe, that of an artificer is to that of a labourer. In China, the great ambition of every man is to get possession of some little bit of land, either in property or in lease; and leases are there said to be granted upon very moderate terms, and to be sufficiently secured to the lessees. The Chinese have little respect for foreign trade. Your beggarly commerce! was the language in which the Mandarins of Pekin used to talk to Mr. de Lange, the Russian envoy, concerning it. Except with Japan, the Chinese carry on, themselves, and in their own bottoms, little or no foreign trade; and it is only into one or two ports of their kingdom that they even admit the ships of foreign nations. Foreign trade, therefore, is, in China, every way confined within a much narrower circle than that to which it would naturally extend itself, if more freedom was allowed to it, either in their own ships, or in those of foreign nations.

Manufactures, as in a small bulk they frequently contain a great value, and can upon that account be transported at less expence from one country to another than most parts of rude produce, are, in almost all countries, the principal support of foreign trade. In countries, besides, less extensive and less favourably circumstanced for interior commerce than China, they generally require the support of foreign trade. Without an extensive foreign market, they could not well flourish, either in countries so moderately extensive as to afford but a narrow home market; or in countries where the communication between one province and another was so difficult, as to render it impossible for the goods of any particular place to enjoy the whole of that home market which the country could afford. The perfection of manufacturing industry, it must be remembered, depends altogether upon the division of labour; and the degree to which the division of labour can be introduced into any manufacture, is necessarily regulated, it has already been shown, by the extent of the market. But the great extent of the empire of China, the vast multitude of its inhabitants, the variety of climate, and consequently of productions in its different provinces, and the easy communication by means of water carriage between the greater part of them, render the home market of that country of so great extent, as to be alone sufficient to support very great manufactures, and to admit of very considerable subdivisions of labour. The home market of China is, perhaps, in extent, not much inferior to the market of all the different countries of Europe put together. A more extensive foreign trade, however, which to this great home market added the foreign market of all the rest of the world; especially if any considerable part of this trade was carried on in Chinese ships; could scarce fail to increase very much the manufactures of China, and to improve very much the productive powers of its manufacturing industry. By a more extensive navigation, the Chinese would naturally learn the art of using and constructing themselves all the different machines made use of in other countries, as well as the other improvements of art and industry which are practised in all the different parts of the world. Upon their present plan they have little opportunity of improving themselves by the example of any other nation; except that of the Japanese. [...]

The greatest and most important branch of the commerce of every nation, it has already been observed, is that which is carried on between the inhabitants of the town and those of the country. The inhabitants of the town draw from the country the rude produce which constitutes both the materials of their work and the fund of their subsistence; and they pay for this rude produce by sending back to the country a certain portion of it manufactured and prepared for immediate use. The trade which is carried on between these two different sets of people, consists ultimately in a certain quantity of rude produce exchanged for a certain quantity of manufactured produce. The dearer the latter, therefore, the cheaper the former; and whatever tends in any country to raise the price of manufactured produce, tends to lower that of the rude produce of the land, and thereby to discourage agriculture. The smaller the quantity of manufactured produce which any given quantity of rude produce, or, what comes to the same thing, which the price of any given quantity of rude produce is capable of purchasing, the smaller the exchangeable value of that given quantity of rude produce; the smaller the encouragement which either the landlord has to increase its quantity by improving, or the farmer by cultivating the land. Whatever, besides, tends to diminish in any country the number of artificers and manufacturers, tends to diminish the home market, the most important of all markets for the rude produce of the land, and thereby still further to discourage agriculture.

Those systems, therefore, which preferring agriculture to all other employments, in order to promote it, impose restraints upon manufactures and foreign trade, act contrary to the very end which they propose, and indirectly discourage that very species of industry which they mean to promote. They are so far, perhaps, more inconsistent than even the mercantile system. That system, by encouraging manufactures and foreign trade more than agriculture, turns a certain portion of the capital of the society from supporting a more advantageous, to support a less advantageous species of industry. But still it really and in the end encourages that species of industry which it means to promote. Those agricultural systems, on the contrary, really and in the end discourage their own favourite species of industry.

169

It is thus that every system which endeavours, either, by extra-ordinary encouragements, to draw towards a particular species of industry a greater share of the capital of the society than what would naturally go to it; or, by extraordinary restraints, to force from a particular species of industry some share of the capital which would otherwise be employed in it; is in reality subversive of the great purpose which it means to promote. It retards, instead of accelerating, the progress of the society towards real wealth and greatness; and diminishes, instead of increasing, the real value of the annual produce of its land and labour.

All systems either of preference or of restraint, therefore, being thus completely taken away, the obvious and simple system of natural liberty establishes itself of its own accord. Every man, as long as he does not violate the laws of justice, is left perfectly free to pursue his own interest his own way, and to bring both his industry and capital into competition with those of any other man, or order of men. The sovereign is completely discharged from a duty, in the attempting to perform which he must always be exposed to innumerable delusions, and for the proper performance of which no human wisdom or knowledge could ever be sufficient; the duty of superintending the industry of private people, and of directing it towards the employments most suitable to the interest of the society. According to the system of natural liberty, the sovereign has only three duties to attend to; three duties of great importance, indeed, but plain and intelligible to common understandings: first, the duty of protecting the society from the violence and invasion of other independent societies; secondly, the duty of protecting, as far as possible, every member of the society from the injustice or oppression of every other member of it, or the duty of establishing an exact administration of justice; and, thirdly, the duty of erecting and maintaining certain publick works and certain publick institutions, which it can never be for the interest of any individual, or small number of individuals, to erect and maintain; because the profit could never repay the expence to any individual or small number of individuals, though it may frequently do much more than repay it to a great society.

The proper performance of those several duties of the sovereign necessarily supposes a certain expence; and this expence again necessarily requires a certain revenue to support it. In the following book, therefore, I shall endeavour to explain; first, what are the necessary expences of the sovereign or common-wealth; and which of those expences ought to be defrayed by the general contribution of the whole society; and which of them, by that of some particular part only, or of some particular members of the society: secondly, what are the different methods in which the whole society may be made to contribute towards defraying the expences incumbent on the whole society, and what are the principal advantages and inconveniences of each of those methods: and, thirdly, what are the reasons and causes which have induced almost all modern governments to mortgage some part of this revenue, or to contract debts, and what have been the effects of those debts upon the real wealth, the annual produce of the land and labour of the society. The following book, therefore, will naturally be divided into three chapters.

Notes
1 Jean Baptiste Colbert (1619–83) was made Controller General of France in 1665.
2 Net.
3 Saving.
4 *Tableau économique* (1757–8).
5 Saleable.
6 i.e. the 'Physiocrats'.
7 *L'ordre naturel et essentiel des sociétés politiques* (1767) by Mercier de la Rivière.
8 Victor Riqueti, Marquis de Mirabeau; French economist, disciple of Quesnai and the 'Physiocratic' school. He was the author of *Man's Friend or a Treatise on Population* (1756).

ADAM SMITH

Of the Expense of Institutions for Education (1776)

(ibid., Book V, Chapter 1) Of the Expences [*sic*] of the Sovereign or Commonwealth, Part III, Of Publick Works and Publick Institutions, Article II, Of the Expence of the Institutions for the Education of Youth.

At the end of Book IV of *The Wealth of Nations* Smith concludes that it is in no way the duty of a sovereign to try to control or direct the kind of work which his subjects undertake. There are, he suggests, three main duties of the sovereign: to protect the nation from invasion; to protect individual subjects from injustice at the hands of others; and to erect and maintain certain public works and institutions.

Smith believed that the state should bear a large part of the expense of institutions for the education of the 'common people' in 'the most essential parts of education'. In the case of the universities, however, Smith thought that public money invested in these institutions, for example, to pay the salaries of professors who would otherwise have to look to their students for their fees, would tend to a reduction in standards of teaching.

The institutions for the education of the youth may, in the same manner, furnish a revenue sufficient for defraying their own expence. The fee or honorary which the scholar pays to the master naturally constitutes a revenue of this kind.

Even where the reward of the master does not arise altogether from this natural revenue, it still is not necessary that it should be derived from that general revenue of society, of which the collection and application is, in most countries, assigned to the executive power. Through the greater part of Europe, accordingly, the endowment of schools and colleges makes either no charge upon that general revenue, or but a very small one. It every where arises chiefly from some local or provincial revenue, from the rent of some landed estate, or from the interest of some sum of money allotted and put under the management of trustees for this particular purpose, sometimes by the sovereign himself, and sometimes by some private donor.

Have those publick endowments contributed in general to promote the end of their institution? Have they contributed to encourage the diligence, and to improve the abilities of the teachers? Have they directed the course of education towards objects more useful, both to the individual and to the publick, than those to which it would naturally have gone of its own accord? It should not seem very difficult to give at least a probable answer to each of those questions.

In every profession, the exertion of the greater part of those who exercise it, is always in proportion to the necessity they are under of making that exertion. This necessity is greatest with those to whom the emoluments of their profession are the only source from which they expect their fortune, or even their ordinary revenue and subsistence. In order to acquire this fortune, or even to get this subsistence, they must, in the course of a year, execute a certain quantity of work of a known value; and, where the competition is free, the rivalship of competitors, who are all endeavouring to justle one another out of employment, obliges every man to endeavour to execute his work with a certain degree of exactness. The greatness of the objects which are to be acquired by success in some particular professions may, no doubt, sometimes animate the exertion of a few men of extraordinary spirit and ambition. Great objects, however, are evidently not necessary in order to occasion the greatest exertions. Rivalship and emulation render excellency, even in mean professions, an object of ambition, and frequently occasion the very greatest exertions. Great objects, on the contrary, alone and unsupported by the necessity of application, have seldom been sufficient to occasion any considerable exertion. In England, success in the profession of the law leads to some very great objects of ambition; and yet how few men, born to easy fortunes, have ever in this country been eminent in that profession!

The endowments of schools and colleges have necessarily diminished more or less the necessity of application in the teachers. Their subsistence, so far as it arises from their salaries, is evidently derived from a fund altogether independent of their success and reputation in their particular professions.

In some universities the salary makes but a part, and frequently but a small part of the emoluments of the teacher, of which the greater part arises from the honoraries or fees of his pupils. The necessity of application, though always more or less diminished, is not in this case entirely taken away. Reputation in his profession is still of some importance to him, and he still has some dependency upon the affection, gratitude, and favourable report of those who have attended upon his instructions; and these favourable sentiments he is likely to gain in no way so well as by deserving them, that is, by the abilities and diligence with which he discharges every part of his duty.

In other universities the teacher is prohibited from receiving any honorary or fee from his pupils, and his salary constitutes the whole of the revenue which he derives from his office. His interest is, in this case, set as directly in opposition to his duty as it is possible to set it. It is the interest of every man to live as much at his ease as he can; and if his emoluments are to be precisely the same, whether he does, or does not perform some very laborious duty, it is certainly his interest, at least as interest is vulgarly understood, either to neglect it altogether, or, if he is subject to some authority which will not suffer him to do this, to perform it in as careless and slovenly a manner as that authority will permit. If he is naturally active and a lover of labour, it is his interest to employ that activity in any way, from which he can derive some advantage, rather than in the performance of his duty, from which he can derive none.

If the authority to which he is subject resides in the body corporate, the college, or university, of which he himself is a member, and in which the greater part of the other members are, like himself, persons who either are, or ought to be teachers; they are likely to make a common cause, to be all very indulgent to one another, and every man to consent that his neighbour may neglect his duty, provided he himself is allowed to neglect his own. In the university of Oxford, the greater part of the publick professors have, for these many years, given up altogether even the pretence of teaching.

If the authority to which he is subject resides, not so much in the body corporate of which he is a member, as in some other extraneous persons, in the bishop of the diocese for example; in the governor of the province; or, perhaps, in some minister of state; it is not indeed in this case very likely that he will be suffered to neglect his duty altogether. All that such superiors, however, can force him to do, is to attend upon his pupils a certain number of hours, that is, to give a certain number of lectures in the week or in the year. What those lectures shall be, must still depend upon the diligence of the teacher; and that diligence is likely to be proportioned to the motives which he has for exerting it. An extraneous jurisdiction of this kind, besides, is liable to be exercised both ignorantly and capriciously. In its nature it is arbitrary and discretionary, and the persons who exercise it, neither attending upon the lectures of the teacher themselves, nor perhaps understanding the sciences[1] which it is his business to teach, are seldom capable of exercising it with judgment. From the insolence of office too they are frequently indifferent how they exercise it, and are very apt to censure or deprive him of his office wantonly, and without any just cause. The person subject to such jurisdiction is necessarily degraded by it, and, instead of being one of the most respectable, is rendered one of the meanest and most contemptible persons in the society. It is by powerful protection only that he can effectually guard himself against the bad usage to which he is at all times exposed; and this protection he is most likely to gain, not by ability or diligence in his profession, but by obsequiousness to the will of his superiors, and by being ready, at all times, to sacrifice to that will the rights, the interest, and the honour of the body corporate of which he is a member. Whoever has attended for any considerable time to the administration of a French university, must have had occasion to remark the effects which naturally result from an arbitrary and extraneous jurisdiction of this kind.

Whatever forces a certain number of students to any college or university, independent of the merit or reputation of the teachers, tends more or less to diminish the necessity of that merit or reputation. [...]

The abilities, both civil and military, of the Greeks and Romans, will readily be allowed to have been, at least, equal to those of any modern nation. Our prejudice is perhaps rather to over rate them. But except in what related to military exercises, the state seems to have been at no pains to form those great abilities: for I cannot be induced to believe that the musical education of the Greeks could be of much consequence in forming them. Masters, however, had been found, it seems, for instructing the better sort of people among those nations in every art and science in which the circumstances of their society rendered it necessary or convenient for them to be instructed. The demand for such instruction produced, what it always produces, the talent for giving it; and the emulation which an unrestrained competition never fails to excite, appears to have brought that talent to a very high degree of perfection. In the attention which the antient philosophers excited, in the empire which they acquired over the opinions and principles of their auditors,[2] in the faculty which they possessed of giving a certain tone and character to the conduct and conversation of those auditors; they appear to have been much superior to any modern teachers. In modern times, the diligence of publick teachers is more or less corrupted by the circumstances, which render them more or less independent of their success and reputation in their particular professions. Their salaries too put the private teacher, who would pretend to come into competition with them, in the same state with a merchant who attempts to trade without a bounty[3] in competition with those who trade with a considerable one. If he sells his goods at nearly the same price, he cannot have the same profit, and poverty and beggary at least, if not bankruptcy and ruin, will infallibly be his lot. If he attempts to sell them much dearer, he is likely to have so few customers that his circumstances will not be much mended. The privileges of graduation, besides, are in many countries necessary, or at least extremely convenient to most men of learned professions, that is, to the far greater part of those who have occasion for a learned education. But those privileges can be obtained only by attending the lectures of the publick teachers. The most careful attendance upon the ablest instructions of any private teacher, cannot always give any title to demand them. It is from these different causes that the private teacher of any of the sciences which are commonly taught in universities, is in modern times generally considered as in the very lowest order of men of letters. A man of real abilities can scarce find out a more humiliating or a more unprofitable employment to turn them to. The endowments of schools and colleges have, in this manner, not only corrupted the diligence of publick teachers, but have rendered it almost impossible to have any good private ones.

Were there no publick institutions for education, no system, no science would be taught for which there was not some demand; or which the circumstances of the times did not render it, either necessary, or convenient, or at least fashionable to learn. A private teacher could never find his account in teaching, either an exploded and antiquated system of a science acknowledged to be useful, or a science universally believed to be a mere useless and pedantick heap of sophistry and nonsense. Such systems, such sciences, can subsist no where, but in those incorporated societies for education where prosperity and revenue are in a great measure independent of their reputation, and altogether independent of their industry. Were there no publick institutions for education, a gentleman, after going through, with application and abilities, the most complete course of education, which the circumstances of the times were supposed to afford, could not come into the world completely ignorant of every thing which is the common subject of conversation among gentlemen and men of the world.

There are no publick institutions for the education of women, and there is accordingly nothing useless, absurd, or fantastical in the common course of their education. They are taught what their parents or guardians judge it necessary or useful for them to learn; and they are taught nothing else. Every part of their education tends evidently to some useful purpose; either to improve the natural attractions of their person, or to form their mind to reserve, to modesty, to chastity, and to œconomy: to render them both likely to become the mistresses of a family, and to behave properly when they have become such. In every part of her life a woman feels some conveniency or advantage from every part of her education. It seldom happens that a man, in any part of his life, derives any conveniency or advantage from some of the most laborious and troublesome parts of his education.

Ought the publick, therefore, to give no attention, it may be asked, to the education of the people? Or if it ought to give any, what are the different parts of education which it ought to attend to in the different orders of the people? and in what manner ought it to attend to them?

In some cases the state of the society necessarily places the greater part of individuals in such situations as naturally form in them, without any attention of government, almost all the abilities and virtues which that state requires, or perhaps can admit of. In other cases the state of the society does not place the greater part of individuals in such situations, and some attention of government is necessary in order to prevent the almost entire corruption and degeneracy of the great body of the people.

In the progress of the division of labour, the employment of the far greater part of those who live by labour, that is, of the great body of the people, comes to be confined to a few very simple operations;

frequently to one or two. But the understandings of the greater part of men are necessarily formed by their ordinary employments. The man whose whole life is spent in performing a few simple operations, of which the effects too are, perhaps, or very nearly the same, always the same, has no occasion to exert his understanding, or to exercise his invention in finding out expedients for removing difficulties which never occur. He naturally loses, therefore, the habit of such exertion, and generally becomes as stupid and ignorant as it is possible for a human creature to become. The torpor of his mind renders him, not only incapable of relishing or bearing a part in any rational conversation, but of conceiving any generous, noble, or tender sentiment, and consequently of forming any just judgment concerning many even of the ordinary duties of private life. Of the great and extensive interests of his country, he is altogether incapable of judging; and unless very particular pains have been taken to render him otherwise, he is equally incapable of defending his country in war. The uniformity of his stationary life naturally corrupts the courage of his mind, and makes him regard with abhorrence the irregular, uncertain, and adventurous life of a soldier. It corrupts even the activity of his body, and renders him incapable of exerting his strength with vigour and perseverance, in any other employment than that to which he has been bred. His dexterity at his own particular trade seems, in this manner, to be acquired at the expence of his intellectual, social, and martial virtues. But in every improved and civilized society this is the state into which the labouring poor, that is, the great body of the people, must necessarily fall, unless government takes some pains to prevent it.

It is otherwise in the barbarous societies, as they are commonly called, of hunters, of shepherds, and even of husbandmen in that rude state of husbandry which precedes the improvement of manufactures, and the extension of foreign commerce. In such societies the varied occupations of every man oblige every man to exert his capacity, and to invent expedients for removing difficulties which are continually occurring. Invention is kept alive, and the mind is not suffered to fall into that drowsy stupidity, which, in a civilized society, seems to benumb the understanding of almost all the inferior ranks of people. In those barbarous societies, as they are called, every man, it has already been observed, is a warrior. Every man too is in some measure a statesman, and can form a tolerable judgment concerning the interest of the society, and the conduct of those who govern it. How far their chiefs are good judges in peace, or good leaders in war, is obvious to the observation of almost every single man among them. In such a society indeed, no man can well acquire that improved and refined understanding, which a few men sometimes possess in a more civilized state. Though in a rude society there is a good deal of variety in the occupations of every individual, there is not a great deal in those of the whole society. Every man does, or is capable of doing, almost every thing which any other man does, or is capable of doing. Every man has a considerable degree of knowledge, ingenuity, and invention; but scarce any man has a great degree. The degree, however, which is commonly possessed, is generally sufficient for conducting the whole simple business of the society. In a civilized state, on the contrary, though there is little variety in the occupations of the greater part of individuals, there is an almost infinite variety in those of the whole society. These varied occupations present an almost infinite variety of objects to the contemplation of those few, who, being attached to no particular occupation themselves, have leisure and inclination to examine the occupations of other people. The contemplation of so great a variety of objects necessarily exercises their minds in endless comparisons and combinations, and renders their understandings, in an extraordinary degree, both acute and comprehensive. Unless those few, however, happen to be placed in some very particular situations, their great abilities, though honourable to themselves, may contribute very little to the good government or happiness of their society. Notwithstanding the great abilities of those few, all the nobler parts of the human character may be, in a great measure, obliterated and extinguished in the great body of the people.

The education of the common people requires, perhaps, in a civilized and commercial society, the attention of the publick more than that of people of some rank and fortune. People of some rank and fortune are generally eighteen or nineteen years of age before they enter upon that particular business, profession, or trade, by which they propose to distinguish themselves in the world. They have before that full time to acquire, or at least to fit themselves for afterwards acquiring, every accomplishment which can recommend them to the publick esteem, or render them worthy of it. Their parents or guardians are generally sufficiently anxious that they should be so accomplished, and are, in most cases, willing enough to lay out the expence which is necessary for that purpose. If they are not always properly educated, it is seldom from the want of expence laid out upon their education; but from the improper application of that expence. It is seldom from the want of masters; but from the negligence and incapacity of the masters who are to be had, and from the difficulty, or rather from the impossibility which there is, in the present state of things, of finding any better. The employments too in which people of some rank or fortune spend the greater part of their lives, are not, like those of the common people, simple and uniform. They are almost all of them extremely complicated, and such as exercise the head more than the hands. The understandings of those who are engaged in such employments can seldom grow torpid for want of exercise. The employments of people of some rank and fortune, besides, are seldom such as harass them from morning to night. They generally have a good deal of leisure, during which they may perfect themselves in every branch either of useful or ornamental knowledge of which they may have laid the foundation, or for which they may have acquired some taste in the earlier part of life.

It is otherwise with the common people. They have little time to spare for education. Their parents can scarce afford to maintain them even in infancy. As soon as they are able to work, they must apply to some trade by which they can earn their subsistence. That trade too is generally so simple and uniform as to give little exercise to the understanding; while, at the same time, their labour is both so constant and so severe, that it leaves them little leisure and less inclination to apply to, or even to think of any thing else.

But though the common people cannot, in any civilized society, be so well instructed as people of some rank and fortune, the most essential parts of education, however, to read, write, and account, can be acquired at so early a period of life, that the greater part even of those who are to be bred to the lowest occupations, have time to acquire them before they can be employed in those occupations. For a very small expence the publick can facilitate, can encourage, and can even impose upon almost the whole body of the people, the necessity of acquiring those most essential parts of education.

The publick can facilitate this acquisition by establishing in every parish or district a little school, where children may be taught for a reward so moderate, that even a common labourer may afford it; the master being partly, but not wholly paid by the publick; because if he was wholly, or even principally paid by it, he would soon learn to neglect his business. In Scotland the establishment of such parish schools has taught almost the whole common people to read, and a very great proportion of them to write and account. In England the establishment of charity schools[4] has had an effect of the same kind, though not so universally, because the establishment is not so universal. If in those little schools the books, by which the children are taught to read, were a little more instructive than they commonly are: and if, instead of a little smattering of Latin; which the children of the common people are sometimes taught there, and which can scarce ever be of any use to them: they were instructed in the elementary parts of geometry and mechanicks, the literary education of this rank of people would perhaps be as complete as it can be. There is scarce a common trade which does not afford some opportunities of applying to it the principles of geometry and mechanicks, and which would not therefore gradually exercise and improve the common people in those principles, the necessary introduction to the most sublime as well as to the most useful sciences.

The publick can encourage the acquisition of those most essential parts of education by giving small premiums, and little badges of distinction, to the children of the common people who excel in them.

The publick can impose upon almost the whole body of the people the necessity of acquiring those most essential parts of education, by obliging every man to undergo an examination or probation in them before he can obtain the freedom in any corporation,[5] or be allowed to set up any trade either in a village or town corporate.

It was in this manner, by facilitating the acquisition of their military and gymnastic exercises, by encouraging it, and even by imposing upon the whole body of the people the necessity of learning those exercises, that the Greek and Roman republicks maintained the martial spirit of their respective citizens. They facilitated the acquisition of those exercises by appointing a certain place for learning and practising them, and by granting to certain masters the privilege of teaching in that place. Those masters do not appear to have had either salaries or exclusive privileges of any kind. Their reward consisted altogether in what they got from their scholars; and a citizen who had learnt his exercises in the publick Gymnasia, had no sort of legal advantage over one who had learnt them privately, provided the latter had learnt them equally well. Those republicks encouraged the acquisition of those exercises, by bestowing little premiums and badges of distinction upon those who excelled in them. To have gained a prize in the Olympic, Isthmian or Nemaean[6] games, gave illustration, not only to the person who gained it, but to his whole family and kindred. The obligation which every citizen was under to serve a certain number of years, if called upon, in the armies of the republick, sufficiently imposed the necessity of learning those exercises without which he could not be fit for that service.

That in the progress of improvement the practice of military exercises, unless government takes proper pains to support it, goes gradually to decay, and, together with it, the martial spirit of the great body of the people, the example of modern Europe sufficiently demonstrates. But the security of every society must always depend, more or less, upon the martial spirit of the great body of the people. In the present times, indeed, that martial spirit alone, and unsupported by a well-disciplined standing army,[7] would not, perhaps, be sufficient for the defence and security of any society. But where every citizen had the spirit of a soldier, a smaller standing army would surely be requisite. That spirit, besides, would necessarily diminish very much the dangers to liberty, whether real or imaginary, which are commonly apprehended from a standing army. As it would very much facilitate the operations of that army against a foreign invader, so it would obstruct them as much if unfortunately they should ever be directed against the constitution of the state.

The antient institutions of Greece and Rome seem to have been much more effectual, for maintaining the martial spirit of the great body of the people, than the establishment of what are called the militias of modern times. They were much more simple. When they were once established, they executed themselves,[8] and it acquired little or no attention from government to maintain them in the most perfect vigour. Whereas to maintain even in tolerable execution the complex regulations of any modern militia, requires the continual and painful attention of government, without which they are constantly falling into total neglect and disuse. The influence, besides, of the antient institutions was much more universal. By means of them the whole body of the people was compleatly instructed in the use of arms. Whereas it is but a very small part of them who can ever be so instructed by the regulations of any modern militia; except, perhaps, that of Switzerland.

But a coward, a man incapable either of defending or of revenging himself, evidently wants one of the most essential parts of the character of a man. He is as much mutilated and deformed in his mind, as another is in his body, who is either deprived of some of its most essential members, or has lost the use of them. He is evidently the more wretched and miserable of the two; because happiness and misery, which reside altogether in the mind, must necessarily depend more upon the healthful or unhealthful, the mutilated or entire state of the mind, than upon that of the body. Even though the martial spirit of the people were of no use towards the defence of the society, yet to prevent that sort of mental mutilation, deformity and wretchedness, which cowardice necessarily involves in it, from spreading themselves through the great body of the people, would still deserve the most serious attention of government; in the same manner as it would deserve its most serious attention to prevent a leprosy or any other loathsome and offensive disease, though neither mortal nor dangerous, from spreading itself among them; though, perhaps, no other publick good might result from such attention besides the prevention of so great a publick evil.

The same thing may be said of the gross ignorance and stupidity which, in a civilized society, seem so frequently to benumb the understandings of all the inferior ranks of people. A man, without the proper use of the intellectual faculties of a man, is, if possible, more contemptible than even a coward, and seems to be mutilated and deformed in a still more essential part of the character of human nature. Though the state was to derive no advantage from the instruction of the inferior ranks of people, it would still deserve its attention that they should not be altogether uninstructed. The state, however, derives no inconsiderable advantage from their instruction. The more they are instructed, the less liable they are to the delusions of enthusiasm and superstition, which, among ignorant nations, frequently occasion the most dreadful disorders. An instructed and intelligent people besides are always more decent and orderly than an ignorant and stupid one. They feel themselves, each individually, more respectable, and more likely to obtain the respect of their lawful superiors, and they are therefore more disposed to respect those superiors. They are more disposed to examine, and more capable of seeing through, the interested complaints of faction and sedition, and they are, upon that accunt, less apt to be misled into any wanton or unnecessary opposition to the measures of government. In free countries, where the safety of government depends very much upon the favourable judgment which the people may form of its conduct, it must surely be of the highest importance that they should not be disposed to judge rashly or capriciously concerning it.

Notes

1   'Sciences' at this period included all sorts of systematic knowledge and inquiry.

2   Listeners.

3   Financial encouragement from the government.

4   Charity schools were elementary schools set up by private charity, though with government encouragement, where poor children were taught reading, writing, simple arithmetic, etc. The first was founded in London in 1685 and by the mid-eighteenth century there were some 1,500, mainly run by Anglicans.

5   To be granted the 'freedom' of a company or corporation was to receive its full privileges. A 'town corporate' is a borough which, by royal charter, is entitled to act in the manner of a 'corporation', i.e. upon the legal fiction that it is a 'person'.

6   All three were Greek festivals and games. The Olympic games were celebrated every four years; the Isthmian games were held in the second and fourth years of each Olympiad on the Isthmus of Corinth, The Nemean games were held every other year in the valley of Nemea.

7   That is, a permanent army of professional soldiers. Such a force was commonly regarded, particularly in Britain, as a potential threat to constitutional liberty.

8   That is, they ran themselves.

Edward Gibbon

The History of the Decline and Fall of the Roman Empire (1776–88)

From Edward Gibbon, *The History of the Decline and Fall of the Roman Empire*, Printed for W. Strahan and T. Cadell, in the Strand London, 1776–88. Reprinted. from edition edited J. B. Bury, Methuen and Co., London, 1909.

In his *History of the Decline and Fall of the Roman Empire* Edward Gibbon (1737–94) surveys the evolution of Europe from the second century A.D. to the dawn of the Renaissance. The present selection, which represents only a small part of the whole work, comprises Chapters I, II, III, IX and XV from Volume One, published in 1776, and the closing section of Chapter XXXVIII from Volume Two, published in 1781. In Chapters I–III, Gibbon describes the 'happy and prosperous' civilization of Europe under the 'enlightened' rule of the Antonine emperors in the second century A.D., a period which he admires, but selectively and with important qualifications. In Chapter IX, scrutinizing the wild Germanic tribes who spilled over the imperial frontiers, he juxtaposes his basic predilection for classical values with the significant recognition that even 'barbarian' societies contained the seeds of life essential to the future development of Europe. The notorious Chapter XV presents Gibbon's treatment of the emergence of Christianity, a subject which he approached in the critical and controversial spirit of voltaire, thereby provoking a furious outcry from the Church of England. Lastly, in the final brief section of Chapter XXXVIII, Gibbon analyses the causes of the collapse of the Western Empire in the fifth century A.D. Looking back complacently from the heights of the late eighteenth century, blithely unconscious of the revolutionary upheavals about to break forth over his head, he provides a comforting assurance of almost limitless Progress within the existing framework of European society.

The Decline and Fall remains a model of historical scholarship. Even in the light of modern research, Gibbon's basic factual accuracy in these chapters can seldom be faulted. His inter-

183

pretations, on the other hand, reveal at least as much about Gibbon himself and the preoccupations of the eighteenth-century mind as they do about the Roman Empire. According to Professor Dawson, 'it is impossible to find any European writer, not even Voltaire himself, whose work reflects more perfectly the spirit of what is called "the Enlightenment", in all its strengths and all its limitations' (Introduction to the Everyman edition, 1956).

Among the many themes shared between Gibbon and other writers in this anthology one might point out the strong influence of Montesquieu (p. 135), particularly in Chapters III and IX, and the common dislike of 'Gothic' barbarity in Gibbon and such art critics as Stuart (Vol. 2 p. 30) and Le Blanc (Vol. 2 p. 42).

Although Gibbon was astonishingly accurate, errors in reference and interpretation do occur in his footnotes and these have spawned, in the many editions since his death, a second set of notes from various editors. In order to save space we have decided to reprint Gibbon and only Gibbon, warts and all, as he appeared in the early editions of *Decline and Fall*. The one exception to this rule is the inclusion of translations (denoted by square brackets) of the main Latin and French quotations included in the footnotes. Those readers wanting to check the accuracy of Gibbon's footnotes should compare the ones printed here with those in a reliable 'modern' edition such as the one by J. B. Bury. In the rare instances where Gibbon's interpretations are positively misleading we have included an editorial note to clarify matters.

CHAPTER I

The Extent and Military Force of the Empire in the Age of the Antonines

Introduction In the second century of the Christian Æra, the empire of Rome comprehended the fairest part of the earth, and the most civilized portion of mankind. The frontiers of that extensive monarchy were guarded by ancient renown and disciplined valour. The gentle, but powerful, influence of laws and manners had gradually cemented the union of the provinces. Their peaceful inhabitants enjoyed and abused the advantages of wealth and luxury. The image of a free constitution was preserved with decent reverence. The Roman senate appeared to possess the sovereign authority, and devolved on the emperors all the executive powers of government. During a happy period of more than A.D. 96–180. fourscore years, the public administration was conducted by the virtue and abilities of Nerva, Trajan, Hadrian, and the two Antonines. It is the design of this and of the two succeeding chapters, to describe the prosperous condition of their empire; and afterwards, from the death of

Marcus Antoninus, to deduce the most important circumstances of its decline and fall: a revolution which will ever be remembered, and is still felt by the nations of the earth.

The principal conquests of the Romans were achieved under the republic; and the emperors, for the most part, were satisfied with preserving those dominions which had been acquired by the policy of the senate, the active emulation of the consuls, and the martial enthusiasm of the people. The seven first centuries were filled with a rapid succession of triumphs; but it was reserved for Augustus to relinquish the ambitious design of subduing the whole earth, and to introduce a spirit of moderation into the public councils. Inclined to peace by his temper and situation, it was easy for him to discover that Rome, in her present exalted situation, had much less to hope than to fear from the chance of arms; and that, in the prosecution of remote wars, the undertaking became every day more difficult, the event more doubtful, and the possession more precarious and less beneficial. The experience of Augustus added weight to these salutary reflections, and effectually convinced him that, by the prudent vigour of his counsels, it would be easy to secure every concession which the safety or the dignity of Rome might require from the most formidable barbarians. Instead of exposing his person and his legions to the arrows of the Parthians, he obtained, by an honourable treaty, the restitution of the standards and prisoners which had been taken in the defeat of Crassus.[1]

His generals, in the early part of his reign, attempted the reduction of Æthiopia and Arabia Felix. They marched near a thousand miles to the south of the tropic; but the heat of the climate soon repelled the invaders and protected the unwarlike natives of those sequestered regions.[2] The northern countries of Europe scarcely deserved the expense and labour of conquest. The forests and morasses of Germany were filled with a hardy race of barbarians, who despised life when it was separated from freedom; and though, on the first attack, they seemed to yield to the weight of the Roman power, they soon, by a signal act of despair, regained their independence, and reminded Augustus of the vicissitude of fortune.[3] On the death of that emperor his testament was publicly read in the senate. He bequeathed, as a valuable legacy to his successors, the advice of confining the empire within those limits which

Moderation of Augustus

---

1 Dion Cassius (l. Liv. p. 736) with the annotations of Reimar, who has collected all that Roman vanity has left upon the subject. The marble of Ancyra, on which Augustus recorded his own exploits, asserts that *he compelled* the Parthians to restore the ensigns of Crassus.

2 Strabo (l. xvi. p. 780) Pliny the elder (Hist. Natur. l. vi. 32, 35) and Dion Cassius (l. liii. p.723, and l. liv p.734 have left us very curious details concerning these wars. The Romans made themselves masters of Mariaba, or Merab, a city of Arabia Felix, well known to the Orientals (see Abulfeda and the Nubian geography, p. 52). They were arrived within three days' journey of the Spice country, the rich object of their invasion.

3 By the slaughter of Varus and his three legions. See the first book of the Annals of Tacitus. Sueton. in August. c. 23, and Velleius Paterculus, l. ii c. 117, &c. Augustus did not receive the melancholy news with all the temper and firmness that might have been expected from his character.

nature seemed to have placed as its permanent bulwarks and boundaries: on the west the Atlantic ocean; the Rhine and Danube on the north; the Euphrates on the east; and towards the south the sandy deserts of Arabia and Africa.[4]

Imitated by his successors Happily for the repose of mankind, the moderate system recommended by the wisdom of Augustus was adopted by the fears and vices of his immediate successors. Engaged in the pursuit of pleasure or in the exercise of tyranny, the first Cæsars seldom showed themselves to the armies, or to the provinces; nor were they disposed to suffer, that those triumphs which *their* indolence neglected should be usurped by the conduct and valour of their lieutenants. The military fame of a subject was considered as an insolent invasion of Imperial prerogative; and it became the duty, as well as interest, of every Roman general, to guard the frontiers intrusted to his care, without aspiring to conquests which might have proved no less fatal to himself than to the vanquished barbarians.[5]

Conquest of Britain was the first exception to it The only accession which the Roman empire received during the first century of the Christian aera, was the province of Britain. In this single instance the successors of Cæsar and Augustus were persuaded to follow the example of the former, rather than the precept of the latter. The proximity of its situation to the coast of Gaul seemed to invite their arms; the pleasing, though doubtful, intelligence of a pearl fishery attracted their avarice;[6] and as Britain was viewed in the light of a distinct and insulated world, the conquest scarcely formed any exception to the general system of continental measures. After a war of about forty years, undertaken by the most stupid,[7] maintained by the most dissolute, and terminated by the most timid of all the emperors, the far greater part of the island submitted to the Roman yoke.[8] The various tribes of Britons possessed valour without conduct, and the love of freedom without the spirit of union. They took up arms with savage fierceness, they laid them down, or turned them against each other,

---

4 Tacit. Annal. l. ii. Dion Cassius, l. lvi. p. 832, and the speech of Augustus himself, in Julian's Cæsars. It receives great light from the learned notes of his French translator, M. Spanheim.

5 Germanicus, Suetonius Paulinus, and Agricola were checked and recalled in the course of their victories. Corbulo was put to death. Military merit, as it is admirably expressed by Tacitus, was, in the strictest sense of the word, *imperatoria virtus*.

6 Cæsar himself conceals that ignoble motive; but it is mentioned by Suetonius, c. 47. The British pearls proved, however, of little value, on account of their dark and livid colour. Tacitus observes, with reason (in Agricola, c. 12), that it was an inherent defect "Ego facilius crediderim naturam margaritis deesse quam nobis avaritiam." [I would more easily believe that it is the quality of the pearls which falls short rather than our own cupidity.]

7 Claudius, Nero, and Domitian. A hope is expressed by Pomponius Mela l. iii. c. 6 (he wrote under Claudius), that, by the success of the Roman arms, the island and its savage inhabitants would soon be better known. It is amusing enough to peruse such passages in the midst of London.

8 See the admirable abridgment, given by Tacitus, in the Life of Agricola, and copiously, though perhaps not completely, illustrated by our own antiquarians, Camden and Horsley.

with wild inconstancy; and while they fought singly, they were successively subdued. Neither the fortitude of Caractacus, nor the despair of Boadicea, nor the fanaticism of the Druids, could avert the slavery of their country, or resist the steady progress of the Imperial generals, who maintained the national glory, when the throne was disgraced by the weakest or the most vicious of mankind. At the very time when Domitian, confined to his palace, felt the terrors which he inspired, his legions, under the command of the virtuous Agricola, defeated the collected force of the Caledonians at the foot of the Grampian hills; and his fleets, venturing to explore an unknown and dangerous navigation, displayed the Roman arms round every part of the island. The conquest of Britain was considered as already achieved; and it was the design of Agricola to complete and ensure his success by the easy reduction of Ireland, for which, in his opinion, one legion and a few auxiliaries were sufficient.[9]. The western isle might be improved into a valuable possession, and the Britons would wear their chains with the less reluctance, if the prospect and example of freedom was on every side removed from before their eyes.

But the superior merit of Agricola soon occasioned his removal from the government of Britain; and for ever disappointed this rational, though extensive, scheme of conquest. Before his departure the prudent general had provided for security as well as for dominion. He had observed that the island is almost divided into two unequal parts by the opposite gulfs or, as they are now called, the Friths of Scotland. Across the narrow interval of about forty miles he had drawn a line of military stations, which was afterwards fortified, in the reign of Antoninus Pius, by a turf rampart, erected on foundations of stone.[10] This wall of Antoninus, at a small distance beyond the modern cities of Edinburgh and Glasgow, was fixed as the limit of the Roman province. The native Caledonians preserved, in the northern extremity of the island, their wild independence, for which they were not less indebted to their poverty than to their valour. Their incursions were frequently repelled and chastised; but their country was never subdued.[11] The masters of the fairest and most wealthy climates of the globe turned with contempt from gloomy hills assailed by the winter tempest, from lakes concealed in a blue mist, and from cold and lonely heaths, over which the deer of the forest were chased by a troop of naked barbarians.[12]

Such was the state of the Roman frontiers, and such the maxims of Imperial policy, from the death of Augustus to the accession of Trajan.

Conquest of Dacia: the second exception [A.D. 101–106]

9 The Irish writers, jealous of their national honour, are extremely provoked on this occasion, both with Tacitus and with Agricola.

10 See Horsley's Britannia Romana, l. i c. 10.

11 The poet Buchanan celebrates, with elegance and spirit (see his Sylvæ, v.), the unviolated independence of his native country. But, if the single testimony of Richard of Cirencester¹ was sufficient to create a Roman province of Vespasiana to the north of the wall, that independence would be reduced within very narrow limits.

12 See Appian (in Prœm.) and the uniform imagery of Ossian's poems, which, according to every hypothesis, were composed by a native Caledonian.

That virtuous and active prince had received the education of a soldier, and possessed the talents of a general.[13] The peaceful system of his predecessors was interrupted by scenes of war and conquest; and the legions, after a long interval, beheld a military emperor at their head. The first exploits of Trajan were against the Dacians, the most warlike of men, who dwelt beyond the Danube, and who, during the reign of Domitian, had insulted, with impunity, the majesty of Rome.[14] To the strength and fierceness of barbarians they added a contempt for life, which was derived from a warm persuasion of the immortality and transmigration of the soul.[15] Decebalus, the Dacian king, approved himself a rival not unworthy of Trajan; nor did he despair of his own and the public fortune, till, by the confession of his enemies, he had exhausted every resource both of valour and policy.[16] This memorable war, with a very short suspension of hostilities, lasted five years; and as the emperor could exert, without control, the whole force of the state, it was terminated by the absolute submission of the barbarians.[17] The new province of Dacia, which formed a second exception to the precept of Augustus, was about thirteen hundred miles in circumference. Its natural boundaries were the Dniester, the Theiss or Tibiscus, the Lower Danube, and the Euxine Sea. The vestiges of a military road may still be traced from the banks of the Danube to the neighbourhood of Bender, a place famous in modern history, and the actual frontier of the Turkish and Russian Empires.[18]

Conquests of Trajan in the east   Trajan was ambitious of fame; and as long as mankind shall continue to bestow more liberal applause on their destroyers than on their benefactors, the thirst of military glory will ever be the vice of the most exalted characters. The praises of Alexander, transmitted by a succession of poets and historians, had kindled a dangerous emulation in the mind of Trajan. Like him, the Roman emperor undertook an expedition against the nations of the east, but he lamented with a sigh that his advanced age scarcely left him any hopes of equalling the renown of the son of Philip.[19] Yet the success of Trajan, however transient, was rapid and specious. The degenerate Parthians, broken by intestine discord, fled before his arms. He descended the river Tigris in triumph, from the mountains of Armenia to the Persian gulf. He enjoyed the honour of being the first, as he was the last, of the Roman generals, who ever navigated that remote sea. His fleets ravished the coasts of Arabia; and Trajan vainly flattered himself that he was approaching towards the

13 See Pliny's Panegyric, which seems founded on facts.
14 Dion Cassius, l. lxvii.
15 Herodotus, l. iv c. 94. Julian in the Cæsars, with Spanheim's observations.
16 Plin. Epist. viii. 9.
17 Dion Cassius, l. lxviii. p. 1123, 1131. Julian in Cæsaribus Eutropius, viii. 2, 6. Aurelius Victor in Epitome.
18 See a Memoir of M. d'Anville, on the Province of Dacia in the Académie des Inscriptions, tom. xxviii. p. 444–468.
19 Trajan's sentiments are represented in a very just and lively manner in the Cæsars of Julian.

confines of India.[20] Every day the astonished senate received the intelligence of new names and new nations that acknowledged his sway. They were informed that the kings of Bosphorus, Colchos, Iberia, Albania, Osrhoene, and even the Parthian monarch himself had accepted their diadems from the hands of the emperor; that the independent tribes of the Median and Carduchian hills had implored his protection; and that the rich countries of Armenia, Mesopotamia, and Assyria, were reduced into the state of provinces.[21] But the death of Trajan soon clouded the splendid prospect; and it was justly to be dreaded that so many distant nations would throw off the unaccustomed yoke, when they were no longer restrained by the powerful hand which had imposed it.

It was an ancient tradition that, when the Capitol was founded by one of the roman kings, the god Terminus (who presided over boundaries, and was represented according to the fashion of that age by a large stone) alone, among all the inferior deities, refused to yield his place to Jupiter himself. A favourable inference was drawn from his obstinacy, which was interpreted by the augurs as a sure presage that the boundaries of the Roman power would never recede.[22] During many ages, the prediction, as it is usual, contributed to its own accomplishment. But though Terminus had resisted the majesty of Jupiter, he submitted to the authority of the emperor Hadrian.[23] The resignation of all the eastern conquests of Trajan was the first measure of his reign. He restored to the Parthians the election of an independent sovereign; withdrew the Roman garrisons from the provinces of Armenia, Mesopotamia, and Assyria; and, in compliance with the precepts of Augustus, once more established the Euphrates as the frontier of the empire.[24] Censure, which arraigns the public actions and the private motives of princes, has ascribed to envy a conduct which might be attributed to the prudence and moderation of Hadrian. The various character of that emperor, capable, by turns, of the meanest and the most generous sentiments, may afford some colour to the suspicion. It was, however, scarcely in his power to place the superiority of his predecessor in a more conspicuous light than by thus confessing himself unequal to the task of defending the conquests of Trajan.

Resigned by his successor Hadrian

The martial and ambitious spirit of Trajan formed a very singular contrast with the moderation of his successor. The restless activity of Hadrian was not less remarkable when compared with the gentle repose of Antoninus Pius. The life of the former was almost a perpetual

Contrast of Hadrian and Antoninus Pius

20 Eutropius and Sextus Rufus have endeavoured to perpetuate the illusion. See a very sensible dissertation of M. Freret, in the Académie des Inscriptions, tom. xxi. p. 55.
21 Dion Cassius, l. lxviii.; and the Abbreviators.
22 Ovid Fast. l. ii. ver. 667. See Livy and Dionysius of Halicarnassus, under the reign of Tarquin.
23 St. Augustin is highly delighted with the proof of the weakness of Terminus, and the vanity of the Augurs. See De Civitate Dei, iv. 29.
24 See the Augustan History, p. 5 Jerome's Chronicle; and all the Epitomisers. It is somewhat surprising that this memorable event should be omitted by Dion, or rather by Xiphilin.

journey; and as he possessed the various talents of the soldier, the statesman, and the scholar, he gratified his curiosity in the discharge of his duty. Careless of the difference of seasons and of climates, he marched on foot, and bareheaded, over the snows of Caledonia, and the sultry plains of the Upper Egypt; nor was there a province of the empire which, in the course of his reign, was not honoured with the presence of the monarch.[25] But the tranquil life of Antoninus Pius was spent in the bosom of Italy; and, during the twenty-three years that he directed the public administration, the longest journeys of that amiable prince extended no farther than from his palace in Rome to the retirement of his Lanuvian villa.[26]

Pacific system of Hadrian and the two Antonines

Notwithstanding this difference in their personal conduct, the general system of Augustus was equally adopted and uniformly pursued by Hadrian and by the two Antonines. They persisted in the design of maintaining the dignity of the empire, without attempting to enlarge its limits. By every honourable expedient they invited the friendship of the barbarians; and endeavoured to convince mankind that the Roman power, raised above the temptation of conquest, was actuated only by the love of order and justice. During a long period of forty-three years their virtuous labours were crowned with success; and, if we except a few slight hostilities that served to exercise the legions of the frontier, the reigns of Hadrian and Antoninus Pius offer the fair prospect of universal peace.[27] The Roman name was revered among the most remote nations of the earth. The fiercest barbarians frequently submitted their differences to the arbitration of the emperor; and we are informed by a contemporary historian that he had seen ambassadors who were refused the honour which they came to solicit, of being admitted into the rank of subjects.[28]

Defensive wars of Marcus Antonius

The terror of the Roman arms added weight and dignity to the moderation of the emperors. They preserved peace by a constant preparation for war; and, while justice regulated their conduct, they announced to the nations on their confines that they were as little disposed to endure as to offer an injury. The military strength, which it had been sufficient for Hadrian and the elder Antoninus to display, was exerted against the Parthians and the Germans by the emperor Marcus. The hostilities of the barbarians provoked the resentment of that philosophic monarch, and, in the prosecution of a just defence, Marcus and his generals obtained many signal victories, both on the Euphrates

---

25 Dion, l. lxix. p. 115. Hist. August. p. 5, 8. If all our historians were lost, medals, inscriptions, and other monuments would be sufficient to record the travels of Hadrian.
26 See the Augustan History and the Epitomes.
27 We must, however, remember that, in the time of Hadrian, a rebellion of the Jews raged with religious fury, though only in a single province. Pausanias (l. viii. c. 43) mentions two necessary and successful wars, conducted by the generals of Pius. 1st, Against the wandering Moors, who were driven into the solitudes of Atlas. 2nd, Against the Brigantes of Britain, who had invaded the Roman province. Both these wars (with several other hostilities) are mentioned in the Augustan History p. 19.
28 Appian of Alexandria, in the preface to his History of the Roman Wars.

and on the Danube.[29] The military establishment of the Roman empire, which thus assured either its tranquillity or success, will now become the proper and important object of our attention.

In the purer ages of the commonwealth, the use of arms was reserved for those ranks of citizens who had a country to love, a property to defend, and some share in enacting those laws which it was their interest, as well as duty, to maintain. But in proportion as the public freedom was lost in extent of conquest, war was gradually improved into an art, and degraded into a trade.[30] The legions themselves, even at the time when they were recruited in the most distant provinces, were supposed to consist of Roman citizens. That distinction was generally considered either as a legal qualification or as a proper recompense for the soldier; but a more serious regard was paid to the essential merit of age, strength, and military stature.[31] In all levies, a just preference was given to the climates of the north over those of the south; the race of men born to the exercise of arms was sought for in the country rather than in cities, and it was very reasonably presumed that the hardy occupations of smiths, carpenters, and huntsmen would supply more vigour and resolution than the sedentary trades which are employed in the service of luxury.[32] After every qualification of property had been laid aside, the armies of the Roman emperors were still commanded, for the most part, by officers of a liberal birth and education; but the common soldiers, like the mercenary troops of modern Europe, were drawn from the meanest, and very frequently from the most profligate, of mankind.

Military establish-ment of the Roman emperors

That public virtue, which among the ancients was denominated patriotism, is derived from a strong sense of our own interest in the preservation and prosperity of the free government of which we are members. Such a sentiment, which had rendered the legions of the republic almost invincible, could make but a very feeble impression on the mercenary servants of a despotic prince; and it became necessary to supply that defect by other motives, of a different, but not less forcible nature – honour and religion. The peasant, or mechanic, imbibed the useful prejudice that he was advanced to the more dignified profession of arms, in which his rank and reputation would depend on his own valour; and that, although the prowess of a private soldier must often escape the notice of fame, his own behaviour might sometimes confer glory or disgrace on the company, the legion, or even the army, to

Discipline

29 Dion, l. lxxi. Hist. August. in Marco. The Parthian victories gave birth to a crowd of contemptible historians, whose memory has been rescued from oblivion, and exposed to ridicule, in a very lively piece of criticism of Lucian.

30 The poorest rank of soldiers possessed above forty pounds sterling (Dionys. Halicarn. iv. 17), a very high qualification, at a time when money was so scarce that an ounce of silver was equivalent to seventy pounds weight of brass. The populace, excluded by the ancient constitution, were indiscriminately admitted by Marius. See Sallust. de Bell. Jugurth. c.91

31 Cæsar formed his legion Alauda of Gauls and strangers; but it was during the licence of civil war; and after the victory he gave them the freedom of the city for their reward.

32 See Vegetius de Re Militari,l. i. c.2–7.

whose honours he was associated. On his first entrance into the service, an oath was administered to him with every circumstance of solemnity. He promised never to desert his standard, to submit his own will to the commands of his leaders, and to sacrifice his life for the safety of the emperor and the empire.[33] The attachment of the Roman troops to their standards was inspired by the united influence of religion and of honour. The golden eagle, which glittered in the front of the legion, was the object of their fondest devotion; nor was it esteemed less impious than it was ignominious, to abandon that sacred ensign in the hour of danger.[34] These motives, which derived their strength from the imagination, were enforced by fears and hopes of a more substantial kind. Regular pay, occasional donatives, and a stated recompense, after the appointed term of service, alleviated the hardships of the military life,[35] whilst, on the other hand, it was impossible for cowardice or disobedience to escape the severest punishment. The centurions were authorized to chastise with blows, the generals had a right to punish with death; and it was an inflexible maxim of Roman discipline that a good soldier should dread his officers far more than the enemy. From such laudable arts did the valour of the Imperial troops receive a degree of firmness and docility, unattainable by the impetuous and irregular passions of barbarians.

Exercises
And yet so sensible were the Romans of the imperfection of valour without skill and practice, that, in their language, the name of an army was borrowed from the word which signified exercise.[36] Military exercises were the important and unremitted object of their discipline. The recruits and young soldiers were constantly trained, both in the morning and in the evening, nor was age or knowledge allowed to excuse the veterans from the daily repetition of what they had completely learnt. Large sheds were erected in the winter-quarters of the troops, that their useful labours might not receive any interruption from the most tempestuous weather; and it was carefully observed that the arms destined to this imitation of war should be of double the weight which was acquired in real action.[37] It is not the purpose of this work to enter into any minute description of the Roman exercises. We shall only remark that they comprehended whatever could add strength

33 The oath of service and fidelity to the emperor was annually renewed by the troops, on the first of January.

34 Tacitus calls the Roman Eagles, Bellorum Deos. They were placed in a chapel in the camp, and with the other deities received the religious worship of the troops.

35 See Gronovius de Pecunia vetere, l. iii p. 120, &c. The emperor Domitian raised the annual stipend of the legionaries to twelve pieces of gold, which, in his time, was equivalent to about ten of our guineas. This pay, somewhat higher than our own, had been and was afterwards, gradually increased, according to the progress of wealth and military government. After twenty years' service the veteran received three thousand denarii (about one hundred pounds sterling) or a proportionable allowance of land. The pay and advantages of the guards were, in general, about double those of the legions.

36 *Exercitus ab exercitando*, Varro de Linguâ Latinâ, l. iv. Cicero in Tusculom. l. ii 37. There is room for a very interesting work which should lay open the connexion between the languages and manners of nations.

37 Vegetius, l. i. c. 11 and the rest of his first book.

to the body, activity to the limbs, or grace to the motions. The soldiers were diligently instructed to march, to run, to leap, to swim, to carry heavy burdens, to handle every species of arms that was used either for offence or for defence, either in distant engagement or in a closer onset; to form a variety of evolutions; and to move to the sound of flutes in the Pyrrhic or martial dance.[38] In the midst of peace, the Roman troops familiarised themselves with the practice of war; and it is prettily remarked by an ancient historian who had fought against them, that the effusion of blood was the only circumstance which distinguished a field of battle from a field of exercise.[39] It was the policy of the ablest generals, and even of the emperors themselves, to encourage these military studies by their presence and example; and we are informed that Hadrian, as well as Trajan, frequently condescended to instruct the inexperienced soldiers, to reward the diligent, and sometimes to dispute with them the prize of superior strength or dexterity.[40] Under the reigns of those princes, the science of tactics was cultivated with success; and as long as the empire retained any vigour, their military instructions were respected as the most perfect model of Roman discipline.

Nine centuries of war had gradually introduced into the service many alterations and improvements. The legions, as they are described by Polybius,[41] in the time of the Punic wars, differed very materially from those which achieved the victories of Cæsar, or defended the monarchy[2] of Hadrian and the Antonines. The constitution of the Imperial legion may be described in a few words.[42] The heavy-armed infantry, which composed its principal strength,[43] was divided into ten cohorts, and fifty-five companies, under the orders of a correspondent number of tribunes and centurions. The first cohort, which always claimed the post of honour and the custody of the eagle, was formed of eleven hundred and five soldiers, the most approved for valour and fidelity. The remaining nine cohorts consisted each of five hundred and fifty-five; and the whole body of legionary infantry amounted to six thousand one hundred men. Their arms were uniform, and admirably adapted to the nature of their service: an open helmet, with a lofty crest; a breast-plate, or coat of mail; greaves on their legs, and an ample buckler on their left arm. The buckler was of an oblong and concave

The legions under the emperors

Arms

---

38 The Pyrrhic Dance is extremely well illustrated by M. le Beau, in the Académie des Inscriptions, tom. xxxv p. 262, &c. That learned academician, in a series of memoirs, has collected all the passages of the ancients that relate to the Roman legion.
39 Joseph. de Bell. Judaico, l. iii. c. 5. We are indebted to this Jew for some very curious details of Roman discipline.
40 Plin. Panegyr. c. 13. Life of Hadrian in the Augustan History.
41 See an admirable digression on the Roman discipline, in the sixth book of his history.
42 Vegetius de Re Militari, l. ii c. 5 &c. Considerable part of his very perplexed abridgment was taken from the regulations of Trajan and Hadrian; and the legion, as he describes it, cannot suit any other age of the Roman empire.
43 Ibid., c. 1. In the purer age of Cæsar and Cicero, the word *miles* was almost confined to the infantry. Under the Lower Empire, and in the times of chivalry, it was appropriated almost as exclusively to the men at arms, who fought on horseback.

figure, four feet in length, and two and a half in breadth, framed of a light wood, covered with a bull's hide, and strongly guarded with plates of brass. Besides a lighter spear, the legionary soldier grasped in his right hand the formidable *pilum*, a ponderous javelin, whose utmost length was about six feet, and which was terminated by a massy triangular point of steel of eighteen inches.[44] This instrument was indeed much inferior to our modern firearms; since it was exhausted by a single discharge, at the distance of only ten or twelve paces. Yet, when it was launched by a firm and skilful hand, there was not any cavalry that durst venture within its reach, nor any shield or corslet that could sustain the impetuosity of its weight. As soon as the Roman had darted his *pilum*, he drew his sword, and rushed forwards to close with the enemy. It was a short well-tempered Spanish blade, that carried a double edge, and was alike suited to the purpose of striking or of pushing; but the soldier was always instructed to prefer the latter use of his weapon, as his own body remained less exposed, whilst he inflicted a more dangerous wound on his adversary.[45] The legion was usually drawn up eight deep; and the regular distance of three feet was left between the files as well as ranks.[46] A body of troops, habituated to preserve this open order, in a long front and a rapid charge, found themselves prepared to execute every disposition which the circumstances of war, or the skill of their leader, might suggest. The soldier possessed a free space for his arms and motions, and sufficient intervals were allowed, through which seasonable reinforcements might be introduced to the relief of the exhausted combatants.[47] The tactics of the Greeks and Macedonians were formed on very different principles. The strength of the phalanx depended on sixteen ranks of long pikes, wedged together in the closest array.[48] But it was soon discovered, by reflection as well as by the event, that the strength of the phalanx was unable to contend with the activity of the legion.[49]

Cavalry   The cavalry, without which the force of the legion would have remained imperfect, was divided into ten troops or squadrons; the first, as the companion of the first cohort, consisted of an hundred and thirty-two men; whilst each of the other nine amounted only to sixty-six. The entire establishment formed a regiment, if we may use the modern expression, of seven hundred and twenty-six horse, naturally connected with its respective legion, but occasionally separated to act

44 In the time of Polybuis and Dionysius of Halicarnassus (l. v. c. 45) the steel point of the *pilum* seems to have been much longer. In the time of Vegetius it was reduced to a foot or even nine inches. I have chosen a mediumn.
45 For the legionary arms, see Lipsius de Militia Romana, l. iii. c. 2–7.
46 See the beautiful comparison of Virgil, Georgic, ii. v. 279.
47 M. Guichard, Mémoires Militaires, tom. i. c. 4, and Nouveaux Mémoires, tom. i. p. 293–311, has treated the subject like a scholar and an officer.
48 See Arrian's Tactics. With the true partiality of a Greek, Arrian rather chose to describe the phalanx of which he had read, than the legions which he had commanded.
49 Polyb. 1. xvii.

in the line, and to compose a part of the wings of the army.[50] The cavalry of the emperors was no longer composed, like that of the ancient republic, of the noblest youths of Rome and Italy, who, by performing their military service on horseback, prepared themselves for the offices of senator and consul; and solicited, by deeds of valour, the future suffrages of their countrymen.[51] Since the alteration of manners and government, the most wealthy of the equestrian order[3] were engaged in the administration of justice, and of the revenue;[52] and whenever they embraced the profession of arms, they were immediately intrusted with a troop of horse, or a cohort of foot.[53] Trajan and Hadrian formed their cavalry from the same provinces, and the same class of their subjects, which recruited the ranks of the legion. The horses were bred, for the most part, in Spain or Cappadocia. The Roman troopers despised the complete armour with which the cavalry of the East was encumbered. *Their* more useful arms consisted in a helmet, an oblong shield, light boots, and a coat of mail. A javelin, and a long broad sword, were their principal weapons of offence. The use of lances and of iron maces they seem to have borrowed from the barbarians.[54]

The safety and honour of the empire was principally intrusted to the legions, but the policy of Rome condescended to adopt every useful instrument of war. Considerable levies were regularly made among the provincials, who had not yet deserved the honourable distinction of Romans. Many dependent princes and communities, dispersed round the frontiers, were permitted, for a while, to hold their freedom and security by the tenure of military service.[55] Even select troops of hostile barbarians were frequently compelled or persuaded to consume their dangerous valour in remote climates, and for the benefit of the state.[56] All these were included under the general name of auxiliaries; and, howsoever they might vary according to the difference of times and circumstances, their numbers were seldom much inferior to those of the legions themselves.[57] Among the auxiliaries, the bravest and most faithful bands were placed under the command of præfects and centurions, and severely trained in the arts of Roman discipline; but the far greater part retained those arms to which the nature of their

Auxiliaries

50 Veget. de Re Militari, 1. ii. c. 6. His positive testimony, which might be supported by circumstantial evidence, ought surely to silence those critics who refuse the Imperial legion its proper body of cavalry.
51 See Livy almost throughout, particularly xlii. 61.
52 Plin. Hist. Natur. xxxiii. 2. The true sense of that very curious passage was first discovered and illustrated by M. de Beaufort, République Romaine, l, ii. c. 2.
53 As in the instance of Horace and Agricola. This appears to have been a defect in the Roman discipline; which Hadrian endeavoured to remedy by ascertaining the legal age of a tribune.
54 See Arrian's Tactics.
55 Such, in particular, was the state of the Batavians. Tacit. Germania, c. 29.
56 Marcus Antoninus obliged the vanquished Quadi and Marcomanni to supply him with a large body of troops, which he immediately sent into Britain. Dion Cassius, l. lxxi.
57 Tacit. Annal. iv. 5. Those who fix a regular proportion of as many foot, and twice as many horse, confound the auxiliaries of the emperors with the Italian allies of the republic.

country, or their early habits of life, more peculiarly adapted them. By this institution, each legion, to whom a certain proportion of auxiliaries was allotted, contained within itself every species of lighter troops, and of missile weapons; and was capable of encountering every nation with the advantages of its respective arms and discipline.[58] Nor was the legion destitute of what, in modern language, would be styled a

Artillery train of artillery. It consisted in ten military engines of the largest, and fifty-five of a smaller size; but all of which either in an oblique or horizontal manner, discharged stones and darts with irresistible violence.[59]

Encampment The camp of a Roman legion presented the appearance of a fortified city.[60] As soon as the space was marked out, the pioneers carefully levelled the ground, and removed every impediment that might interrupt its perfect regularity. Its form was an exact quadrangle; and we may calculate that a square of about seven hundred yards was sufficient for the encampment of twenty thousand Romans; though a similar number of our own troops would expose to the enemy a front of more than treble that extent. In the midst of the camp, the prætorium, or general's quarters, rose above the others; the cavalry, the infantry, and the auxiliaries occupied their respective stations; the streets were broad and perfectly straight, and a vacant space of two hundred feet was left on all sides, between the tents and the rampart. The rampart itself was usually twelve feet high, armed with a line of strong and intricate palisades, and defended by a ditch of twelve feet in depth as well as in breadth. This important labour was performed by the hands of the legionaries themselves; to whom the use of the spade and the pick-axe was no less familiar than that of the sword or *pilum*. Active valour may often be the present of nature; but such patient diligence can be the fruit only of habit and discipline.[61]

March Whenever the trumpet gave the signal of departure, the camp was almost instantly broken up, and the troops fell into their ranks without delay or confusion. Besides their arms, which the legionaries scarcely considered as an encumbrance, they were laden with their kitchen furniture, the instruments of fortification, and the provision of many

58 Vegetius, ii. 2. Arrian, in his order of march and battle against the Alani.

59 The subject of the ancient machines is treated with great knowledge and ingenuity by the Chevalier Folard – (Polybe, tom. ii. p. 233–290). He prefers them in many respects to our modern cannon and mortars. We may observe that the use of them in the field gradually became more prevalent, in proportion as personal valour and military skill declined with the Roman empire. When men were no longer found, their place was supplied by machines. See Vegetius, ii. 25. Arrian.

60 Vegetius finishes his second book, and the description of the legion, with the following emphatic words: "Universa quæ in quoque belli genere necessaria esse creduntur, secum legio debet ubique portare, ut in quovis loco fixerit castra, armatam faciat civitatem." [The generally accepted method in that war was that the legion should carry essentials with it everywhere, so that in whatever place it struck camp, it might make a fortified city.]

61 For the Roman Castrametation, see Polybius, l. vi., with Lipsius de Militiâ Romanâ, Joseph. de Bell. Jud. l. iii. c. 5, Vegetius, i. 21–25, iii. 9, and Mémoires de Guichard, tom. i. c. 1.

days.[62] Under this weight, which would oppress the delicacy of a modern soldier, they were trained by a regular step to advance, in about six hours, near twenty miles.[63] On the appearance of an enemy, they threw aside their baggage, and, by easy and rapid evolutions, converted the column of march into an order of battle.[64] The slingers and archers skirmished in the front; the auxiliaries formed the first line, and were seconded or sustained by the strength of the legions; the cavalry covered the flanks, and the military engines were placed in the rear.

Such were the arts of war, by which the Roman emperors defended their extensive conquests, and preserved a military spirit, at a time when every other virtue was oppressed by luxury and despotism. If, in the consideration of their armies, we pass from their discipline to their numbers, we shall not find it easy to define them with any tolerable accuracy. We may compute, however, that the legion, which was itself a body of six thousand eight hundred and thirty-one Romans, might, with its attendant auxiliaries, amount to about twelve thousand five hundred men. The peace establishment of Hadrian and his successors was composed of no less than thirty of these formidable brigades; and most probably formed a standing force of three hundred and seventy-five thousand men. Instead of being confined within the walls of fortified cities, which the Romans considered as the refuge of weakness or pusillanimity, the legions were encamped on the banks of the great rivers, and along the frontiers of the barbarians. As their stations, for the most part, remained fixed and permanent, we may venture to describe the distribution of the troops. Three legions were sufficient for Britain. The principal strength lay upon the Rhine and Danube, and consisted of sixteen legions, in the following proportions: two in the Lower, and three in the Upper Germany; one in Rhætia, one in Noricum, four in Pannonia, three in Mæsia, and two in Dacia. The defence of the Euphrates was intrusted to eight legions, six of whom were planted in Syria, and the other two in Cappadocia. With regard to Egypt, Africa and Spain, as they were far removed from any important scene of war, a single legion maintained the domestic tranquillity of each of those great provinces. Even Italy was not left destitute of a military force. Above twenty thousand chosen soldiers, distinguished by the titles of City Cohorts and Prætorian Guards, watched over the safety of the monarch and the capital. As the authors of almost every revolution that distracted the empire, the Prætorians will very soon and very loudly demand our attention; but, in their arms and institutions, we cannot find any circumstance which discriminated them from the legions, unless it were a more splendid appearance, and a less rigid discipline.[65]

Number and disposition of the legion

62 Cicero in Tusculan. ii. 37. – Joseph. de Bell. Jud. l. iii. 5. Frontinus, iv. 1.
63 Vegetius, i. 9. See Mémoires de l'Académie des Inscriptions, tom. xxv. p. 187.
64 See those evolutions admirably well explained by M. Guichard, Nouveaux Mémoires, tom. i. p. 141–234.
65 Tacitus (Annal. iv. 5) has given us a state of the legions under Tiberius; and Dion Cassius (l. lv. p. 794) under Alexander Severus. I have endeavoured to fix on the proper medium between these two periods. See likewise Lipsius de Magnitudine Româ, l. i. c. 4, 5.

197

Navy   The navy maintained by the emperors might seem inadequate to their greatness; but it was fully sufficient for every useful purpose of government. The ambition of the Romans was confined to the land; nor was that warlike people ever actuated by the enterprising spirit which had prompted the navigators of Tyre, of Carthage, and even of Marseilles, to enlarge the bounds of the world, and to explore the most remote coasts of the ocean. To the Romans the ocean remained an object of terror rather than of curiosity;[66] the whole extent of the Mediterranean, after the destruction of Carthage and the extirpation of the pirates, was included within their provinces. The policy of the emperors was directed only to preserve the peaceful dominion of that sea, and to protect the commerce of their subjects. With these moderate views, Augustus stationed two permanent fleets in the most convenient ports of Italy, the one at Ravenna, on the Adriatic, the other at Misenum, in the bay of Naples. Experience seems at length to have convinced the ancients that, as soon as their galleys exceeded two, or at the most three ranks of oars; they were suited rather for vain pomp than for real service. Augustus himself, in the victory of Actium, had seen the superiority of his own light frigates (they were called Liburnians) over the lofty but unwieldy castles of his rival.[67] Of these Liburnians he composed the two fleets of Ravenna and Misenum, destined to command, the one the eastern, the other the western division of the Mediterranean; and to each of the squadrons he attached a body of several thousand marines. Besides these two ports, which may be considered as the principal seats of the Roman navy, a very considerable force was stationed at Frejus, on the coast of Provence, and the Euxine was guarded by forty ships and three thousand soldiers. To all these we add the fleet which preserved the communication between Gaul and Britain, and a great number of vessels constantly maintained on the Rhine and Danube, to harass the country, or to intercept the passage of the barbarians.[68] If we review this general state of the Imperial forces, of the cavalry as well as infantry, of the legions, the auxiliaries, the guards,

Amount of the whole establish- ment   and the navy, the most liberal computation will not allow us to fix the entire establishment by sea and by land at more than four hundred and fifty thousand men: a military power which, however formidable it may seem, was equalled by a monarch of the last century, whose kingdom was confined within a single province of the Roman empire.[69]

View of the provinces of the Roman Empire   We have attempted to explain the spirit which moderated, and the strength which supported, the power of Hadrian and the Antonines. We shall now endeavour, with clearness and precision, to describe the

66 The Romans tried to disguise, by the pretence of religious awe, their ignorance and terror. See Tacit. Germania, c. 34.

67 Plutarch. in Marc. Anton. And yet if we may credit Orosius, these monstrous castles were no more than ten feet above the water, vi. 19.

68 See Lipsius de Magnitud. Rom. l. i. c. 5. The sixteen last chapters of Vegetius relate to naval affairs.

69 Voltaire, Siècle de Louis XIV. c. 29. It must, however, be remembered, that France still feels that extraordinary effort.

provinces once united under their sway, but, at present, divided into so many independent and hostile states.

Spain, the western extremity of the empire, of Europe, and of the ancient world, has, in every age, invariably preserved the same natural limits: the Pyrenean mountains, the Mediterranean, and the Atlantic Ocean. That great peninsula, at present so unequally divided between two sovereigns, was distributed by Augustus into three provinces, Lusitania, Bætica, and Tarraconensis. The kingdom of Portugal now fills the place of the warlike country of the Lusitanians; and the loss sustained by the former, on the side of the East, is compensated by an accession of territory towards the North. The confines of Grenada and Andalusia correspond with those of ancient Bætica. The remainder of Spain – Gallicia, and the Asturias, Biscay, and Navarre, Leon, and the two Castilles, Murcia, Valencia, Catalonia, and Arragon – all contributed to form the third and most considerable of the Roman governments, which, from the name of its capital, was styled the province of Tarragona.[70] Of the native barbarians, the Celtiberians were the most powerful, as the Cantabrians and Asturians proved the most obstinate. Confident in the strength of their mountains, they were the last who submitted to the arms of Rome, and the first who threw off the yoke of the Arabs.

Ancient Gaul, as it contained the whole country between the Pyrenees, the Alps, the Rhine, and the Ocean, was of greater extent than modern France. To the dominions of that powerful monarchy, with its recent acquisitions of Alsace and Lorraine, we must add the duchy of Savoy, the cantons of Switzerland, the four electorates of the Rhine, and the territories of Liege, Luxemburg, Hainault, Flanders and Brabant. When Augustus gave laws to the conquests of his father, he introduced a division of Gaul equally adapted to the progress of the legions, to the course of the rivers, and to the principal national distinctions, which had comprehended above an hundred independent states.[71] The sea-coast of the Mediterranean, Languedoc, Provence, and Dauphiné, received their provincial appellation from the colony of Narbonne. The government of Aquitaine was extended from the Pyrenees to the Loire. The country between the Loire and the Seine was styled the Celtic Gaul, and soon borrowed a new denomination from the celebrated colony of Lugdunum, or Lyons. The Belgic lay beyond the Seine, and in more ancient times had been bounded only by the Rhine; but a little before the age of Cæsar, the Germans, abusing their superiority of valour, had occupied a considerable portion of the Belgic

Spain (margin)

Gaul (margin)

70 See Strabo, l. ii. It is natural enough to suppose, that Arragon is derived from Tarraconensis, and several moderns who have written in Latin use those words as synonymous. It is, however, certain, that the Arragon, a little stream which falls from the Pyrenees into the Ebro, first gave its name to a country, and gradually to a kingdom. See d'Anville, Géographie du Moyen Age, p. 181.
71 One hundred and fifteen *cities* appear in the Notitia of Gaul; and it is well known that this appellation was applied not only to the capital town, but to the whole territory of each state. But Plutarch and Appian increase the number of tribes to three or four hundred.

territory. The Roman conquerors very eagerly embraced so flattering a circumstance, and the Gallic frontier of the Rhine, from Basil to Leyden, received the pompous names of the Upper and the Lower Germany.[72] Such, under the reign of the Antonines, were the six provinces of Gaul: the Narbonnese, Aquitaine, the Celtic, or Lyonnese, the Belgic, and the two Germanies.

Britain   We have already had occasion to mention the conquest of Britain, and to fix the boundary of the Roman province in this island. It comprehended all England, Wales, and the Lowlands of Scotland, as far as the Friths of Dumbarton and Edinburgh. Before Britain lost her freedom, the country was irregularly divided between thirty tribes of barbarians, of whom the most considerable were the Belgæ in the West, the Brigantes in the North, the Silures in South Wales, and the Iceni in Norfolk and Suffolk.[73] As far as we can either trace or credit the resemblance of manners and language, Spain, Gaul and Britain were peopled by the same hardy race of savages. Before they yielded to the Roman arms, they often disputed the field, and often renewed the contest. After their submission they constituted the western division of the European provinces, which extended from the columns of Hercules to the wall of Antoninus, and from the mouth of the Tagus to the sources of the Rhine and Danube.

Before the Roman conquest, the country which is now called Italy Lombardy was not considered as a part of Italy. It had been occupied by a powerful colony of Gauls, who, settling themselves along the banks of the Po, from Piedmont to Romagna, carried their arms and diffused their name from the Alps to the Apennine. The Ligurians dwelt on the rocky coast, which now forms the republic of Genoa. Venice was yet unborn; but the territories of that state, which lie to the east of the Adige, were inhabited by the Venetians.[74] The middle part of the peninsula, that now composes the duchy of Tuscany and the ecclesiastical state, was the ancient seat of the Etruscans and Umbrians; to the former of whom Italy was indebted for the first rudiments of civilized life.[75] The Tiber rolled at the foot of the seven hills of Rome, and the country of the Sabines, the Latins, and the Volsci, from that river to the frontiers of Naples, was the theatre of her infant victories. On that celebrated ground the first consuls deserved triumphs, their successors adorned villas, and *their* posterity have erected convents.[76] Capua and Campania possessed the immediate territory of Naples; the rest of the kingdom was inhabited by many warlike nations, the Marsi, the Samnites, the Apulians, and the Lucanians; and the sea-coasts had been covered by the flourishing colonies of the Greeks. We may remark that,

72 D'Anville, Notice de l'Ancienne Gaule.
73 Whitaker's History of Manchester, vol. i. c. 3.
74 The Italian Veneti, though often confounded with the Gauls, were more probably of Illyrian origin. See M. Freret, Mémoires de l'Académie des Inscriptions, tom. xviii.
75 See Maffei, Verona illustrata, l. 1.
76 The first contrast was observed by the ancients. See Florus, i. 11. The second must strike every modern traveller.

when Augustus divided Italy into eleven regions, the little province of Istria was annexed to that seat of Roman sovereignty.[77]

The European provinces of Rome were protected by the course of the Rhine and the Danube. The latter of those mighty streams, which rises at the distance of only thirty miles from the former, flows above thirteen hundred miles, for the most part to the south-east, collects the tribute of sixty navigable rivers, and is, at length, through six mouths, received into the Euxine, which appears scarcely equal to such an accession of waters.[78] The provinces of the Danube soon acquired the general appellation of Illyricum, or the Illyrian frontier,[79] and were esteemed the most warlike of the empire; but they deserve to be more particularly considered under the names of Rhætia, Noricum, Pannonia, Dalmatia, Dacia, Mæsia, Thrace, Macedonia, and Greece. *(margin: The Danube and Illyrian frontier)*

The province of Rhæti, which soon extinguished the name of the Vindelicians, extended from the summit of the Alps to the banks of the Danube; from its source, as far as its conflux with the Inn. The greatest part of the flat country is subject to the elector of Bavaria; the city of Augsburg is protected by the constitution of the German empire; the Grisons are safe in their mountains; and the country of Tyrol is ranked among the numerous provinces of the house of Austria. *(margin: Rhaetia)*

The wide extent of territory which is included between the Inn, the Danube, and the Save, – Austria, Styria, Carinthia, Carniola, the Lower Hungary, and Sclavonia, – was known to the ancients under the names of Noricum and Pannonia. In their original state of independence their fierce inhabitants were intimately connected. Under the Roman government they were frequently united, and they still remain the patrimony of a single family. They now contain the residence of a German prince, who styles himself Emperor of the Romans, and form the centre, as well as strength, of the Austrian power. It may not be improper to observe that, if we except Bohemia, Moravia, the northern skirts of Austria, and a part of Hungary, between the Theiss and the Danube, all the other dominions of the house of Austria were comprised within the limits of the Roman empire. *(margin: Noricum and Pannonia)*

Dalmatia, to which the name of Illyricum more properly belonged, was a long, but narrow tract, between the Save and the Adriatic. The best part of the sea-coast, which still retains its ancient appellation, is a province of the Venetian state, and the seat of the little republic of Ragusa. The inland parts have assumed the Sclavonian names of Croatia and Bosnia; the former obeys an Austrian governor, the latter a Turkish pasha; but the whole country is still infested by tribes of barbarians, whose savage independence irregularly marks the doubtful limit of the Christian and Mahometan power.[80] *(margin: Dalmatia)*

---

77 Pliny (Hist. Natur. l. iii., follows the division of Italy by Augustus.
78 Tournefort, Voyages en Grèce et Asie Mineure, lettre xviii.
79 The name of Illyricum originally belonged to the sea-coast of the Adriatic, and was gradually extended by the Romans from the Alps to the Euxine Sea. See Severini, Pannonia, l. i. c. 3.
80 A Venetian traveller, the Abbate Fortis, has lately given us some account of those very

Maesia and
Dacia

After the Danube had received the waters of the Theiss and the Save, it acquired, at least among the Greeks, the name of Ister.[81] It formerly divided Mæsia and Dacia, the latter of which, as we have already seen, was a conquest of Trajan, and the only province beyond the river. If we inquire into the present state of those countries, we shall find that, on the left hand of the Danube, Temeswar and Transylvania have been annexed, after many revolutions, to the crown of Hungary; whilst the principalities of Moldavia and Wallachia acknowledge the supremacy of the Ottoman Porte. On the right hand of the Danube, Mæsia, which during the middle ages was broken into the barbarian kingdoms of Servia and Bulgaria, is again united in Turkish slavery.

Thrace,
Macedonia
and Greece

The appellation of Roumelia, which is still bestowed by the Turks on the extensive countries of Thrace, Macedonia, and Greece, preserves the memory of their ancient state under the Roman empire. In the time of the Antonines, the martial regions of Thrace, from the mountains of Hæmus and Rhodope to the Bosphorus and the Hellespont, had assumed the form of a province. Notwithstanding the change of masters and of religion, the new city of Rome, founded by Constantine on the banks of the Bosphorus, has ever since remained the capital of a great monarchy. The kingdom of Macedonia, which, under the reign of Alexander, gave laws to Asia, derived more solid advantages from the policy of the two Philips; and, with its dependencies of Epirus and Thessaly, extended from the Ægean to the Ionian sea. When we reflect on the fame of Thebes and Argos, of Sparta and Athens, we can scarcely persuade ourselves that so many immortal republics of ancient Greece were lost in a single province of the Roman empire, which, from the superior influence of the Achæan league, was usually denominated the province of Achaia.

Asia Minor

Such was the state of Europe under the Roman emperors. The provinces of Asia, without excepting the transient conquests of Trajan, are all comprehended within the limits of the Turkish power. But, instead of following the arbitrary divisions of despotism and ignorance, it will be safer for us, as well as more agreeable, to observe the indelible characters of nature. The name of Asia Minor is attributed, with some propriety, to the peninsula which, confined between the Euxine and the Mediterranean, advances from the Euphrates towards Europe. The most extensive and flourishing district westward of Mount Taurus and the river Halys, was dignified by the Romans with the exclusive title of Asia. The jurisdiction of that province extended over the ancient monarchies of Troy, Lydia, and Phrygia, the maritime countries of the Pamphylians, Lycians, and Carians, and the Grecian colonies of Ionia, which equalled in arts, though not in arms, the glory of their parent. The kingdoms of Bithynia and Pontus possessed the northern side of the peninsula from Constantinople to Trebizond. On the opposite side

obscure countries. But the geography and antiquities of the western Illyricum can be expected only from the munificence of the emperor, its sovereign.

81 The Save rises near the confines of *Istria*, and was considered by the more early Greeks as the principal stream of the Danube.

the province of Cilicia was terminated by the mountains of Syria: the inland country, separated from the Roman Asia by the river Halys, and from Armenia by the Euphrates, had once formed the independent kingdom of Cappadocia. In this place we may observe that the northern shores of the Euxine, beyond Trebizond in Asia and beyond the Danube in Europe, acknowledged the sovereignty of the emperors, and received at their hands either tributary princes or Roman garrisons. Budzak, Crim Tartary, Circassia, and Mingrelia are the modern appellations of those savage countries.[82]

Under the successors of Alexander, Syria was the seat of the Seleucidæ, who reigned over Upper Asia, till the successful revolt of the Parthians confined their dominions between the Euphrates and the Mediterranean. When Syria became subject to the Romans, it formed the eastern frontier of their empire; nor did that province, in its utmost latitude, know any other bounds than the mountains of Cappadocia to the north, and, towards the south, the confines of Egypt and the Red Sea. Phœnicia and Palestine were sometimes annexed to, and sometimes separated from, the jurisdiction of Syria. The former of these was a narrow and rocky coast; the latter was a territory scarcely superior to Wales, either in fertility or extent. Yet Phœnicia and Palestine will for ever live in the memory of mankind; since America, as well as Europe, has received letters from the one, and religion from the other.[83] A sandy desert, alike destitute of wood and water, skirts along the doubtful confine of Syria, from the Euphrates to the Red Sea. The wandering life of the Arabs was inseparably connected with their independence, and wherever, on some spots less barren than the rest, they ventured to form any settled habitations, they soon became subjects to the Roman empire.[84] *(margin: Syria, Phoenicia, and Palestine)*

The geographers of antiquity have frequently hesitated to what portion of the globe they should ascribe Egypt.[85] By its situation that celebrated kingdom is included within the immense peninsula of Africa; but it is accessible only on the side of Asia, whose revolutions, in almost every period of history, Egypt has humbly obeyed. A Roman præfect was seated on the splendid throne of the Ptolemies; and the iron sceptre of the Mamalukes is now in the hands of a Turkish pasha. The Nile flows down the country, about five hundred miles from the tropic of Cancer to the Mediterranean, and marks on either side, the *(margin: Egypt)*

82 See the Periplus of Arrian. He examined the coasts of the Euxine, when he was governor of Cappadocia.
83 The progress of religion is well known. The use of letters was introduced among the savages of Europe about fifteen hundred years before Christ; and the Europeans carried them to America, about fifteen centuries after the Christian æra. But in a period of three thousand years, the Phœnician alphabet received considerable alterations, as it passed through the hands of the Greeks and Romans.
84 Dion Cassius, lxviii. p. 1131.
85 Ptolemy and Strabo, with the modern geographers, fix the Isthmus of Suez as the boundary of Asia and Africa. Dionysius, Mela, Pliny, Sallust, Hirtius, and Solinus, have preferred for that purpose the western branch of the Nile, or even the great Catabathmus, or descent, which last would assign to Asia not only Egypt, but part of Libya.

extent of fertility by the measure of its inundations. Cyrene, situated towards the west and along the sea-coast, was first a Greek colony, afterwards a province of Egypt, and is now lost in the desert of Barca.

Africa   From Cyrene to the ocean, the coast of Africa extends above fifteen hundred miles; yet so closely is it pressed between the Mediterranean and the Sahara, or sandy desert, that its breadth seldom exceeds fourscore or an hundred miles. The eastern division was considered by the Romans as the more peculiar and proper province of Africa. Till the arrival of the Phœnician colonies, that fertile country was inhabited by the Libyans, the most savage of mankind. Under the immediate jurisdiction of Carthage it became the centre of commerce and empire; but the republic of Carthage is now degenerated into the feeble and disorderly states of Tripoli and Tunis. The military government of Algiers oppresses the wide extent of Numidia, as it was once united under Massinissa and Jugurtha: but in the time of Augustus the limits of Numidia were contracted; and at least two-thirds of the country acquiesced in the name of Mauritania, with the epithet of Cæsariensis. The genuine Mauritania, or country of the Moors, which, from the ancient city of Tingi, or Tangier, was distinguished by the appellation of Tingitana, is represented by the modern kingdom of Fez. Sallè, on the Ocean, so infamous at present for its piratical depredations, was noticed by the Romans, as the extreme object of their power, and almost of their geography. A city of their foundation may still be discovered near Mequinez, the residence of the barbarian whom we condescend to style the Emperor of Morocco; but it does not appear that his more southern dominions, Morocco itself, and Segelmessa, were ever comprehended within the Roman province. The western parts of Africa are intersected by the branches of Mount Atlas, a name so idly celebrated by the fancy of poets;[86] but which is now diffused over the immense ocean that rolls between the ancient and the new continent.[87]

The Mediterranean with its islands   Having now finished the circuit of the Roman empire, we may observe that Africa is divided from Spain by a narrow strait of about twelve miles, through which the Atlantic flows into the Mediterranean. The columns of Hercules, so famous among the ancients, were two mountains which seemed to have been torn asunder by some convulsion of the elements; and at the foot of the European mountain the fortress of Gibraltar is now seated. The whole extent of the Mediterranean Sea, its coasts and its islands, were comprised within the Roman dominion. Of the larger islands, the two Baleares, which derive their names of Majorca and Minorca from their respective size, are

---

86 The long range, moderate height, and gentle declivity of Mount Atlas (see Shaw's Travels, p. 5) are very unlike a solitary mountain which rears its head into the clouds, and seems to support the heavens. The peak of Teneriff, on the contrary, rises a league and a half above the surface of the sea, and, as it was frequently visited by the Phœnicians, might engage the notice of the Greek poets. See Buffon, Histoire Naturelle, tom. i. p. 312. Histoire des Voyages, tom. ii.

87 M. de Voltaire, tom. xiv. p. 297, unsupported by either fact or probability, has generously bestowed the Canary Islands on the Roman empire.

subject at present, the former to Spain, the latter to Great Britain. It is easier to deplore the fate than to describe the actual condition of Corsica. Two Italian sovereigns assume a regal title from Sardinia and Sicily. Crete, or Candia, with Cyprus, and most of the smaller islands of Greece and Asia, have been subdued by the Turkish arms; whilst the little rock of Malta defies their power, and has emerged, under the government of its military Order, into fame and opulence.

This long enumeration of provinces, whose broken fragments have formed so many powerful kingdoms, might almost induce us to forgive the vanity or ignorance of the ancients. Dazzled with the extensive sway, the irresistible strength, and the real or affected moderation of the emperors, they permitted themselves to despise, and sometimes to forget, the outlying countries which had been left in the enjoyment of a barbarous independence; and they gradually assumed the licence of confounding the Roman monarchy with the globe of the earth.[88] But the temper, as well as knowledge, of a modern historian require a more sober and accurate language. He may impress a juster image of the greatness of Rome by observing that the empire was above two thousand miles in breadth, from the wall of Antoninus and the northern limits of Dacia to Mount Atlas and the tropic of Cancer; that it extended in length more than three thousand miles, from the Western Ocean to the Euphrates; that it was situated in the finest part of the Temperate Zone, between the twenty-fourth and fifty-sixth degrees of northern latitude; and that it was supposed to contain above sixteen hundred thousand square miles, for the most part of fertile and well-cultivated land.[89]

General idea of the Roman empire

88 Bergier, Hist. des Grands Chemins, l. iii. c. 1, 2, 3, 4: a very useful collection.
89 See Templeman's Survey of the Globe; but I distrust both the doctor's learning and his maps.

CHAPTER II

Of the Union and Internal Prosperity of the Roman Empire, in the Age of the Antonines

It is not alone by the rapidity or extent of conquest that we should estimate the greatness of Rome. The sovereign of the Russian deserts commands a larger portion of the globe. In the seventh summer after his passage of the Hellespont, Alexander erected the Macedonian trophies on the banks of the Hyphasis.[1] Within less than a century, the irresistible Zingis, and the Mogul princes of his race, spread their cruel devastations and transient empire from the sea of China to the confines of Egypt and Germany.[2] But the firm edifice of Roman power was raised

Principles of government

1 They were erected about the midway between Lahor and Delhi. The conquests of Alexander in Hindostan were confined to the Punjab, a country watered by the five great streams of the Indus.
2 See M. de Guignes, Histoire des Huns, l. xv. xvi. and xvii.

and preserved by the wisdom of ages. The obedient provinces of Trajan and the Antonines were united by laws and adorned by arts. They might occasionally suffer from the partial abuse of delegated authority; but the general principle of government was wise, simple, and beneficient. They enjoyed the religion of their ancestors, whilst in civil honours and advantages they were exalted, by just degrees, to an equality with their conquerors.

Universal spirit of toleration

I. The policy of the emperors and the senate, as far as it concerned religion, was happily seconded by the reflections of the enlightened, and by the habits of the superstitious, part of their subjects. The various modes of worship which prevailed in the Roman world were all considered by the people as equally true; by the philosopher as equally false; and by the magistrate[4] as equally useful. And thus toleration produced not only mutual indulgence, but even religious concord.

Of the people

The superstition of the people was not embittered by any mixture of theological rancour; nor was it confined by the chains of any speculative system. The devout polytheist, though fondly attached to his national rites, admitted with implicit faith the different religions of the earth.[3] Fear, gratitude, and curiosity, a dream or an omen, a singular disorder, or a distant journey, perpetually disposed him to multiply the articles of his belief, and to enlarge the list of his protectors. The thin texture of the pagan mythology was interwoven with various but not discordant materials. As soon as it was allowed that sages and heroes, who had lived or who had died for the benefit of their country, were exalted to a state of power and immortality, it was universally confessed that they deserved, if not the adoration, at least the reverence of all mankind. The deities of a thousand groves and a thousand streams possessed in peace their local and respective influence; nor could the Roman who deprecated the wrath of the Tiber deride the Egyptian who presented his offering to the beneficent genius of the Nile. The visible powers of Nature, the planets, and the elements, were the same throughout the universe. The invisible governors of the moral world were inevitably cast in a similar mould of fiction and allegory. Every virtue, and even vice, acquired its divine representative; every art and profession its patron, whose attributes in the most distant ages and countries were uniformly derived from the character of their peculiar votaries. A republic of gods of such opposite tempers and interests required, in every system, the moderating hand of a supreme magistrate, who, by the progress of knowledge and of flattery, was gradually invested with the sublime perfections of an Eternal Parent and Omnipotent

3 There is not any writer who describes in so lively a manner as Herodotus the true genius of Polytheism. The best commentary may be found in Mr. Hume's Natural History of Religion; and the best contrast in Bossuet's Universal History. Some obscure traces of an intolerant spirit appear in the conduct of the Egyptians (see Juvenal, Sat. xv.); and the Christians as well as Jews, who lived under the Roman empire, formed a very important exception; so important indeed, that the discussion will require a distinct chapter of this work.

Monarch.[4] Such was the mild spirit of antiquity, that the nations were less attentive to the difference than to the resemblance of their less religious worship. The Greek, the Roman, and the Barbarian, as they met before their respective altars, easily persuaded themselves that, under various names and with various ceremonies, they adored the same deities. The elegant mythology of Homer gave a beautiful and almost a regular form to the polytheism of the ancient world.[5]

The philosophers of Greece deduced their morals from the nature of man rather than from that of God. They meditated, however, on the divine Nature as a very curious and important speculation, and in the profound inquiry they displayed the strength and weakness of the human understanding.[6] Of the four most celebrated schools, the Stoics and the Platonists endeavoured to reconcile the jarring interests of reason and piety. They have left us the most sublime proofs of the existence and perfections of the first cause; but, as it was impossible for them to conceive the creation of matter, the workman in the Stoic philosophy was not sufficiently distinguished from the work; whilst, on the contrary, the spiritual God of Plato and his disciples resembled an idea rather than a substance. The opinions of the Academics and Epicureans were of a less religious cast; but, whilst the modest science of the former induced them to doubt, the positive ignorance of the latter urged them to deny, the providence of a Supreme Ruler. The spirit of inquiry, prompted by emulation and supported by freedom, had divided the public teachers of philosophy into a variety of contending sects; but the ingenuous youth, who from every part resorted to Athens and the other seats of learning in the Roman empire, were alike instructed in every school to reject and to despise the religion of the multitude. How, indeed, was it possible that a philosopher should accept as divine truths the idle tales of the poets, and the incoherent traditions of antiquity; or that he should adore, as gods, those imperfect beings whom he must have despised, as men! Against such unworthy adversaries, Cicero condescended to employ the arms of reason and eloquence; but the satire of Lucian was a much more adequate as well as more efficacious weapon. We may be well assured that a writer conversant with the world would never have ventured to expose the gods of his country to public ridicule, had they not already been the objects of secret contempt among the polished and enlightened orders of society.[7]

Notwithstanding the fashionable irreligion which prevailed in the

Of philosophers

---

4 The rights, power, and pretensions of the sovereign of Olympus are very clearly described in the xvth book of the Iliad: in the Greek original, I mean; for Mr. Pope, without perceiving it, has improved the theology of Homer.

5 See, for instance, Cæsar de Bell. Gall. vi. 17. Within a century or two the Gauls themselves applied to their gods the names of Mercury, Mars, Apollo, &c.

6 The admirable work of Cicero de Naturâ Deorum is the best clue we have to guide us through the dark and profound abyss. He represents with candour, and confutes with subtlety, the opinions of the philosophers.

7 I do not pretend to assert that, in this irreligious age, the natural terrors of superstition, dreams, omens, apparitions,&c., had lost their efficacy.

age of the Antonines, both the interests of the priests and the credulity of the people were sufficiently respected. In their writings and conversation the philosophers of antiquity asserted the independent dignity of reason; but they resigned their actions to the commands of law and of custom. Viewing with a smile of pity and indulgence the various errors of the vulgar, they diligently practised the ceremonies of their fathers, devoutly frequented the temples of the gods; and, sometimes condescending to act a part on the theatre of superstition, they concealed the sentiments of an Atheist under the sacerdotal robes. Reasoners of such a temper were scarcely inclined to wrangle about their respective modes of faith or of worship. It was indifferent to them what shape the folly of the multitude might choose to assume; and they approached, with the same inward contempt and the same external reverence, the altars of the Libyan, the Olympian, or the Capitoline Jupiter.[8]

Of the magistrate It is not easy to conceive from what motives a spirit of persecution could introduce itself into the Roman councils. The magistrates could not be actuated by a blind though honest bigotry, since the magistrates were themselves philosophers; and the schools of Athens had given laws to the senate. They could not be impelled by ambition or avarice, as the temporal and ecclesiastical powers were united in the same hands. The pontiffs[5] were chosen among the most illustrious of the senators; and the office of Supreme Pontiff was constantly exercised by the emperors themselves. They knew and valued the advantages of religion, as it is connected with civil government. they encouraged the public festivals which humanize the manners of the people. They managed the arts of divination as a convenient instrument of policy; and they respected, as the firmest bond of society, the useful persuasion that, either in this or in a future life, the crime of perjury is most assuredly punished by the avenging gods.[9] But, whilst they acknowledged the general advantages of religion, they were convinced that the various modes of worship contributed alike to the same salutary purposes; and that, in every country, the form of superstition which had received the sanction of time and experience was the best adapted to the climate and to its inhabitants. Avarice and taste very frequently despoiled the vanquished nations of the elegant statues of their gods and the rich ornaments of their temples;[10] but, in the exercise of the

In the provinces religion which they derived from their ancestors, they uniformly experienced the indulgence, and even protection, of the Roman conquerors. The province of Gaul seems, and indeed only seems, an exception to this universal toleration. Under the specious pretext of

8 Socrates, Epicurus, Cicero, and Plutarch, always inculcated a decent reverence for the religion of their own country, and of mankind. The devotion of Epicurus was assiduous and exemplary. Diogen. Laert. x. 10.

9 Polybius, l. vi. c. 56. Juvenal, Sat. xiii., laments that in his time this apprehension had lost much of its effect.

10 See the fate of Syracuse, Tarentum, Ambracia, Corinth, &c., the conduct of Verres, in Cicero (Actio ii. Orat. 4), and the usual practice of governors, in the viiith Satire of Juvenal.

abolishing human sacrifices, the emperors Tiberius and Claudius suppressed the dangerous power of the Druids;[11] but the priests themselves, their gods, and their altars, subsisted in peaceful obscurity till the final destruction of Paganism.[12]

Rome, the capital of a great monarchy, was incessantly filled with **at Rome** subjects and strangers from every part of the world,[13] who all introduced and enjoyed the favourite superstitions of their native country.[14] Every city in the empire was justified in maintaining the purity of its ancient ceremonies; and the Roman senate, using the common privilege, sometimes interposed to check this inundation of foreign rites. The Egyptian superstition, of all the most contemptible and abject, was frequently prohibited; the temples of Serapis and Isis demolished, and their worshippers banished from Rome and Italy.[15] But the zeal of fanaticism prevailed over the cold and feeble efforts of policy. The exiles returned, the proselytes multiplied, the temples were restored with increasing splendour, and Isis and Serapis at length assumed their place among the Roman deities.[16] Nor was this indulgence a departure from the old maxims of government. In the purest ages of the commonwealth, Cybele and Æsculapius had been invited by solemn embassies;[17] and it was customary to tempt the protectors of besieged cities by the promise of more distinguished honours than they possessed in their native country.[18] Rome gradually became the common temple of her subjects; and the freedom of the city was bestowed on all the gods of mankind.[19]

II. The narrow policy of preserving without any foreign mixture the **Freedom** pure blood of the ancient citizens, had checked the fortune, and **of Rome** hastened the ruin, of Athens and Sparta. The aspiring genius of Rome sacrificed vanity to ambition, and deemed it more prudent, as well as honourable, to adopt virtue and merit for her own wheresoever they were found, among slaves or strangers, enemies or barbarians.[20] During

---

11 Sueton. in Claud. – Plin. Hist. Nat. xxx. i.

12 Pelloutier, Histoire des Celtes, tom. vi. p. 230–252.

13 Seneca Consolat. ad Helviam, p. 74. Edit. Lips.

14 Dionysius Halicarn. Antiquitat. Roman. l. ii.

15 In the year of Rome 701, the temple of Isis and Serapis was demolished by the order of the senate (Dion Cassius, l. xl. p. 252), and even by the hands of the consul (Valerius Maximus, 1, 3). After the death of Cæsar, it was restored at the public expense (Dion, l. xlvii. p.501). When Augustus was in Egypt, he revered the majesty of Serapis (Dion, l. li. .p. 647); but in the Pomærium of Rome, and a mile round it, he prohibited the worship of the Egyptian gods (Dion, l. liii. p. 697, l. liv. p. 735). They remained, however, very fashionable under his reign (Ovid. de Art. Amand. l. i) and that of his successor, till the justice of Tiberius was provoked to some acts of severity. (See Tacit. Annal. ii. 85, Joseph. Antiquit. l. xviii. c. 3.)

16 Tertullian, in Apologetic. c. 6, p. 74. Edit. Havercamp. I am inclined to attribute their establishment to the devotion of the Flavian family.

17 See Livy, l. xi. and xxix.

18 Macrob. Saturnalia, l. iii. c. 9. He gives us a form of evocation.

19 Minucius Felix in Octavio, p. 54. Arnobius, l. vi. p. 115.

20 Tacit. Annal. xi. 24. The Orbis Romanus of the learned Spanheim is a complete history of the progressive admission of Latium, Italy, and the provinces to the freedom of Rome.

the most flourishing æra of the Athenian commonwealth the number of citizens gradually decreased from about thirty [21] to twenty-one thousand.[22] If, on the contrary, we study the growth of the Roman republic, we may discover that, notwithstanding the incessant demands of wars and colonies, the citizens, who, in the first census of Servius Tullius, amounted to no more than eighty-three thousand, were multiplied, before the commencement of the social war, to the number of four hundred and sixty-three thousand men able to bear arms in the service of their country.[23] When the allies of Rome claimed an equal share of honours and privileges, the senate indeed preferred the chance of arms to an ignominious concession. The Samnites and the Lucanians paid the severe penalty of their rashness; but the rest of the Italian states, as they successively returned to their duty, were admitted into the bosom of the republic,[24] and soon contributed to the ruin of public freedom. Under a democratical government the citizens exercise the powers of sovereignty; and those powers will be first abused, and afterwards lost, if they are committed to an unwieldy multitude. But, when the popular assemblies had been suppressed by the administration of the emperors, the conquerors were distinguished from the vanquished nations only as the first and most honourable order of subjects; and their increase, however rapid, was no longer exposed to the same dangers. Yet the wisest princes who adopted the maxims of Augustus guarded with the strictest care the dignity of the Roman name, and diffused the freedom of the city with a prudent liberality.[25]

Italy   Till the privileges of Romans had been progressively extended to all the inhabitants of the empire, an important distinction was preserved between Italy and the provinces. The former was esteemed the centre of public unity, and the firm basis of the constitution. Italy claimed the birth, or at least the residence, of the emperors and the senate.[26] The estates of the Italians were exempt from taxes, their persons from the arbitrary jurisdiction of governors. Their municipal corporations, formed after the perfect model of the capital, were intrusted, under the immediate eye of the supreme power, with the execution of the laws. From the foot of the Alps to the extremity of Calabria, all the natives of Italy were born citizens of Rome. Their partial distinctions were obliterated, and they insensibly coalesced into one great nation, united

---

21 Herodotus, v. 97. It should seem, however, that he followed a large and popular estimation.

22 Athenæus Deipnosophist, l. vi. p. 272, Edit. Casaubon. Meursius de Fortunâ Atticâ, c. 4.

23 See a very accurate collection of the numbers of each Lustrum in M. de Beaufort, République Romaine, l. iv. c. 4.

24 Appian de Bell. Civil. l. i. Velleius Paterculus, l. ii. c. 15, 16, 17.

25 Mæcenas had advised him to declare, by one edict, all his subjects citizens. But we may justly suspect that the historian Dion was the author of a counsel, so much adapted to the practice of his own age, and so little to that of Augustus.

26 The senators were obliged to have one-third of their own landed property in Italy. See Plin. l. vi. ep. 19. The qualification was reduced by Marcus to one-fourth. Since the reign of Trajan, Italy had sunk nearer to the level of the provinces.

by language, manners, and civil institutions, and equal to the weight of a powerful empire. The republic gloried in her generous policy, and was frequently rewarded by the merit and services of her adopted sons. Had she always confined the distinction of Romans to the ancient families within the walls of the city, that immortal name would have been deprived of some of its noblest ornaments. Virgil was a native of Mantua; Horace was inclined to doubt whether he should call himself an Apulian or a Lucanian; it was in Padua that an historian[6] was found worthy to record the majestic series of Roman victories. The patriot family of the Catos emerged from Tusculum; and the little town of Arpinum claimed the double honour of producing Marius and Cicero, the former of whom deserved, after Romulus and Camillus, to be styled the Third Founder of Rome; and the latter, after saving his country from the designs of Catiline, enabled her to contend with Athens for the palm of eloquence.[27]

The provinces of the empire (as they have been described in the preceding chapter) were destitute of any public force or constitutional freedom. In Etruria, in Greece,[28] and in Gaul,[29] it was the first care of the senate to dissolve those dangerous confederacies which taught mankind that, as the Roman arms prevailed by division, they might be resisted by union. Those princes whom the ostentation of gratitude or generosity permitted for a while to hold a precarious sceptre were dismissed from their thrones, as soon as they had performed their appointed task of fashioning to the yoke the vanquished nations. The free states and cities which had embraced the cause of Rome were rewarded with a nominal alliance, and insensibly sunk into real servitude. The public authority was everywhere exercised by the ministers of the senate and of the emperors, and that authority was absolute and without control. But the same salutary maxims of government, which had secured the peace and obedience of Italy, were extended to the most distant conquests. A nation of Romans was gradually formed in the provinces, by the double expedient of introducing colonies, and of admitting the most faithful and deserving of the provincials to the freedom of Rome. *The provinces*

"Wheresoever the Roman conquers, he inhabits," is a very just observation of Seneca,[30] confirmed by history and experience. The natives of Italy, allured by pleasure or by interest, hastened to enjoy the advantages of victory; and we may remark that, about forty years after the reduction of Asia, eighty thousand Romans were massacred in one *Colonies and municipal towns*

27 The first part of the Verona Illustrata of the Marquis Maffei gives the clearest and most comprehensive view of the state of Italy under the Cæsars.
28 See Pausanias, l. vii. The Romans condescended to restore the names of those assemblies, when they could no longer be dangerous.
29 They are frequently mentioned by Cæsar. The Abbé Dubos attempts, with very little success, to prove that the assemblies of Gaul were continued under the emperors. Histoire de l'Etablissement de la Monarchie Françoise, l. i. c. 4.
30 Seneca in Consolat. ad Helviam, c. 6.

day by the cruel orders of Mithridates.[31] These voluntary exiles were engaged for the most part in the occupations of commerce, agriculture, and the farm of the revenue. But after the legions were rendered permanent by the emperors, the provinces were peopled by a race of soldiers; and the veterans, whether they received the reward of their service in land or in money, usually settled with their families in the country where they had honourably spent their youth. Throughout the empire, but more particularly in the western parts, the most fertile districts and the most convenient situations were reserved for the establishment of colonies; some of which were of a civil and others of a military nature. In their manners and internal policy, the colonies formed a perfect representation of their great parent; and [as] they were soon endeared to the natives by the ties of friendship and alliance, they effectually diffused a reverence for the Roman name, and a desire which was seldom disappointed of sharing, in due time, its honours and advantages.[32] The municipal cities insensibly equalled the rank and splendour of the colonies; and in the reign of Hadrian it was disputed which was the preferable condition, of those societies which had issued from, or those which had been received into, the bosom of Rome.[33] The right of Latium, as it was called, conferred on the cities to which it had been granted a more partial favour. The magistrates only, at the expiration of their office, assumed the quality of Roman citizens; but as those offices were annual, in a few years they circulated round the principal families.[34] Those of the provincials who were permitted to bear arms in the legions;[35] those who exercised any civil employment; all, in a word, who performed any public service, or displayed any personal talents, were rewarded with a present, whose value was continually diminished by the increasing liberality of the emperors. Yet even in the age of the Antonines, when the freedom of the city had been bestowed on the greater number of their subjects, it was still accompanied with very solid advantages. The bulk of the poeple acquired, with that title, the benefit of the Roman laws, particularly in the interesting articles of marriage, testaments, and inheritances; and the road of fortune was open to those whose pretensions were seconded by favour or merit. The grandsons of the Gauls who had besieged Julius Cæsar in Alesia commanded legions, governed provinces, and were admitted

31 Memnon apud Photium, c. 33. Valer. Maxim. ix. 2. Plutarch and Dion Cassius swell the massacre to 150,000 citizens; but I should esteem the smaller number to be more than sufficient.
32 Twenty-five colonies were settled in Spain (see Plin. Hist. Natur. iii. 3, 4, iv. 35): and nine in Britain, of which London, Colchester, Lincoln, Chester, Gloucester, and Bath, still remain considerable cities (see Richard of Cirencester;[7] p. 36, and Whitaker's History of Manchester, l. i. c. 3).
33 Aul. Gell. Noctes Atticæ, xvi. 13. The Emperor Hadrian expressed his surprise that the cities of Utica, Gades, and Italica, which already enjoyed the rights of *Municipia*, should solicit the title of *colonies*. Their example, however, became fashionable, and the empire was filled with honorary colonies. See Spanheim, de Usu Numismatum, Dissertat. xiii.
34 Spanheim, Orbis Roman. c. 8, p. 62.
35 Aristid. in Romæ Encomio, tom. i. p. 218. Edit. Jebb.

into the senate of Rome.[36] Their ambition, instead of disturbing the tranquillity of the state, was intimately connected with its safety and greatness.

So sensible were the Romans of the influence of language over national manners, that it was their most serious care to extend, with the progress of their arms, the use of the Latin tongue.[37] The ancient dialects of Italy, the Sabine, the Etruscan, and the Venetian, sunk into oblivion; but in the provinces, the east was less docile than the west to the voice of its victorious preceptors. This obvious difference marked the two portions of the empire with a distinction of colours, which, though it was in some degree concealed during the meridian splendour of prosperity, became gradually more visible as the shades of night descended upon the Roman world. The western countries were civilized by the same hands which subdued them. As soon as the barbarians were reconciled to obedience, their minds were opened to any new impressions of knowledge and politeness. The language of Virgil and Cicero, though with some inevitable mixture of corruption, was so universally adopted in Africa, Spain, Gaul, Britain, and Pannonia,[38] that the faint traces of the Punic or Celtic idioms were preserved only in the mountains, or among the peasants.[39] Education and study insensibly inspired the natives of those countries with the sentiments of Romans; and Italy gave fashions, as well as laws, to her Latin provincials. They solicited with more ardour, and obtained with more facility, the freedom and honours of the state; supported the national dignity in letters[40] and in arms; and, at length, in the person of Trajan, produced an emperor whom the Scipios would not have disowned for their countryman. The situation of the Greeks was very different from that of the barbarians. The former had been long since civilized and corrupted. They had too much taste to relinquish their language, and too much vanity to adopt any foreign institutions. Still preserving the prejudices, after they had lost the virtues, of their ancestors, they affected to despise the unpolished manners of the Roman conquerors, whilst they were compelled to respect their superior wisdom and power.[41] Nor was the influence of the Grecian language and sentiments confined to the narrow limits of that once celebrated country. Their

Divisions of the Latin and the Greek provinces

36 Tacit. Annal. xi. 23, 24. Hist. iv. 74.
37 See Plin. Hist. Natur. iii. 5. Augustin. de Civitate Dei, xix. 7. Lipsius de pronunciatione Linguæ Latinæ, c. 3.
38 Apuleius and Augustin will answer for Africa; Strabo for Spain and Gaul; Tacitus, in the life of Agricola, for Britain; and Velleius Paterculus, for Pannonia. To them we may add the language of the Inscriptions.
39 The Celtic was preserved in the mountains of Wales, Cornwall, and Armorica. We may observe that Apuleius reproaches an African youth, who lived among the populace, with the use of the Punic; whilst he had almost forgot Greek, and neither could nor would speak Latin (Apolog. p. 596). The greater part of St. Austin's congregations were strangers to the Punic.
40 Spain alone produced Columella, the Senecas, Lucan, Martial, and Quintilian.
41 There is not, I believe, from Dionysius to Libanius, a single Greek critic who mentions Virgil or Horace. They seem ignorant that the Romans had any good writers.

empire, by the progress of colonies and conquest, had been diffused from the Hadriatic to the Euphrates and the Nile. Asia was covered with Greek cities, and the long reign of the Macedonian kings had introduced a silent revolution into Syria and Egypt. In their pompous courts those princes united the elegance of Athens with the luxury of the East, and the example of the court was imitated, at an humble distance, by the higher ranks of their subjects. Such was the general division of the Roman empire into the Latin and Greek languages. To these we may add a third distinction for the body of the natives in Syria, and especially in Egypt. The use of their ancient dialects, by secluding them from the commerce of mankind, checked the improvements of those barbarians.[42] The slothful effeminacy of the former exposed them to the contempt, the sullen ferociousness of the latter excited the aversion, of the conquerors.[43] Those nations had submitted to the Roman power, but they seldom desired or deserved the freedom of the city; and it was remarked that more than two hundred and thirty years elapsed after the ruin of the Ptolemies, before an Egyptian was admitted into the senate of Rome.[44]

General uses of both languages

It is a just though trite observation, that victorious Rome was herself subdued by the arts of Greece. Those immortal writers who still command the admiration of modern Europe soon became the favourite object of study and imitation in Italy and the western provinces. But the elegant amusements of the Romans were not suffered to interfere with their sound maxims of policy. Whilst they acknowledged the charms of the Greek, they asserted the dignity of the Latin, tongue, and the exclusive use of the latter was inflexibly maintained in the administration of civil as well as military government.[45] The two languages exercised at the same time their separate jurisdiction throughout the empire: the former, as the natural idiom of science; the latter, as the legal dialect of public transactions. Those who united letters with business were equally conversant with both; and it was almost impossible, in any province, to find a Roman subject, of a liberal education, who was at once a stranger to the Greek and to the Latin language.

Slaves

It was by such institutions that the nations of the empire insensibly melted away into the Roman name and people. But there still remained, in the centre of every province and of every family, an unhappy condition of men who endured the weight, without sharing the benefits, of society. In the free states of antiquity the domestic slaves were exposed to the wanton rigour of despotism. The perfect settlement of the Roman empire was preceded by ages of violence and rapine.

Their treatment

---

42 The curious reader may see in Dupin (Bibliothèque Ecclésiastique, tom. xix. p. 1, c. 8) how much the use of the Syriac and Egyptian languages was still preserved.
43 See Juvenal, Sat. iii. and xv. Ammian. Marcellin. xxii. 16.
44 Dion Cassius, l. lxxvi. p. 1275. The first instance happened under the reign of Septimius Severus.
45 See Valerius Maximus, l. ii. c. 2, n. 2. The Emperor Claudius disfranchised an eminent Grecian for not understanding Latin. He was probably in some public office. Suetonius in Claud. c. 16.

The slaves consisted, for the most part, of barbarian captives, taken in thousands by the chance of war, purchased at a vile price,[46] accustomed to a life of independence, and impatient to break and to revenge their fetters. Against such internal enemies, whose desperate insurrections had more than once reduced the republic to the brink of destruction,[47] the most severe regulations[48] and the most cruel treatment seemed almost justified by the great law of self-preservation. But when the principal nations of Europe, Asia, and Africa were united under the laws of one sovereign, the source of foreign supplies flowed with much less abundance, and the Romans were reduced to the milder but more tedious method of propagation. In their numerous families, and particularly in their country estates, they encouraged the marriage of their slaves. The sentiments of nature, the habits of education, and the possession of a dependent species of property, contributed to alleviate the hardships of servitude.[49] The existence of a slave became an object of greater value, and, though his happiness still depended on the temper and circumstances of the master, the humanity of the latter, instead of being restrained by fear, was encouraged by the sense of his own interest. The progress of manners was accelerated by the virtue or policy of the emperors; and by the edicts of Hadrian and the Antonines the protection of the laws was extended to the most abject part of mankind. The jurisdiction of life and death over the slaves, a power long exercised and often abused, was taken out of private hands, and reserved to the magistrates alone. The subterraneous prisons were abolished; and, upon a just complaint of intolerable treatment, the injured slave obtained either his deliverance or a less cruel master.[50]

Hope, the best comfort of our imperfect condition, was not denied to the Roman slave; and, if he had any opportunity of making himself either useful or agreeable, he might very naturally expect that the diligence and fidelity of a few years would be rewarded with the inestimable gift of freedom. The benevolence of the master was so frequently prompted by the meaner suggestions of vanity and avarice, that the laws found it more necessary to restrain than to encourage a profuse and undistinguishing liberality, which might degenerate into a very dangerous abuse.[51] It was a maxim of ancient jurisprudence that a slave had not any country of his own; he acquired with his liberty an admission into the political society of which his patron was a member. The consequences of this maxim would have prostituted the privileges

Enfranchisement

---

46 In the camp of Lucullus, an ox sold for a drachma, and a slave for four drachmæ, or about three shillings. Plutarch. in Lucull. p. 580.

47 Diodorus Siculus in Eclog. Hist. l. xxxiv. and xxxvi. Florus, iii. 19, 20.

48 See a remarkable instance of severity, in Cicero in Verrem, v. 3.

49 See in Gruter, and the other collectors, a great number of inscriptions addressed by slaves to their wives, children, fellow-servants, masters, &c. They are all most probably of the Imperial age.

50 See the Augustan History, and a dissertation of M. de Burigny, in the xxxvth volume of the Academy of Inscriptions, upon the Roman slaves.

51 See another dissertation of M. de Burigny in the xxxviith volume, on the Roman freedmen.

of the Roman city to a mean and promiscuous multitude. Some seasonable exceptions were therefore provided; and the honourable distinction was confined to such slaves only as, for just causes, and with the approbation of the magistrate, should receive a solemn and legal manumission. Even these chosen freedmen obtained no more than the private rights of citizens, and were rigorously excluded from civil or military honours. Whatever might be the merit or fortune of their sons, *they* likewise were esteemed unworthy of a seat in the senate; nor were the traces of a servile origin allowed to be completely obliterated till the third or fourth generation.[52] Without destroying the distinction of ranks, a distant prospect of freedom and honours was presented, even to those whom pride and prejudice almost disdained to number among the human species.

Numbers   It was once proposed to discriminate the slaves by a peculiar habit, but it was justly apprehended that there might be some danger in acquainting them with their own numbers.[53] Without interpreting, in their utmost strictness, the liberal appellations of legions and myriads,[54] we may venture to pronounce that the proportion of slaves, who were valued as property, was more considerable than that of servants, who can be computed only as an expense.[55] The youths of a promising genius were instructed in the arts and sciences, and their price was ascertained by the degree of their skill and talents.[56] Almost every profession, either liberal[57] or mechanical, might be found in the household of an opulent senator. The ministers of pomp and sensuality were multiplied beyond the conception of modern luxury.[58] It was more for the interest of the merchant or manufacturer to purchase than to hire his workmen; and in the country slaves were employed as the cheapest and most laborious instruments of agriculture. To confirm the general observation, and to display the multitude of slaves, we might allege a variety of particular instances. It was discovered, on a very melancholy occasion, that four hundred slaves were maintained in a single palace of Rome.[59] The same number of four hundred belonged to an estate, which an African widow, of a very private condition, resigned to her son, whilst she reserved for herself a much larger share

52 Spanheim, Orbis Roman. l. i. c. 16, p. 124, &c.
53 Seneca de Clementiâ, l. i. c. 24. The original is much stronger, "Quantum periculum immineret si servi nostri numerare nos cœpissent". [How great would be the danger threatening us if our slaves began to count us.]
54 See Pliny (Hist. Natur. l. xxxiii.) and Athenæus (Deipnosophist, l. vi. p. 272). The latter boldly asserts that he knew very many (πάμπολλοι) Romans who possessed, not for use, but ostentation, ten and even twenty thousand slaves.
55 In Paris there are not more than 43,700 domestics of every sort, and not a twelfth part of the inhabitants. Messange, Recherches sur la Population, p. 186.
56 A learned slave sold for many hundred pounds sterling; Atticus always bred and taught them himself. Cornel. Nepos in Vit. c. 18.
57 Many of the Roman physicians were slaves. See Dr. Middleton's Dissertation and Defence.
58 Their ranks and offices are very copiously enumerated by Pignorius de Servis.
59 Tacit. Annal. xiv. 43. They all were executed for not preventing their master's murder.

of her property.[60] A freedman, under the reign of Augustus, though his fortune had suffered great losses in the civil wars, left behind him three thousand six hundred yoke of oxen, two hundred and fifty thousand head of smaller cattle, and, what was almost included in the description of cattle, four thousand one hundred and sixteen slaves.[61]

The number of subjects who acknowledged the laws of Rome, of citizens, of provincials, and of slaves, cannot now be fixed with such a degree of accuracy as the importance of the object would deserve. We are informed that, when the emperor Claudius exercised the office of censor, he took an account of six millions nine hundred and forty-five thousand Roman citizens, who, with the proportion of women and children, must have amounted to about twenty millions of souls. The multitude of subjects of an inferior rank was uncertain and fluctuating. But, after weighing with attention every circumstance which could influence the balance, it seems probable that there existed, in the time of Claudius, about twice as many provincials as there were citizens, of either sex and of every age; and that the slaves were at least equal in number to the free inhabitants of the Roman world. The total amount of this imperfect calculation would rise to about one hundred and twenty millions of persons: a degree of population which possibly exceeds that of modern Europe,[62] and forms the most numerous society that has ever been united under the same system of government.

Populousness of the Roman empire

Domestic peace and union were the natural consequences of the moderate and comprehensive policy embraced by the Romans. If we turn our eyes towards the monarchies of Asia, we shall behold despotism in the centre and weakness in the extremities; the collection of the revenue, or the administration of justice, enforced by the presence of an army; hostile barbarians, established in the heart of the country, hereditary satraps usurping the dominion of the provinces, and subjects, inclined to rebellion, though incapable of freedom. But the obedience of the Roman world was uniform, voluntary, and permanent. The vanquished nations, blended into one great people, resigned the hope, nay even the wish, of resuming their independence, and scarcely considered their own existence as distinct from the existence of Rome. The established authority of the emperors pervaded without an effort the wide extent of their dominions, and was exercised with the same facility on the banks of the Thames, or of the Nile, as on those of the Tiber. The legions were destined to serve against the public enemy, and the civil magistrate seldom required the aid of a military force.[63] In this state of general security, the leisure as

Obedience and union

60 Apuleius in Apolog. p. 548. Edit. Delphin.
61 Plin. Hist. Natur. l. xxxiii. 47.
62 Compute twenty millions in France, twenty-two in Germany, four in Hungary, ten in Italy with its islands, eight in Great Britain and Ireland, eight in Spain and Portugal, ten or twelve in the European Russia, six in Poland, six in Greece and Turkey, four in Sweden, three in Denmark and Norway, four in the Low Countries. The whole would amount to one hundred and five, or one hundred and seven millions. See Voltaire, de l'Histoire Générale.
63 Joseph. de Bell. Judaico, l. ii. c.16. The oration of Agrippa, or rather of the historian, is a fine picture of the Roman empire.

well as opulence both of the prince and people were devoted to improve and to adorn the Roman empire.

Roman monuments

Among the innumerable monuments of architecture constructed by the Romans, how many have escaped the notice of history, how few have resisted the ravages of time and barbarism! And yet even the majestic ruins that are still scattered over Italy and the provinces would be sufficient to prove that those countries were once the seat of a polite and powerful empire. Their greatness alone, or their beauty, might deserve our attention; but they are rendered more interesting by two important circumstances, which connect the agreeable history of the arts with the more useful history of human manners. Many of those works were erected at private expense, and almost all were intended for public benefit.

Many of them erected at private expense

It is natural to suppose that the greatest number, as well as the most considerable of the Roman edifices, were raised by the emperors, who possessed so unbounded a command both of men and money. Augustus was accustomed to boast that he had found his capital of brick, and that he had left it of marble.[64] The strict economy of Vespasian was the source of his magnificence. The works of Trajan bear the stamp of his genius. The public monuments with which Hadrian adorned every province of the empire were executed not only by his orders, but under his immediate inspection. He was himself an artist; and he loved the arts, as they conduced to the glory of the monarch. They were encouraged by the Antonines, as they contributed to the happiness of the people. But if the emperors were the first, they were not the only architects of their dominions. Their example was universally imitated by their principal subjects, who were not afraid of declaring that they had spirit to conceive, and wealth to accomplish, the noblest undertakings. Scarcely had the proud structure of the Coliseum been dedicated at Rome, before the edifices of a smaller scale indeed, but of the same design and materials, were erected for the use, and at the expense, of the cities of Capua and Verona.[65] The inscription of the stupendous bridge of Alcantara attests that it was thrown over the Tagus by the contribution of a few Lusitanian communities. When Pliny was intrusted with the government of Bithynia and Pontus, provinces by no means the richest or most considerable of the empire, he found the cities within his jurisdiction striving with each other in every useful and ornamental work that might deserve the curiosity of strangers or the gratitude of their citizens. It was the duty of the Proconsul to supply their deficiencies, to direct their taste, and sometimes to moderate their emulation.[66] The opulent senators of

64 Sueton. in August. c. 28. Augustus built in Rome the temple and forum of Mars the Avenger; the Temple of Jupiter Tonans in the Capitol; that of Apollo Palatine, with public libraries; the portico and basilica of Caius and Lucius; the porticoes of Livia and Octavia, and the theatre of Marcellus. The example of the sovereign was imitated by his ministers and generals; and his friend Agrippa left behind him the immortal monument of the Pantheon.
65 See Maffei, Verona illustrata, l. iv. p. 68.
66 See the xth book of Pliny's Epistles. He mentions the following works, carried on at

218

Rome and the provinces esteemed it an honour, and almost an obligation, to adorn the splendour of their age and country; and the influence of fashion very frequently supplied the want of taste or generosity. Among a crowd of these private benefactors, we may select Herodes Atticus, an Athenian citizen, who lived in the age of the Antonines. Whatever might be the motive of his conduct, his magnificence would have been worthy of the greatest kings.

The family of Herod, at least after it had been favoured by fortune, was lineally descended from Cimon and Miltiades, Theseus and Cecrops, Æacus and Jupiter. But the posterity of so many gods and heroes was fallen into the most abject state. His grandfather had suffered by the hands of justice, and Julius Atticus, his father, must have ended his life in poverty and contempt, had he not discovered an immense treasure buried under an old house, the last remains of his patrimony. According to the rigour of law, the emperor might have asserted his claim; and the prudent Atticus prevented, by a frank confession, the officiousness of informers. But the equitable Nerva, who then filled the throne, refused to accept any part of it, and commanded him to use, without scruple, the present of fortune. The cautious Athenian still insisted that the treasure was too considerable for a subject, and that he knew not how to *use it*. *Abuse it then*, replied the monarch, with a good-natured peevishness; for it is your own.[67] Many will be of opinion that Atticus literally obeyed the emperor's last instructions, since he expended the greatest part of his fortune, which was much increased by an advantageous marriage, in the service of the Public. He had obtained for his son Herod the prefecture of the free cities of Asia; and the young magistrate, observing that the town of Troas was indifferently supplied with water, obtained from the munificence of Hadrian three hundred myriads of drachms (about a hundred thousand pounds) for the construction of a new aqueduct. But in the execution of the work the charge amounted to more than double the estimate, and the officers of the revenue began to murmur, till the generous Atticus silenced their complaints by requesting that he might be permitted to take upon himself the whole additional expense.[68]

Example of Herodes Atticus

The ablest preceptors of Greece and Asia had been invited by liberal rewards to direct the education of young Herod. Their pupil soon became a celebrated orator according to the useless rhetoric of that age, which, confining itself to the schools, disdained to visit either the Forum or the Senate. He was honoured with the consulship at Rome; but the greatest part of his life was spent in a philosophic retirement at Athens, and his adjacent villas; perpetually surrounded by sophists,

His reputation

the expense of the cities. At Nicomedia, a new forum, an aqueduct, and a canal, left unfinished by a king; at Nice, a gymnasium and a theatre, which had already cost near ninety thousand pounds; baths at Prusa and Claudiopolis; and an aqueduct of sixteen miles in length for the use of Sinope.
67 Hadrian afterwards made a very equitable regulation, which divided all treasure trove between the right of property and that of discovery. Hist. August. p. 9.
68 Philostrat. in Vit. Sophist. l. ii. p. 548.

who acknowledged, without reluctance, the superiority of a rich and generous rival.[69] The monuments of his genius have perished; some remains still preserve the fame of his taste and munificence: modern travellers have measured the remains of the stadium which he constructed at Athens. It was six hundred feet in length, built entirely of white marble, capable of admitting the whole body of the people, and finished in four years, whilst Herod was president of the Athenian games. To the memory of his wife Regilla he dedicated a theatre, scarcely to be paralleled in the empire: no wood except cedar very curiously carved was employed in any part of the building. The Odeum, designed by Pericles for musical performances and the rehearsal of new tragedies, had been a trophy of the victory of the arts over barbaric greatness; as the timbers employed in the construction consisted chiefly of the masts of the Persian vessels. Notwithstanding the repairs bestowed on that ancient edifice by a king of Cappadocia, it was again fallen to decay. Herod restored its ancient beauty and magnificence. Nor was the liberality of that illustrious citizen confined to the walls of Athens. The most splendid ornaments bestowed on the temple of Neptune in the Isthmus, a theatre at Corinth, a stadium at Delphi, a bath at Thermopylæ, and an aqueduct at Canusium in Italy, were insufficient to exhaust his treasures. The people of Epirus, Thessaly, Eubœa, Bœotia, and Peloponnesus experienced his favours; and many inscriptions of the cities of Greece and Asia gratefully style Herodes Atticus their patron and benefactor.[70]

Most of the Roman monuments for public use: temples, theatres, aqueducts, &c. In the commonwealths of Athens and Rome, the modest simplicity of private houses announced the equal condition of freedom; whilst the sovereignty of the people was represented in the majestic edifices destined to the public use:[71] nor was this republican spirit totally extinguished by the introduction of wealth and monarchy. It was in works of national honour and benefit that the most virtuous of the emperors affected to display their magnificence. The golden palace of Nero excited a just indignation, but the vast extent of ground which had been usurped by his selfish luxury was more nobly filled under the succeeding reigns by the Coliseum, the baths of Titus, the Claudian portico, and the temples dedicated to the goddess of Peace and to the genius of Rome.[72] These monuments of architecture, the property of the Roman people, were adorned with the most beautiful productions of Grecian painting and sculpture; and in the temple of Peace a very curious library was opened to the curiosity of the learned. At a small

---

69 Aulus Gellius, in Noct. Attic. i. 2, ix. 2, xviii. 10, xix. 12. Philostrat. p. 564.
70 See Philostrat. l. ii. p. 548, 560. Pausanias, l. i. and vii. 20. The life of Herodes, in the xxxth volume of the Memoirs of the Academy of Inscriptions.
71 It is particularly remarked of Athens by Dicæarchs, de Statu Græciæ, p. 8, inter Geographos Minores, edit. Hudson.
72 Donatus de Roma Vetere, l. iii. c. 4, 5, 6; Nardini, Roma Antica, l. iii. 11, 12, 13, and an MS. description of ancient Rome by Bernardus Oricellarius, or Rucellai, of which I obtained a copy from the library of the Canon Ricadi at Florence. Two celebrated pictures of Timanthes and of Protogenes are mentioned by Pliny as in the Temple of Peace; and the Laocoon was found in the baths of Titus.

distance from thence was situated the Forum of Trajan. It was surrounded with a lofty portico in the form of a quadrangle, into which four triumphal arches opened a noble and spacious entrance: in the centre arose a column of marble, whose height of one hundred and ten feet denoted the elevation of the hill that had been cut away. This column, which still subsists in its ancient beauty, exhibited an exact representation of the Dacian victories of its founder. The veteran soldier contemplated the story of his own campaigns, and, by an easy illusion of national vanity, the peaceful citizen associated himself to the honours of the triumph. All the other quarters of the capital, and all the provinces of the empire, were embellished by the same liberal spirit of public magnificence, and were filled with amphitheatres, theatres, temples, porticos, triumphal arches, baths and aqueducts, all variously conducive to the health, the devotion, and the pleasures of the meanest citizen. The last mentioned of those edifices deserve our peculiar attention. The boldness of the enterprise, the solidity of the execution, and the uses to which they were subservient, rank the aqueducts among the noblest monuments of Roman genius and power. The aqueducts of the capital claim a just pre-eminence; but the curious traveller, who, without the light of history, should examine those of Spoleto, of Metz, or of Segovia, would very naturally conclude that those provincial towns had formerly been the residence of some potent monarch. The solitudes of Asia and Africa were once covered with flourishing cities, whose populousness, and even whose existence, was derived from such artificial supplies of a perennial stream of fresh water.[73]

We have computed the inhabitants, and contemplated the public works, of the Roman empire. The observation of the number and greatness of its cities will serve to confirm the former and to multiply the latter. It may not be unpleasing to collect a few scattered instances relative to that subject, without forgetting, however, that, from the vanity of nations and the poverty of language, the vague appellation of city has been indifferently bestowed on Rome and upon Laurentum. I. *Ancient* Italy is said to have contained eleven hundred and ninety-seven cities; and, for whatsoever aera of antiquity the expression might be intended,[74] there is not any reason to believe the country less populous in the age of the Antonines, than in that of Romulus. The petty states of Latium were contained within the metropolis of the empire, by whose superior influence they had been attracted. Those parts of Italy which have so long languished under the lazy tyranny of priests and viceroys had been afflicted only by the more tolerable calamities of war; and the first symptoms of decay which *they* experienced were amply compensated by the rapid improvements of the Cisalpine Gaul. The splendour of Verona may be traced in its remains: yet Verona was less celebrated than Aquileia or Padua, Milan or Ravenna. II. The spirit of

[margin: Number and greatness of the cities of the empire]

[margin: In Italy]

[margin: Gaul and Spain]

---

73 Montfaucon, l'Antiquité Expliquée, tom. iv. p. 2, l. i. c. 9. Fabretti has composed a very learned treatise on the aqueducts of Rome.
74 Ælian, Hist. Var. l. ix. c. 16. He lived in the time of Alexander Severus. See Fabricius, Biblioth. Græca, l. iv. c. 21.

improvement had passed the Alps, and been felt even in the woods of Britain, which were gradually cleared away to open a free space for convenient and elegant habitations. York was the seat of government; London was already enriched by commerce; and Bath was celebrated for the salutary effects of its medicinal waters. Gaul could boast of her twelve hundred cities;[75] and, though, in the northern parts, many of them, without excepting Paris itself, were little more than the rude and imperfect townships of a rising people, the southern provinces imitated the wealth and elegance of Italy.[76] Many were the cities of Gaul, Marseilles, Arles, Nismes, Narbonne, Toulouse, Bordeaux, Autun, Vienne, Lyons, Langres, and Treves, whose ancient condition might sustain an equal, and perhaps advantageous, comparison with their present state. With regard to Spain, that country flourished as a province, and has declined as a kingdom. Exhausted by the abuse of her strength, by America, and by superstition, her pride might possibly be confounded, if we required such a list of three hundred and sixty cities as Pliny has exhibited under the reign of Vespasian.[77] III. Three hundred African cities had once acknowledged the authority of Carthage,[78] nor is it likely that their numbers diminished under the administration of the emperors: Carthage itself rose with new splendour from its ashes; and that capital, as well as Capua and Corinth, soon recovered all the advantages which can be separated from independent sovereignty. IV. The provinces of the east present the contrast of Roman magnificence with Turkish barbarism. The ruins of antiquity, scattered over uncultivated fields, and ascribed by ignorance to the power of magic, scarcely afford a shelter to the oppressed peasant or wandering Arab. Under the reign of the Cæsars, the proper Asia alone contained five hundred populous cities,[79] enriched with all the gifts of nature, and adorned with all the refinements of art. Eleven cities of Asia had once disputed the honour of dedicating a temple to Tiberius, and their respective merits were examined by the senate.[80] Four of them were immediately rejected as unequal to the burden; and among these was Laodicea, whose splendour is still displayed in its ruins.[81] Laodicea collected a very considerable revenue from its flocks of sheep, cele-

Africa (margin note)

Asia (margin note)

---

75 Joseph. de Bell. Jud. ii. 16. The number, however, is mentioned and should be received with a degree of latitude.

76 Plin. Hist. Natur. iii. 5.

77 Plin. Hist. Natur. iii. 3, 4, iv. 35. The list seems authentic and accurate: the division of the provinces and the different condition of the cities are minutely distinguished.

78 Strabon. Geograph. l. xvii. p. 1189.

79 Joseph. de Bell. Jud. ii. 16. Philostrat. in Vit. Sophist. l. ii. p. 548. Edit. Olear.

80 Tacit. Annal. iv. 55. I have taken some pains in consulting and comparing modern travellers, with regard to the fate of those eleven cities of Asia; seven or eight are totally destroyed, Hypæpe, Tralles, Laodicea, Ilium, Halicarnassus, Miletus, Ephesus, and we may add Sardis. Of the remaining three, Pergamus is a straggling village of two or three thousand inhabitants; Magnesia, under the name of Guzel-hissar, a town of some consequence; and Smyrna, a great city, peopled by a hundred thousand souls. But even at Smyrna, while the Franks have maintained commerce, the Turks have ruined the arts.

81 See a very exact and pleasing description of the ruins of Laodicea, in Chandler's Travels through Asia Minor, p. 225, &c.

brated for the fineness of their wool, and had received, a little before the contest, a legacy of above four hundred thousand pounds by the testament of a generous citizen.[82] If such was the poverty of Laodicea, what must have been the wealth of those cities, whose claim appeared preferable, and particularly of Pergamus, of Smyrna, and of Ephesus, who so long disputed with each other the titular primacy of Asia?[83] The capitals of Syria and Egypt held a still superior rank in the empire: Antioch and Alexandria looked down with disdain on a crowd of dependent cities,[84] and yielded with reluctance to the majesty of Rome itself.

All these cities were connected with each other, and with the capital, by the public highways, which, issuing from the Forum of Rome, traversed Italy, pervaded the provinces, and were terminated only by the frontiers of the empire. If we carefully trace the distance from the wall of Antoninus to Rome, and from thence to Jerusalem, it will be found that the great chain of communication, from the north-west to the south-east point of the empire, was drawn out to the length of four thousand and eighty Roman miles.[85] The public roads were accurately divided by milestones, and ran in a direct line from one city to another, with very little respect for the obstacles either of nature or private property. Mountains were perforated, and bold arches thrown over the broadest and most rapid streams.[86] The middle part of the road was raised into a terrace which commanded the adjacent country, consisted of several strata of sand, gravel, and cement, and was paved with large stones, or, in some places near the capital, with granite.[87] Such was the solid construction of the Roman highways, whose firmness has not entirely yielded to the effort of fifteen centuries. They united the subjects of the most distant provinces by an easy and familiar intercourse; but their primary object had been to facilitate the marches of the legions; nor was any country considered as completely subdued, till it had been rendered, in all its parts, pervious to the arms and authority of the conqueror. The advantage of receiving the earliest intelligence, and of conveying their orders with celerity, induced the emperors to

Roman roads

Posts

---

82 Strabo, l. xii. p. 866. He had studied at Tralles.

83 See a dissertation of M. de Bose, Mém. de l'Académie, tom. xviii. Aristides pronounced an oration which is still extant, to recommend concord to the rival cities.

84 The inhabitants of Egypt, exclusive of Alexandria, amounted to seven millions and a half (Joseph. de Bell. Jud. ii. 16). Under the military government of the Mamalukes, Syria was supposed to contain sixty thousand villages (Histoire de Timur Bec, l. v. c. 20).

85 The following Itinerary may serve to convey some idea of the direction of the road, and of the distance between the principal towns. I. From the wall of Antoninus to York, 222 Roman miles. II. London 227. III. Rhutupiæ or Sandwich 67. IV. The navigation to Boulogne 45. V. Rheims 174. VI. Lyons 330. VII. Milan 324. VIII. Rome 426. IX. Brundusium 360. X. The navigation to Dyrrachium 40. XI. Byzantium 711. XII. Ancyra 283. XIII. Tarsus 301. XIV. Antioch 141. XV. Tyre 252. XVI. Jerusalem 168. In all 4080 Roman, or 3740 English miles. See the Itineraries published by Wesseling, his annotations; Gale and Stukeley for Britain, and M. d'Anville for Gaul and Italy.

86 Montfaucon (l'Antiquité Expliquée, tom. iv. p. 2, l. i. c. 5) has described the bridges of Narni, Alcantara, Nismes, &c.

87 Bergier, Histoire des grands Chemins de l'Empire Romain, l. ii. c. 1–28.

establish, throughout their extensive dominions, the regular institution of posts.[88] Houses were everywhere erected at the distance only of five or six miles; each of them was constantly provided with forty horses, and, by the help of these relays, it was easy to travel an hundred miles in a day along the Roman roads.[89] The use of the posts was allowed to those who claimed it by an Imperial mandate; but, though originally intended for the public service, it was sometimes indulged to the

Navigation business or conveniency of private citizens.[90] Nor was the communication of the Roman empire less free and open by sea than it was by land. The provinces surrounded and enclosed the Mediterranean; and Italy, in the shape of an immense promontory, advanced into the midst of that great lake. The coasts of Italy are, in general, destitute of safe harbours; but human industry had corrected the deficiencies of nature; and the artificial port of Ostia, in particular, situate at the mouth of the Tiber, and formed by the Emperor Claudius, was an useful monument of Roman greatness.[91] From this port, which was only sixteen miles from the capital, a favourable breeze frequently carried vessels in seven days to the columns of Hercules, and in nine or ten to Alexandria in Egypt.[92]

Improve-
ment of
agriculture Whatever evils either reason or declamation have imputed to
in the extensive empire, the power of Rome was attended with some beneficial consequences to mankind; and the same freedom of intercourse which extended the vices, diffused likewise the improvements, of social
western life. In the more remote ages of antiquity, the world was unequally
countries divided. The east was in the immemorial possession of arts and luxury;
of the em- whilst the west was inhabited by rude and warlike barbarians, who
pire either disdained agriculture, or to whom it was totally unknown. Under the protection of an established government, the productions of happier climates and the industry of more civilized nations were gradually introduced into the western countries of Europe; and the natives were encouraged, by an open and profitable commerce, to multiply the former as well as to improve the latter. It would be almost impossible to enumerate all the articles, either of the animal or the vegetable reign, which were successively imported into Europe from Asia and Egypt;[93] but it will not be unworthy of the dignity, and much less of the utility, of an historical work, slightly to touch on a few of the

Introduc- principal heads. 1. Almost all the flowers, the herbs, and the fruits that
tion of
fruits, &c. 88 Procopius in Hist. Arcanâ, c. 30. Bergier, Hist. des grands Chemins, l. iv. Codex Theodosian. l. viii. tit. v. vol. ii. p. 506–563, with Godefroy's learned commentary.

89 In the time of Theodosius, Cæsarius, a magistrate of high rank, went post from Antioch to Constantinople. He began his journey at night, was in Cappadocia (165 miles from Antioch) the ensuing evening, and arrived at Constantinople the sixth day about noon. The whole distance was 725 Roman, or 665 English miles. See Libanius, Orat. xxii. and the Itineraria, p. 572–581.

90 Pliny, though a favourite and a minister, made an apology for granting post horses to his wife on the most urgent business, Epist. x. 121, 122.

91 Bergier, Hist. des grands Chemins, l. iv. c. 49.

92 Plin. Hist. Natur. xix. l.

93 It is not improbable that the Greeks and Phœnicians introduced some new arts and productions into the neighbourhood of Marseilles and Gades.

grow in our European gardens are of foreign extraction, which, in many cases, is betrayed even by their names: the apple was a native of Italy, and, when the Romans had tasted the richer flavour of the apricot, the peach, the pomegranate, the citron, and the orange, they contented themselves with applying to all these new fruits the common denomination of apple, discriminating them from each other by the additional epithet of their country. 2. In the time of Homer, the vine grew wild in The vine the island of Sicily and most probably in the adjacent continent; but it was not improved by the skill, nor did it afford a liquor grateful to the taste, of the savage inhabitants.[94] A thousand years afterwards, Italy could boast that, of the four-score most generous and celebrated wines, more than two-thirds were produced from her soil.[95] The blessing was soon communicated to the Narbonnese province of Gaul; but so intense was the cold to the north of the Cevennes that, in the time of Strabo, it was thought impossible to ripen the grapes in those parts of Gaul.[96] This difficulty, however, was gradually vanquished; and there is some reason to believe that the vineyards of Burgundy are as old as the age of the Antonines.[97] 3. The olive, in the western world, followed the The olive progress of peace, of which it was considered as the symbol. Two centuries after the foundation of Rome, both Italy and Africa were strangers to that useful plant; it was naturalized in those countries; and at length carried into the heart of Spain and Gaul. The timid errors of the ancients, that it required a certain degree of heat, and could only flourish in the neighbourhood of the sea, were insensibly exploded by industry and experience.[98] 4. The cultivation of flax was transported Flax from Egypt to Gaul, and enriched the whole country, however it might impoverish the particular lands on which it was sown.[99] 5. The use of Artificial artificial grasses became familiar to the farmers both of Italy and the grasses provinces, particularly the Lucerne, which derived its name and origin from Media.[100] The assured supply of wholesome and plentiful food for the cattle during winter multiplied the number of the flocks and herds, which in their turn contributed to the fertility of the soil. To all these improvements may be added an assiduous attention to mines and fisheries, which, by employing a multitude of laborious hands, serve to increase the pleasures of the rich and the subsistence of the poor. The General elegant treatise of Columella describes the advanced state of the plenty Spanish husbandry, under the reign of Tiberius; and it may be observed

94 See Homer Odyss. l. ix. v. 358.
95 Plin. Hist. Natur. l. xiv.
96 Strab. Geograph. l. iv. p. 223. The intense cold of a Gallic winter was almost proverbial among the ancients.
97 In the beginning of the ivth century, the orator Eumenius (Panegyric. Veter. viii. 6, edit. Delphin) speaks of the vines in the territory of Autun, which were decayed through age, and the first plantation of which was totally unknown. The Pagus Arebrignus is supposed by M. d'Anville to be the district of Beaune, celebrated, even at present, for one of the first growths of Burgundy.
98 Plin. Hist. Natur. l. xv.
99 Plin. Hist. Natur. l. xix.
100 See the agreeable Essays on Agriculture by Mr. Harte, in which he has collected all that the ancients and moderns have said of Lucerne.

that those famines which so frequently afflicted the infant republic were seldom or never experienced by the extensive empire of Rome. The accidental scarcity, in any single province, was immediately relieved by the plenty of its more fortunate neighbours.

Arts of luxury Agriculture is the foundation of manufactures; since the productions of nature are the materials of art. Under the Roman empire, the labour of an industrious and ingenious people was variously, but incessantly, employed in the service of the rich. In their dress, their table, their houses, and their furniture, the favourites of fortune united every refinement of conveniency, of elegance, and of splendour, whatever could soothe their pride or gratify their sensuality. Such refinements, under the odious name of luxury, have been severely arraigned by the moralists of every age; and it might perhaps be more conducive to the virtue, as well as happiness, of mankind, if all possessed the necessaries, and none the superfluities, of life. But in the present imperfect condition of society, luxury, though it may proceed from vice or folly, seems to be the only means that can correct the unequal distribution of property. The diligent mechanic, and the skilful artist, who have obtained no share in the division of the earth, receive a voluntary tax from the possessors of land; and the latter are prompted, by a sense of interest, to improve those estates, with whose produce they may purchase additional pleasures. This operation, the particular effects of which are felt in every society, acted with much more diffusive energy in the Roman world. The provinces would soon have been exhausted of their wealth, if the manufactures and commerce of luxury had not insensibly restored to the industrious subjects the sums which were exacted from them by the arms and authority of Rome. As long as the circulation was confined within the bounds of the empire, it impressed the political machine with a new degree of activity, and its consequences, sometimes beneficial, could never become pernicious.

Foreign trade But it is no easy task to confine luxury within the limits of an empire. The most remote countries of the ancient world were ransacked to supply the pomp and delicacy of Rome. The forest of Scythia afforded some valuable furs. Amber was brought over land from the shores of the Baltic to the Danube; and the barbarians were astonished at the price which they received in exchange for so useless a commodity.[101] There was a considerable demand for Babylonian carpets, and other manufactures of the East; but the most important and unpopular branch of foreign trade was carried on with Arabia and India. Every year, about the time of the summer solstice, a fleet of an hundred and twenty vessels sailed from Myos-hormos, a port of Egypt, on the Red Sea. By the periodical assistance of the monsoons, they traversed the ocean in about forty days. The coast of Malabar, or the island of Ceylon,[102] was

101 Tacit. Germania, c. 45. Plin. Hist. Natur. xxxvii. 11. The latter observed, with some humour, that even fashion had not yet found out the use of amber. Nero sent a Roman knight to purchase great quantities on the spot, where it was produced; the coast of modern Prussia.
102 Called Taprobana by the Romans, and Serendib by the Arabs. It was discovered under the reign of Claudius, and gradually became the principal mart of the east.

the usual term of their navigation, and it was in those markets that the merchants from the more remote countries of Asia expected their arrival. The return of the fleet of Egypt was fixed to the months of December or January; and as soon as their rich cargo had been transported on the backs of camels from the Red Sea to the Nile, and had descended that river as far as Alexandria, it was poured, without delay, into the capital of the empire.[103] The objects of oriental traffic were splendid and trifling: silk, a pound of which was esteemed not inferior in value to a pound of gold;[104] precious stones, among which the pearl claimed the first rank after the diamond;[105] and a variety of aromatics, that were consumed in religious worship and the pomp of funerals. The labour and risk of the voyage was rewarded with almost incredible profit; but the profit was made upon Roman subjects, and a few individuals were enriched at the expense of the Public. As the natives of Arabia and India were contented with the productions and manufactures of their own country, silver, on the side of the Romans, was the principal, if not the only, instrument of commerce. It was a complaint worthy of the gravity of the senate, that, in the purchase of female ornaments, the wealth of the state was irrecoverably given away to foreign and hostile nations.[106] The annual loss is computed, by a writer of an inquisitive but censorious temper, at upwards of eight hundred thousand pounds sterling.[107] Such was the style of discontent, brooding over the dark prospect of approaching poverty. And yet, if we compare the proportion between gold and silver, as it stood in the time of Pliny, and as it was fixed in the reign of Constantine, we shall discover within that period a very considerable increase.[108] There is not the least reason to suppose that gold was become more scarce; it is therefore evident that silver was grown more common; that whatever might be the amount of the Indian and Arabian exports, they were far from exhausting the wealth of the Roman world; and that the produce of the mines abundantly supplied the demands of commerce.

Gold and silver

Notwithstanding the propensity of mankind to exalt the past, and to depreciate the present, the tranquil and prosperous state of the empire was warmly felt and honestly confessed, by the provincials as well as Romans. "They acknowledged that the true principles of social life, laws, agriculture, and science, which had been first invented by the wisdom of Athens, were now firmly established by the power of Rome,

General felicity

---

103 Plin. Hist. Natur. l. vi. Strabo, l. xvii.

104 Hist. August. p. 224. A silk garment was considered as an ornament to a woman, but as a disgrace to a man.

105 The two great pearl fisheries were the same as at present, Ormuz and Cape Comorin. As well as we can compare ancient with modern geography, Rome was supplied with diamonds from the mine of Sumelpur, in Bengal, which is described in the Voyages de Tavernier, tom. ii. p. 281.

106 Tacit. Annal. iii. 53. In a speech of Tiberius.

107 Plin. Hist. Natur. xii. 18. In another place he computes half that sum; Quingenties HS for India exclusive of Arabia.

108 The proportion which was 1 to 10, and 12½, rose to 14²/₅, the legal regulation of Constantine. See Arbuthnot's Table of ancient Coins, c. v.

under whose auspicious influence the fiercest barbarians were united by an equal government and common language. They affirm that, with the improvement of arts, the human species was visibly multiplied. They celebrate the increasing splendour of the cities, the beautiful face of the country, cultivated and adorned like an immense garden; and the long festival of peace, which was enjoyed by so many nations, forgetful of their ancient animosities, and delivered from the apprehension of future danger."[109] Whatever suspicions may be suggested by the air of rhetoric and declamation which seems to prevail in these passages, the substance of them is perfectly agreeable to historic truth.

Decline of courage; It was scarcely possible that the eyes of contemporaries should discover in the public felicity the latent causes of decay and corruption. This long peace, and the uniform government of the Romans, introduced a slow and secret poison into the vitals of the empire. The minds of men were gradually reduced to the same level, the fire of genius was extinguished, and even the military spirit evaporated. The natives of Europe were brave and robust. Spain, Gaul, Britain, and Illyricum supplied the legions with excellent soldiers, and constituted the real strength of the monarchy. Their personal valour remained, but they no longer possessed that public courage which is nourished by the love of independence, the sense of national honour, the presence of danger, and the habit of command. They received laws and governors from the will of their sovereign, and trusted for their defence to a mercenary army. The posterity of their boldest leaders was contented with the rank of citizens and subjects. The most aspiring spirits resorted to the court or standard of the emperors; and the deserted provinces, deprived of political strength or union, insensibly sunk into the languid indifference of private life.

of genius The love of letters, almost inseparable from peace and refinement, was fashionable among the subjects of Hadrian and the Antonines, who were themselves men of learning and curiosity. It was diffused over the whole extent of their empire; the most northern tribes of Britons had acquired a taste for rhetoric; Homer as well as Virgil were transcribed and studied on the banks of the Rhine and Danube; and the most liberal rewards sought out the faintest glimmerings of literary merit.[110] The sciences of physic and astronomy were successfully cultivated by the

109 Among many other passages, see Pliny (Hist. Natur. iii. 5), Aristides (de Urbe Româ) and Tertullian (de Animâ, c. 30).
110 Herodes Atticus gave the sophist Polemo above eight thousand pounds for three declamations. See Philostrat. l. i. p. 558. The Antonines founded a school at Athens, in which professors of grammar, rhetoric, politics, and the four great sects of philosophy, were maintained at the public expense for the instruction of youth. The salary of a philosopher was ten thousand drachmæ, between three and four hundred pounds a year. Similar establishments were formed in the other great cities of the empire. See Lucian in Eunuch. tom. ii. p. 353, edit. Reitz. Philostrat. l. ii. p. 566. Hist. August. p. 21. Dion Cassius, l. lxxxi. p. 1195. Juvenal himself, in a morose satire, which in every line betrays his own disappointment and envy, is obliged, however, to say – O Juvenes, circumspicit et agitat [leg. stimulat] vos, Materiamque sibi Ducis indulgentia quaerit – Satir. vii. 20. [Young men, he (i.e. the Emperor) is looking around and urging you on, searching in your verses for talent that he can encourage.]

Greeks; the observations of Ptolemy and the writings of Galen are studied by those who have improved their discoveries and corrected their errors; but, if we except the inimitable Lucian, this age of indolence passed away without having produced a single writer of original genius or who excelled in the arts of elegant composition. The authority of Plato and Aristotle, of Zeno and Epicurus, still reigned in the schools, and their systems, transmitted with blind deference from one generation of disciples to another, precluded every generous attempt to exercise the powers, or enlarge the limits, of the human mind. The beauties of the poets and orators, instead of kindling a fire like their own, inspired only cold and servile imitations: or, if any ventured to deviate from those models, they deviated at the same time from good sense and propriety. On the revival of letters, the youthful vigour of the imagination after a long repose, national emulation, a new religion, new languages, and a new world, called forth the genius of Europe. But the provincials of Rome, trained by a uniform artificial foreign education, were engaged in a very unequal competition with those bold ancients, who, by expressing their genuine feelings in their native tongue, had already occupied every place of honour. The name of Poet was almost forgotten; that of Orator was usurped by the sophists. A cloud of critics, of compilers, of commentators, darkened the face of learning, and the decline of genius was soon followed by the corruption of taste.

The sublime Longinus, who in somewhat a later period, and in the court of a Syrian queen, preserved the spirit of ancient Athens, observes and laments this degeneracy of his contemporaries, which debased their sentiments, enervated their courage, and depressed their talents. "In the same manner," says he, "as some children always remain pigmies, whose infant limbs have been too closely confined; thus our tender minds, fettered by the prejudices and habits of a just servitude, are unable to expand themselves, or to attain that well-proportioned greatness which we admire in the ancients, who, living under a popular government, wrote with the same freedom as they acted."[111] This diminutive stature of mankind, if we pursue the metaphor, was daily sinking below the old standard, and the Roman world was indeed peopled by a race of pigmies, when the fierce giants of the north broke in and mended the puny breed. They restored a manly spirit of freedom; and, after the revolution of ten centuries, freedom became the happy parent of taste and science.

Degeneracy

---

111 Longin. de Sublim. c. 43, p. 229, edit. Toll. Here too we may say of Longinus, "his own example strengthens all his laws". Instead of proposing his sentiments with a manly boldness, he insinuates them with the most guarded caution, puts them into the mouth of a friend, and, as far as we can collect from a corrupted text, makes a show of refuting them himself.

CHAPTER III

*Of the Constitution of the Roman Empire, in the
Age of the Antonines*

Idea of a monarchy The obvious definition of a monarchy seems to be that of a state, in which a single person, by whatsoever name he may be distinguished, is intrusted with the execution of the laws, the management of the revenue, and the command of the army. But unless public liberty is protected by intrepid and vigilant guardians, the authority of so formidable a magistrate will soon degenerate into despotism. The influence of the clergy, in an age of superstition, might be usefully employed to assert the rights of mankind; but so intimate is the connexion between the throne and the altar, that the banner of the church has very seldom been seen on the side of the people. A martial nobility and stubborn commons, possessed of arms, tenacious of property, and collected into constitutional assemblies, form the only balance capable of preserving a free constitution against enterprises of an aspiring prince.

Situation of Augustus Every barrier of the Roman constitution had been levelled by the vast ambition of the dictator; every fence had been extirpated by the cruel hand of the triumvir. After the victory of Actium, the fate of the Roman world depended on the will of Octavianus, surnamed Cæsar by his uncle's adoption, and afterwards Augustus, by the flattery of the senate. The conqueror was at the head of forty-four veteran legions,[1] conscious of their own strength and of the weakness of the con- stitution, habituated during twenty years' civil war to every act of blood and violence, and passionately devoted to the house of Cæsar, from whence alone they had received and expected the most lavish rewards. The provinces, long oppressed by the ministers of the republic, sighed for the government of a single person, who would be the master, not the accomplice, of those petty tyrants. The people of Rome, viewing with a secret pleasure the humiliation of the aristocracy,[8] demanded only bread and public shows, and were supplied with both by the liberal hand of Augustus. The rich and polite Italians, who had almost universally embraced the philosophy of Epicurus, enjoyed the present blessings of ease and tranquillity, and suffered not the pleasing dream to be interrupted by the memory of their old tumultuous freedom. With its power, the senate had lost its dignity; many of the most noble families were extinct. The republicans of spirit and ability had perished in the field of battle, or in the proscription. The door of the assembly had been designedly left open for a mixed multitude of more than a thousand persons, who reflected disgrace upon their rank, instead of deriving honour from it.[2]

He reforms the senate The reformation of the senate, was one of the first steps in which

1 Orosius, vi. 18.
2 Julius Cæsar introduced soldiers, strangers and half-barbarians, into the senate. (Sueton. in Cæsar. c. 80.) The abuse became still more scandalous after his death.

230

Augustus laid aside the tyrant, and professed himself the father of his country. He was elected censor; and, in concert with his faithful Agrippa, he examined the list of the senators, expelled a few members, whose vices or whose obstinacy required a public example, persuaded near two hundred to prevent the shame of an expulsion by a voluntary retreat, raised the qualification of a senator to about ten thousand pounds, created a sufficient number of patrician families, and accepted for himself the honourable title of Prince of the Senate, which had always been bestowed by the censors on the citizen the most eminent for his honours and services.[3] But, whilst he thus restored the dignity, he destroyed the independence, of the senate. The principles of a free constitution are irrecoverably lost, when the legislative power is nominated by the executive.

Before an assembly thus modelled and prepared, Augustus pronounced a studied oration, which displayed his patriotism, and disguised his ambition. "He lamented, yet excused, his past conduct. Filial piety had required at his hands the revenge of his father's murder; the humanity of his own nature had sometimes given way to the stern laws of necessity, and to a forced connexion with two unworthy colleagues: as long as Antony lived, the republic forbad him to abandon her to a degenerate Roman and a barbarian queen. He was now at liberty to satisfy his duty and his inclination. He solemnly restored the senate and people to all their ancient rights; and wished only to mingle with the crowd of his fellow-citizens, and to share the blessings which he had obtained for his country."[4] *Resigns his usurped power*

It would require the pen of Tacitus (if Tacitus had assisted at this assembly) to describe the various emotions of the senate; those that were suppressed, and those that were affected. It was dangerous to trust the sincerity of Augustus; to seem to distrust it was still more dangerous. The respective advantages of monarchy and a republic have often divided speculative inquirers; the present greatness of the Roman state, the corruption of manners, and the licence of the soldiers, supplied new arguments to the advocates of monarchy; and these general views of government were again warped by the hopes and fears of each individual. Amidst this confusion of sentiments, the answer of the senate was unanimous and decisive. They refused to accept the resignation of Augustus; they conjured him not to desert the republic which he had saved. After a decent resistance the crafty tyrant submitted to the orders of the senate; and consented to receive the government of the provinces, and the general command of the Roman armies, under the well-known names of PROCONSUL[9] and IMPERATOR.[5] *Is prevailed upon to resume it under the title of emperor or general*

3 Dion Cassius, l. iii. p. 693, Suetonius in August. c. 35.
4 Dion, l. liii. p. 6983, gives us a prolix and bombastic speech on this great occasion. I have borrowed from Suetonius and Tacitus the general language of Augustus.
5 *Imperator* (from which we have derived emperor) signified under the republic no more than *general*, and was emphatically bestowed by the soldiers, when on the field of battle they proclaimed their victorious leader worthy of that title. When the Roman *emperors* assumed it in that sense, they placed it after their name, and marked how often they had taken it.

But he would receive them only for ten years. Even before the expiration of that period, he hoped that the wounds of civil discord would be completely healed, and that the republic, restored to its pristine health and vigour, would no longer require the dangerous interposition of so extraordinary a magistrate. The memory of this comedy, repeated several times during the life of Augustus, was preserved to the last ages of the empire by the peculiar pomp with which the perpetual monarchs of Rome always solemnized the tenth years of their reign.[6]

Power of the Roman generals Without any violation of the principles of the constitution, the general of the Roman armies might receive and exercise an authority almost despotic over the soldiers, the enemies, and the subjects of the republic. With regard to the soldiers, the jealousy of freedom had, even from the earliest ages of Rome, given way to the hopes of conquest and a just sense of military discipline. The dictator, or consul, had a right to command the service of the Roman youth, and to punish an obstinate or cowardly disobedience by the most severe and ignominious penalties, by striking the offender out of the list of citizens, by confiscating his property, and by selling his person to slavery.[7] The most sacred rights of freedom, confirmed by the Porcian and Sempronian laws, were suspended by the military engagement. In his camp the general exercised an absolute power of life and death; his jurisdiction was not confined by any forms of trial or rules of proceeding, and the execution of the sentence was immediate and without appeal.[8] The choice of the enemies of Rome was regularly decided by the legislative authority. The most important resolutions of peace and war were seriously debated in the senate, and solemnly ratified by the people. But when the arms of the legions were carried to a great distance from Italy, the generals assumed the liberty of directing them against whatever people, and in whatever manner, they judged most advantageous for the public service. It was from the success, not from the justice, of their enterprises, that they expected the honours of a triumph. In the use of victory, especially after they were no longer controlled by the commissioners of the senate, they exercised the most unbounded despotism. When Pompey commanded in the East, he rewarded his soldiers and allies, dethroned princes, divided kingdoms, founded colonies, and distributed the treasures of Mithridates. On his return to Rome he obtained, by a single act of the senate and people, the universal ratification of all his proceedings.[9] Such was the power over the soldiers, and over the enemies of Rome, which was either granted to, or

6 Dion, l. liii. p. 703, &c.
7 Liv. Epitom. l. xiv. Valer. Maxim. vi. 3.
8 See in the viiith book of Livy, the conduct of Manlius Torquatus and Papirius Cursor. They violated the laws of nature and humanity, but they asserted those of military discipline; and the people, who abhorred the action, were obliged to respect the principle.
9 By the lavish but unconstrained suffrages of the people, Pompey had obtained a military command scarcely inferior to that of Augustus. Among the extraordinary acts of power executed by the former, we may remark the foundation of twenty-nine cities, and

assumed by, the generals of the republic. They were, at the same time, the governors, or rather monarchs, of the conquered provinces, united the civil with the military character, administered justice as well as the finances, and exercised both the executive and legislative power of the state.

From what has been already observed in the first chapter of this work, some notion may be formed of the armies and provinces thus intrusted to the ruling hand of Augustus. But, as it was impossible that he could personally command the legions of so many distant frontiers, he was indulged by the senate, as Pompey had already been, in the permission of devolving the execution of his great office on a sufficient number of lieutenants. In rank and authority these officers seemed not inferior to the ancient proconsuls; but their station was dependent and precarious. They received and held their commissions at the will of a superior, to whose *auspicious* influence the merit of their action was legally attributed.[10] They were the representatives of the emperor. The emperor alone was the general of the republic, and his jurisdiction, civil as well as military, extended over all the conquests of Rome. It was some satisfaction, however, to the senate that he always delegated his power to the members of their body. The imperial lieutenants were of consular or prætorian dignity; the legions were commanded by senators, and the præfecture of Egypt was the only important trust committed to a Roman knight. *(marginal note: Lieutenants of the emperor)*

Within six days after Augustus had been compelled to accept so very liberal a grant, he resolved to gratify the pride of the senate by an easy sacrifice. He represented to them that they had enlarged his powers, even beyond that degree which might be required by the melancholy condition of the times. They had not permitted him to refuse the laborious command of the armies and the frontiers; but he must insist on being allowed to restore the more peaceful and secure provinces to the mild administration of the civil magistrate. In the division of the provinces Augustus provided for his own power and for the dignity of the republic. The proconsuls of the senate, particularly those of Asia, Greece, and Africa, enjoyed a more honourable character than the lieutenants of the emperor, who commanded in Gaul and Syria. The former were attended by lictors, the latter by soldiers. A law was passed that, wherever the emperor was present, his extraordinary commission should supersede the ordinary jurisdiction of the governor; a custom was introduced that the new conquests belonged to the imperial portion; and it was soon discovered that the authority of the *Prince*, the favourite epithet of Augustus, was the same in every part of the empire. *(marginal note: Division of the provinces between the emperor and the senate)*

the distribution of three or four millions sterling to his troops. The ratification of his acts met with some opposition and delays in the senate. See Plutarch, Appian, Dion Cassius, and the first book of the epistles to Atticus.

10 Under the commonwealth, a triumph could only be claimed by the general, who was authorized to take the Auspices in the name of the people. By an exact consequence, drawn from this principle of policy and religion, the triumph was reserved to the emperor, and his most successful lieutenants were satisfied with some marks of distinction, which, under the name of triumphal honours, were invented in their favour.

The former preserves his military command, and guards, in Rome itself

In return for this imaginary concession, Augustus obtained an important privilege, which rendered him master of Rome and Italy. By a dangerous exception to the ancient maxims, he was authorized to preserve his military command, supported by a numerous body of guards, even in time of peace, and in the heart of the capital. His command, indeed, was confined to those citizens who were engaged in the service by the military oath; but such was the propensity of the Romans to servitude, that the oath was voluntarily taken by the magistrates, the senators, and the equestrian order, till the homage of flattery was insensibly converted into an annual and solemn protestation of fidelity.

Consular and tribunitian powers

Although Augustus considered a military force as the firmest foundation, he wisely rejected it as a very odious instrument, of government. It was more agreeable to his temper, as well as to his policy, to reign under the venerable names of ancient magistracy, and artfully to collect in his own person all the scattered rays of civil jurisdiction. With this view, he permitted the senate to confer upon him, for his life, the powers of the consular[11] and tribunitian offices,[12] which were, in the same manner, continued to all his successors. The consuls had succeeded to the kings of Rome, and represented the dignity of the state. They superintended the ceremonies of religion, levied and commanded the legions, gave audience to foreign ambassadors, and presided in the assemblies both of the senate and people. The general control of the finances was intrusted to their care; and, though they seldom had leisure to administer justice in person, they were considered as the supreme guardians of law, equity, and the public peace. Such was their ordinary jurisdiction; but, whenever the senate empowered the first magistrate to consult the safety of the commonwealth, he was raised by that decree above the laws, and exercised, in the defence of liberty, a temporary despotism.[13] The character of the tribunes was, in every respect, different from that of the consuls. The appearance of the former was modest and humble; but their persons were sacred and inviolable. Their force was suited rather for opposition than for action. They were instituted to defend the oppressed, to pardon offences, to arraign the enemies of the people, and, when they judged it necessary, to stop, by a single word,[10] the whole machine of government. As long as the republic subsisted, the dangerous influence

11 Cicero (de Legibus, iii. 3) gives the consular office the name of *Regia potestas*: and Polybius (l. vi. c. 3) observes three powers in the Roman constitution. The monarchical was represented and exercised by the consuls.
12 As the tribunitian power (distinct from the annual office) was first invented for the dictator Cæsar (Dion, l. xliv. p. 384), we may easily conceive, that it was given as a reward for having so nobly asserted, by arms, the sacred rights of the tribunes and people. See his own commentaries, de Bell. Civil. l. i.
13 Augustus exercised nine annual consulships without interruption. He then most artfully refused that magistracy as well as the dictatorship, absented himself from Rome, and waited till the fatal effects of tumult and faction forced the senate to invest him with a perpetual consulship. Augustus, as well as his successors, affected, however, to conceal so invidious a title.

which either the consul or the tribune might derive from their respective jurisdiction was diminished by several important restrictions. Their authority expired with the year in which they were elected; the former office was divided between two, the latter among ten, persons; and, as both in their private and public interest they were adverse to each other, their mutual conflicts contributed, for the most part, to strengthen rather than to destroy the balance of the constitution. But when the consular and tribunitian powers were united, when they were vested for life in a single person, when the general of the army was, at the same time, the minister of the senate and the representative of the Roman people, it was impossible to resist the exercise, nor was it easy to define the limits, of his imperial prerogative.

To these accumulated honours the policy of Augustus soon added the splendid as well as important dignities of supreme pontiff, and of censor. By the former he acquired the management of the religion, and by the latter a legal inspection over the manners and fortunes, of the Roman people. If so many distinct and independent powers did not exactly unite with each other, the complaisance of the senate was prepared to supply every deficiency by the most ample and extraordinary concessions. The emperors, as the first ministers of the republic, were exempted from the obligation and penalty of many inconvenient laws: they were authorized to convoke the senate, to make several motions in the same day, to recommend candidates for the honours of the state, to enlarge the bounds of the city, to employ the revenue at their discretion, to declare peace and war, to ratify treaties; and, by a most comprehensive clause, they were empowered to execute whatsoever they should judge advantageous to the empire, and agreeable to the majesty of things private or public, human or divine.[14] *Imperial prerogatives*

When all the various powers of executive government were committed to the *Imperial magistrate*, the ordinary magistrates of the commonwealth languished in obscurity, without vigour, and almost without business. The names and forms of the ancient administration were preserved by Augustus with the most anxious care. The usual number of consuls, prætors, and tribunes[15] were annually invested with their respective ensigns of office, and continued to discharge some of their least important functions. Those honours still attracted the vain ambition of the Romans; and the emperors themselves, though invested for life with the powers of the consulship, frequently aspired to *The magistrates*

14 See a fragment of a Decree of the Senate, conferring on the Emperor Vespasian all the powers granted to his predecessors, Augustus, Tiberius, and Claudius. This curious and important monument is published in Gruter's Inscriptions, No. ccxlii.
15 Two consuls were created on the Calends of January; but in the course of the year others were substituted in their places, till the annual number seems to have amounted to no less than twelve. The prætors were usually sixteen or eighteen (Lipsius in Excurs. D. ad Tacit. Annal. l. i.). I have not mentioned the Ædiles or Quæstors. Officers of the police or revenue easily adapt themselves to any form of government. In the time of Nero the tribunes legally possessed the right of intercession, though it might be dangerous to exercise it (Tacit. Annal. xvi. 26). In the time of Trajan, it was doubtful whether the tribuneship was an office or a name (Plin. Epist. 123).

the title of that annual dignity, which they condescended to share with the most illustrious of their fellow-citizens.[16] In the election of these magistrates, the people, during the reign of Augustus, were permitted to expose all the inconveniences of a wild democracy. That artful prince, instead of discovering the least symptom of impatience, humbly solicited their suffrages for himself or his friends, and scrupulously practised all the duties of an ordinary candidate.[17] But we may venture to ascribe to his councils the first measure of the succeeding reign, by which the elections were transferred to the senate.[18] The assemblies of the people were for ever abolished, and the emperors were delivered from a dangerous multitude, who, without restoring liberty, might have disturbed, and perhaps endangered, the established government.

The senate   By declaring themselves the protectors of the people, Marius and Cæsar had subverted the constitution of their country. But as soon as the senate had been humbled and disarmed, such an assembly, consisting of five or six hundred persons, was found a much more tractable and useful instrument of dominion. It was on the dignity of the senate that Augustus and his successors founded their new empire; and they affected, on every occasion, to adopt the language and principles of Patricians. In the administration of their own powers, they frequently consulted the great national council, and *seemed* to refer to its decision the most important concerns of peace and war. Rome, Italy, and the internal provinces were subject to the immediate jurisdiction of the senate. With regard to civil objects, it was the supreme court of appeal; with regard to criminal matters, a tribunal, constituted for the trial of all offences that were committed by men in any public station, or that affected the peace and majesty of the Roman people. The exercise of the judicial power became the most frequent and serious occupation of the senate; and the important causes that were pleaded before them afforded a last refuge to the spirit of ancient eloquence. As a council of state, and as a court of justice, the senate possessed very considerable prerogatives; but in its legislative capacity, in which it was supposed virtually to represent the people, the rights of sovereignty were acknowledged to reside in that assembly. Every power was derived from their authority, every law was ratified by their sanction. Their regular meetings were held on three stated days in every month, the Calends,

16 The tyrants themselves were ambitious of the consulship. The virtuous princes were moderate in the pursuit, and exact in the discharge, of it. Trajan revived the ancient oath, and swore before the consul's tribunal that he would observe the laws (Plin. Panegyric. c. 64).

17 Quoties magistratuum comitiis interesset, tribus cum candidatis suis circuibat; supplicabatque more solemni. Ferebat et ipse suffragium in tribubus, ut unus e populo. Suetonius in August. c. 56. [Whenever he had an interest in the election of magistrates he toured the tribes (i.e. the electors) with his candidates and canvassed in the traditional way. He used also to cast his vote in his own tribe as if he were an ordinary man.]

18 Tum primum Comitia e campo ad patres translata sunt. Tacit. Annal. i. 15. [Then the elections were transferred from the Assembly to the Senate.] The word *primum* seems to allude to some faint and unsuccessful efforts, which were made towards restoring them to the people.[11]

the Nones, and the Ides. The debates were conducted with decent freedom; and the emperors themselves, who gloried in the name of senators, sat, voted, and divided with their equals.

To resume, in a few words, the system of the Imperial government, as it was instituted by Augustus, and maintained by those princes who understood their own interest and that of the people, it may be defined an absolute monarchy disguised by the forms of a commonwealth. The masters of the Roman world surrounded their throne with darkness, concealed their irresistible strength, and humbly professed themselves the accountable ministers of the senate, whose supreme decrees they dictated and obeyed.[19] *General idea of the Imperial system*

The face of the court corresponded with the forms of the administration. The emperors, if we except those tyrants whose capricious folly violated every law of nature and decency, disdained that pomp and ceremony which might offend their countrymen, but could add nothing to their real power. In all the offices of life, they affected to confound themselves with their subjects, and maintained with them an equal intercourse of visits and entertainments. Their habit, their palace, their table, were suited only to the rank of an opulent senator. Their family, however numerous or splendid, was composed entirely of their domestic slaves and freedmen.[20] Augustus or Trajan would have blushed at employing the meanest of the Romans in those menial offices which, in the household and bedchamber of a limited monarch, are so eagerly solicited by the proudest nobles of Britain. *Court of the emperors*

The deification of the emperors[21] is the only instance in which they departed from their accustomed prudence and modesty. The Asiatic Greeks were the first inventors, the successors of Alexander the first objects, of this servile and impious mode of adulation. It was easily transferred from the kings to the governors of Asia; and the Roman magistrates very frequently were adored as provincial deities, with the pomp of altars and temples, of festivals and sacrifices.[22] It was natural that the emperors should not refuse what the proconsuls had accepted; and the divine honours which both the one and the other received from the provinces attested rather the despotism than the servitude of Rome. But the conquerors soon imitated the vanquished nations in the arts of flattery; and the imperious spirit of the first Cæsar too easily *Deification*

19 Dion Cassius (l. liii. p. 703–714) has given a very loose and partial sketch of the Imperial system. To illustrate and often to correct him, I have meditated Tacitus, examined Suetonius, and consulted the following moderns: the Abbé de la Blèterie in the Mémoires de l'Académie des Inscriptions, tom. xix. xxi. xxiv. xxv. xxvii. Beaufort, République Romaine, tom. i. p. 255–275. The dissertations of Noodt and Gronovius, *de lege Regia*: printed at Leyden, in the year 1731. Gravina de Imperio Romano, p. 479–544 of his Opuscula. Maffei, Verona Illustrata, p. i. p. 245, &c.
20 A weak prince will always be governed by his domestics. The power of slaves aggravated the shame of the Romans; and the senate paid court to a Pallas or a Narcissus. There is a chance that a modern favourite may be a gentleman.
21 See a treatise of Van Dale de Consecratione Principum. It would be easier for me to copy, than it has been to verify, the quotations of that learned Dutchman.
22 See a dissertation of the Abbé Mongault in the first volume of the Academy of Inscriptions.

consented to assume, during his life time, a place among the tutelar deities of Rome. The milder temper of his successor declined so dangerous an ambition, which was never afterwards revived, except by the madness of Caligula and Domitian. Augustus permitted indeed some of the provincial cities to erect temples to his honour, on condition that they should associate the worship of Rome with that of the sovereign; he tolerated private superstition, of which he might be the object;[23] but he contented himself with being revered by the senate and people in his human character, and wisely left to his successor the care of his public deification. A regular custom was introduced that, on the decease of every emperor who had neither lived nor died like a tyrant, the senate by a solemn decree should place him in the number of the gods; and the ceremonies of his apotheosis were blended with those of his funeral. This legal and, as it should seem, injudicious profanation, so abhorrent to our stricter principles, was received with a very faint murmur[24] by the easy nature of Polytheism; but it was received as an institution, not of religion, but of policy. We should disgrace the virtues of the Antonines by comparing them with the vices of Hercules or Jupiter. Even the characters of Cæsar or Augustus were far superior to those of the popular deities. But it was the misfortune of the former to live in an enlightened age, and their actions were too faithfully recorded to admit of such a mixture of fable and mystery as the devotion of the vulgar requires. As soon as their divinity was established by law, it sunk into oblivion, without contributing either to their own fame or to the dignity of succeeding princes.

Titles of *Augustus* and *Caesar*   In the consideration of the Imperial government, we have frequently mentioned the artful founder, under his well-known title of Augustus, which was not however conferred upon him till the edifice was almost completed. The obscure name of Octavianus he derived from a mean family in the little town of Aricia. It was stained with the blood of the proscription; and he was desirous, had it been possible, to erase all memory of his former life. The illustrious surname of Cæsar he had assumed, as the adopted son of the dictator; but he had too much good sense either to hope to be confounded, or to wish to be compared, with that extraordinary man. It was proposed in the senate to dignify their minister with a new appellation; and, after a very serious discussion, that of Augustus was chosen, among several others, as being the most expressive of the character of peace and sanctity which he uniformly affected.[25] *Augustus* was therefore a personal, *Caesar* a family, distinction. The former should naturally have expired with the prince on whom it was bestowed; and, however the latter was diffused by adoption and female alliance, Nero was the last prince who could allege any

---

23 Jurandasque tuum per nomen ponimus *aras* [We set up altars in your name for taking oaths], says Horace to the emperor himself, and Horace was well acquainted with the court of Augustus.

24 See Cicero in Philippic. i. 6. Julian. in Cæsaribus. Inque Deûm templis jurabit Roma per umbras [And Rome will swear by the shades in the temples of the gods] is the indignant expression of Lucan; but it is a patriotic rather than a devout indignation.

25 Dion Cassius, l. liii. p. 710, with the curious Annotations of Reimar.

hereditary claim to the honours of the Julian line. But, at the time of his death, the practice of a century had inseparably connected those appellations with the Imperial dignity, and they have been preserved by a long succession of emperors, – Romans, Greeks, Franks, and Germans, – from the fall of the republic to the present time. A distinction was, however, soon introduced. The sacred title of Augustus was always reserved for the monarch, whilst the name of Cæsar was more freely communicated to his relations; and, from the reign of Hadrian at least, was appropriated to the second person in the state, who was considered as the presumptive heir of the empire.

The tender respect of Augustus for a free constitution which he had destroyed can only be explained by an attentive consideration of the character of that subtle tyrant. A cool head, an unfeeling heart, and a cowardly disposition prompted him at the age of nineteen to assume the mask of hypocrisy, which he never afterwards laid aside. With the same hand, and probably with the same temper, he signed the proscription of Cicero and the pardon of Cinna. His virtues, and even his vices, were artificial; and according to the various dictates of his interest, he was at first the enemy, and at last the father, of the Roman world.[26] When he framed the artful system of the Imperial authority, his moderation was inspired by his fears. He wished to deceive the people by an image of civil liberty, and the armies by an image of civil government. *(margin: Character and policy of Augustus)*

I. The death of Cæsar was ever before his eyes. He had lavished wealth and honours on his adherents; but the most favoured friends of his uncle were in the number of the conspirators. The fidelity of the legions might defend his authority against open rebellion, but their vigilance could not secure his person from the dagger of a determined republican; and the Romans, who revered the memory of Brutus,[27] would applaud the imitation of his virtue. Cæsar had provoked his fate as much by the ostentation of his power as by his power itself. The consul or the tribune might have reigned in peace. The title of king had armed the Romans against his life. Augustus was sensible that mankind is governed by names; nor was he deceived in his expectation that the senate and people would submit to slavery, provided they were respectfully assured that they still enjoyed their ancient freedom. A feeble senate and enervated people cheerfully acquiesced in the pleasing illusion, as long as it was supported by the virtue, or by even the prudence, of the succesors of Augustus. It was a motive of self-preservation, not a principle of liberty, that animated the conspirators against Caligula, Nero, and Domitian. They attacked the person of the *(margin: Image of liberty for the people)*

26 As Octavianus advanced to the banquet of the Cæsars, his colour changed like that of the chameleon; pale at first, then red, afterwards black, he at last assumed the mild livery of Venus and the Graces (Cæsars, p. 309). This image, employed by Julian in his ingenious fiction, is just and elegant; but, when he considers this change of character as real, and ascribes it to the power of philosophy, he does too much honour to philosophy and to Octavianus.

27 Two centuries after the establishment of monarchy, the emperor Marcus Antoninus recommends the character of Brutus as a perfect model of Roman virtue.

GIBBON

tyrant, without aiming their blow at the authority of the emperor.

Attempts of the senate after the death of Caligula

There appears, indeed, *one* memorable occasion, in which the senate, after seventy years of patience, made an ineffectual attempt to re-assume its long-forgotten rights. When the throne was vacant by the murder of Caligula, the consuls convoked that assembly in the Capitol, condemned the memory of the Cæsars, gave the watchword *liberty* to the few cohorts who faintly adhered to their standard, and during eight and forty hours, acted as the independent chiefs of a free common-wealth. But while they deliberated, the prætorian guards had resolved. The stupid Claudius, brother of Germanicus, was already in their camp, invested with the Imperial purple, and prepared to support his election by arms. The dream of liberty was at an end; and the senate awoke to all the horrors, of inevitable servitude. Deserted by the people, and threatened by a military force, that feeble assembly was compelled to ratify the choice of the prætorians, and to embrace the benefit of an amnesty, which Claudius had the prudence to offer, and the generosity to observe.[28]

Image of govern-ment for the armies

II. The insolence of the armies inspired Augustus with fears of a still more alarming nature. The despair of the citizens could only attempt what the power of the soldiers was, at any time, able to execute. How precarious was his own authority over men whom he had taught to violate every social duty! He had heard their seditious clamours; he dreaded their calmer moments of reflection. One revolution had been purchased by immense rewards; but a second revolution might double those rewards. The troops professed the fondest attachment to the house of Cæsar; but the attachments of the multitude are capricious and inconstant. Augustus summoned to his aid whatever remained in those fierce minds of Roman prejudices; enforced the rigour of discipline by the sanction of law; and, interposing the majesty of the senate between the emperor and the army, boldly claimed their allegiance as the first magistrate of the republic.[29]

Their obedience

During a long period of two hundred and twenty years, from the establishment of this artful system to the death of Commodus, the dangers inherent to a military government were, in a great measure, suspended. The soldiers were seldom roused to that fatal sense of their own strength, and of the weakness of the civil authority, which was, before and afterwards, productive of such dreadful calamities. Caligula and Domitian were assassinated in their palace by their own domestics: the convulsions which agitated Rome on the death of the former were confined to the walls of the city. But Nero involved the whole empire in his ruin. In the space of eighteen months four princes perished by the sword; and the Roman world was shaken by the fury of the contending

28 It is much to be regretted that we have lost the part of Tacitus which treated of that transaction. We are forced to content ourselves with the popular rumours of Josephus, and the imperfect hints of Dion and Suetonius.
29 Augustus restored the ancient severity of discipline. After the civil wars, he dropped the endearing name of Fellow-Soldiers, and called them only Soldiers (Sueton. in August. c. 25). See the use Tiberius made of the senate in the mutiny of the Pannonian legions (Tacit. Annal. i.).

armies. Excepting only this short, though violent, eruption of military licence, the two centuries from Augustus to Commodus passed away, unstained with civil blood, and undisturbed by revolutions. The emperor was elected by the *authority of the senate* and *the consent of the soldiers.*[30] The legions respected their oath of fidelity; and it requires a minute inspection of the Roman annals to discover three inconsiderable rebellions, which were all suppressed in a few months, and without even the hazard of a battle.[31]

In elective monarchies, the vacancy of the throne is a moment big Designa-with danger and mischief. The Roman emperors, desirous to spare the tion of a legions that interval of suspense, and the temptation of an irregular successor choice, invested their designed successor with so large a share of present power, as should enable him, after their decease, to assume the remainder without suffering the empire to perceive the change of masters. Thus Augustus, after all his fairer prospects had been snatched Of Tiberius from him by untimely deaths, rested his last hopes on Tiberius, obtained for his adopted son the censorial and tribunitian powers, and dictated a law, by which the future prince was invested with an authority equal to his own over the provinces and the armies.[32] Thus Vespasian subdued the generous mind of his eldest son. Titus was adored by the Of Titus eastern legions, which, under his command, had recently achieved the conquest of Judea. His power was dreaded, and, as his virtues were clouded by the intemperance of youth, his designs were suspected. Instead of listening to such unworthy suspicions, the prudent monarch associated Titus to the full powers of the Imperial dignity; and the grateful son ever approved himself the humble and faithful minister of so indulgent a father.[33]

The good sense of Vespasian engaged him indeed to embrace every The race of measure that might confirm his recent and precarious elevation. The the Caesars military oath, and the fidelity of the troops, had been consecrated, by and the the habits of an hundred years, to the name and family of the Cæsars; family and, although that family had been continued only by the fictitious rite of adoption, the Romans still revered, in the person of Nero, the grandson of Germanicus, and the lineal successor of Augustus. It was not without reluctance and remorse that the prætorian guards had been persuaded to abandon the cause of the tyrant.[34] The rapid downfall of Galba, Otho, and Vitellius, taught the armies to consider the emperors as the creatures of *their* will, and the instruments of *their* licence. The

---

30 These words seem to have been the constitutional language. See Tacit. Annal. xiii. 4.
31 The first was Camillus Scribonianus, who took up arms in Dalmatia against Claudius, and was deserted by his own troops in five days; the second, L. Antonius, in Germany, who rebelled against Domitian; and the third, Avidius Cassius, in the reign of M. Antonnius. The two last reigned but a few months and were cut off by their own adherents. We may observe that both Camillus and Cassius coloured their ambition with the design of restoring the republic, a task, said Cassius, peculiarly reserved for his name and family.
32 Velleius Paterculus, l. ii. c. 121. Sueton. in Tiber. c. 20.
33 Sueton. in Tit. c. 6. Plin. in Præfat. Hist. Natur.
34 This idea is frequently and strongly inculcated by Tacitus. See Hist. i. 5, 16, ii. 76.

birth of Vespasian was mean; his grandfather had been a private soldier, his father a petty officer of the revenue,[35] his own merit had raised him, in an advanced age, to the empire; but his merit was rather useful than shining, and his virtues were disgraced by a strict and even sordid parsimony. Such a prince consulted his true interest by the association of a son whose more splendid and amiable character might turn the public attention from the obscure origin to the future glories of the Flavian house. Under the mild administration of Titus, the Roman world enjoyed a transient felicity, and his beloved memory served to protect, above fifteen years, the vices of his brother Domitian.

A.D. 96.
Adoption and character of Trajan

Nerva had scarcely accepted the purple from the assassins of Domitian before he discovered that his feeble age was unable to stem the torrent of public disorders which had multiplied under the long tyranny of his predecessor. His mild disposition was respected by the good; but the degenerate Romans required a more vigorous character, whose justice should strike terror into the guilty. Though he had several relations, he fixed his choice on a stranger. He adopted Trajan, then about forty years of age, and who commanded a powerful army in the Lower Germany; and immediately, by a decree of the senate,

A.D.98 declared him his colleague and successor in the empire.[36] It is sincerely to be lamented, that, whilst we are fatigued with the disgustful relation of Nero's crimes and follies, we are reduced to collect the actions of Trajan from the glimmerings of an abridgement, or the doubtful light of a panegyric. There remains, however, one panegyric far removed beyond the suspicion of flattery. Above two hundred and fifty years after the death of Trajan, the senate, in pouring out the customary acclamations on the accession of a new emperor, wished that he might surpass the felicity of Augustus, and the virtue of Trajan.[37]

A.D. 117.
Of Hadrian

We may readily believe that the father of his country hesitated whether he ought to intrust the various and doubtful character of his kinsman Hadrian with sovereign power. In his last moments, the arts of the empress Plotina either fixed the irresolution of Trajan, or boldly supposed a fictitious adoption,[38] the truth of which could not be safely disputed; and Hadrian was peaceably acknowledged as his lawful successor. Under his reign, as has been already mentioned, the empire flourished in peace and prosperity. He encouraged the arts, reformed the laws, asserted military discipline, and visited all his provinces in person. His vast and active genius was equally suited to the most

---

35 The emperor Vespasian, with his usual good sense, laughed at the genealogists, who deduced his family from Flavius, the founder of Reate (his native country), and one of the companions of Hercules. Sueton. in Vespasian. c. 12.

36 Dio. l. lxviii. p. 1121. Plin. Secund. in Panegyric.

37 Felicior Augusto, MELIOR TRAJANO. [Happier than Augustus, better than Trajan.] Eutrop. viii. 5.

38 Dion (l. lxix. p. 1249) affirms the whole to have been a fiction, on the authority of his father, who, being governor of the province where Trajan died, had very good opportunities of sifting this mysterious transaction. Yet Dodwell (Prælect. Camden. xvii.) has maintained that Hadrian was called to the certain hope of the empire during the life-time of Trajan.

enlarged views and the minute details of civil policy. But the ruling passions of his soul were curiosity and vanity. As they prevailed, and as they were attracted by different objects, Hadrian was, by turns, an excellent prince, a ridiculous sophist, and a jealous tyrant. The general tenor of his conduct deserved praise for its equity and moderation. Yet, in the first days of his reign, he put to death four consular senators, his personal enemies, and men who had been judged worthy of empire; and the tediousness of a painful illness rendered him, at last, peevish and cruel. The senate doubted whether they should pronounce him a god or a tyrant; and the honours decreed to his memory were granted to the prayers of the pious Antoninus.[39]

The caprice of Hadrian influenced his choice of a successor. After revolving in his mind several men of distinguished merit, whom he esteemed and hated, he adopted Ælius Verus, a gay and voluptuous nobleman, recommended by uncommon beauty to the lover of Antinous.[40] But, whilst Hadrian was delighting himself with his own applause and the acclamations of the soldiers, whose consent had been secured by an immense donative, the new Cæsar[41] was ravished from his embraces by an untimely death. He left only one son. Hadrian commended the boy to the gratitude of the Antonines. He was adopted by Pius; and, on the accession of Marcus, was invested with an equal share of sovereign power. Among the many vices of this younger Verus, he possessed one virtue – a dutiful reverence for his wiser colleague, to whom he willingly abandoned the ruder cares of empire. The philosophic emperor dissembled his follies, lamented his early death, and cast a decent veil over his memory.

Adoption of the elder and younger Verus

As soon as Hadrian's passion was either gratified or disappointed, he resolved to deserve the thanks of posterity by placing the most exalted merit on the Roman throne. His discerning eye easily discovered a senator about fifty years of age, blameless in all the offices of life; and a youth of about seventeen, whose riper years opened the fair prospect of every virtue: the elder of these was declared the son and successor of Hadrian, on condition, however, that he himself should immediately adopt the younger. The two Antonines (for it is of them that we are now speaking) governed the Roman world forty-two years with the same invariable spirit of wisdom and virtue. Although Pius had two sons,[42] he preferred the welfare of Rome to the interest of his family, gave his daughter Faustina in marriage to young Marcus, obtained from the senate the tribunitian and proconsular powers, and, with a noble disdain, or rather ignorance, of jealousy, associated him to all the

Adoption of the two Antonines

A.D. 138–180

39 Dion. l. lxx. p. 1171. Aurel. Victor.
40 The deification of Antinous, his medals, statutes, temples, city, oracles, and constellation, are well known, and still dishonour the memory of Hadrian. Yet we may remark that of the first fifteen emperors Claudius was the only one whose taste in love was entirely correct. For the honours of Antinous, see Spanheim, Commentaires sur les Cæsars de Julien, p. 80.
41 Hist. August. p. 13. Aurelius Victor in Epitom.
42 Without the help of medals and inscriptions, we should be ignorant of this fact, so honourable to the memory of Pius.

labours of government. Marcus, on the other hand, revered the character of his benefactor,loved him as a parent, obeyed him as a sovereign,[43] and, after he was no more, regulated his own administration by the example and maxims of his predecessor. Their united reigns are possibly the only period of history in which the happiness of a great people was the sole object of government.

Character and reign of Pius   Titus Antoninus Pius has been justly denominated a second Numa. The same love of religion, justice, and peace, was the distinguishing characteristic of both princes. But the situation of the latter opened a much larger field for the exercise of those virtues. Numa could only prevent a few neighbouring villages from plundering each other's harvests. Antoninus diffused order and tranquillity over the greatest part of the earth. His reign is marked by the rare advantage of furnishing very few materials for history; which is, indeed, little more than the register of the crimes, follies, and misfortunes of mankind. In private life he was an amiable as well as a good man. The native simplicity of his virtue was a stranger to vanity or affectation. He enjoyed with moderation the conveniences of his fortune, and the innocent pleasures of society;[44] and the benevolence of his soul displayed itself in a cheerful serenity of temper.

Of Marcus   The virtue of Marcus Aurelius Antoninus was of a severer and more laborious kind.[45] It was the well-earned harvest of many a learned conference, of many a patient lecture, and many a midnight lucubration. At the age of twelve years he embraced the rigid system of the Stoics, which taught him to submit his body to his mind, his passions to his reason; to consider virtue as the only good, vice as the only evil, all things external as things indifferent.[46] His Meditations, composed in the tumult of a camp, are still extant; and he even condescended to give lessons on philosophy, in a more public manner than was perhaps consistent with the modesty of a sage or the dignity of an emperor.[47] But his life was the noblest commentary on the precepts of Zeno. He was

43 During the twenty-three years of Pius's reign, Marcus was only two nights absent from the palace, and even those were at different times. Hist. August. p. 25.
44 He was fond of the theatre and not insensible to the charms of the fair sex. Marcus Antoninus, i. 16. Hist. August. p. 20, 21. Julian. in Cæsar.
45 The enemies of Marcus charged him with hypocrisy and with a want of that simplicity which distinguished Pius and even Verus (Hist. Aug. p. 34). This suspicion, unjust as it was, may serve to account for the superior applause bestowed upon personal qualifications, in preference to the social virtues. Even Marcus Antoninus has been called a hypocrite; but the wildest scepticism never insinuated that Cæsar might possibly be a coward, or Tully a fool. Wit and valour are qualifications more easily ascertained than humanity or the love of justice.
46 Tacitus has characterized, in a few words, the principles of the Portico: Doctores sapientiæ secutus est, qui sola bona quæ honesta, mala tantum quæ turpia; potentiam, nobilitatem, cæteraque extra animum, neque bonis neque malis adnumerant. Tacit. Hist. iv. 5. [He followed the teachers of wisdom who consider that moral virtue is the only good just as wickedness alone is evil and that power, noble rank and other things outside the spirit are neither good nor evil.]
47 Before he went on the second expedition against the Germans, he read lectures of philosophy to the Roman people, during three days. He had already done the same in the cities of Greece and Asia. Hist. August. p. 41, in Cassio, c. 3.

severe to himself, indulgent to the imperfection of others, just and beneficent to all mankind. He regretted that Avidius Cassius, who excited a rebellion in Syria, had disappointed him, by a voluntary death, of the pleasure of converting an enemy into a friend; and he justified the sincerity of that sentiment by moderating the zeal of the senate against the adherents of the traitor.[48] War he detested, as the disgrace and calamity of human nature; but when the necessity of a just defence called upon him to take up arms, he readily exposed his person to eight winter campaigns on the frozen banks of the Danube, the severity of which was at last fatal to the weakness of his constitution. His memory was revered by a grateful posterity, and above a century after his death many persons preserved the image of Marcus Antoninus among those of their household gods.[49]

If a man were called to fix the period in the history of the world during which the condition of the human race was most happy and prosperous, he would, without hesitation, name that which elapsed from the death of Domitian to the accession of Commodus. The vast extent of the Roman empire was governed by absolute power, under the guidance of virtue and wisdom. The armies were restrained by the firm but gentle hand of four successive emperors, whose characters and authority commanded involuntary respect. The forms of the civil administration were carefully preserved by Nerva, Trajan, Hadrian, and the Antonines, who delighted in the image of liberty, and were pleased with considering themselves as the accountable ministers of the laws. Such princes deserved the honour of restoring the republic, had the Romans of their days been capable of enjoying a rational freedom. *Happiness of the Romans* *A.D. 96–180*

The labours of these monarchs were over-paid by the immense reward that inseparably waited on their success; by the honest pride of virtue, and by the exquisite delight of beholding the general happiness of which they were the authors. A just but melancholy reflection embittered, however, the noblest of human enjoyments. They must often have recollected the instability of a happiness which depended on the character of a single man. The fatal moment was perhaps approaching, when some licentious youth, or some jealous tyrant, would abuse, to the destruction, that absolute power which they had exerted for the benefit of their people. The ideal restraints of the senate and the laws might serve to display the virtues, but could never correct the vices, of the emperor. The military force was a blind and irresistible instrument of oppression; and the corruption of Roman manners would always supply flatterers eager to applaud, and ministers prepared to serve, the fear or the avarice, the lust or the cruelty, of their masters. *Its precarious nature*

These gloomy apprehensions had been already justified by the experience of the Romans. The annals of the emperors exhibit a strong and various picture of human nature, which we should vainly seek among the mixed and doubtful characters of modern history. In the *Memory of Tiberius, Caligula, Nero, and Domitian*

---

48 Dio. l. lxxi. p. 1190. Hist. August. in Avid. Cassio.
49 Hist. August. in Marc. Antonin. c. 18.

conduct of those monarchs we may trace the utmost lines of vice and virtue; the most exalted perfection and the meanest degeneracy of our own species. The golden age of Trajan and the Antonines had been preceded by an age of iron. It is almost superfluous to enumerate the unworthy successors of Augustus. Their unparalleled vices, and the splendid theatre on which they were acted, have saved them from oblivion. The dark unrelenting Tiberius, the furious Caligula, the stupid Claudius, the profligate and cruel Nero, the beastly Vitellius,[50] and the timid inhuman Domitian are condemned to everlasting infamy. During fourscore years (excepting only the short and doubtful respite of Vespasian's reign),[51] Rome groaned beneath an unremitting tyranny, which exterminated the ancient families of the republic, and was fatal to almost every virtue and every talent that arose in that unhappy period.

Peculiar misery of the Romans under their tyrants

Under the reign of these monsters the slavery of the Romans was accompanied with two peculiar circumstances, the one occasioned by their former liberty, the other by their extensive conquests, which rendered their condition more wretched than that of the victims of tyranny in any other age or country. From these causes were derived, 1. The exquisite sensibility of the sufferers; and 2. The impossibility of escaping from the hand of the oppressor.

Insensibility of the Orientals

I. When Persia was governed by the descendants of Sefi, a race of princes whose wanton cruelty often stained their divan, their table, and their bed with the blood of their favourites, there is a saying recorded of a young nobleman, That he never departed from the sultan's presence without satisfying himself whether his head was still on his shoulders. The experience of every day might almost justify the scepticism of Rustan.[52] Yet the fatal sword, suspended above him by a single thread, seems not to have disturbed the slumbers, or interrupted the tranquillity, of the Persian. The monarch's frown, he well knew, could level him with the dust; but the stroke of lightning or apoplexy might be equally fatal; and it was the part of a wise man to forget the inevitable calamities of human life in the enjoyment of the fleeting hour. He was dignified with the appellation of the king's slave; had, perhaps, been purchased from obscure parents, in a country which he had never known; and was trained up from his infancy in the severe discipline of the seraglio.[53] His

50 Vitellius consumed in mere eating at least six millions of our money, in about seven months. It is not easy to express his vices with dignity, or even decency. Tacitus fairly calls him a hog; but it is by substituting for a coarse word a very fine image. "At Vitellius, umbraculis hortorum abditus, ut *ignava animalia*, quibus si cibum suggeras jacent torpentque, praeterita, instantia, futura, pari oblivione dimiserat. Atque illum nemore Aricino desidem et marcentem," &c. [And Vitellius, withdrawn to the shady places of his country seat, dismissed past, present, and future to complete oblivion, just as idle beasts lie torpid if someone throws food to them. So in sylvan Aricia, apathetic and sated, this man...] Tacit. Hist. iii. 36, ii. 95. Sueton. in Vitell. c. 13. Dio Cassius, 1. lxv. p. 1062.
51 The execution of Helvidius Priscus and of the virtuous Eponina disgraced the reign of Vespasian.
52 Voyage de Chardin en Perse, vol. iii. p. 293.
53 The practice of raising slaves to the great offices of state is still more common among the Turks than among the Persians. The miserable countries of Georgia and Circassia

name, his wealth, his honours, were the gift of a master, who might, without injustice, resume what he had bestowed. Rustan's knowledge, if he possessed any, could only serve to confirm his habits by prejudices. His language afforded not words for any form of government, except absolute monarchy. The history of the East informed him that such had ever been the condition of mankind.[54] The Koran, and the interpreters of that divine book, inculcated to him that the sultan was the descendant of the prophet, and the viceregent of heaven; that patience was the first virtue of a Mussulman, and unlimited obedience the great duty of a subject.

The minds of the Romans were very differently prepared for slavery. Oppressed beneath the weight of their own corruption and of military violence, they for a long while preserved the sentiments, or at least the ideas, of their freeborn ancestors. The education of Helvidius and Thrasea, of Tacitus and Pliny, was the same as that of Cato and Cicero. From Grecian philosophy they had imbibed the justest and most liberal notions of the dignity of human nature and the origin of civil society. The history of their own country had taught them to revere a free, a virtuous, and a victorious commonwealth; to abhor the successful crimes of Cæsar and Augustus; and inwardly to despise those tyrants whom they adored with the most abject flattery. As magistrates and senators, they were admitted into the great council which had once dictated laws to the earth, whose name gave still a sanction to the acts of the monarch, and whose authority was so often prostituted to the vilest purposes of tyranny. Tiberius, and those emperors who adopted his maxims, attempted to disguise their murders by the formalities of justice, and perhaps enjoyed a secret pleasure in rendering the senate their accomplice as well as their victim. By this assembly the last of the Romans were condemned for imaginary crimes and real virtues. Their infamous accusers assumed the language of independent patriots, who arraigned a dangerous citizen before the tribunal of his country; and the public service was rewarded by riches and honours.[55] The servile judges professed to assert the majesty of the commonwealth, violated in the person of its first magistrate,[56] whose clemency they most applauded when they trembled the most at his inexorable and impending cruelty.[57]

Knowledge and free spirit of the Romans

supply rulers to the greatest part of the East.

54 Chardin says that European travellers have diffused among the Persians some ideas of the freedom and mildness of our governments. They have done them a very ill office.

55 They alleged the example of Scipio and Cato (Tacit. Annal. iii. 66). Marcellus Eprius and Crispius Vibius had acquired two millions and a half under Nero. Their wealth, which aggravated their crimes, protected them under Vespasian. See Tacit. Hist. iv. 43, Dialog. de Orator. c. 8. For one accusation, Regulus, the just object of Pliny's satire, received from the senate the consular ornaments, and a present of sixty thousand pounds.

56 The crime of *majesty* was formerly a treasonable offence against the Roman people. As tribunes of the people, Augustus and Tiberius applied it to their own persons, and extended it to an infinite latitude.

57 After the virtuous and unfortunate widow of Germanicus had been put to death, Tiberius received the thanks of the senate for his clemency. She had not been publicly strangled; nor was the body drawn with a hook to the Gemoniæ, where those of common malefactors were exposed. See Tacit. Annal. vi. 25. Sueton. in Tiberio, c. 53.

The tyrant beheld their baseness with just contempt, and encountered their secret sentiments of detestation with sincere and avowed hatred for the whole body of the senate.

Extent of their empire left them no place of refuge

II. The division of Europe into a number of independent states, connected, however, with each other, by the general resemblance of religion, language and manners, is productive of the most beneficial consequences to the liberty of mankind. A modern tyrant, who should find no resistance either in his own breast or in his people, would soon experience a gentle restraint from the example of his equals, the dread of present censure, the advice of his allies, and the apprehension of his enemies. The object of his displeasure, escaping from the narrow limits of his dominions, would easily obtain, in a happier climate, a secure refuge, a new fortune adequate to his merit, the freedom of complaint, and perhaps the means of revenge. But the empire of the Romans filled the world, and, when that empire fell into the hands of a single person, the world became a safe and dreary prison for his enemies. The slave of Imperial despotism, whether he was condemned to drag his gilded chain in Rome and the senate, or to wear out a life of exile on the barren rock of Seriphus or the frozen banks of the Danube, expected his fate in silent despair.[58] To resist was fatal, and it was impossible to fly. On every side he was encompassed with a vast extent of sea and land, which he could never hope to traverse without being discovered, seized, and restored to his irritated master. Beyond the frontiers, his anxious view could discover nothing, except the ocean, inhospitable deserts, hostile tribes of barbarians, of fierce manners and unknown language, or dependent kings, who would gladly purchase the emperor's protection by the sacrifice of an obnoxious fugitive.[59] "Wherever you are," said Cicero to the exiled Marcellus, "remember that you are equally within the power of the conqueror."[60]

58 Seriphus was a small rocky island in the Ægean Sea, the inhabitants of which were despised for their ignorance and obscurity. The place of Ovid's exile is well known by his just but unmanly lamentations. It should seem that he only received an order to leave Rome in so many days, and to transport himself to Tomi. Guards and gaolers were unnecessary.
59 Under Tiberius, a Roman knight attempted to fly to the Parthians. He was stopt in the straits of Sicily; but so little danger did there appear in the example, that the most jealous of tyrants disdained to punish it. Tacit. Annal. vi. 14.
60 Cicero ad Familiares, iv. 7.

CHAPTER IX

The State of Germany till the Invasion of the Barbarians, in the Time of the Emperor Decius

The government and religion of Persia have deserved some notice from their connexion with the decline and fall of the Roman empire. We shall occasionally mention the Scythian or Sarmatian tribes, which, with their arms and horses, their flocks and herds, their wives and families, wandered over the immense plains which spread themselves from the Caspian Sea to the Vistula, from the confines of Persia to those of Germany. But the warlike Germans, who first resisted, then invaded, and at length overturned, the Western monarchy of Rome, will occupy a much more important place in this history, and possess a stronger, and, if we may use the expression, a more domestic, claim to our attention and regard. The most civilized nations of modern Europe issued from the woods of Germany, and in the rude institutions of those barbarians we may still distinguish the original principles of our present laws and manners. In their primitive state of simplicity and independence, the Germans were surveyed by the discerning eye, and delineated by the masterly pencil, of Tacitus, the first of historians who applied the science of philosophy to the study of facts. The expressive conciseness of his descriptions has deserved to exercise the diligence of innumerable antiquarians, and to excite the genius and penetration of the philosophic historians of our own times. The subject, however various and important, has already been so frequently, so ably, and so successfully discussed, that it is now grown familiar to the reader, and difficult to the writer. We shall therefore content ourselves with observing, and indeed with repeating, some of the most important circumstances of climate, of manners, and of institutions, which rendered the wild barbarians of Germany such formidable enemies to the Roman power.

Ancient Germany, excluding from its independent limits the province westward of the Rhine, which had submitted to the Roman yoke, extended itself over a third part of Europe. Almost the whole of modern Germany, Denmark, Norway, Sweden, Finland, Livonia, Prussia, and the greater part of Poland, were peopled by the various tribes of one great nation, whose complexion, manners, and language denoted a common origin, and preserved a striking resemblance. On the west, ancient Germany was divided by the Rhine from the Gallic, and on the south by the Danube from the Illyrian, provinces of the empire. A ridge of hills, rising from the Danube, and called the Carpathian Mountains, covered Germany on the side of Dacia or Hungary. The eastern frontier was faintly marked by the mutual fears of the Germans and the Sarmatians, and was often confounded by the mixture of warring and confederating tribes of the two nations. In the remote darkness of the north the ancients imperfectly descried a frozen ocean that lay beyond the Baltic Sea and beyond the peninsula, or islands,[1] of Scandinavia.

Extent of Germany

---

1 The modern philosophers of Sweden seem agreed that the waters of the Baltic gradually sink in a regular proportion, which they have ventured to estimate at half an inch every year. Twenty centuries ago, the flat country of Scandinavia must have been covered by the sea; while the high lands rose above the waters, as so many islands of various forms and dimensions. Such indeed is the notion given us by Mela, Pliny, and Tacitus, of the vast countries round the Baltic. See in the Bibliothèque Raisonnée, tom. xl. and xlv., a large abstract of Dalin's History of Sweden, composed in the Swedish language.

Climate   Some ingenious writers[2] have suspected that Europe was much colder formerly than it is at present; and the most ancient descriptions of the climate of Germany tend exceedingly to confirm their theory. The general complaints of intense frost and eternal winter are perhaps little to be regarded, since we have no method of reducing to the accurate standard of the thermometer the feelings or the expressions of an orator born in the happier regions of Greece or Asia. But I shall select two remarkable circumstances of a less equivocal nature. 1. The great rivers which covered the Roman provinces, the Rhine and the Danube, were frequently frozen over, and capable of supporting the most enormous weights. The barbarians, who often chose that severe season for their inroads, transported, without apprehension or danger, their numerous armies, their cavalry, and their heavy waggons, over a vast and solid bridge of ice.[3] Modern ages have not presented an instance of a like phenomenon. 2. The reindeer, that useful animal, from whom the savage of the North derives the best comforts of his dreary life, is of a constitution that supports, and even requires, the most intense cold. He is found on the rock of Spitzberg, within ten degrees of the pole; he seems to delight in the snows of Lapland and Siberia; but at present he cannot subsist, much less multiply, in any country to the south of the Baltic.[4] In the time of Cæsar, the reindeer, as well as the elk and the wild bull, was a native of the Hercynian forest, which then overshadowed a great part of Germany and Poland.[5] The modern improvements sufficiently explain the causes of the diminution of the cold. These immense woods have been gradually cleared, which intercepted from the earth the rays of the sun.[6] The morasses have been drained, and, in proportion as the soil has been cultivated, the air has become more temperate. Canada, at this day, is an exact picture of ancient Germany. Although situate in the same parallel with the finest provinces of France and England, that country experiences the most rigorous cold. The reindeer are very numerous, the ground is covered with deep and lasting snow, and the great river of St. Lawrence is regularly frozen, in a season when the waters of the Seine and the Thames are usually free from ice.[7]

Its effects on the natives   It is difficult to ascertain, and easy to exaggerate, the influence of the climate of ancient Germany over the minds and bodies of the natives.

2 In particular, Mr. Hume, and the Abbé du Bos, and M. Pelloutier, Hist. des Celtes, tom. i.
3 Diodorus Siculus, l. v. p. 340, edit. Wessel. Herodian l. vi. p. 221. Jornandes, c. 55. On the banks of the Danube, the wine, when brought to table, was frequently frozen into great lumps, *frusta vini*. Ovid Epist. ex Ponto, l. iv. 7, 7–10. Virgil Georgic. l. iii. 355. The fact is confirmed by a soldier and a philosopher, who had experienced the intense cold of Thrace. See Xenophon, Anabasis, l. vii. p. 560, edit. Hutchinson.
4 Buffon, Histoire Naturelle, tom. xii. p. 79, 116.
5 Cæsar de Bell. Gallic. vi. 23, &c. The most inquisitive of the Germans were ignorant of its utmost limits, although some of them had travelled in it more than sixty days' journey.
6 Cluverius (Germania Antiqua, l. iii. c. 47) investigates the small and scattered remains of the Hercynian Wood.
7 Charlevoix, Histoire du Canada.

Many writers have supposed, and most have allowed, though, as it should seem, without any adequate proof, that the rigorous cold of the North was favourable to long life and generative vigour, that the women were more fruitful, and the human species more prolific, than in warmer or more temperate climates.[8] We may assert, with greater confidence, that the keen air of Germany formed the large and masculine limbs of the natives, who were, in general, of a more lofty stature than the people of the South,[9] gave them a kind of strength better adapted to violent exertions than to patient labour, and inspired them with constitutional bravery, which is the result of nerves and spirits. The severity of a winter campaign, that chilled the courage of the Roman troops, was scarcely felt by these hardy children of the North,[10] who, in their turn, were unable to resist the summer heats, and dissolved away in languor and sickness under the beams of an Italian sun.[11]

There is not anywhere upon the globe a large tract of country which we have discovered destitute of inhabitants or whose first population can be fixed with any degree of historical certainty. And yet, as the most philosophic minds can seldom refrain from investigating the infancy of great nations, our curiosity consumes itself in toilsome and disappointed efforts. When Tacitus considered the purity of the German blood, and the forbidding aspect of the country, he was disposed to pronounce those barbarians *Indigenoe*, or natives of the soil. We may allow with safety, and perhaps with truth, that ancient Germany was not originally peopled by any foreign colonies already formed into a political society;[12] but that the name and nation received their existence from the gradual union of some wandering savages of the Hercynian woods. To assert those savages to have been the spontaneous production of the earth which they inhabited would be a rash inference, condemned by religion, and unwarranted by reason. *Origin of the Germans*

Such rational doubt is but ill suited with the genius of popular vanity. Among the nations who have adopted the Mosaic history of the world, the ark of Noah has been of the same use, as was formerly to the Greeks and Romans the siege of Troy. On a narrow basis of acknowledged truth, an immense but rude superstructure of fable has been erected; *Fables and conjectures*

---

8 Olaus Rudbeck asserts that the Swedish women often bear ten or twelve children, and not uncommonly twenty or thirty; but the authority of Rudbeck is much to be suspected.
9 In hos artus, in hæc corpora, quæ miramur, excrescunt. [They develop those limbs and that physique which we so much admire.] Tacit. Germania, c. 20. Cluver. l. i. c. 14.
10 Plutarch. in Mario. The Cimbri, by way of amusement, often slid down mountains of snow on their broad shields.
11 The Romans made war in all climates, and by their excellent discipline were in a great measure preserved in health and vigour. It may be remarked that man is the only animal which can live and multiply in every country from the equator to the poles. The hog seems to approach the nearest to our species in that privilege.
12 Tacit. German. c. 3. The emigration of the Gauls followed the course of the Danube, and discharged itself on Greece and Asia. Tacitus could discover only one inconsiderable tribe that retained any traces of a Gallic origin.

and the wild Irishman,[13] as well as the wild Tartar,[14] could point out the individual son of Japhet from whose loins his ancestors were lineally descended. The last century abounded with antiquarians of profound learning and easy faith, who, by the dim light of legends and traditions, of conjectures and etymologies, conducted the great-grandchildren of Noah from the Tower of Babel to the extremities of the globe. Of these judicious critics, one of the most entertaining was Olaus Rudbeck, professor in the university of Upsal.[15] Whatever is celebrated either in history or fable, this zealous patriot ascribes to his country. From Sweden (which formed so considerable a part of ancient Germany) the Greeks themselves derived their alphabetical characters, their astronomy, and their religion. Of that delightful region (for such it appeared to the eyes of a native) the Atlantis of Plato, the country of the Hyperboreans, the gardens of the Hesperides, the Fortunate Islands, and even the Elysian Fields, were all but faint and imperfect transcripts. A clime so profusely favoured by Nature could not long remain desert after the flood. The learned Rudbeck allows the family of Noah a few years to multiply from eight to about twenty thousand persons. He then disperses them into small colonies to replenish the earth, and to propagate the human species. The German or Swedish detachment (which marched, if I am not mistaken, under the command of Askenaz the son of Gomer, the son of Japhet) distinguished itself by a more than common diligence in the prosecution of this great work. The northern hive cast its swarms over the greatest part of Europe, Africa, and Asia; and (to use the author's metaphor) the blood circulated back from the extremities to the heart.

The Germans ignorant of letters   But all this well-laboured system of German antiquities is annihilated by a single fact, too well attested to admit of any doubt, and of too decisive a nature to leave room for any reply. The Germans, in the age of Tacitus, were unacquainted with the use of letters;[16] and the use of letters is the principal circumstance that distinguishes a civilized people

13 According to Dr. Keating (History of Ireland, p. 13, 14), the giant Partholanus, who was the son of Seara, the son of Esra, the son of Sru, the son of Framant, the son of Fathaclan, the son of Magog, the son of Japhet, the son of Noah, landed on the coast of Munster, the 14th day of May in the year of the world one thousand nine hundred and seventy-eight. Though he succeeded in his great enterprise, the loose behaviour of his wife rendered his domestic life very unhappy, and provoked him to such a degree, that he killed – her favourite greyhound. This, as the learned historian very properly observes, was the *first* instance of female falsehood and infidelity ever known in Ireland.

14 Genealogical History of the Tartars by Abulghazi Bahadur Khan.

15 His work, entitled Atlantica, is uncommonly scarce. Bayle has given two most curious extracts from it. République des Lettres, Janvier et Février, 1685.

16 Tacit. Germ. ii. 19. Literarum secreta viri pariter ac fœminæ ignorant. [Both the men and women are equally ignorant of the mysteries of the alphabet.] We may rest contented with this decisive authority, without entering into the obscure disputes concerning the antiquity of the Runic characters. The learned Celsius, a Swede, a scholar and a philosopher, was of opinion, that they were nothing more than the Roman letters, with the curves changed into straight lines for the ease of engraving. See Pelloutier, Histoire des Celtes, l. ii. c. 11. Dictionnaire Diplomatique, tom. i. p. 223. We may add, that the oldest Runic inscriptions are supposed to be of the third century, and the most ancient writer who mentions the Runic characters is Venantius Fortunatus (Carm. vii. 18), who

from a herd of savages, incapable of knowledge or reflection. Without that artificial help the human memory soon dissipates or corrupts the ideas intrusted to her charge; and the nobler faculties of the mind, no longer supplied with models or with materials, gradually forget their powers: the judgment becomes feeble and lethargic, the imagination languid or irregular. Fully to apprehend this important truth, let us attempt, in an improved society, to calculate the immense distance between the man of learning and the *illiterate* peasant. The former, by reading and reflection, multiplies his own experience, and lives in distant ages and remove countries; whilst the latter, rooted to a single spot, and confined to a few years of existence, surpasses but very little his fellow-labourer the ox in the exercise of his mental faculties. The same and even a greater difference will be found between nations than between individuals; and we may safely pronounce that without some species of writing no people has ever preserved the faithful annals of their history, ever made any considerable progress in the abstract sciences, or ever possessed, in any tolerable degree of perfection, the useful and agreeable arts of life.

Of these arts the ancient Germans were wretchedly destitute. They passed their lives in a state of ignorance and poverty, which it has pleased some declaimers to dignify with the appellation of virtuous simplicity. Modern Germany is said to contain about two thousand three hundred walled towns.[17] In a much wider extent of country the geographer Ptolemy could discover no more than ninety places which he decorates with the name of cities;[18] though, according to our ideas, they would but ill deserve that splendid title. We can only suppose them to have been rude fortifications, constructed in the centre of the woods, and designed to secure the women, children, and cattle, whilst the warriors of the tribe marched out to repel a sudden invasion.[19] But Tacitus asserts, as a well-known fact, that the Germans, in his time, had *no* cities;[20] and that they affected to despise the works of Roman industry as places of confinement rather than of security.[21] Their edifices were not even contiguous, or formed into regular villas;[22] each barbarian fixed his independent dwelling on the spot to which a plain, a wood, or a stream of fresh water had induced him to give the

of arts and agriculture

lived towards the end of the sixth century.

Barbara fraxineis pingatur RUNA tabellis. [There are strange Runic inscriptions on ashwood tablets.]

17 Recherches Philosophiques sur les Américains, tom. iii. p. 228. The author of that very curious work is, if I am not misinformed, a German by birth.

18 The Alexandrian Geographer is often criticized by the accurate Cluverius.

19 See Cæsar, and the learned Mr. Whitaker in his history of Manchester, vol. i.

20 Tacit. Germ. 16.

21 When the Germans commanded the Ubii of Cologne to cast off the Roman yoke, and with their new freedom to resume their ancient manners, they insisted on the immediate demolition of the walls of the colony. "Postulamus a vobis, muros coloniæ, munimenta servitii, detrahatis; etiam fera animalia, si clausa teneas, virtutis obliviscuntur." [We ask you to demolish the walls of the colonia[12] which keeps you in servitude; for even wild animals forget their courage if they are kept in captivity.] Tacit. Hist. iv. 64.

22 The straggling villages of Silesia are several miles in length. See Cluver.l. i. c. 13.

preference. Neither stone, nor brick, nor tiles were employed in these slight habitations.[23] They were indeed no more than low huts of a circular figure, built of rough timber, thatched with straw, and pierced at the top to leave a free passage for the smoke. In the most inclement winter, the hardy German was satisfied with a scanty garment made of the skin of some animal. The nations who dwelt towards the North clothed themselves in furs; and the women manufactured for their own use a coarse kind of linen.[24] The game of various sorts with which the forests of Germany were plentifully stocked supplied its inhabitants with food and exercise.[25] Their monstrous herds of cattle, less remarkable indeed for their beauty than for their utility,[26] formed the principal object of their wealth. A small quantity of corn was the only produce exacted from the earth: the use of orchards or artificial meadows was unknown to the Germans; nor can we expect any improvements in agriculture from a people whose property every year experienced a general change by a new division of the arable lands, and who, in that strange operation, avoided disputes by suffering a great part of their territory to lie waste and without tillage.[27]

and of the use of metals Gold, silver, and iron were extremely scarce in Germany. Its barbarous inhabitants wanted both skill and patience to investigate those rich veins of silver, which have so liberally rewarded the attention of the princes of Brunswick and Saxony. Sweden, which now supplies Europe with iron, was equally ignorant of its own riches; and the appearance of the arms of the Germans furnished a sufficient proof how little iron they were able to bestow on what they must have deemed the noblest use of that metal. The various transactions of peace and war had introduced some Roman coins (chiefly silver) among the borderers of the Rhine and Danube; but the more distant tribes were absolutely unacquainted with the use of money, carried on their confined traffic by the exchange of commodities, and prized their rude earthen vessels as of equal value with the silver vases, the presents of Rome to their princes and ambassadors.[28] To a mind capable of reflection such leading facts convey more instruction than a tedious detail of subordinate circumstances. The value of money has been settled by general consent to express our wants and our property, as letters were invented to express our ideas; and both these institutions, by giving more active energy to the powers and passions of human nature, have contributed to multiply the objects they were designed to represent. The use of gold and silver is in a great measure factitious; but it would be impossible to enumerate the important and various services which agriculture, and all the arts, have received from iron, when tempered and fashioned by the

23 One hundred and forty years after Tacitus a few more regular structures were erected near the Rhine and Danube. Herodian, l. vii. p. 234.
24 Tacit. Germ. 17.
25 Tacit. Germ. 5.
26 Cæsar de Bell. Gall. vi. 21.
27 Tacit. Germ. 26. Cæsar, vi. 22.
28 Tacit. Germ. 5.

operation of fire and the dexterous hand of man. Money, in a word, is the most universal incitement, iron the most powerful instrument, of human industry; and it is very difficult to conceive by what means a people, neither actuated by the one nor seconded by the other, could emerge from the grossest barbarism.[29]

If we contemplate a savage nation in any part of the globe, a supine indolence and a carelessness of futurity will be found to constitute their general character. In a civilized state every faculty of man is expanded and exercised; and the great chain of mutual dependence connects and embraces the several members of society. The most numerous portion of it is employed in constant and useful labour. The select few, placed by fortune above that necessity, can, however, fill up their time by the pursuits of interest or glory, by the improvement of their estate or of their understanding, by the duties, the pleasures, and even the follies, of social life. The Germans were not possessed of these varied resources. The care of the house and family, the management of the land and cattle, were delegated to the old and the infirm, to women and slaves. The lazy warrior, destitute of every art that might employ his leisure hours, consumed his days and nights in the animal gratifications of sleep and food. And yet, by a wonderful diversity of nature (according to the remark of a writer who had pierced into its darkest recesses), the same barbarians are by turns the most indolent and the most restless of mankind. They delight in sloth, they detest tranquillity.[30] The languid soul, oppressed with its own weight, anxiously required some new and powerful sensation; and war and danger were the only amusements adequate to its fierce temper. The sound that summoned the German to arms was grateful to his ear. It roused him from his uncomfortable lethargy, gave him an active pursuit, and, by strong exercise of the body, and violent emotions of the mind, restored him to a more lively sense of his existence. In the dull intervals of peace these barbarians were immoderately addicted to deep gaming and excessive drinking; both of which, by different means, the one by inflaming their passions, the other by extinguishing their reason, alike relieved them from the pain of thinking. They gloried in passing whole days and nights at table; and the blood of friends and relations often stained their numerous and drunken assemblies.[31] Their debts of honour (for in that light they have transmitted to us those of play) they discharged with the most romantic fidelity. The desperate gamester, who had staked his person and liberty on a last throw of the dice, patiently submitted to the decision of fortune, and suffered himself to be bound, chastised, and sold into remote slavery, by his weaker but more lucky antagonist.[32]

Their indolence

29 It is said that the Mexicans and Peruvians, without the use of either money or iron, had made a very great progress in the arts. Those arts, and the monuments they produced, have been strangely magnified. See Recherches sur les Américains, tom. ii. p. 153, &c.
30 Tacit. Germ. 15.
31 Tacit. Germ. 22, 23.
32 Tacit. Germ. 24. The Germans might borrow the *arts* of play from the Romans, but the *passion* is wonderfully inherent in the human species.

Their taste for strong liquors   Strong beer, a liquor extracted with very little art from wheat or barley, and *corrupted* (as it is strongly expressed by Tacitus) into a certain semblance of wine, was sufficient for the gross purposes of German debauchery. But those who had tasted the rich wines of Italy, and afterwards of Gaul, sighed for that more delicious species of intoxication. They attempted not, however (as has since been executed with so much success), to naturalize the vine on the banks of the Rhine and Danube; nor did they endeavour to procure by industry the materials of an advantageous commerce. To solicit by labour what might be ravished by arms was esteemed unworthy of the German spirit.[33] The intemperate thirst of strong liquors often urged the barbarians to invade the provinces on which art or nature had bestowed those much envied presents. The Tuscan who betrayed his country to the Celtic nations attracted them into Italy by the prospect of the rich fruits and delicious wines, the productions of a happier climate.[34] And in the same manner the German auxiliaries, invited into France during the civil wars of the sixteenth century, were allured by the promise of plenteous quarters in the provinces of Champagne and Burgundy.[35] Drunkenness, the most illiberal but not the most dangerous of *our* vices, was sometimes capable, in a less civilized state of mankind, of occasioning a battle, a war, or a revolution.

State of population   The climate of ancient Germany has been mollified, and the soil fertilized, by the labour of ten centuries from the time of Charlemagne. The same extent of ground, which at present maintains, in ease and plenty, a million of husbandmen and artificers, was unable to supply an hundred thousand lazy warriors with the simple necessaries of life.[36] The Germans abandoned their immense forests to the exercise of hunting, employed in pasturage the most considerable part of their lands, bestowed on the small remainder a rude and careless cultivation, and then accused the scantiness and sterility of a country that refused to maintain the multitude of its inhabitants. When the return of famine severely admonished them of the importance of the arts, the national distress was sometimes alleviated by the emigration of a third, perhaps, or a fourth part of their youth.[37] The possession and the enjoyment of property are the pledges which bind a civilized people to an improved country. But the Germans, who carried with them what they most valued, their arms, their cattle, and their women, cheerfully abandoned the vast silence of their woods for the unbounded hopes of plunder and conquest. The innumerable swarms, that issued, or seemed to issue,

33 Tacit. Germ. 14.
34 Plutarch. in Camillo. T. Liv. v. 33.
35 Dubos, Hist. de la Monarchie Françoise, tom. i. p. 193.
36 The Helvetian nation, which issued from the country called Switzerland, contained, of every age and sex, 368,000 persons (Cæsar de Bell. Gall. i. 29). At present, the number of people in the Pays de Vaud (a small district on the banks of the Leman Lake, much more distinguished for politeness than for industry) amounts to 112,591. See an excellent Tract of M. Muret, in the Mémoires de la Société de Berne.
37 Paul Diaconus, c. 1, 2, 3. Machiavel, Davila, and the rest of Paul's followers, represent these emigrations too much as regular and concerted measures.

from the great storehouse of nations, were multiplied by the fears of the vanquished and by the credulity of succeeding ages. And from facts thus exaggerated, an opinion was gradually established, and has been supported by writers of distinguished reputation, that, in the age of Cæsar and Tacitus, the inhabitants of the North were far more numerous than they are in our days.[38] A more serious inquiry into the causes of population seems to have convinced modern philosophers of the falsehood, and indeed the impossibility, of the supposition. To the names of Mariana and of Machiavel[39] we can oppose the equal names of Robertson and Hume.[40]

A warlike nation like the Germans, without either cities, letters, arts, or money, found some compensation for this savage state in the enjoyment of liberty. Their poverty secured their freedom, since our desires and our possessions are the strongest fetters of despotism. "Among the Suiones (says Tacitus) riches are held in honour. They are *therefore* subject to an absolute monarch, who instead of intrusting his people with the free use of arms, as is practised in the rest of Germany, commits them to the safe custody, not of a citizen, or even of a freedman, but of a slave. The neighbours of the Suiones, the Sitones, are sunk even below servitude; they obey a woman."[41] In the mention of these exceptions, the great historian sufficiently acknowledges the general theory of government. We are only at a loss to conceive by what means riches and despotism could penetrate into a remote corner of the North, and extinguish the generous flame that blazed with such fierceness on the frontier of the Roman provinces, or how the ancestors of those Danes and Norwegians, so distinguished in later ages by their unconquered spirit, could thus tamely resign the great character of German liberty.[42] Some tribes, however, on the coast of the Baltic, acknowledged the authority of kings, though without relinquishing the rights of men;[43] but in the far greater part of Germany the form of government was a democracy, tempered, indeed, and controlled, not so much by general and positive laws as by the occasional ascendant of birth or valour, of eloquence or superstition.[44]

Civil governments, in their first institutions, are voluntary associ-

German freedom

Assemblies of the people

38 Sir William Temple and Montesquieu have indulged, on this subject, the usual liveliness of their fancy.
39 Machiavel, Hist. di Firenze, l. i. Mariana, Hist. Hispan. l. v. c. l.
40 Robertson's Cha. V. Hume's Politic. Ess.
41 Tacit. Germ. 44, 45. Freinshemius (who dedicated his supplement to Livy, to Christina of Sweden) thinks proper to be very angry with the Roman who expressed so very little reverence for Northern queens.
42 May we not suspect that superstition was the parent of despotism? The descendants of Odin (whose race was not extinct till the year 1060) are said to have reigned in Sweden above a thousand years. The temple of Upsal was the ancient seat of religion and empire. In the year 1153 I find a singular law prohibiting the use and possession of arms to any, except the king's guards. Is it not probable that it was coloured by the pretence of reviving an old institution? See Dalin's History of Sweden in the Bibliothèque Raisonnée, tom. xi. and xiv.
43 Tacit. Germ. c. 43.
44 Id. c. 11, 12, 13, &c.

ations for mutual defence. To obtain the desired end it is absolutely necessary that each individual should conceive himself obliged to submit his private opinion and actions to the judgment of the greater number of his associates. The German tribes were contented with this rude but liberal outline of political society. As soon as a youth, born of free parents, had attained the age of manhood, he was introduced into the general council of his countrymen, solemnly invested with a shield and spear, and adopted as an equal and worthy member of the military commonwealth. The assembly of the warriors of the tribe was convened at stated seasons, or on sudden emergencies. The trial of public offences, the election of magistrates, and the great business of peace and war, were determined by its independent voice. Sometimes, indeed, these important questions were previously considered and prepared in a more select council of the principal chieftains.[45] The magistrates might deliberate and persuade, the people only could resolve and execute; and the resolutions of the Germans were for the most part hasty and violent. Barbarians accustomed to place their freedom in gratifying the present passion, and their courage in overlooking all future consequences, turned away with indignant contempt from the remonstrances of justice and policy, and it was the practice to signify by a hollow murmur their dislike of such timid councils. But, whenever a more popular orator proposed to vindicate the meanest citizen from either foreign or domestic injury, whenever he called upon his fellow-countrymen to assert the national honour, or to pursue some enterprise full of danger and glory, a loud clashing of shields and spears expressed the eager applause of the assembly. For the Germans always met in arms, and it was constantly to be dreaded lest an irregular multitude, inflamed with faction and strong liquors, should use those arms to enforce, as well as to declare, their furious resolves. We may recollect how often the diets of Poland have been polluted with blood, and the more numerous party has been compelled to yield to the more violent and seditious.[46]

Authority of the princes and magistrates

A general of the tribe was elected on occasions of danger; and, if the danger was pressing and extensive, several tribes concurred in the choice of the same general. The bravest warrior was named to lead his countrymen into the field, by his example rather than by his commands. But this power, however limited, was still invidious. It expired with the war, and in time of peace, the German tribes acknowledged not any supreme chief.[47] *Princes* were, however, appointed, in the general assembly, to administer justice, or rather to compose differences,[48] in their respective districts. In the choice of these magistrates as much

---

45 Grotius changes an expression of Tacitus, pertractantur into prætractantur.[13] The correction is equally just and ingenious.

46 Even in *our* ancient parliament, the barons often carried a question not so much by the number of votes as by that of their armed followers.

47 Cæsar de Bell. Gall. vi. 23.

48 Minuunt controversias is a very happy expression of Cæsar's.

regard was shown to birth as to merit.[49] To each was assigned, by the public, a guard, and a council of an hundred persons, and the first of the princes appears to have enjoyed a pre-eminence of rank and honour which sometimes tempted the Romans to compliment him with the regal title.[50]

The comparative view of the powers of the magistrates, in two remarkable instances, is alone sufficient to represent the whole system of German manners. The disposal of the landed property within their district was absolutely vested in their hands, and they distributed it every year according to a new division.[51] At the same time they were not authorized to punish with death, to imprison, or even to strike a private citizen.[52] A people thus jealous of their persons, and careless of their possessions, must have been totally destitute of industry and the arts, but animated with a high sense of honour and independence. *more absolute over the property than over the persons of the Germans*

The Germans respected only those duties which they imposed on themselves. The most obscure soldier resisted with disdain the authority of the magistrates. "The noblest youths blushed not to be numbered among the faithful companions of some renowned chief, to whom they devoted their arms and service. A noble emulation prevailed, among the companions to obtain the first place in the esteem of their chief; amongst the chiefs, to acquire the greatest number of valiant companions. To be ever surrounded by a band of select youths was the pride and strength of the chiefs, their ornament in peace, their defence in war. The glory of such distinguished heroes diffused itself beyond the narrow limits of their own tribe. Presents and embassies solicited their friendship, and the fame of their arms often ensured victory to the party which they espoused. In the hour of danger it was shameful for the chief to be surpassed in valour by his companions; shameful for the companions not to equal the valour of their chief. To survive his fall in battle was indelible infamy. To protect his person, and to adorn his glory with the trophies of their own exploits, were the most sacred of their duties. The chiefs combated for victory, the companions for the chief. The noblest warriors, whenever their native country was sunk in the laziness of peace, maintained their numerous bands in some distant scene of action, to exercise their restless spirit, and to acquire renown by voluntary dangers. Gifts worthy of soldiers, the warlike steed, the bloody and ever victorious lance, were the rewards which the companions claimed from the liberality of their chief. The rude plenty of his hospitable board was the only pay that *he* could bestow, or they would accept. War, rapine, and the free-will offerings of his friends, supplied the materials of this munificence."[53] This institution, however it might accidentally weaken the several republics, invigorated the general *Voluntary engagements*

---

49 Reges ex nobilitate, duces ex virtute sumunt [They choose their kings for their noble birth, their military leaders for their courage.] Tacit. Germ. 7.
50 Cluver, Germ. Ant. l. i. c. 38.
51 Cæsar, vi. 22. Tacit. Germ. 26.
52 Tacit. Germ. 7.
53 Tacit. Germ. 13, 14.

character of the Germans, and even ripened amongst them all the virtues of which barbarians are susceptible – the faith and valour, the hospitality and the courtesy, so conspicuous long afterwards in the ages of chivalry. The honourable gifts, bestowed by the chief on his brave companions, have been supposed, by an ingenious writer, to contain the first rudiments of the fiefs, distributed after the conquest of the Roman provinces, by the barbarian lords among their vassals, with a similar duty of homage and military service.[54] These conditions are, however, very repugnant to the maxims of the ancient Germans, who delighted in mutual presents; but without either imposing or accepting the weight of obligations.[55]

German chastity "In the days of chivalry, or more properly of romance, all the men were brave, and all the women were chaste;" and, notwithstanding the latter of these virtues is acquired and preserved with much more difficulty than the former, it is ascribed, almost without exception, to the wives of the ancient Germans. Polygamy was not in use, except among the princes, and among them only for the sake of multiplying their alliances. Divorces were prohibited by manners rather than by laws. Adulteries were punished as rare and inexpiable crimes; nor was seduction justified by example and fashion.[56] We may easily discover that Tacitus indulges an honest pleasure in the contrast of barbarian virtue with the dissolute conduct of the Roman ladies: yet there are some striking circumstances that give an air of truth, or at least of probability, to the conjugal faith and chastity of the Germans.

Its probable causes Although the progress of civilization has undoubtedly contributed to assuage the fiercer passions of human nature, it seems to have been less favourable to the virtue of chastity, whose most dangerous enemy is the softness of the mind. The refinements of life corrupt while they polish the intercourse of the sexes. The gross appetite of love becomes most dangerous, when it is elevated, or rather, indeed, disguised, by sentimental passion. The elegance of dress, of motion, and of manners, gives a lustre to beauty, and inflames the senses through the imagination. Luxurious entertainments, midnight dances, and licentious spectacles present at once temptation and opportunity to female frailty.[57] From such dangers the unpolished wives of the barbarians were secured by poverty, solitude, and the painful cares of a domestic life. The German huts, open on every side to the eye of indiscretion or

---

54 Esprit des Loix, l. xxx. c. 3. The brilliant imagination of Montesquieu is corrected, however, by the dry cold reason of the Abbé de Mably. Observations sur l'Histoire de France, tom. i. p. 356.

55 Gaudent muneribus, sed nec data imputant, nec acceptis obligantur. [They enjoy presents but expect no return, nor do they feel obligation in receiving.] Tacit. Germ. c. 21.

56 The adulteress was whipped through the village. Neither wealth nor beauty could inspire compassion, or procure her a second husband. Tacit. Germ. C. 18, 19

57 Ovid employs two hundred lines in the research of places the most favourable to love. Above all he considers the theatre as the best adapted to collect the beauties of Rome, and to melt them into tenderness and sensuality.

jealousy, were a better safeguard of conjugal fidelity than the walls, the bolts, and the eunuchs of a Persian haram. To this reason another may be added of a more honourable nature. The Germans treated their women with esteem and confidence, consulted them on every occasion of importance, and fondly believed that in their breasts resided a sanctity and wisdom more than human. Some of these interpreters of fate, such as Velleda, in the Batavian war, governed, in the name of the deity, the fiercest nations of Germany.[58] The rest of the sex, without being adored as goddesses, were respected as the free and equal companions of soldiers; associated even by the marriage ceremony to a life of toil, of danger, and of glory.[59] In their great invasions, the camps of the barbarians were filled with a multitude of women, who remained firm and undaunted amidst the sound of arms, the various forms of destruction, and the honourable wounds of their sons and husbands.[60] Fainting armies of Germans have more than once been driven back upon the enemy by the generous despair of the women, who dreaded death much less than servitude. If the day was irrecoverably lost, they well knew how to deliver themselves and their children, with their own hands, from an insulting victor.[61] Heroines of such a cast may claim our admiration; but they were most assuredly neither lovely nor very susceptible of love. Whilst they affected to emulate the stern virtues of *man*, they must have resigned that attractive softness in which principally consist the charm and weakness of *woman*. Conscious pride taught the German females to suppress every tender emotion that stood in competition with honour, and the first honour of the sex has ever been that of chastity. The sentiments and conduct of these high-spirited matrons may, at once, be considered as a cause, as an effect, and as a proof, of the general character of the nation. Female courage, however it may be raised by fanaticism, or confirmed by habit, can only be a faint and imperfect imitation of the manly valour that distinguishes the age or country in which it may be found.

The religious system of the Germans (if the wild opinions of savages **Religion** can deserve that name) was dictated by their wants, their fears, and their ignorance.[62] They adored the great visible objects and agents of Nature, the Sun and the Moon, the Fire and the Earth; together with those imaginary deities who were supposed to preside over the most important occupations of human life. They were persuaded that, by some ridiculous arts of divination, they could discover the will of the superior

---

58 Tacit. Hist. iv. 61, 65.

59 The marriage present was a yoke of oxen, horses, and arms. See Germ. c. 18. Tacitus is somewhat too florid on the subject.

60 The change of *exigere* into *exugere* is a most excellent correction.[14]

61 Tacit. Germ. c. 7. Plutarch. in Mario. Before the wives of the Teutones destroyed themselves and their children, they had offered to surrender, on condition that they should be received as the slaves of the vestal virgins.

62 Tacitus has employed a few lines, and Cluverius one hundred and twenty-four pages, on this obscure subject. The former discovers in Germany the gods of Greece and Rome. The latter is positive that, under the emblems of the sun, the moon, and the fire, his pious ancestors worshipped the Trinity in unity.

beings, and that human sacrifices were the most precious and acceptable offering to their altars. Some applause has been hastily bestowed on the sublime notion entertained by that people of the Deity whom they neither confined within the walls of a temple nor represented by any human figure; but when we recollect that the Germans were unskilled in architecture, and totally unacquainted with the art of sculpture, we shall readily assign the true reason of a scruple, which arose not so much from a superiority of reason as from a want of ingenuity. The only temples in Germany were dark and ancient groves, consecrated by the reverence of succeeding generations. Their secret gloom, the imagined residence of an invisible power, by presenting no distinct object of fear or worship, impressed the mind with a still deeper sense of religious horror;[63] and the priests, rude and illiterate as they were, had been taught by experience the use of every artifice that could preserve and fortify impressions so well suited to their own interest.

Its effects in peace   The same ignorance which renders barbarians incapable of conceiving or embracing the useful retraints of laws exposes them naked and unarmed to the blind terrors of superstition. The German priests, improving this favourable temper of their countrymen, had assumed a jurisdiction even in temporal concerns which the magistrate could not venture to exercise; and the haughty warrior patiently submitted to the lash of correction, when it was inflicted, not by any human power, but by the immediate order of the god of war.[64] The defects of civil policy were sometimes supplied by the interposition of ecclesiastical authority. The latter was constantly exerted to maintain silence and decency in the popular assemblies; and was sometimes extended to a more enlarged concern for the national welfare. A solemn procession was occasionally celebrated in the present countries of Mecklenburgh and Pomerania. The unknown symbol of the *Earth*, covered with a thick veil, was placed on a carriage drawn by cows; and in this manner the goddess, whose common residence was in the isle of Rugen, visited several adjacent tribes of her worshippers. During her progress, the sound of war was hushed, quarrels were suspended, arms laid aside, and the restless Germans had an opportunity of tasting the blessings of peace and harmony.[65] The *truce of God*, so often and so ineffectually proclaimed by the clergy of the eleventh century, was an obvious imitation of this ancient custom.[66]

in war   But the influence of religion was far more powerful to inflame than to moderate the fierce passions of the Germans. Interest and fanaticism often prompted its ministers to sanctify the most daring and the most unjust enterprises, by the approbation of Heaven, and full assurances of success. The consecrated standards, long revered in the groves of superstition were placed in the front of the battle;[67] and the hostile army

63 The sacred wood, described with such sublime horror by Lucan, was in the neighbourhood of Marseilles; bu there were many of the same kind in Germany.
64 Tacit. Germania, c. 7.
65 Tacit. Germania, c. 40.
66 See Dr. Robertson's History of Charles V. vol. i. note 10.
67 Tacit. Germ. c. 7. These standards were only the heads of wild beasts.

was devoted with dire execrations to the gods of war and of thunder.[68] In the faith of soldiers (and such were the Germans) cowardice is the most unpardonable of sins. A brave man was the worthy favourite of their martial deities; the wretch who had lost his shield was alike banished from the religious and the civil assemblies of his countrymen. Some tribes of the north seem to have embraced the doctrine of transmigration,[69] others imagined a gross paradise of immortal drunkenness.[70] All agreed that a life spent in arms, and a glorious death in battle, were the best preparations for a happy futurity, either in this or in another world.

The immortality so vainly promised by the priests was, in some degree, conferred by the bards. That singular order of men has most deservedly attracted the notice of all who have attempted to investigate the antiquities of the Celts, the Scandinavians, and the Germans. Their genius and character, as well as the reverence paid to that important office, have been sufficiently illustrated. But we cannot so easily express, or even conceive, the enthusiasm of arms and glory which they kindled in the breast of their audience. Among a polished people, a taste for poetry is rather an amusement of the fancy than a passion of the soul. And yet, when in calm retirement we peruse the combats described by Homer or Tasso, we are insensibly seduced by the fiction, and feel a momentary glow of martial ardour. But how faint, how cold is the sensation which a peaceful mind can receive from solitary study! It was in the hour of battle, or in the feast of victory, that the bards celebrated the glory of heroes of ancient days, the ancestors of those warlike chieftains who listened with transport to their artless but animated strains. The view of arms and of danger heightened the effect of the military song; and the passions which it tended to excite, the desire of fame and the contempt of death, were the habitual sentiments of a German mind.[71] *The bards*

Such was the situation and such were the manners of the ancient Germans. Their climate, their want of learning, of arts, and of laws, their notions of honour, of gallantry, and of religion, their sense of freedom, impatience of peace, and thirst of enterprise, all contributed to form a people of military heroes. And yet we find that, during more than two hundred and fifty years that elapsed from the defeat of Varus *Causes which checked the progress of the Germans*

68 See an instance of this custom, Tacit. Annal. xiii. 57.
69 Cæsar, Diodorus, and Lucan seem to ascribe this doctrine to the Gauls, but M. Pelloutier (Histoire des Celtes, l. iii. c. 18) labours to reduce their expressions to a more orthodox sense.
70 Concerning this gross but alluring doctrine of the Edda, see Fable xx in the curious version of that book, published by M. Mallet, in his Introduction to the History of Denmark.
71 See Tacit. Germ. c. 3. Diodor. Sicul. l. v. Strabo, l. iv. p. 197. The classical reader may remember the rank of Demodocus in the Phæacian court, and the ardour infused by Tyrtæus into the fainting Spartans. Yet there is little probability that the Greeks and the Germans were the same people. Much learned trifling might be spared, if our antiquarians would condescend to reflect that similar manners will naturally be produced by similar situations.

to the reign of Decius, these formidable barbarians made few considerable attempts, and not any material impression, on the luxurious and
enslaved provinces of the empire. Their progress was checked by their
want of arms and discipline, and their fury was diverted by the intestine
division of ancient Germany.

Want of arms I. It has been observed, with ingenuity, and not without truth, that
the command of iron soon gives a nation the command of gold. But the
rude tribes of Germany, alike destitute of both those valuable metals,
were reduced slowly to acquire, by their unassisted strength, the
possession of the one as well as the other. The face of a German army
displayed their poverty of iron. Swords and the longer kind of lances
they could seldom use. Their *frameoe* (as they called them in their own
language) were long spears headed with a sharp but narrow iron point,
and which, as occasion required, they either darted from a distance, or
pushed in close onset. With this spear and with a shield their cavalry was
contented. A multitude of darts, scattered[72] with incredible force, were
an additional resource of the infantry. Their military dress, when they
wore any, was nothing more than a loose mantle. A variety of colours
was the only ornament of their wooden or their osier shields. Few of the
chiefs were distinguished by cuirasses, scarce any by helmets. Though
the horses of Germany were neither beautiful, swift, nor practised in
the skilful evolutions of the Roman manage, several of the nations
obtained renown by their cavalry; but, in general, the principal strength
of the Germans consisted in their infantry[73] which was drawn up in
and of dis- several deep columns, according to the distinction of tribes and
cipline families. Impatient of fatigue or delay, these half-armed warriors
rushed to battle with dissonant shouts and disordered ranks; and
sometimes, by the effort of native valour, prevailed over the constrained and more artificial bravery of the Roman mercenaries. But as
the barbarians poured forth their whole souls on the first onset, they
knew not how torally or to retire. A repulse was a sure defeat; and a
defeat was most commonly total destruction. When we recollect the
complete armour of the Roman soldiers, their discipline, exercises,
evolutions, fortified camps, and military engines, it appears a just
matter of surprise how the naked and unassisted valour of the
barbarians could dare to encounter in the field the strength of the
legions and the various troops of the auxiliaries, which seconded their
operations. The contest was too unequal, till the introduction of luxury
had enervated the vigour, and a spirit of disobedience and sedition had
relaxed the discipline, of the Roman armies. The introduction of
barbarian auxiliaries into those armies was a measure attended with
very obvious dangers, as it might gradually instruct the Germans in the
arts of war and of policy. Although they were admitted in small numbers

72 Missilia spargunt, Tacit. Germ. c. 6. Either that historian used a vague expression, or
he meant that they were thrown at random.
73 It was the principal distinction from the Sarmatians, who generally fought on
horseback.

and with the strictest precaution, the example of Civilis was proper to convince the Romans that the danger was not imaginary, and that their precautions were not always sufficient.[74] During the civil wars that followed the death of Nero, that artful and intrepid Batavian, whom his enemies condescended to compare with Hannibal and Sertorius,[75] formed a great design of freedom and ambition. Eight Batavian cohorts, renowned in the wars of Britain and Italy, repaired to his standard. He introduced an army of Germans into Gaul, prevailed on the powerful cities of Treves and Langres to embrace his cause, defeated the legions, destroyed their fortified camps, and employed against the Romans the military knowledge which he had acquired in their service. When at length, after an obstinate struggle, he yielded to the power of the empire, Civilis secured himself and his country by an honourable treaty. The Batavians still continued to occupy the islands of the Rhine,[76] the allies, not the servants, of the Roman monarchy.

II. The strength of ancient Germany appears formidable when we consider the effects that might have been produced by its united effort. The wide extent of country might very possibly contain a million of warriors, as all who were of an age to bear arms were of a temper to use them. But this fierce multitude, incapable of concerting or executing any plan of national greatness, was agitated by various and often hostile intentions. Germany was divided into more than forty independent states; and even in each state the unions of the several tribes was extremely loose and precarious. The barbarians were easily provoked; they knew not how to forgive an injury, much less an insult; their resentments were bloody and implacable. The casual disputes that so frequently happened in their tumultuous parties of hunting or drinking were sufficient to inflame the minds of whole nations; the private feud of any considerable chieftains diffused itself among their followers and allies. To chastise the insolent, or to plunder the defenceless, were alike causes of war. The most formidable states of Germany affected to encompass their territories with a wide frontier of solitude and devastation. The awful distance preserved by their neighbours attested the terror of their arms, and in some measure defended them from the danger of unexpected incursions.[77] {Civil dissensions of Germany}

"The Bructeri (it is Tacitus who now speaks) were totally exterminated by the neighbouring tribes,[78] provoked by their insolence, allured by the hopes of spoil, and perhaps inspired by the tutelar deities of the empire. Above sixty thousand barbarians were destroyed, not by the {Fomented by the policy of Rome}

74 The relation of this enterprise occupies a great part of the fourth and fifth books of the History of Tacitus, and is more remarkable for its eloquence than perspicuity. Sir Henry Saville has observed several inaccuracies.
75 Tacit. Hist. iv. 13. Like them, he had lost an eye.
76 It was contained between the two branches of the old Rhine, as they subsisted before the face of the country was changed by art and nature. See Cluver. German. Antiq. l. iii. c. 30, 37.
77 Cæsar de Bell. Gall. l. vi. 23.
78 They are mentioned however in the ivth and vth centuries by Nazarius, Ammianus, Claudian, &c., as a tribe of Franks. See Cluver. Germ. Antiq. l. iii. c. 13.

Roman arms, but in our sight, and for our entertainment. May the nations, enemies of Rome, ever preserve this enmity to each other! We have now attained the utmost verge of prosperity,[79] and have nothing left to demand of fortune except the discord of the barbarians."[80] These sentiments, less worthy of the humanity than of the patriotism of Tacitus, express the invariable maxims of the policy of his countrymen. They deemed it a much safer expedient to divide than to combat the barbarians, from whose defeat they could derive neither honour nor advantage. The money and negotiations of Rome insinuated themselves into the heart of Germany, and every art of seduction was used with dignity to conciliate those nations whom their proximity to the Rhine or Danube might render the most useful friends as well as the most troublesome enemies. Chiefs of renown and power were flattered by the most trifling presents, which they received either as marks of distinction or as the instruments of luxury. In civil dissensions, the weaker faction endeavoured to strengthen its interest by entering into secret connexions with the governors of the frontier provinces. Every quarrel among the Germans was fomented by the intrigues of Rome; and every plan of union and public good was defeated by the stronger bias of private jealousy and interest.[81]

Transient union agaínts Marcus Antonius   The general conspiracy which terrified the Romans under the reign of Marcus Antoninus comprehended almost all the nations of Germany, and even Sarmatia, from the mouth of the Rhine to that of the Danube.[82] It is impossible for us to determine whether this hasty confederation was formed by necessity, by reason, or by passion; but we may rest assured, that the barbarians were neither allured by the indolence or provoked by the ambition of the Roman monarch. This dangerous invasion required all the firmness and vigilance of Marcus. He fixed generals of ability in the several stations of attack, and assumed in person the conduct of the most important province on the Upper Danube. After a long and doubtful conflict, the spirit of the barbarians was subdued. The Quadi and the Marcomanni,[83] who had taken the lead in the war, were the most severely punished in its catastrophe. They were commanded to retire five miles[84] from their own banks of the Danube, and to deliver up the flower of the youth,

---

79   *Urgentibus* is the common reading, but good sense; Lipsius, and some MSS declare for *Vergentibus.*

80   Tacit. Germania, c. 33. The pious Abbé de la Blèterie is very angry with Tacitus, talks of the devil who was a murderer from the beginning, &c., &c.

81   Many traces of this policy may be discovered in Tacitus and Dion; and many more may be inferred from the principles of human nature.

82   Hist. August. p. 31. Ammian. Marcellin. l. xxxi. c. 5. Aurel. Victor. The Emperor Marcus was reduced to sell the rich furniture of the palace, and to enlist slaves and robbers.

83   The Marcomanni, a colony, who, from the banks of the Rhine, occupied Bohemia and Morovia, had once erected a great and formidable monarchy under their king Maroboduus. See Strabo, l. vii. Vell. Pat. ii. 105. Tacit. Annal. ii. 63.

84   Mr. Wotton (History of Rome, p. 166) increases the prohibition to ten times the distance. His reasoning is specious but not conclusive. Five miles were sufficient for a fortified barrier.

who were immediately sent into Britain, a remote island, where they might be secure as hostages and useful as soldiers.[85] On the frequent rebellions of the Quadi and Marcomanni, the irritated emperor resolved to reduce their country into the form of a province. His designs were disappointed by death. This formidable league, however, the only one that appears in the two first centuries of the Imperial history, was entirely dissipated without leaving any traces behind in Germany.

In the course of this introductory chapter, we have confined ourselves to the general outlines of the manners of Germany, without attempting to describe or to distinguish the various tribes which filled that great country in the time of Cæsar, of Tacitus, or of Ptolemy. As the ancient or as new tribes successively present themselves in the series of this history, we shall concisely mention their origin, their situation, and their particular character. Modern nations are fixed and permanent societies, connected among themselves by laws and government, bound to their native soil by arts and agriculture. The German tribes were voluntary and fluctuating associations of soldiers, almost of savages. The same territory often changed its inhabitants in the tide of conquest and emigration. The same communities, uniting in a plan of defence or invasion, bestowed a new title on their new confederacy. The dissolution of an ancient confederacy restored to the independent tribes their peculiar but long forgotten appellation. A victorious state often communicated its own name to a vanquished people. Sometimes crowds of volunteers flocked from all parts to the standard of a favourite leader; his camp became their country, and some circumstance of the enterprise soon gave a common denomination to the mixed multitude. The distinctions of the ferocious invaders were perpetually varied by themselves, and confounded by the astonished subjects of the Roman empire.[86]

Wars and the administration of public affairs are the principal subjects of history; but the number of persons interested in these busy scenes is very different, according to the different condition of mankind. In great monarchies millions of obedient subjects pursue their useful occupations in peace and obscurity. The attention of the writer, as well as of the reader, is solely confined to a court, a capital, a regular army, and the districts which happen to be the occasional scene of military operations. But a state of freedom and barbarism, the season of civil commotions, or the situation of petty republics,[87] raises almost every member of the community into action and consequently into notice. The irregular divisions and the restless motions of the people of Germany dazzle our imagination, and seem to multiply their numbers. The profuse enumeration of kings and warriors, of armies and nations,

85 Dion, l. lxxi. and lxxii.
86 See an excellent dissertation on the origin and migrations of nations, in the Mémoires de l'Académie des Inscriptions, tom. xviii. p. 48–71. It is seldom that the antiquarian and the philosopher are so happily blended.
87 Should we suspect that Athens contained only 21,000 citizens, and Sparta no more than 39,000? See Hume and Wallace on the number of mankind in ancient and modern times.

inclines us to forget that the same objects are continually repeated under a variety of appellations, and that the most splendid appellations have been frequently lavished on the most inconsiderable objects.

CHAPTER XV

The Progress of the Christian Religion, and the Sentiments, Manners, Numbers, and Condition, of the Primitive Christians

Import-
ance of the
inquiry

A candid but rational inquiry into the progress and establishment of Christianity may be considered as a very essential part of the history of the Roman empire. While that great body was invaded by open violence, or undermined by slow decay, a pure and humble religion gently insinuated itself into the minds of men, grew up in silence and obscurity, derived new vigour from opposition, and finally erected the triumphant banner of the cross on the ruins of the Capitol. Nor was the influence of Christianity confined to the period or to the limits of the Roman empire. After a revolution of thirteen or fourteen centuries, that religion is still professed by the nations of Europe, the most distinguished portion of human kind in arts and learning as well as in arms. By the industry and zeal of the Europeans it has been widely diffused to the most distant shores of Asia and Africa; and by the means of their colonies has been firmly established from Canada to Chili, in a world unknown to the ancients.

Its diffi-
culties

But this inquiry, however useful or entertaining, is attended with two peculiar difficulties. The scanty and suspicious materials ofsiastical history seldom enable us to dispel the dark cloud that hangs over the first age of the church. The great law of impartiality too often obliges us to reveal the imperfections of the uninspired teachers and believers of the gospel; and, to a careless observer, *their* faults may seem to cast a shade on the faith which they professed. But the scandal of the pious Christian, and the fallacious triumph of the Infidel, should cease as soon as they recollect not only *by whom*, but likewise *to whom*, the Divine Revelation was given. The theologian may indulge the pleasing task of describing Religion as she descended from Heaven, arrayed in her native purity. A more melancholy duty is imposed on the historian. He must discover the inevitable mixture of error and corruption which she contracted in a long residence upon earth, among a weak and degenerate race of human beings.

Five causes
of the
growth of
Christian-
ity

Our curiosity is naturally prompted to inquire by what means the Christian faith obtained so remarkable a victory over the established religions of the earth. To this inquiry, an obvious but satisfactory answer may be returned; that it was owing to the convincing evidence of the doctrine itself, and to the ruling providence of its great Author. But, as truth and reason seldom find so favourable a reception in the world, and as the wisdom of Providence frequently condescends to use the passions of the human heart, and the general circumstances of mankind, as instruments to execute its purpose; we may still be permitted, though with becoming submission, to ask not indeed what were the first, but what were the secondary causes of the rapid growth of the Christian church. It will, perhaps, appear that it was most effectually favoured and assisted by the five following causes: I. The inflexible, and, if we may use the expression, the intolerant zeal of the Christians, derived, it is true, from the Jewish religion, but purified from the narrow and unsocial spirit which, instead of inviting, had deterred the Gentiles from embracing the law of Moses. II. The doctrine of a future life, improved by every additional circumstance which could give weight and efficacy to that important truth. III. The miraculous powers ascribed to the primitive church. IV. The pure and austere morals of the Christians. V. The union and discipline of the Christian republic, which gradually formed an independent and increasing state in the heart of the Roman empire.

I. We have already described the religious harmony of the ancient world, and the facility with which the most different and even hostile nations embraced, or at least respected, each other's superstitions. A single people refused to join in the common intercourse of mankind. The Jews, who, under the Assyrian and Persian monarchies, had languished for many ages the most despised portion of their slaves,[1] emerged from obscurity under the successors of Alexander; and, as they multiplied to a surprising degree in the East, and afterwards in the West, they soon excited the curiosity and wonder of other nations.[2] The sullen obstinacy with which they maintained their peculiar rites and unsocial manners seemed to mark them out a distinct species of men, who boldly professed, or who faintly disguised, their implacable hatred to the rest of human kind.[3] Neither the violence of Antiochus, nor the arts of Herod, nor the example of the circumjacent nations, could ever persuade the Jews to associate with the institutions of Moses the elegant mythology of the Greeks.[4] According to the maxims of universal

THE FIRST CAUSE. Zeal of the Jews

---

1 Dum Assyrios penes, Medosque, et Persas Oriens fuit, despectissima pars servientium. [While the East was dominated by the Assyrians, Medes and Persians, they (i.e. the Jews) were despised and kept in complete subjection.] Tacit. Hist. v. 8. Herodotus, who visited Asia whilst it obeyed the last of those empires, slightly mentions the Syrians of Palestine, who, according to their own confession, had received from Egypt the rite of circumcision. See 1. ii. c. 104.

2 Diodorus Siculus, l. xl. Dion Cassius, l. xxxvii. p. 121. Tacit. Hist. v. 1–9. Justin, xxxvi. 2, 3.

3 Tradidit arcano quæcunque volumine Moses:
Non monstrare vias eadem nisi sacra colenti,
Quæsitum ad fontem solos deducere verpos. [Moses taught in that secret book of his, not to show the way except to fellow believers and to check they are circumcised if they want the fountain. (Juvenal xiv: 102).] The letter of this law is not to be found in the present volume of Moses. But the wise, the humane Maimonides openly teaches that, if an idolater fall into the water, a Jew ought not to save him from instant death. See Basnage, Histoire des Juifs, l. vi. c. 28.

4 A Jewish sect, which indulged themselves in a sort of occasional conformity, derived from Herod, by whose example and authority they had been seduced, the name of Herodians. But their numbers were so inconsiderable, and their duration so short, that

toleration, the Romans protected a superstition which they despised.[5] The polite Augustus condescended to give orders that sacrifices should be offered for his prosperity in the temple of Jerusalem;[6] while the meanest of the posterity of Abraham, who should have paid the same homage to the Jupiter of the Capitol, would have been an object of abhorrence to himself and to his brethren. But the moderation of the conquerors was insufficient to appease the jealous prejudices of their subjects, who were alarmed and scandalized at the ensigns of paganism, which necessarily introduced themselves into a Roman province.[7] The mad attempt of Caligula to place his own statue in the temple of Jerusalem was defeated by the unanimous resolution of a people who dreaded death much less than such an idolatrous profanation.[8] Their attachment to the law of Moses was equal to their detestation of foreign religions. The current of zeal and devotion, as it was contracted into a narrow channel, ran with the strength, and sometimes with the fury, of a torrent.

Its gradual increase

This inflexible perseverance, which appeared so odious, or so ridiculous, to the ancient world, assumes a more awful character, since Providence has deigned to reveal to us the mysterious history of the chosen people. But the devout, and even scrupulous, attachment to the Mosaic religion, so conspicuous among the Jews who lived under the second temple, becomes still more surprising, if it is compared with the stubborn incredulity of their forefathers. When the law was given in thunder from Mount Sinai; when the tides of the ocean and the course of the planets were suspended for the convenience of the Israelites; and when temporal rewards and punishments were the immediate consequences of their piety or disobedience; they perpetually relapsed into rebellion against the visible majesty of their Divine King, placed the idols of the nations in the sanctuary of Jehovah, and imitated every fantastic ceremony that was practised in the tents of the Arabs or in the cities of Phœnicia.[9] As the protection of Heaven was deservedly withdrawn from the ungrateful race, their faith acquired a proportionable degree of vigour and purity. The contemporaries of Moses

Josephus has not thought them worthy of his notice. See Prideaux's Connection, vol. ii. p. 285.

5 Cicero pro Flacco, c. 28.

6 Philo de Legatione. Augustus left a foundation for a perpetual sacrifice. Yet he approved of the neglect which his grandson Caius expressed towards the temple of Jerusalem. See Sueton. in August. c. 93, and Casaubon's notes on that passage.

7 See, in particular, Joseph. Antiquitat. xvii. 6, xviii. 3, and de Bel. Judaic. i. 33, and ii. 9. Edit. Havercamp.

8 Jussi a Caio Cæsare, effigiem ejus in templo locare arma potius sumpsere. [When ordered by Gaius Caesar to put up his statue in the temple, they chose rather to revolt.] Tacit. Hist. v. 9. Philo and Josephus gave a very circumstantial, but a very rhetorical, account of this transaction, which exceedingly perplexed the governor of Syria. At the first mention of this idolatrous proposal, King Agrippa fainted away; and did not recover his senses till the third day.

9 For the enumeration of the Syrian and Arabian deities, it may be observed that Milton has comprised, in one hundred and thirty very beautiful lines, the two large and learned syntagmas which Selden had composed on that abstruse subject.

and Joshua had beheld, with careless indifference, the most amazing miracles. Under the pressure of every calamity, the belief of those miracles has preserved the Jews of a later period from the universal contagion of idolatry; and, in contradiction to every known principle of the human mind, that singular people seems to have yielded a stronger and more ready assent to the traditions of their remote ancestors than to the evidence of their own senses.[10]

The Jewish religion was admirably fitted for defence, but it was never designed for conquest; and it seems probable that the number of proselytes was never much superior to that of apostates. The divine promises were originally made, and the distinguishing rite of circumcision was enjoined, to a single family. When the posterity of Abraham had multiplied like the sands of the sea, the Deity, from whose mouth they received a system of laws and ceremonies, declared himself the proper and, as it were, the national God of Israel; and, with the most jealous care, separated his favourite people from the rest of mankind. The conquest of the land of Canaan was accompanied with so many wonderful and with so many bloody circumstances that the victorious Jews were left in a state of irreconcilable hostility with all their neighbours. They had been commanded to extirpate some of the most idolatrous tribes; and the execution of the Divine will had seldom been retarded by the weakness of humanity. With the other nations they were forbidden to contract any marriages or alliances; and the prohibition of receiving them into the congregation, which, in some cases, was perpetual, almost always extended to the third, to the seventh, or even to the tenth generation. The obligation of preaching to the Gentiles the faith of Moses had never been inculcated as a precept of the law, nor were the Jews inclined to impose it on themselves as a voluntary duty. In the admission of new citizens, that unsocial people was actuated by the selfish vanity of the Greeks, rather than by the generous policy of Rome. The descendants of Abraham were flattered by the opinion that they alone were the heirs of the covenant; and they were apprehensive of diminishing the value of their inheritance, by sharing it too easily with the strangers of the earth. A larger acquaintance with mankind extended their knowledge without correcting their prejudices; and whenever the God of Israel acquired any new votaries, he was much more indebted to the inconstant humour of polytheism than to the active zeal of his own missionaries.[11] The religion of Moses seems to be instituted for a particular country, as well as for a single nation; and, if a strict obedience had been paid to the order that every male, three times in the year, should present himself before the Lord Jehovah, it would have been impossible that the Jews could ever have

Their religion better suited to defence than to conquest

10 "How long will this people provoke me? and how long will it be ere they *believe* me, for all the *signs* which I have shewn among them?" (Numbers xiv. 11). It would be easy, but it would be unbecoming, to justify the complaint of the Deity, from the whole tenor of the Mosaic history.
11 All that relates to the Jewish proselytes has been very ably treated by Basnage, Hist. des Juifs, l. vi. c. 6, 7.

spread themselves beyond the narrow limits of the promised land.[12] That obstacle was indeed removed by the destruction of the temple of Jerusalem; but the most considerable part of the Jewish religion was involved in its destruction; and the Pagans, who had long wondered at the strange report of an empty sanctuary,[13] were at a loss to discover what could be the object, or what could be the instruments, of a worship which was destitute of temples and of altars, of priests and of sacrifices. Yet even in their fallen state, the Jews, still asserting their lofty and exclusive privileges, shunned, instead of courting, the society of strangers. They still insisted with inflexible rigour on those parts of the law which it was in their power to practise. Their peculiar distinctions of days, of meats, and a variety of trivial though burdensome observances, were so many objects of disgust and aversion for the other nations, to whose habits and prejudices they were diametrically opposite. The painful and even dangerous rite of circumcision was alone capable of repelling a willing proselyte from the door of the synagogue.[14]

More liberal zeal of Chirstianity Under these circumstances, Christianity offered itself to the world, armed with the strength of the Mosaic law, and delivered from the weight of its fetters. An exclusive zeal for the truth of religion and the unity of God was as carefully inculcated in the new as in the ancient system; and whatever was now revealed to mankind, concerning the nature and designs of the Supreme Being, was fitted to increase their reverence for that mysterious doctrine. The divine authority of Moses and the prophets was admitted, and even established, as the firmest basis of Christianity. From the beginning of the world, an uninterrupted series of predictions had announced and prepared the long expected coming of the Messiah, who, in compliance with the gross apprehensions of the Jews, had been more frequently represented under the character of a King and Conqueror, than under that of a Prophet, a Martyr, and the Son of God. By his expiatory sacrifice, the imperfect sacrifices of the temple were at once consummated and abolished. The ceremonial law, which consisted only of types and figures, was succeeded by a pure and spiritual worship, equally adapted to all climates, as well as to every condition of mankind; and to the initiation of blood was substituted a more harmless initiation of water. The promise of divine favour, instead of being partially confined to the posterity of Abraham, was universally proposed to the freeman and the slave, to the Greek and

12 See Exod. xxiv. 23, Deut. xvi. 16, the commentators, and a very sensible note in the Universal History, vol. i. p. 603, edit. fol.
13 When Pompey, using or abusing the right of conquest, entered into the Holy of Holies, it was observed with amazement, "Nullâ intus Deûm effigie, vacuam sedem et inania arcana." [There is no statue of a god in there, the sanctuary was vacant and the Holy of Holies empty.] Tacit. Hist. v. 9. It was a popular saying, with regard to the Jews,
Nil præter nubes et cæli numen adorant. [They worship a spirit in the sky which is nothing except the clouds.]
14 A second kind of circumcision was inflicted on a Samaritan or Egyptian proselyte. The sullen indifference of the Talmudists, with respect to the conversion of strangers, may be seen in Basnage, Histoire des Juifs, l. vi. c. 6.

to the barbarian, to the Jew and to the Gentile. Every privilege that could raise the proselyte from earth to Heaven, that could exalt his devotion, secure his happiness, or even gratify that secret pride which, under the semblance of devotion, insinuates itself into the human heart, was still reserved for the members of the Christian church; but at the same time all mankind was permitted, and even solicited, to accept the glorious distinction, which was not only proffered as a favour, but imposed as an obligation. It became the most sacred duty of a new convert to diffuse among his friends and relations the inestimable blessing which he had received, and to warn them against a refusal that would be severely punished as a criminal disobedience to the will of a benevolent but all-powerful deity.

The enfranchisement of the church from the bonds of the synagogue was a work however of some time and of some difficulty. The Jewish converts, who acknowledged Jesus in the character of the Messiah foretold by their ancient oracles, respected him as a prophetic teacher of virtue and religion; but they obstinately adhered to the ceremonies of their ancestors, and were desirous of imposing them on the Gentiles, who continually augmented the number of believers. These Judaizing Christians seem to have argued with some degree of plausibility from the divine origin of the Mosaic law, and from the immutable perfections of its great Author. They affirmed *that*, if the Being, who is the same through all eternity, had designed to abolish those sacred rites which had served to distinguish his chosen people, the repeal of them would have been no less clear and solemn than their first promulgation: *that*, instead of those frequent declarations, which either suppose or assert the perpetuity of the Mosaic religion, it would have been represented as a provisionary scheme intended to last only till the coming of the Messiah, who should instruct mankind in a more perfect mode of faith and of worship:[15] *that* the Messiah himself, and his disciples who conversed with him on earth, instead of authorizing by their example the most minute observances of the Mosaic law,[16] would have published to the world the abolition of those useless and obsolete ceremonies, without suffering Christianity to remain during so many years obscurely confounded among the sects of the Jewish church. Arguments like these appear to have been used in the defence of the expiring cause of the Mosaic law; but the industry of our learned divines has abundantly

Obstinacy and reasons of the believing Jews

---

15 These arguments were urged with great ingenuity by the Jew Orobio, and refuted with equal ingenuity and candour by the Christian Limborch. See the Amica Callano (it well deserves that name) or account of the dispute between them.

16 Jesus . . . circumcisus erat; cibis utebatur Judaicis; vestitû simili; purgatos scabie mittebat ad sacerdotes; Paschata et alios dies festos religiose observabat si quos sanavit sabbato, ostendit non tantum ex lege, sed et ex receptis sententiis talia opera sabbato non interdicta. [Jesus . . . had been circumcised; he used Jewish food; similarly with clothing. He used to send those cleansed from leprosy to the priests; and he painstakingly observed the Passover and the days of other festivals. If he healed them on the sabbath he showed not so much from the law but from traditional beliefs that such deeds were not forbidden on the sabbath.] Grotius de veritate Religionis Christianæ, l. v. c. 7. A little afterwards (c. 12) he expatiates on the condescension of the apostles.

explained the ambiguous language of the Old Testament, and the ambiguous conduct of the apostolic teachers. It was proper gradually to unfold the system of the Gospel, and to pronounce, with the utmost caution and tenderness, a sentence of condemnation so repugnant to the inclination and prejudices of the believing Jews.

The Naza-rene church of Jerusalem The history of the church of Jerusalem affords a lively proof of the necessity of those precautions, and of the deep impression which the Jewish religion had made on the minds of its sectaries. The first fifteen bishops of Jerusalem were all circumcised Jews; and the congregation over which they presided, united the law of Moses with the doctrine of Christ.[17] It was natural that the primitive tradition of a church which was founded only forty days after the death of Christ, and was governed almost as many years under the immediate inspection of his apostle, should be received as the standard of orthodoxy.[18] The distant churches very frequently appealed to the authority of their venerable Parent, and relieved her distresses by a liberal contribution of alms. But, when numerous and opulent societies were established in the great cities of the empire, in Antioch, Alexandria, Ephesus, Corinth, and Rome, the reverence which Jerusalem had inspired to all the Christian colonies insensibly diminished. The Jewish converts, or, as they were afterwards called, the Nazarenes, who had laid the foundations of the church, soon found themselves overwhelmed by the increasing multitudes that from all the various religions of polytheism inlisted under the banner of Christ; and the Gentiles, who with the approbation of their peculiar apostle had rejected the intolerable weight of Mosaic ceremonies, at length refused to their more scrupulous brethren the same toleration which at first they had humbly solicited for their own practice. The ruin of the temple, of the city, and of the public religion of the Jews, was severely felt by the Nazarenes; as in their manners, though not in their faith, they maintained so intimate a connexion with their impious countrymen, whose misfortunes were attributed by the Pagans to the contempt, and more justly ascribed by the Christians to the wrath, of the Supreme Deity. The Nazarenes retired from the ruins of Jerusalem to the little town of Pella beyond the Jordan, where that ancient church languished above sixty years in solitude and obscurity.[19] They still enjoyed the comfort of making frequent and devout visits to the *Holy City*, and the hope of being one day restored to those seats which both nature and religion taught them to love as well as to revere. But at

17 Pæne omnes Christum Deum sub legis observatione credebant. [Almost everyone who believed in Christ did so under the traditional law.] Sulpicius Severus, ii. 31. See Eusebius, Hist. Ecclesiast. l. iv. c. 5.
18 Mosheim de Rebus Christianis ante Constantinum Magnum, p. 153. In this masterly performance, which I shall often have occasion to quote, he enters much more fully into the state of the primitive church than he has an opportunity of doing in his General History.
19 Eusebius, l. iii. c. 5. Le Clerc, Hist. Ecclesiast. p. 605. During this occasional absence, the bishop and church of Pella still retained the title of Jerusalem. In the same manner, the Roman pontiffs resided seventy years at Avignon; and the patriarchs of Alexandria have long since transferred their episcopal seat to Cairo.

length, under the reign of Hadrian, the desperate fanaticism of the Jews filled up the measure of their calamities; and the Romans, exasperated by their repeated rebellions, exercised the rights of victory with unusual rigour. The emperor founded, under the name of Ælia Capitolina, a new city on Mount Sion,[20] to which he gave the privileges of a colony; and, denouncing the severest penalties against any of the Jewish people who should dare to approach its precincts, he fixed a vigilant garrison of a Roman cohort to enforce the execution of his orders. The Nazarenes had only one way left to escape the common proscription, and the force of truth was, on this occasion, assisted by the influence of temporal advantages. They elected Marcus for their bishop, a prelate of the race of the Gentiles, and most probably a native either of Italy or of some of the Latin provinces. At his persuasion, the most considerable part of the congregation renounced the Mosaic law, in the practice of which they had persevered above a century. By this sacrifice of their habits and prejudices they purchased a free admission into the colony of Hadrian, and more firmly cemented their union with the Catholic church.[21]

When the name and honours of the church of Jerusalem had been The restored to Mount Sion, the crimes of heresy and schism were imputed Ebionites to the obscure remnant of the Nazarenes which refused to accompany their Latin bishop. They still preserved their former habitation of Pella, spread themselves into the villages adjacent to Damascus, and formed an inconsiderable church in the city of Berœa, or, as it is now called, of Aleppo, in Syria.[22] The name of Nazarenes was deemed too honourable for those Christian Jews, and they soon received from the supposed poverty of their understanding, as well as of their condition, the contemptuous epithet of Ebionites.[23] In a few years after the return of the church of Jerusalem, it became a matter of doubt and controversy whether a man who sincerely acknowledged Jesus as the Messiah, but who still continued to observe the law of Moses, could possibly hope for salvation. The humane temper of Justin Martyr inclined him to answer this question in the affirmative; and, though he expressed himself with the most guarded diffidence, he ventured to determine in favour of

20 Dion Cassius, l. xix. The exile of the Jewish nation from Jerusalem is attested by Aristo of Pella (apud Euseb. l. iv. c. 6), and is mentioned by several ecclesiastical writers; though some of them too hastily extend this interdiction to the whole country of Palestine.
21 Eusebius, l. iv. c. 6. Sulpicius Severus, ii. 31. By comparing their unsatisfactory accounts, Mosheim (p. 327, &c.) has drawn out a very distinct representation of the circumstances and motives of this revolution.
22 Le Clerc (Hist. Ecclesiast. p. 477, 535) seems to have collected from Eusebius, Jerome, Epiphanius, and other writers, all the principal circumstances that relate to the Nazarenes, or Ebionites. The nature of their opinions soon divided them into a stricter and a milder sect; and there is some reason to conjecture that the family of Jesus Christ remained members, at least, of the latter and more moderate party.
23 Some writers have been pleased to create an Ebion, the imaginary author of their sect and name. But we can more safely rely on the learned Eusebius than on the vehement Tertullian or the credulous Epiphanius. According to Le Clerc, the Hebrew word *Ebjonim* may be translated into Latin by that of *Pauperes*. See Hist. Ecclesiast. p. 477.

such an imperfect Christian, if he were content to practise the Mosaic ceremonies, without pretending to assert their general use or necessity. But, when Justin was pressed to declare the sentiment of the church, he confessed that there were very many among the orthodox Christians, who not only excluded their Judaizing brethren from the hope of salvation, but who declined any intercourse with them in the common offices of friendship, hospitality, and social life.[24] The more rigorous opinion prevailed, as it was natural to expect, over the milder; and an external bar of separation was fixed between the disciples of Moses and those of Christ. The unfortunate Ebionites, rejected from one religion as apostates, and from the other as heretics, found themselves compelled to assume a more decided character; and, although some traces of that obsolete sect may be discovered as late as the fourth century, they insensibly melted away either into the church or the synagogue.[25]

The Gnostics   While the orthodox church preserved a just medium between excessive veneration and improper contempt for the law of Moses, the various heretics deviated into equal but opposite extremes of error and extravagance. From the acknowledged truth of the Jewish religion the Ebionites had concluded that it could never be abolished. From its supposed imperfections the Gnostics as hastily inferred that it never was instituted by the wisdom of the Deity. There are some objections against the authority of Moses and the prophets, which too readily present themselves to the sceptical mind; though they can only be derived from our ignorance of remote antiquity, and from our incapacity to form an adequate judgment of the divine œconomy. These objections were eagerly embraced, and as petulantly urged, by the vain science of the Gnostics.[26] As those heretics were, for the most part, averse to the pleasures of sense, they morosely arraigned the polygamy of the patriarchs, the gallantries of David, and the seraglio of Solomon. The conquest of the land of Canaan, and the extirpation of the unsuspecting natives, they were at a loss how to reconcile with the common notions of humanity and justice. But, when they recollected the sanguinary list of murders, of executions, and of massacres, which stain almost every page of the Jewish annals, they acknowledged that

24 See the very curious Dialogue of Justin Martyr with the Jew Tryphon. The conference between them was held at Ephesus, in the reign of Antoninus Pius, and about twenty years after the return of the church of Pella to Jerusalem. For this date consult the accurate note of Tillemont, Mémoires Ecclésiastiques, tom. ii. p. 511.
25 Of all the systems of Christianity, that of Abyssinia is the only one which still adheres to the Mosaic rites (Geddes's Church History of Æthiopia, and Dissertations de La Grand sur la Relation du P. Lobo). The eunuch of the queen Candace might suggest some suspicions; but, as we are assured (Socrates, i. 19, Sozomen, ii. 24, Ludolphus, p. 281) that the Æthiopians were not converted till the fourth century, it is more reasonable to believe that they respected the Sabbath, and distinguished the forbidden meats, in imitation of the Jews, who, in a very early period, were seated on both sides of the Red Sea. Circumcision had been practised by the most ancient Æthiopians, from motives of health and cleanliness, which seem to be explained in the Recherches Philosophiques sur les Américains, tom. ii. p. 117.
26 Beausobre, Histoire du Manichéisme, l. i. c. 3, has stated their objections, particularly those of Faustus, the adversary of Augustin, with the most learned impartiality.

the barbarians of Palestine had exercised as much compassion towards their idolatrous enemies as they had ever shewn to their friends or countrymen.[27] Passing from the sectaries of the law to the law itself, they asserted that it was impossible that a religion which consisted only of bloody sacrifices and trifling ceremonies, and whose rewards as well as punishments were all of a carnal and temporal nature, could inspire the love of virtue, or restrain the impetuosity of passion. The Mosaic account of the creation and fall of man was treated with profane derision by the Gnostics, who would not listen with patience to the repose of the Deity after six days' labour, to the rib of Adam, the garden of Eden, the trees of life and of knowledge, the speaking serpent, the forbidden fruit, and the condemnation pronounced against human kind for the venial offence of their first progenitors.[28] The God of Israel was impiously represented by the Gnostics as a being liable to passion and to error, capricious in his favour, implacable in his resentment, meanly jealous of his superstitious worship, and confining his partial providence to a single people and to this transitory life. In such a character they could discover none of the features of the wise and omnipotent father of the universe.[29] They allowed that the religion of the Jews was somewhat less criminal than the idolatry of the Gentiles; but it was their fundamental doctrine that the Christ whom they adored as the first and brightest emanation of the Deity appeared upon earth to rescue mankind from their various errors, and to reveal a *new* system of truth and perfection. The most learned of the fathers, by a very singular condescension, have imprudently admitted the sophistry of the Gnostics. Acknowledging that the literal sense is repugnant to every principle of faith as well as reason, they deem themselves secure and invulnerable behind the ample veil of allegory, which they carefully spread over every tender part of the Mosaic dispensation.[30]

It has been remarked, with more ingenuity than truth, that the virgin purity of the church was never violated by schism or heresy before the reign of Trajan or Hadrian, about one hundred years after the death of Christ.[31] We may observe, with much more propriety, that, during that period, the disciples of the Messiah were indulged in a freer latitude both of faith and practice than has ever been allowed in succeeding

Their sects, progress, and influence

---

27 Apud ipsos fides obstinata, misericordia in promptû: adversus omnes alios hostile odium. [Among themselves their loyalty is firm and compassion manifest; but against everyone else they show hatred as though to enemies.] Tacit. Hist. v. 4. Surely Tacitus had seen the Jews with too favourable an eye. The perusal of Josephus must have destroyed the antithesis.

28 Dr. Burnet (Archæologia, l. ii. c. 7) has discussed the first chapters of Genesis with too much wit and freedom.

29 The milder Gnostics considered Jehovah, the Creator, as a Being of a mixed nature between God and the Dæmon. Others confounded him with the evil principle. Consult the second century of the general history of Mosheim, which gives a very distinct, though concise, account of their strange opinions on this subject.

30 See Beausobre, Hist. du Manichéisme, l. i. c. 4. Origen and St. Augustin were among the Allegorists.

31 Hegesippus, ap. Euseb. l. iii. 32, iv. 22. Clemens, Alexandrin. Stromat. vii. 17.

ages. As the terms of communion were insensibly narrowed, and the spiritual authority of the prevailing party was exercised with increasing severity, many of its most respectable adherents, who were called upon to renounce, were provoked to assert, their private opinions, to pursue the consequences of their mistaken principles, and openly to erect the standard of rebellion against the unity of the church. The Gnostics were distinguished as the most polite, the most learned, and the most wealthy of the Christian name, and that general appellation which expressed a superiority of knowledge was either assumed by their own pride or ironically bestowed by the envy of their adversaries. They were almost without exception of the race of the Gentiles, and their principal founders seem to have been natives of Syria or Egypt, where the warmth of the climate disposes both the mind and the body to indolent and contemplative devotion. The Gnostics blended with the faith of Christ many sublime but obscure tenets which they derived from oriental philosophy, and even from the religion of Zoroaster, concerning the eternity of matter, the existence of two principles, and the mysterious hierarchy of the invisible world.[32] As soon as they launched out into that vast abyss, they delivered themselves to the guidance of a disordered imagination; and, as the paths of error are various and infinite, the Gnostics were imperceptibly divided into more than fifty particular sects,[33] of whom the most celebrated appear to have been the Basilidians, the Valentinians, the Marcionites, and, in a still later period, the Manichæans. Each of these sects could boast of its bishops and congregations, of its doctors and martyrs,[34] and, instead of the four gospels adopted by the church, the heretics produced a multitude of histories, in which the actions and discourses of Christ and of his apostles were adapted to their respective tenets.[35] The success of the Gnostics was rapid and extensive.[36] They covered Asia and Egypt,

32 In the account of the Gnostics of the second and third centuries, Mosheim is ingenious and candid; Le Clerc dull, but exact; Beausobre almost always an apologist; and it is much to be feared that the primitive fathers are very frequently calumniators.

33 See the catalogues of Irenæus and Epiphanius. It must indeed be allowed that those writers were inclined to multiply the number of sects which opposed the *unity* of the church.

34 Eusebius, l. iv. c. 15. Sozomen, l. ii. c. 32. See in Bayle, in the article of *Marcion*, a curious detail of a dispute on that subject. It should seem that some of the Gnostics (the Basilidians) declined, and even refused, the honour of martyrdom. Their reasons were singular and abstruse. See Mosheim, p. 359.

35 See a very remarkable passage of Origen (Proem. ad Lucam). That indefatigable writer, who had consumed his life in the study of the scriptures, relies for their authenticity on the inspired authority of the church. It was impossible that the Gnostics could receive our present gospels, many parts of which (particularly in the resurrection of Christ) are directly, and as it might seem designedly, pointed against their favourite tenets. It is therefore somewhat singular that Ignatius (Epist. ad Smyrn. Patr. Apostol. tom. ii. p. 34), should choose to employ a vague and doubtful tradition, instead of quoting the certain testimony of the evangelists.

36 Faciunt favos et vespæ; faciunt ecclesias et Marcionitæ [As wasps make honeycombs, so the Marcionites make Congregations] is the strong expression of Tertullian, which I am obliged to quote from memory. In the time of Epiphanius (advers. Hæreses, p. 302), the Marcionites were very numerous in Italy, Syria, Egypt, Arabia, and Persia.

established themselves in Rome, and sometimes penetrated into the provinces of the West. For the most part they arose in the second century, flourished during the third, and were suppressed in the fourth or fifth, by the prevalence of more fashionable controversies, and by the superior ascendant of the reigning power. Though they constantly disturbed the peace, and frequently disgraced the name, of religion, they contributed to assist rather than to retard the progress of Christianity. The Gentile converts, whose strongest objections and prejudices were directed against the law of Moses, could find admission into many Christian societies, which required not from their untutored mind any belief of an antecedent revelation. Their faith was insensibly fortified and enlarged, and the church was ultimately benefited by the conquests of its most inveterate enemies.[37]

But, whatever difference of opinion might subsist between the Orthodox, the Ebionites, and the Gnostics, concerning the divinity or the obligation of the Mosaic law, they were all equally animated by the same exclusive zeal and by the same abhorrence for idolatry which had distinguished the Jews from the other nations of the ancient world. The philosopher, who considered the system of polytheism as a composition of human fraud and error, could disguise a smile of contempt under the mask of devotion, without apprehending that either the mockery or the compliance would expose him to the resentment of any invisible, or, as he conceived them, imaginary powers. But the established religions of Paganism were seen by the primitive Christians in a much more odious and formidable light. It was the universal sentiment both of the church and of heretics that the dæmons were the authors, the patrons, and the objects of idolatry.[38] Those rebellious spirits who had been degraded from the rank of angels, and cast down into the infernal pit, were still permitted to roam upon earth, to torment the bodies, and to seduce the minds, of sinful men. The dæmons soon discovered and abused the natural propensity of the human heart towards devotion, and, artfully withdrawing the adoration of mankind from their Creator, they usurped the place and honours of the Supreme Deity. By the success of their malicious contrivances, they at once gratified their own vanity and revenge, and obtained the only comfort of which they were yet susceptible, the hope of involving the human species in the participation of their guilt and misery. It was confessed, or at least it was imagined, that they had distributed among themselves the most important characters of polytheism, one dæmon assuming the name and attributes of Jupiter, another of Æsculapius, a third of Venus, and a fourth perhaps of Apollo;[39] and that, by the advantage of their

The dæmons considered as the gods of antiquity

---

37 Augustin is a memorable instance of this gradual progress from reason to faith. He was, during several years, engaged in the Manichæan sect.

38 The unanimous sentiment of the primitive church is very clearly explained by Justin Martyr, Apolog. Major, by Athenagoras Legat. c. 22 &c., and by Lactantius, Institut. Divin. ii. 14–19.

39 Tertullian (Apolog. c. 23) alleges the confession of the Dæmons themselves as often as they were tormented by the Christian exorcists.

long experience and aerial nature, they were enabled to execute, with sufficient skill and dignity, the parts which they had undertaken. They lurked in the temples, instituted festivals and sacrifices, invented fables, pronounced oracles, and were frequently allowed to perform miracles. The Christians, who, by the interposition of evil spirits, could so readily explain every præternatural appearance, were disposed and even desirous to admit the most extravagant fictions of the Pagan mythology. But the belief of the Christian was accompanied with horror. The most trifling mark of respect to the national worship he considered as a direct homage yielded to the dæmon, and as an act of rebellion against the majesty of God.

Abhor-
rence of the
Christians
for idolatry
In consequence of this opinion, it was the first but arduous duty of a Christian to preserve himself pure and undefiled by the practice of idolatry. The religion of the nations was not merely a speculative doctrine professed in the schools or preached in the temples. The innumerable deities and rites of polytheism were closely interwoven with every circumstance of business or pleasure, of public or of private life; and it seemed impossible to escape the observance of them, without, at the same time, renouncing the commerce of mankind and Ceremonies all the offices and amusements of society.[40] The important transactions of peace and war were prepared or concluded by solemn sacrifices, in which the magistrate, the senator, and the soldier were obliged to preside or to participate.[41] The public spectacles were an essential part of the cheerful devotion of the Pagans, and the gods were supposed to accept, as the most grateful offering, the games that the prince and people celebrated in honour of their peculiar festivals.[42] The Christian, who with pious horror avoided the abomination of the circus or the theatre, found himself encompassed with infernal snares in every convivial entertainment, as often as his friends, invoking the hospitable deities, poured out libations to each other's happiness.[43] When the bride, struggling with well-affected reluctance, was forced in hymenæal pomp over the threshold of her new habitation,[44] or when the sad

40 Tertullian has written a most severe treatise against idolatry, to caution his brethren against the hourly danger of incurring that guilt. Recogita silvam, et quantæ latitant spinæ. De Coronâ Militis, c. 10. [Consider a wood and how great those lushes are which conceal themselves there.]
41 The Roman senate was always held in a temple or consecrated place (Aulus Gellius, xiv. 7). Before they entered on business, every senator dropped some wine and frankincense on the altar. Sueton. in August. c. 35.
42 See Tertullian de Spectaculis. This severe reformer shews no more indulgence to a tragedy of Euripides than to a combat of gladiators. The dress of the actors particularly offends him. By the use of the lofty buskin, they impiously strive to add a cubit to their stature, c. 23.
43 The ancient practice of concluding the entertainment with libations may be found in every classic. Socrates and Seneca, in their last moments, made a noble application of this custom. Postquam stagnum calidæ aquæ introiit, respergens proximos servorum, additâ voce, libare se liquorem illum Jovi Liberatori, [Then he got into a bath of warm water and sprinkled some on the slaves attending him saying that the water was his libation to Jove the Liberator.] Tacit. Annal. xv. 64.
44 See the elegant but idolatrous hymn of Catullus, on the nuptials of Manlius and Julia. O Hymen, Hymenæe iö! Quis huic Deo compararier ausit? [O Hymen Hymenaeus[15] Io! Who may dare to make comparison with this god?]

procession of the dead slowly moved towards the funeral pile;[45] the Christian, on these interesting occasions, was compelled to desert the persons who were the dearest to him, rather than contract the guilt inherent to those impious ceremonies. Every art and every trade that Arts was in the least concerned in the framing or adorning of idols was polluted by the stain of idolatry;[46] a severe sentence, since it devoted to eternal misery the far greater part of the community, which is employed in the exercise of liberal or mechanic professions. If we cast our eyes over the numerous remains of antiquity, we shall perceive that, besides the immediate representations of the Gods and the holy instruments of their worship, the elegant forms and agreeable fictions, consecrated by the imagination of the Greeks, were introduced as the richest ornaments of the houses, the dress, and the furniture, of the Pagans.[47] Even the arts of music and painting, of eloquence and poetry, flowed from the same impure origin. In the style of the fathers, Apollo and the Muses were the organs of the infernal spirit, Homer and Virgil were the most eminent of his servants, and the beautiful mythology which pervades and animates the compositions of their genius is destined to celebrate the glory of the dæmons. Even the common language of Greece and Rome abounded with familiar but impious expressions, which the imprudent Christian might too carelessly utter, or too patiently hear.[48]

The dangerous temptations which on every side lurked in ambush Festivals to surprise the unguarded believer assailed him with redoubled violence on the days of solemn festivals. So artfully were they framed and disposed throughout the year that superstition always wore the appearance of pleasure, and often of virtue.[49] Some of the most sacred festivals in the Roman ritual were destined to salute the new calends of January with vows of public and private felicity, to indulge the pious remembrance of the dead and living, to ascertain the inviolable bounds of property, to hail, on the return of spring, the genial powers of fecundity, to perpetuate the two memorable æras of Rome, the foundation of the city and that of the republic, and to restore, during the humane license of the Saturnalia, the primitive equality of mankind. Some idea may be conceived of the abhorrence of the Christians for such impious ceremonies, by the

45 The ancient funerals (in those of Misenus and Pallas) are no less accurately described by Virgil than they are illustrated by his commentator Servius. The pile itself was an altar, the flames were fed with the blood of victims, and all the assistants were sprinkled with lustral water.

46 Tertullian de Idololatria, c. 11.

47 See every part of Montfaucon's Antiquities. Even the reverses of the Greek and Roman coins were frequently of an idolatrous nature. Here indeed the scruples of the Christian were suspended by a stronger passion.

48 Tertullian de Idololatria, c. 20, 21, 22. If a Pagan friend (on the occasion perhaps of sneezing) used the familiar expression of "Jupiter bless you," the Christian was obliged to protest against the divinity of Jupiter.

49 Consult the most laboured work of Ovid, his imperfect *Fasti*. He finished no more than the first six months of the year. The compilation of Macrobius is called the *Saturnalia*, but it is only a small part of the first book that bears any relation to the title.

scrupulous delicacy which they displayed on a much less alarming occasion. On days of general festivity, it was the custom of the ancients to adorn their doors with lamps and with branches of laurel, and to crown their heads with a garland of flowers. This innocent and elegant practice might, perhaps, have been tolerated as a mere civil institution. But it most unluckily happened that the doors were under the protection of the household gods, that the laurel was sacred to the lover of Daphne, and that garlands of flowers, though frequently worn as a symbol either of joy or mourning, had been dedicated in their first origin to the service of superstition. The trembling Christians, who were persuaded in this instance to comply with the fashion of their country and the commands of the magistrate, laboured under the most gloomy apprehensions, from the reproaches of their own conscience, the censures of the church, and the denunciations of divine vengeance.[50]

Zeal for Christianity

Such was the anxious diligence which was required to guard the chastity of the gospel from the infectious breath of idolatry. The superstitious observances of public or private rites were carelessly practised, from education and habit, by the followers of the established religion. But, as often as they occurred, they afforded the Christians an opportunity of declaring and confirming their zealous opposition. By these frequent protestations, their attachment to the faith was continually fortified, and, in proportion to the increase of zeal, they combated with the more ardour and success in the holy war which they had undertaken against the empire of the dœmons.

THE SECOND CAUSE. The doctrine of the immortality of the soul among the philosophers

II. The writings of Cicero[51] represent, in the most lively colours, the ignorance, the errors, and the uncertainty of the ancient philosophers, with regard to the immortality of the soul. When they are desirous of arming their disciples against the fear of death, they inculcate, as an obvious though melancholy position, that the fatal stroke of our dissolution releases us from the calamities of life, and that those can no longer suffer who no longer exist. Yet there were a few sages of Greece and Rome who had conceived a more exalted, and, in some respects, a juster idea of human nature; though it must be confessed that, in the sublime inquiry, their reason had been often guided by their imagination, and that their imagination had been prompted by their vanity. When they viewed with complacency the extent of their own mental powers when they

---

50 Tertullian has composed a defence, or rather panegyric, of the rash action of a Christian soldier who, by throwing away his crown of laurel, had exposed himself and his brethren to the most imminent danger. By the mention of the *emperors* (Severus and Caracalla) it is evident, notwithstanding the wishes of M. de Tillemont, that Tertullian composed his treatise De Coronâ long before he was engaged in the errors of the Montanists. See Mémoires Ecclésiastiques, tom. iii. p. 384.

51 In particular, the first book of the Tusculan Questions, and the treatise De Senectute, and the Somnium Scipionis contain, in the most beautiful language, everything that Grecian philosophy, or Roman good sense, could possibly suggest on this dark but important object.

exercised the various faculties of memory, of fancy, and of judgment, in the most profound speculations, or the most important labours, and when they reflected on the desire of fame, which transported them into future ages far beyond the bounds of death and of the grave; they were unwilling to confound themselves with the beasts of the field, or to suppose that a being, for whose dignity they entertained the most sincere admiration, could be limited to a spot of earth and to a few years of duration. With this favourable prepossession, they summoned to their aid the science, or rather the language, of Metaphysics. They soon discovered that, as none of the properties of matter will apply to the operations of the mind, the human soul must consequently be a substance distinct from the body, pure, simple, and spiritual, incapable of dissolution, and susceptible of a much higher degree of virtue and happiness after the release from its corporeal prison. From these spacious and noble principles, the philosophers who trod in the footsteps of Plato deduced a very unjustifiable conclusion, since they asserted, not only the future immortality, but the past eternity of the human soul, which they were too apt to consider as a portion of the infinite and self-existing spirit which pervades and sustains the universe.[52] A doctrine thus removed beyond the senses and the experience of mankind might serve to amuse the leisure of a philosophic mind; or, in the silence of solitude, it might sometimes impart a ray of comfort to desponding virtue; but the faint impression which had been received in the schools was soon obliterated by the commerce and business of active life. We are sufficiently acquainted with the eminent persons who flourished in the age of Cicero, and of the first Cæsars, with their actions, their characters, and their motives, to be assured that their conduct in this life was never regulated by any serious conviction of the rewards or punishments of a future state. At the bar and in the senate of Rome the ablest orators were not apprehensive of giving offence to their hearers by exposing that doctrine as an idle and extravagant opinion, which was rejected with contempt by every man of a liberal education and understanding.[53]

Since, therefore, the most sublime efforts of philosophy can extend no further than feebly to point out the desire, the hope, or at most the probability, of a future state, there is nothing, except a divine revelation, that can ascertain the existence, and describe the condition, of the invisible country which is destined to receive the

among the Pagans of Greece and Rome

---

52 The pre-existence of human souls, so far at least as that doctrine is compatible with religion, was adopted by many of the Greek and Latin fathers. See Beausobre, Hist. du Manichéisme, 1. vi. c. 4.

53 See Cicero pro Cluent. c. 61. Cæsar ap. Sallust. de Bell. Catilin. c. 50. Juvenal. Satir. ii. 149.

Esse aliquos manes, et subterranea regna,

[. . .]

Nec pueri credunt, nisi qui nondum ære lavantur. [That there are such things as spirits of the dead and kingdoms in the underworld . . . not even boys believe, except those who aren't yet old enough to pay to get into the baths.[16]]

souls of men after their separation from the body. But we may perceive several defects inherent to the popular religions of Greece and Rome, which rendered them very unequal to so arduous a task. 1. The general system of their mythology was unsupported by any solid proofs; and the wisest among the Pagans had already disclaimed its usurped authority. 2. The description of the infernal regions had been abandoned to the fancy of painters and of poets, who peopled them with so many phantoms and monsters, who dispensed their rewards and punishments with so little equity, that a solemn truth, the most congenial to the human heart, was oppressed and disgraced by the absurd mixture of the wildest fictions.[54] 3. The doctrine of a future state was scarcely considered among the devout polytheists of Greece and Rome as a fundamental article of faith. The providence of the gods, as it related to public communities rather than to private individuals, was principally displayed on the visible theatre of the present world. The petitions which were offered on the altars of Jupiter or Apollo expressed the anxiety of their worshippers for temporal happiness, and their ignorance or indifference concerning a future life.[55] The important truth of the immortality of the soul was inculcated with more diligence as well as success in India, in Assyria, in Egypt, and in Gaul; and, since we cannot attribute such a difference to the among the superior knowledge of the barbarians, we must ascribe it to the Barbarians influence of an established priesthood, which employed the motives of virtue as the instrument of ambition.[56]

among the   We might naturally expect that a principle, so essential to Jews   religion, would have been revealed in the clearest terms to the chosen people of Palestine, and that it might safely have been intrusted to the hereditary priesthood of Aaron. It is incumbent on us to adore the mysterious dispensations of Providence,[57] when we discover that the doctrine of the immortality of the soul is omitted

---

54 The xith book of the Odyssey gives a very dreary and incoherent account of the infernal shades. Pindar and Virgil have embellished the picture; but even those poets, though more correct than their great model, are guilty of very strange inconsistencies. See Bayle, Responses aux Questions d'un Provincial, part iii. c. 22.

55 See the xvith epistle of the first book of Horace, the xiiith Satire of Juvenal, and the iind Satire of Persius: these popular discourses express the sentiment and language of the multitude.

56 If we confine ourselves to the Gauls, we may observe that they intrusted, not only their lives, but even their money, to the security of another world. Vetus ille mos Gallorum occurrit (says Valerius Maximus, 1. ii. c. 6, p. 10), quos, memoria proditum est, pecunias mutuas, quæ his apud inferos redderentur, dare solitos. [This ancient custom is found among the Gauls, so runs the tradition, that they habitually lend money which will be repayed to them in the underworld.] The same custom is more darkly insinuated by Mela, 1. iii. c. 2. It is almost needless to add that the profits of trade hold a just proportion to the credit of the merchant, and that the Druids derived from their holy profession a character of responsibility which could scarcely be claimed by any other order of men.

57 The right reverend author of the Divine Legation of Moses assigns a very curious reason for the omission, and most ingeniously retorts it on the unbelievers.

in the law of Moses; it is darkly insinuated by the prophets, and during the long period which elapsed between the Egyptian and the Babylonian servitudes, the hopes as well as fears of the Jews appear to have been confined within the narrow compass of the present life.[58] After Cyrus had permitted the exiled nation to return into the promised land, and after Ezra had restored the ancient records of their religion, two celebrated sects, the Sadducees and the Pharisees, insensibly arose at Jerusalem.[59] The former, selected from the more opulent and distinguished ranks of society, were strictly attached to the literal sense of the Mosaic law, and they piously rejected the immortality of the soul, as an opinion that received no countenance from the Divine book, which they revered as the only rule of their faith. To the authority of scripture the Pharisees added that of tradition, and they accepted, under the name of traditions, several speculative tenets from the philosophy or religion of the eastern nations. The doctrines of fate or predestination, of angels and spirits, and of a future state of rewards and punishments, were in the number of these new articles of belief; and, as the Pharisees, by the austerity of their manners, had drawn into their party the body of the Jewish people, the immortality of the soul became the prevailing sentiment of the synagogue, under the reign of the Asmonæan princes and pontiffs. The temper of the Jews was incapable of contenting itself with such a cold and languid assent as might satisfy the mind of a Polytheist; and, as soon as they admitted the idea of a future state, they embraced it with the zeal which has always formed the characteristic of the nation. Their zeal, however, added nothing to its evidence, or even probability: and it was still necessary that the doctrine of life and immortality, which had been dictated by nature, approved by reason, and received by superstition, should obtain the sanction of Divine truth from the authority and example of Christ.

When the promise of eternal happiness was proposed to mankind, on condition of adopting the faith and of observing the precepts of the gospel, it is no wonder that so advantageous an offer should have been accepted by great numbers of every religion, of every rank, and of every province in the Roman empire. The ancient Christians were animated by a contempt for their present existence, and by a just confidence of immortality, of which the doubtful and imperfect faith of modern ages cannot give us any adequate notion. In the primitive church, the influence of truth was very powerfully

among the Christians

Approaching end of the world

---

58 See Le Clerc (Prolegomena ad Hist. Ecclesiast. sect. 1, c. 8). His authority seems to carry the greater weight, as he has written a learned and judicious commentary on the books of the Old Testament.

59 Joseph. Antiquitat. 1. xiii. c. 10. De Bell. Jud. ii. 8. According to the most natural interpretation of his words, the Sadducees admitted only the Pentateuch; but it has pleased some modern critics to add the prophets to their creed, and to suppose that they contented themselves with rejecting the traditions of the Pharisees. Dr. Jortin has argued that point in his Remarks on Ecclesiastical History, vol. ii, p. 103.

strengthened by an opinion which, however it may deserve respect for its usefulness and antiquity, has not been found agreeable to experience. It was universally believed that the end of the world and the kingdom of Heaven were at hand. The near approach of this wonderful event had been predicted by the apostles; the tradition of it was preserved by their earliest disciples, and those who understood in their literal sense the discourses of Christ himself were obliged to expect the second and glorious coming of the Son of Man in the clouds, before that generation was totally extinguished, which had beheld his humble condition upon earth, and which might still be witness of the calamities of the Jews under Vespasian or Hadrian. The revolution of seventeen centuries has instructed us not to press too closely the mysterious language of prophecy and revelation; but, as long as, for wise purposes, this error was permitted to subsist in the church, it was productive of the most salutary effects on the faith and practice of Christians, who lived in the awful expectation of that moment when the globe itself, and all the various race of mankind, should tremble at the appearance of their divine judge.[60]

Doctrine of the Millennium The ancient and popular doctrine of the Millennium was intimately connected with the second coming of Christ. As the works of the creation had been finished in six days, their duration in their present state, according to a tradition which was attributed to the prophet Elijah, was fixed to six thousand years.[61] By the same analogy it was inferred that this long period of labour and contention, which was now almost elapsed,[62] would be succeeded by a joyful Sabbath of a thousand years; and that Christ, with the triumphant band of the saints and the elect who had escaped death, or who had been miraculously revived, would reign upon earth till the time appointed for the last and general resurrection. So pleasing was this hope to the mind of believers that the *New Jerusalem*, the seat of this blissful kingdom, was quickly adorned with all the gayest colours of the imagination. A felicity consisting only of pure and spiritual pleasure would have appeared too refined for its inhabitants, who were still supposed to possess their human nature

60 This expectation was countenanced by the twenty-fourth chapter of St. Matthew, and by the first epistle of St. Paul to the Thessalonians. Erasmus removes the difficulty by the help of allegory and metaphor; and the learned Grotius ventures to insinuate that, for wise purposes, the pious deception was permitted to take place.
61 See Burnet's Sacred Theory, part iii. c. 5. This tradition may be traced as high as the author of the Epistle of Barnabas, who wrote in the first century, and who seems to have been half a Jew.
62 The primitive church of Antioch computed almost 6000 years from the creation of the world to the birth of Christ. Africanus, Lactantius, and the Greek church have reduced that number to 5500, and Eusebius has contented himself with 5200 years. These calculations were formed on the Septuagint, which was universally received during the six first centuries. The authority of the Vulgate and of the Hebrew text has determined the moderns, Protestants as well as Catholics, to prefer a period of about 4000 years; though, in the study of profane antiquity, they often find themselves straitened by those narrow limits.

and senses. A garden of Eden, with the amusements of the pastoral life, was no longer suited to the advanced state of society which prevailed under the Roman empire. A city was therefore erected of gold and precious stones, and a supernatural plenty of corn and wine was bestowed on the adjacent territory; in the free enjoyment of whose spontaneous productions the happy and benevolent people was never to be restrained by any jealous laws of exclusive property.[63] The assurance of such a Millennium was carefully inculcated by a succession of fathers from Justin Martyr[64] and Irenæus, who conversed with the immediate disciples of the apostles, down to Lactantius, who was preceptor to 'the son of Constantine.[65] Though it might not be universally received, it appears to have been the reigning sentiment of the orthodox believers; and it seems so well adapted to the desires and apprehensions of mankind that it must have contributed, in a very considerable degree, to the progress of the Christian faith. But, when the edifice of the church was almost completed, the temporary support was laid aside. The doctrine of Christ's reign upon earth was at first treated as a profound allegory, was considered by degrees as a doubtful and useless opinion, and was at length rejected as the absurd invention of heresy and fanaticism.[66] A mysterious prophecy, which still forms a part of the sacred canon, but which was thought to favour the exploded sentiment, has very narrowly escaped the proscription of the church.[67]

Whilst the happiness and glory of a temporal reign were promised to the disciples of Christ, the most dreadful calamities

Conflagra-
tion
of Rome
and of the
world

63 Most of these pictures were borrowed from a misinterpretation of Isaiah, Daniel, and the Apocalypse. One of the grossest images may be found in Irenæus (l. 5, p. 455), the disciple of Papias, who had seen the apostle St. John.

64 See the second dialogue of Justin with Tryphon and the seventh book of Lactantius. It is unnecessary to allege all the intermediate fathers, as the fact is not disputed. Yet the curious reader may consult Daillé de Usu Patrum, l. iii. c. 4.

65 The testimony of Justin, of his own faith and that of his orthodox brethren, in the doctrine of a Millennium, is delivered in the clearest and most solemn manner (Dialog. cum Tryphonte Jud. P. 177, 178, edit. Benedictin). If in the beginning of this important passage there is anything like an inconsistency, we may impute it, as we think proper, either to the author or to his transcribers.

66 Dupin, Bibliothèque Ecclésiastique, tom. i. p. 223, tom. ii. p. 366, and Mosheim, p. 720; though the latter of these learned divines is not altogether candid on this occasion.

67 In the Council of Laodicea (about the year 360) the Apocalypse was tacitly excluded from the sacred canon, by the same churches of Asia to which it is addressed; and we may learn from the complaint of Sulpicius Severus that their sentence had been ratified by the greater number of Christians of his time. From what causes, then, is the Apocalypse at present so generally received by the Greek, the Roman, and the Protestant churches? The following ones may be assigned. 1. The Greeks were subdued by the authority of an impostor who, in the sixth century, assumed the character of Dionysius the Areopagite. 2. A just apprehension, that the grammarians might become more important than the theologians, engaged the Council of Trent to fix the seal of their infallibility on all the books of Scripture, contained in the Latin Vulgate, in the number of which the Apocalypse was fortunately included (Fra Paolo, Istoria del Concilio Tridentino, l. ii.). 3. The advantage of turning those mysterious prophecies against the See of Rome

were denounced against an unbelieving world. The edification of the new Jerusalem was to advance by equal steps with the destruction of the mystic Babylon; and, as long as the emperors who reigned before Constantine persisted in the profession of idolatry, the epithet of Babylon was applied to the city and to the empire of Rome. A regular series was prepared of all the moral and physical evils which can afflict a flourishing nation; intestine discord, and the invasion of the fiercest barbarians from the unknown regions of the North; pestilence and famine, comets and eclipses, earthquakes and inundations.[68] All these were only so many preparatory and alarming signs of the great catastrophe of Rome, when the country of the Scipios and Cæsars should be consumed by a flame from Heaven, and the city of the seven hills, with her palaces, her temples, and her triumphal arches, should be buried in a vast lake of fire and brimstone. It might, however, afford some consolation to Roman vanity, that the period of their empire would be that of the world itself; which, as it had once perished by the element of water, was destined to experience a second and a speedy destruction from the element of fire. In the opinion of a general conflagration, the faith of the Christian very happily coincided with the tradition of the East, the philosophy of the Stoics, and the analogy of Nature; and even the country which, from religious motives, had been chosen for the origin and principal scene of the conflagration, was the best adapted for that purpose by natural and physical causes; by its deep caverns, beds of sulphur, and numerous volcanoes, of which those of Ætna, of Vesuvius, and of Lipari, exhibit a very imperfect representation. The calmest and most intrepid sceptic could not refuse to acknowledge that the destruction of the present system of the world by fire was in itself extremely probable. The Christian, who founded his belief much less on the fallacious arguments of reason than on the authority of tradition and the interpretation of scripture, expected it with terror and confidence, as a certain and approaching event; and, as his mind was perpetually filled with the solemn idea, he considered every disaster that happened to the empire as an infallible symptom of an expiring world.[69]

The Pagans devoted to eternal punishment

The condemnation of the wisest and most virtuous of the Pagans, on account of their ignorance or disbelief of the divine truth, seems to offend the reason and the humanity of the present age.[70] But the primitive church, whose faith was of a much firmer

inspired the Protestants with uncommon veneration for so useful an ally. See the ingenious and elegant discourses of the present bishop of Lichfield on that unpromising subject.

68 Lactantius (Institut. Divin. vii. 15, &c.) relates the dismal tale of futurity with great spirit and eloquence.

69 On this subject every reader of taste will be entertained with the third part of Burnet's Sacred Theory. He blends philosophy, scripture, and tradition into one magnificent system; in the description of which he displays a strength of fancy not inferior to that of Milton himself.

70 And yet, whatever may be the language of individuals, it is still the public doctrine of

consistence, delivered over, without hesitation, to eternal torture the far greater part of the human species. A charitable hope might perhaps be indulged in favour of Socrates, or some other sages of antiquity, who had consulted the light of reason before that of the gospel had arisen.[71] But it was unanimously affirmed that those who, since the birth or the death of Christ, had obstinately persisted in the worship of the dæmons, neither deserved, nor could expect, a pardon from the irritated justice of the Deity. These rigid sentiments, which had been unknown to the ancient world, appear to have infused a spirit of bitterness into a system of love and harmony. The ties of blood and friendship were frequently torn asunder by the difference of religious faith; and the Christians, who, in this world, found themselves oppressed by the power of the Pagans, were sometimes seduced by resentment and spiritual pride to delight in the prospect of their future triumph. "You are fond of spectacles," exclaims the stern Tertullian; "except the greatest of all spectacles, the last and eternal judgment of the universe. How shall I admire, how laugh, how rejoice, how exult, when I behold so many proud monarchs, and fancied gods, groaning in the lowest abyss of darkness; so many magistrates, who persecuted the name of the Lord, liquefying in fiercer fires than they ever kindled against the Christians; so many sage philosophers blushing in red hot flames, with their deluded scholars; so many celebrated poets trembling before the tribunal, not of Minos, but of Christ; so many tragedians, more tuneful in the expression of their own sufferings; so many dancers —!" But the humanity of the reader will permit me to draw a veil over the rest of this infernal description, which the zealous African pursues in a long variety of affected and unfeeling witticisms.[72]

Doubtless there were many among the primitive Christians of a temper more suitable to the meekness and charity of their profession. There were many who felt a sincere compassion for the danger of their friends and countrymen, and who exerted the most benevolent zeal to save them from the impending destruction. The

Were often converted by their fears

all the Christian churches; nor can even our own refuse to admit the conclusions which must be drawn from the viiith and the xviiith of her Articles. The Jansenists, who have so diligently studied the works of the fathers, maintain this sentiment with distinguished zeal; and the learned M. de Tillemont never dismisses a virtuous emperor without pronouncing his damnation. Zuinglius is perhaps the only leader of a party who has ever adopted the milder sentiment, and he gave no less offence to the Lutherans than to the Catholics. See Bossuet, Histoire des Variations des Eglises Protestantes, 1. ii. c. 19-22.
71 Justin and Clemens of Alexandria allow that some of the philosophers were instructed by the Logos; confounding its double signification of the human reason and of the Divine Word.
72 Tertullian de Spectaculis, c. 30. In order to ascertain the degree of authority which the zealous African had acquired, it may be sufficient to allege the testimony of Cyprian, the doctor and guide of all the western churches. (See Prudent. Hymn. xiii. 100.) As often as he applied himself to his daily study of the writings of Tertullian, he was accustomed to say, "*Da mihi magistrum*; Give me my master". (Hieronym. de Viris Illustribus, tom. i. p. 284.)

careless Polytheist, assailed by new and unexpected terrors, against which neither his priests nor his philosophers could afford him any certain protection, was very frequently terrified and subdued by the menace of eternal tortures. His fears might assist the progress of his faith and reason; and, if he could once persuade himself to suspect that the Christian religion might possibly be true, it became an easy task to convince him that it was the safest and most prudent party that he could possibly embrace.

THE THIRD CAUSE. Miraculous powers of the primitive church   III. The supernatural gifts, which even in this life were ascribed to the Christians above the rest of mankind, must have conduced to their own comfort, and very frequently to the conviction of infidels. Besides the occasional prodigies, which might sometimes be affected by the immediate interposition of the Deity when he suspended the laws of Nature for the service of religion, the Christian church, from the time of the apostles and their first disciples,[73] has claimed an uninterrupted succession of miraculous powers, the gift of tongues, of vision and of prophecy, the power of expelling dæmons, of healing the sick, and of raising the dead. The knowledge of foreign languages was frequently communicated to the contemporaries of Irenæus, though Irenæus himself was left to struggle with the difficulties of a barbarous dialect whilst he preached the gospel to the natives of Gaul.[74] The divine inspiration, whether it was conveyed in the form of a waking or of a sleeping vision, is described as a favour very liberally bestowed on all ranks of the faithful, on women as on elders, on boys as well as upon bishops. When their devout minds were sufficiently prepared by a course of prayer, of fasting, and of vigils, to receive the extraordinary impulse, they were transported out of their senses, and delivered in extasy what was inspired, being mere organs of the Holy Spirit, just as a pipe or flute is of him who blows into it.[75] We may add that the design of these visions was, for the most part, either to disclose the future history, or to guide the present administration, of the church. The expulsion of the dæmons from the bodies of those unhappy persons whom they had been permitted to torment was considered as a signal, though ordinary, triumph of religion, and is repeatedly alleged by the ancient apologists as the most convincing evidence of the truth of Christianity. The awful ceremony was usually performed in a public manner, and in the presence of a great number of spectators; the patient was relieved by the power or skill of the exorcist, and the

---

73 Notwithstanding the evasions of Dr. Middleton, it is impossible to overlook the clear traces of visions and inspiration, which may be found in the apostolic fathers.

74 Irenæus adv. Hæres. Proem. p. 3. Dr. Middleton (Free Inquiry, p. 96, &c.) observes that, as this pretension of all others was the most difficult to support by art, it was the soonest given up. The observation suits his hypothesis.

75 Athenagoras in Legatione. Justin Martyr, Cohort. ad Gentes. Tertullian advers. Marcionit. l. iv. These descriptions are not very unlike the prophetic fury for which Cicero (de Divinat. ii. 54) expresses so little reverence.

vanquished dæmon was heard to confess that he was one of the fabled gods of antiquity, who had impiously usurped the adoration of mankind.[76] But the miraculous cure of diseases, of the most inveterate or even præternatural kind, can no longer occasion any surprise, when we recollect that in the days of Irenæus, about the end of the second century, the resurrection of the dead was very far from being esteemed an uncommon event; that the miracle was frequently performed on necessary occasions, by great fasting and the joint supplication of the church of the place, and that the persons thus restored to their prayers had lived afterwards among them many years.[77] At such a period, when faith could ·boast of so many wonderful victories over death, it seems difficult to account for the scepticism of those philosophers who still rejected and derided the doctrine of the resurrection. A noble Grecian had rested on this important ground the whole controversy, and promised Theophilus, bishop of Antioch, that, if he could be gratified with the sight of a single person who had been actually raised from the dead, he would immediately embrace the Christian religion. It is somewhat remarkable that the prelate of the first eastern church, however anxious for the conversion of his friend, thought proper to decline this fair and reasonable challenge.[78]

The miracles of the primitive church, after obtaining the sanction of ages, have been lately attacked in a very free and ingenious inquiry;[79] which, though it has met with the most favourable reception from the Public, appears to have excited a general scandal among the divines of our own as well as of the other Protestant churches of Europe.[80] Our different sentiments on this subject will be much less influenced by any particular arguments than by our habits of study and reflection; and, above all, by the degree of the evidence which we have accustomed ourselves to require for the proof of a miraculous event. The duty of an historian does not call upon him to interpose his private judgment in this nice and important controversy; but he ought not to dissemble the difficulty of adopting such a theory as may reconcile the interest of religion with that of reason, of making a proper application of that theory, and of defining with precision the limits of that happy period, exempt from error and from deceit, to which we might be disposed to extend the gift of supernatural powers. From the first of

Their truth contested

Our perplexity in defining the miraculous period

***

76 Tertullian (Apolog. c. 23) throws out a bold defiance to the Pagan magistrates. Of the primitive miracles, the power of exorcising is the only one which has been assumed by Protestants.

77 Irenæus adv. Hæreses, l. ii. 56, 57; l. v. c. 6. Mr. Dodwell (Dissertat. ad Irenæum, ii. 42) concludes that the second century was still more fertile in miracles than the first.

78 Theophilus ad Autolycum, l. i. p. 345. Edit. Benedictin. Paris, 1742.

79 Dr. Middleton sent out his Introduction in the year 1747, published his Free Inquiry in 1749, and before his death, which happened in 1750, he had prepared a vindication of it against his numerous adversaries.

80 The University of Oxford conferred degrees on his opponents. From the indignation of Mosheim (p. 221), we may discover the sentiments of Lutheran divines.

the fathers to the last of the popes, a succession of bishops, of saints, of martyrs, and of miracles is continued without interruption, and the progress of superstition was so gradual and almost imperceptible that we know not in what particular link we should break the chain of tradition. Every age bears testimony to the wonderful events by which it was distinguished, and its testimony appears no less weighty and respectable than that of the preceding generation, till we are insensibly led on to accuse our own inconsistency, if in the eighth or in the twelfth century we deny to the venerable Bede, or to the holy Bernard, the same degree of confidence which, in the second century, we had so liberally granted to Justin or to Irenæus.[81] If the truth of any of those miracles is appreciated by their apparent use and propriety, every age had unbelievers to convince, heretics to confute, and idolatrous nations to convert; and sufficient motives might always be produced to justify the interposition of Heaven. And yet, since every friend to revelation is persuaded of the reality, and every reasonable man is convinced of the cessation, of miraculous powers, it is evident that there must have been *some period* in which they were either suddenly or gradually withdrawn from the Christian church. Whatever æra is chosen for that purpose, the death of the apostles, the conversion of the Roman empire, or the extinction of the Arian heresy,[82] the insensibility of the Christians who lived at that time will equally afford a just matter of surprise. They still supported their pretensions after they had lost their power. Credulity performed the office of faith; fanaticism was permitted to assume the language of inspiration, and the effects of accident or contrivance were ascribed to supernatural causes. The recent experience of genuine miracles should have instructed the Christian world in the ways of Providence, and habituated their eye (if we may use a very inadequate expression) to the style of the divine artist. Should the most skilful painter of modern Italy presume to decorate his feeble imitations with the name of Raphael or of Correggio, the insolent fraud would be soon discovered and indignantly rejected.

Use of the primitive miracles   Whatever opinion may be entertained of the miracles of the primitive church since the time of the apostles, this unresisting softness of temper, so conspicuous among the believers of the second and third centuries, proved of some accidental benefit to the cause of truth and religion. In modern times, a latent, and even involuntary, scepticism adheres to the most pious dispositions.

---

81 It may seem somewhat remarkable that Bernard of Clairvaux, who records so many miracles of his friend St. Malachi, never takes any notice of his own, which, in their turn, however, are carefully related by his companions and disciples. In the long series of ecclesiastical history, does there exist a single instance of a saint asserting that he himself possessed the gift of miracles?

82 The conversion of Constantine is the æra which is most usually fixed by Protestants. The more rational divines are unwilling to admit the miracles of the fourth, whilst the more credulous are unwilling to reject those of the fifth, century.

Their admission of supernatural truths is much less an active consent than a cold and passive acquiescence. Accustomed long since to observe and to respect the invariable order of Nature, our reason, or at least our imagination, is not sufficiently prepared to sustain the visible action of the Deity. But, in the first ages of Christianity, the situation of mankind was extremely different. The most curious, or the most credulous, among the Pagans were often persuaded to enter into a society which asserted an actual claim of miraculous powers. The primitive Christians perpetually trod on mystic ground, and their minds were exercised by the habits of believing the most extraordinary events. They felt, or they fancied, that on every side they were incessantly assaulted by dæmons, comforted by visions, instructed by prophecy, and surprisingly delivered from danger, sickness, and from death itself, by the supplications of the church. The real or imaginary prodigies, of which they so frequently conceived themselves to be the objects, the instruments, or the spectators, very happily disposed them to adopt, with the same ease, but with far greater justice, the authentic wonders of the evangelic history; and thus miracles that exceeded not the measure of their own experience inspired them with the most lively assurance of mysteries which were acknowledged to surpass the limits of their understanding. It is this deep impression of supernatural truths which has been so much celebrated under the name of faith; a state of mind described as the surest pledge of the divine favour and of future felicity, and recommended as the first or perhaps the only merit of a Christian. According to the more rigid doctors, the moral virtues, which may be equally practised by infidels, are destitute of any value or efficacy in the work of our justification.

IV. But the primitive Christian demonstrated his faith by his virtues; and it was very justly supposed that the divine persuasion, which enlightened or subdued the understanding, must, at the same time, purify the heart, and direct the actions, of the believer. The first apologists of Christianity who justify the innocence of their brethren, and the writers of a later period who celebrate the sanctity of their ancestors, display, in the most lively colours, the reformation of manners which was introduced into the world by the preaching of the gospel. As it is my intention to remark only such human causes as were permitted to second the influence of revelation, I shall slightly mention two motives which might naturally render the lives of the primitive Christians much purer and more austere than those of their Pagan contemporaries, or their degenerate successors; repentance for their past sins, and the laudable desire of supporting the reputation of the society in which they were engaged. *THE FOURTH CAUSE. Virtues of the first Christians*

It is a very ancient reproach, suggested by the ignorance or the malice of infidelity, that the Christians allured into their party the most atrocious criminals, who, as soon as they were touched by a *Effects of their re-pentance* sense of remorse, were easily persuaded to wash away, in the water of baptism, the guilt of their past conduct, for which the temples of the gods refused to grant them any expiation. But this reproach, when it is cleared from misrepresentation, contributes as much to the honour as it did to the increase of the church.[83] The friends of Christianity may acknowledge without a blush that many of the most eminent saints had been before their baptism the most abandoned sinners. Those persons who in the world had followed, though in an imperfect manner, the dictates of benevolence and propriety, derived such a calm satisfaction from the opinion of their own rectitude, as rendered them much less susceptible of the sudden emotions of shame, of grief, and of terror, which have given birth to so many wonderful conversions. After the example of their Divine Master, the missionaries of the gospel disdained not the society of men, and especially of women, oppressed by the consciousness, and very often by the effects, of their vices. As they emerged from sin and superstition to the glorious hope of immortality, they resolved to devote themselves to a life, not only of virtue, but of penitence. The desire of perfection became the ruling passion of their soul; and it is well known that, while reason embraces a cold mediocrity, our passions hurry us, with rapid violence, over the space which lies between the most opposite extremes.

Care of their reputation

When the new converts had been enrolled in the number of the faithful and were admitted to the sacraments of the church, they found themselves restrained from relapsing into their past disorders by another consideration of a less spiritual, but of a very innocent and respectable nature. Any particular society that has departed from the great body of the nation or the religion to which it belonged immediately becomes the object of universal as well as invidious observation. In proportion to the smallness of its numbers, the character of the society may be affected by the virtue and vices of the persons who compose it; and every member is engaged to watch with the most vigilant attention over his own behaviour and over that of his brethren, since, as he must expect to incur a part of the common disgrace, he may hope to enjoy a share of the common reputation. When the Christians of Bithynia were brought before the tribunal of the younger Pliny, they assured the pro-consul that, far from being engaged in any unlawful conspiracy, they were bound by a solemn obligation to abstain from the commission of those crimes which disturb the private or public peace of society, from theft, robbery, adultery, perjury, and fraud.[84] Near a century afterwards, Tertullian, with an honest pride, could boast that very few Christians had suffered by the hand of the

83 The imputations of Celsus and Julian, with the defence of the fathers, are very fairly stated by Spanheim, Commentaire sur les Césars de Julian, p. 468.
84 Plin. Epist. x. 97.

executioner, except on account of their religion.[85] Their serious and sequestered life, averse to the gay luxury of the age, insured them to chastity, temperance, economy, and all the sober and domestic virtues. As the greater number were of some trade or profession, it was incumbent on them, by the strictest integrity and the fairest dealing, to remove the suspicions which the profane are too apt to conceive against the appearances of sanctity. The contempt of the world exercised them in the habits of humility, meekness, and patience. The more they were persecuted, the more closely they adhered to each other. Their mutual charity and unsuspecting confidence has been remarked by infidels, and was too often abused by perfidious friends.[86]

It is a very honourable circumstance for the morals of the primitive Christians, that even their faults, or rather errors, were derived from an excess of virtue. The bishops and doctors of the church, whose evidence attests, and whose authority might influence, the professions, the principles, and even the practice, of their contemporaries, had studied the scriptures with less skill than devotion, and they often received, in the most literal sense, those rigid precepts of Christ and the apostles to which the prudence of succeeding commentators has applied a looser and more figurative mode of interpretation. Ambitious to exalt the perfection of the gospel above the wisdom of philosophy, the zealous fathers have carried the duties of self-mortification, of purity, and of patience, to a height which it is scarcely possible to attain, and much less to preserve, in our present state of weakness and corruption. A doctrine so extraordinary and so sublime must inevitably command the veneration of the people; but it was ill calculated to obtain the suffrage of those worldly philosophers who, in the conduct of this transitory life, consult only the feelings of nature and the interest of society.[87] *Mortality of the fathers*

There are two very natural propensities which we may distinguish in the most virtuous and liberal dispositions, the love of pleasure and the love of action. If the former be refined by art and learning, improved by the charms of social intercourse, and corrected by a just regard to economy, to health, and to reputation, it is productive of the greatest part of the happiness of private life. The love of action is a principle of a much stronger and more doubtful nature. It often leads to anger, to ambition, and to revenge; but, when it is guided by the sense of propriety and benevolence, it becomes the parent of every virtue; and, if those virtues are accompanied with equal abilities, a family, a state, or an *Principles of human nature*

85 Tertullian, Apolog. c. 44. He adds, however, with some degree of hesitation, "Aut si aliud, jam non Christianus". [And if for any other reason, then they were not Christians.]
86 The philosopher Peregrinus (of whose life and death Lucian has left us so entertaining an account) imposed, for a long time, on the credulous simplicity of the Christians of Asia.
87 See a very judicious treatise of Barbeyrac sur la Morale des Pères.

empire may be indebted for their safety and prosperity to the undaunted courage of a single man. To the love of pleasure we may therefore ascribe most of the agreeable, to the love of action we may attribute most of the useful and respectable, qualifications. The character in which both the one and the other should be united and harmonized would seem to constitute the most perfect idea of human nature. The insensible and inactive disposition, which should be supposed alike destitute of both, would be rejected, by the common consent of mankind, as utterly incapable of procuring any happiness to the individual, or any public benefit to the world. But it was not in *this* world that the primitive Christians were desirous of making themselves either agreeable or useful.

The primitive Christians condemn pleasure and luxury   The acquisition of knowledge, the exercise of our reason or fancy, and the cheerful flow of unguarded conversation, may employ the leisure of a liberal mind. Such amusements, however, were rejected with abhorrence, or admitted with the utmost caution, by the severity of the fathers, who despised all knowledge that was not useful to salvation, and who considered all levity of discourse as a criminal abuse of the gift of speech. In our present state of existence, the body is so inseparably connected with the soul that it seems to be our interest to taste, with innocence and moderation, the enjoyments of which that faithful companion is susceptible. Very different was the reasoning of our devout predecessors; vainly aspiring to imitate the perfection of angels, they disdained, or they affected to disdain, every earthly and corporeal delight.[88] Some of our senses indeed are necessary for our preservation, others for our subsistence, and others again for our information, and thus far it was impossible to reject the use of them. The first sensation of pleasure was marked as the first moment of their abuse. The unfeeling candidate for Heaven was instructed, not only to resist the grosser allurements of the taste or smell, but even to shut his ears against the profane harmony of sounds, and to view with indifference the most finished productions of human art. Gay apparel, magnificent houses, and elegant furniture were supposed to unite the double guilt of pride and of sensuality: a simple and mortified appearance was more suitable to the Christian who was certain of his sins and doubtful of his salvation. In their censures of luxury, the fathers are extremely minute and circumstantial;[89] and among the various articles which excite their pious indignation, we may enumerate false hair, garments of any colour except white, instruments of music, vases of gold or silver, downy pillows (as Jacob reposed his head on a stone), white bread, foreign wines, public salutations, the use of warm baths, and the practice of shaving the beard, which, according to the expression of Tertullian, is a lie against our own faces, and an

88 Lactant. Institut. Divin. l. vi. c. 20, 21, 22.
89 Consult a work of Clemens of Alexandria, intitled the Pædagogue, which contains the rudiments of ethics, as they were taught in the most celebrated of the Christian schools.

impious attempt to improve the works of the Creator.[90] When
Christianity was introduced among the rich and the polite, the
observation of these singular laws was left, as it would be at present,
to the few who were ambitious of superior sanctity. But it is always
easy, as well as agreeable, for the inferior ranks of mankind to claim
a merit from the contempt of that pomp and pleasure which fortune
has placed beyond their reach. The virtue of the primitive
Christians, like that of the first Romans, was very frequently
guarded by poverty and ignorance.

The chaste severity of the fathers, in whatever related to the
commerce of the two sexes, flowed from the same principle; their
abhorrence of every enjoyment which might gratify the sensual, and
degrade the spiritual, nature of man. It was their favourite opinion
that, if Adam had preserved his obedience to the Creator, he would
have lived for ever in a state of virgin purity, and that some
harmless mode of vegetation might have peopled paradise with a
race of innocent and immortal beings.[91] The use of marriage was
permitted only to his fallen posterity, as a necessary expedient to
continue the human species, and as a restraint, however imperfect,
on the natural licentiousness of desire. The hesitation of the
orthodox casuists on this interesting subject betrays the perplexity
of men, unwilling to approve an institution which they were
compelled to tolerate.[92] The enumeration of the very whimsical
laws, which they most circumstantially imposed on the marriage-
bed, would force a smile from the young, and a blush from the fair.
It was their unanimous sentiment that a first marriage was adequate
to all the purposes of nature and of society. The sensual connexion
was refined into a resemblance of the mystic union of Christ with
his church, and was pronounced to be indissoluble either by divorce
or by death. The practice of second nuptials was branded with the
name of a legal adultery; and the persons who were guilty of so
scandalous an offence against Christian purity were soon excluded
from the honours, and even from the alms, of the church.[93] Since
desire was imputed as a crime, and marriage was tolerated as a
defect, it was consistent with the same principles to consider a state
of celibacy as the nearest approach to the divine perfection. It was
with the utmost difficulty that ancient Rome could support the
institution of six vestals;[94] but the primitive church was filled with a
great number of persons of either sex who had devoted themselves

*Their sen-
timents
concerning
marriage
and
chastity*

90 Tertullian de Spectaculis, c. 23. Clemens Alexandrin. Pædagog. l. iii. c. 8.
91 Beausobre, Hist. Critique du Manichéisme, l. vii. c. 3. Justin, Gregory of Nyssa,
Augustin, &c., strongly inclined to this opinion.
92 Some of the Gnostic heretics were more consistent; they rejected the use of marriage.
93 See a chain of tradition, from Justin Martyr to Jerome, in the Morale des Pères; c. iv. 6-
26.
94 See a very curious Dissertation on the Vestals, in the Mémoires de l'Académie des
Inscriptions, tom. iv. p. 161-227. Notwithstanding the honours and rewards which were
bestowed on those virgins, it was difficult to procure a sufficient number; nor could the
dread of the most horrible death always restrain their incontinence.

to the profession of perpetual chastity.[95] A few of these, among whom we may reckon the learned Origen,[17] judged it the most prudent to disarm the tempter.[96] Some were insensible and some were invincible against the assaults of the flesh. Disdaining an ignominious flight, the virgins of the warm climate of Africa encountered the enemy in the closest engagement; they permitted priests and deacons to share their bed, and gloried amidst the flames in their unsullied purity. But insulted Nature sometimes vindicated her rights, and this new species of martyrdom served only to introduce a new scandal into the church.[97] Among the Christian ascetics, however (a name which they soon acquired from their painful exercise), many, as they were less presumptuous, were probably more successful. The loss of sensual pleasure was supplied and compensated by spiritual pride. Even the multitude of Pagans were inclined to estimate the merit of the sacrifice by its apparent difficulty; and it was in the praise of these chaste spouses of Christ that the fathers have poured forth the troubled stream of their eloquence.[98] Such are the early traces of monastic principles and institutions which, in a subsequent age, have counterbalanced all the temporal advantages of Christianity.[99]

Their aversion to the business of war and government

The Christians were not less averse to the business than to the pleasures of this world. The defence of our persons and property they knew not how to reconcile with the patient doctrine which enjoined an unlimited forgiveness of past injuries and commanded them to invite the repetition of fresh insults. Their simplicity was offended by the use of oaths, by the pomp of magistracy, and by the active contention of public life, nor could their humane ignorance be convinced that it was lawful on any occasion to shed the blood of our fellow-creatures, either by the sword of justice or by that of war; even though their criminal or hostile attempts should threaten the peace and safety of the whole community.[100] It was acknowledged

---

95 Cupiditatem procreandi aut unam scimus aut nullam. [We understand either a single desire for procreation or none.] Minucius Felix, c. 31. Justin Apolog. Major. Athenagoras in Legat. c. 28. Tertullian de Cultu Femin. l. ii.

96 Eusebius, l. vi. 8. Before the fame of Origen had excited envy and persecution, this extraordinary action was rather admired than censured. As it was his general practice to allegorize scripture, it seems unfortunate that, in this instance only, he should have adopted the literal sense.

97 Cyprian, Epist. 4. and Dodwell, Dissertat. Cyprianic. iii. Something like this rash attempt was long afterwards imputed to the founder of the order of Fontevrault. Bayle has amused himself and his readers on that very delicate subject.

98 Dupin (Bibliothèque Ecclésiastique, tom. i. p. 195) gives a particular account of the dialogue of the ten virgins, as it was composed by Methodius, bishop of Tyre. The praises of virginity are excessive.

99 The Ascetics (as early as the second century) made a public profession of mortifying their bodies, and of abstaining from the use of flesh and wine. Mosheim, p. 310.

100 See the Morale des Pères. The same patient principles have been revived since the Reformation by the Socinians, the modern Anabaptists, and the Quakers. Barclay, the apologist of the Quakers, has protected his brethren by the authority of the primitive Christians, p. 542-549.

that, under a less perfect law, the powers of the Jewish constitution had been exercised, with the approbation of Heaven, by inspired prophets and by anointed kings. The Christians felt and confessed that such institutions might be necessary for the present system of the world, and they cheerfully submitted to the authority of their Pagan governors. But, while they inculcated the maxims of passive obedience, they refused to take any active part in the civil administration or the military defence of the empire. Some indulgence might perhaps be allowed to those persons who, before their conversion, were already engaged in such violent and sanguinary occupations;[101] but it was impossible that the Christians, without renouncing a more sacred duty, could assume the character of soldiers, of magistrates, or of princes.[102] This indolent, or even criminal, disregard to the public welfare exposed them to the contempt and reproaches of the Pagans, who very frequently asked, What must be the fate of the empire, attacked on every side by the barbarians, if all mankind should adopt the pusillanimous sentiments of the new sect?[103] To this insulting question the Christian apologists returned obscure and ambiguous answers, as they were unwilling to reveal the secret cause of their security: the expectation that, before the conversion of mankind was accomplished, war, government, the Roman empire and the world itself would be no more. It may be observed that, in this instance likewise, the situation of the first Christians coincided very happily with their religious scruples, and that their aversion to an active life contributed rather to excuse them from the service, than to exclude them from the honours, of the state and army.

V. But the human character, however it may be exalted or depressed by a temporary enthusiasm, will return, by degrees, to its proper and natural level, and will resume those passions that seem the most adapted to its present condition. The primitive Christians were dead to the business and pleasures of the world; but their love of action, which could never be entirely extinguished, soon revived, and found a new occupation in the government of the church. A separate society, which attacked the established religion of the empire, was obliged to adopt some form of internal policy, and to appoint a sufficient number of ministers, intrusted not only with the spiritual functions, but even with the temporal direction, of the Christian commonwealth. The safety of that society, its honour, its aggrandisement, were productive, even in the most pious minds, of a spirit of patriotism, such as the first of the Romans had felt for the republic, and sometimes, of a similar indiffer-

THE FIFTH CAUSE. The Christians active in the government of the church

---

101 Tertullian, Apolog. c. 21, De Idololatriâ, c. 17, 18. Origen contra Celsum, l. v. p. 253, l. vii. p. 348, l. viii. p.423-428.
102 Tertullian (De Coronâ Militis, c. 11) suggests to them the expedient of deserting; a counsel which, if it had been generally known, was not very proper to conciliate the favour of the emperors towards the Christian sect.
103 As well as we can judge from the mutilated representation of Origen (l. viii. p. 423), his adversary, Celsus, had urged his objection with great force and candour.

ence in the use of whatever means might probably conduce to so desirable an end. The ambition of raising themselves or their friends to the honours and offices of the church was disguised by the laudable intention of devoting to the public benefit the power and consideration which, for that purpose only, it became their duty to solicit. In the exercise of their functions, they were frequently called upon to detect the errors of heresy, or the arts of faction, to oppose the designs of perfidious brethren, to stigmatize their characters with deserved infamy, and to expel them from the bosom of a society whose peace and happiness they had attempted to disturb. The ecclesiastical governors of the Christians were taught to unite the wisdom of the serpent with the innocence of the dove; but, as the former was refined, so the latter was insensibly corrupted, by the habits of government. In the church as well as in the world the persons who were placed in any public station rendered themselves considerable by their eloquence and firmness, by their knowledge of mankind, and by their dexterity in business; and, while they concealed from others, and, perhaps, from themselves, the secret motives of their conduct, they too frequently relapsed into all the turbulent passions of active life, which were tinctured with an additional degree of bitterness and obstinacy from the infusion of spiritual zeal.

Its primitive freedom and equality The government of the church has often been the subject, as well as the prize, of religious contention. The hostile disputants of Rome, of Paris, of Oxford and of Geneva have alike struggled to reduce the primitive and apostolic model[104] to the respective standards of their own policy. The few who have pursued this inquiry with more candour and impartiality are of opinion[105] that the apostles declined the office of legislation, and rather chose to endure some partial scandals and divisions than to exclude the Christians of a future age from the liberty of varying their forms of ecclesiastical government according to the changes of times and circumstances. The scheme of policy which, under their approbation, was adopted for the use of the first century may be discovered from the practice of Jerusalem, of Ephesus, or of Corinth. The societies which were instituted in the cities of the Roman empire were united only by the ties of faith and charity. Independence and equality formed the basis of their internal constitution. The want of discipline and human learning was supplied by the occasional assistance of the *prophets*,[106] who were called to that function, without distinction of age, of sex, or of natural abilities, and who, as often as they felt the divine impulse, poured forth the effusions of the spirit in the assembly of the faithful. But these extraordinary gifts were frequently abused or

104 The aristocratical party in France, as well as in England, has strenuously maintained the divine origin of bishops. But the Calvinistical presbyters were impatient of a superior; and the Roman Pontiff refused to acknowledge an equal. See Fra Paolo.
105 In the history of the Christian hierarchy, I have, for the most part, followed the learned and candid Mosheim.
106 For the prophets of the primitive church, see Mosheim, Dissertationes ad Hist. Eccles. pertinentes, tom. ii. p. 132–208.

misapplied by the prophetic teachers. They displayed them at an improper season, presumptuously disturbed the service of the assembly, and by their pride or mistaken zeal they introduced, particularly into the apostolic church of Corinth, a long and melancholy train of disorders.[107] As the institution of prophets became useless, and even pernicious, their powers were withdrawn and their office abolished. The public functions of religion were solely intrusted to the established ministers of the church, the *bishops* and the *presbyters*; two appellations which, in their first origin, appear to have distinguished the same office and the same order of persons. The name of Presbyter was expressive of their age, or rather of their gravity and wisdom. The title of Bishop denoted their inspection over the faith and manners of the Christians who were committed to their pastoral care. In proportion to the respective numbers of the faithful, a larger or smaller number of these *episcopal presbyters* guided each infant congregation with equal authority and with united councils.[108]

But the most perfect equality of freedom requires the directing hand of a superior magistrate; and the order of public deliberations soon introduces the office of a president, invested at least with the authority of collecting the sentiments, and of executing the resolutions, of the assembly. A regard for the public tranquility, which would so frequently have been interrupted by annual or by occasional elections, induced the primitive Christians to constitute an honourable and perpetual magistracy, and to choose one of the wisest and most holy among their presbyters to execute, during his life, the duties of their ecclesiastical governor. It was under these circumstances that the lofty title of Bishop began to raise itself above the humble appellation of presbyter; and, while the latter remained the most natural distinction for the members of every Christian senate, the former was appropriated to the dignity of its new president.[109] The advantages of this episcopal form of government, which appears to have been introduced before the end of the first century,[110] were so obvious, and so important for the future greatness, as well as the present peace, of Christianity, that it was adopted without delay by all the societies which were already scattered over the empire, had acquired in a very early period the sanction of antiquity,[111] and is

Institution of bishops as presidents of the college of presbyters

---

107 See the Epistles of St. Paul, and of Clemens, to the Corinthians.

108 Hooker's Ecclesiastical Polity, l. vii.

109 See Jerome ad Titum, c. 1, and Epistol. 85 (in the Benedictine edition, 101), and the elaborate apology of Blondel, pro sententiâ Hieronymi. The ancient state, as it is described by Jerome, of the bishop and presbyters of Alexandria receives a remarkable confirmation from the patriarch Eutychius (Annal. tom. i. p. 330, Vers. Pocock), whose testimony I know not how to reject, in spite of all the objections of the learned Pearson in his Vindiciæ Ignatianæ, part i. c. 11.

110 See the introduction to the Apocalypse. Bishops, under the name of angels, were already instituted in seven cities of Asia. And yet the epistle of Clemens (which is probably of as ancient a date) does not lead us to discover any traces of episcopacy either at Corinth or Rome.

111 Nulla Ecclesia sine Episcopo [No congregation without a bishop], has been a fact as well as a maxim since the time of Tertullian and Irenæus.

still revered by the most powerful churches, both of the East and of the West, as a primitive and even as a divine establishment.[112] It is needless to observe that the pious and humble presbyters who were first dignified with the episcopal title could not possess, and would probably have rejected, the power and pomp which now encircles the tiara of the Roman pontiff, or the mitre of a German prelate. But we may define, in a few words, the narrow limits of their original jurisdiction, which was chiefly of a spiritual, though in some instances of a temporal, nature.[113] It consisted in the administration of the sacraments and discipline of the church, the superintendency of religious ceremonies, which imperceptibly increased in number and variety, the consecration of ecclesiastical ministers, to whom the bishop assigned their respective functions, the management of the public fund, and the determination of all such differences as the faithful were unwilling to expose before the tribunal of an idolatrous judge. These powers, during a short period, were exercised according to the advice of the presbyteral college, and with the consent and approbation of the assembly of Christians. The primitive bishops were considered only as the first of their equals, and the honourable servants of a free people. Whenever the episcopal chair became vacant by death, a new president was chosen among the presbyters by the suffrage of the whole congregation, every member of which supposed himself invested with a sacred and sacerdotal character.[114]

Provincial councils   Such was the mild and equal constitution by which the Christians were governed more than a hundred years after the death of the apostles. Every society formed within itself a separate and independent republic: and, although the most distant of these little states maintained a mutual as well as friendly intercourse of letters and deputations, the Christian world was not yet connected by any supreme authority or legislative assembly. As the numbers of the faithful were gradually multiplied, they discovered the advantages that might result from a closer union of their interest and designs. Towards the end of the second century, the churches of Greece and Asia adopted the useful institutions of provincial synods, and they may justly be supposed to have borrowed the model of a representative council from the celebrated examples of their own country, the Amphictyons, the Achæan league, or the assemblies of the Ionian cities. It was soon established as a custom and as a law that the bishops of the independent churches

112 After we have passed the difficulties of the first century, we find the episcopal government universally established, till it was interrupted by the republican genius of the Swiss and German reformers.

113 See Mosheim in the first and second centuries. Ignatius (ad Smyrnæos, c. 3, &c.) is fond of exalting the episcopal dignity. Le Clerc (Hist. Eccles. p. 569) very bluntly censures his conduct. Mosheim, with a more critical judgment (p. 161), suspects the purity even of the smaller epistles.

114 Nonne et Laici sacerdotes sumus? [Surely we are both laymen and priests?] Tertullian, Exhort. ad Castitat. c. 7. As the human heart is still the same, several of the observations which Mr. Hume has made on Enthusiasm (Essays, vol. i. p. 76, quarto edit.) may be applied even to real inspiration.

should meet in the capital of the province at the stated periods of spring and autumn. Their deliberations were assisted by the advice of a few distinguished presbyters, and moderated by the presence of a listening multitude.[115] Their decrees, which were styled Canons, regulated every important controversy of faith and discipline; and it was natural to believe that a liberal effusion of the Holy Spirit would be poured on the united assembly of the delegates of the Christian people. The institution of synods was so well suited to private ambition and to public interest that in the space of a few years it was received throughout the whole empire. A regular correspondence was established between the provincial councils, which mutually communicated and approved their respective proceedings; and the Catholic church soon assumed the form, and acquired the strength, of a great federative republic.[116] Union of the church

As the legislative authority of the particular churches was insensibly superseded by the use of councils, the bishops obtained by their alliance a much larger share of executive and arbitrary power; and, as soon as they were connected by a sense of their common interest, they were enabled to attack, with united vigour, the original rights of their clergy and people. The prelates of the third century imperceptibly changed the language of exhortation into that of command, scattered the seeds of future usurpations, and supplied, by scripture allegories and declamatory rhetoric, their deficiency of force and of reason. They exalted the unity and power of the church, as it was represented in the EPISCOPAL OFFICE, of which every bishop enjoyed an equal and undivided portion.[117] Princes and magistrates, it was often repeated, might boast an earthly claim to a transitory dominion; it was the episcopal authority alone which was derived from the Deity, and extended itself over this and over another world. The bishops were the viceregents of Christ, the successors of the apostles, and the mystic substitutes of the high priest of the Mosaic law. Their exclusive privilege of conferring the sacerdotal character invaded the freedom both of clerical and of popular elections; and if, in the administration of the church, they still consulted the judgment of the presbyters or the inclination of the people, they most carefully inculcated the merit of such a voluntary condescension. The bishops acknowledged the supreme authority which resided in the assembly of their brethren; but, in the government of his peculiar diocese, each of them exacted from his *flock* the same implicit obedience as if that favourite metaphor had been literally just, and as if the shepherd had been of a more exalted nature than that of his Progress of episcopal authority

115 Acta Concil. Carthag. apud Cyprian. Edit. Fell, p. 158. This council was composed of eighty-seven bishops from the provinces of Mauritania, Numidia, and Africa; some presbyters and deacons assisted at the assembly; præsente plebis maximâ parte. [The greatest part of the people being present.]

116 Aguntur præterea per Græcias illas, certis in locis concilia, &c. [Councils in certain places were after this in operation throughout Greece.] Tertullian de Jejuniis, c. 13. The African mentions it as a recent and foreign institution. The coalition of the Christian churches is very ably explained by Mosheim, p. 164-170.

117 Cyprian, in his admired treatise De Unitate Ecclesiæ, p. 75-86.

sheep.[118] This obedience, however, was not imposed without some efforts on one side, and some resistance on the other. The democratical part of the constitution was, in many places, very warmly supported by the zealous or interested opposition of the inferior clergy. But their patriotism received the ignominious epithets of faction and schism; and the episcopal cause was indebted for its rapid progress to the labours of many active prelates, who, like Cyprian of Carthage, could reconcile the arts of the most ambitious statesman with the Christian virtues which seem adapted to the character of a saint and martyr.[119]

Pre-eminence of the metropolitan churches

The same causes which at first had destroyed the equality of the presbyters introduced among the bishops a pre-eminence of rank, and from thence a superiority of jurisdiction. As often as in the spring and autumn they met in provincial synod, the difference of personal merit and reputation was very sensibly felt among the members of the assembly, and the multitude was governed by the wisdom and eloquence of the few. But the order of public proceedings required a more regular and less invidious distinction; the office of perpetual presidents in the councils of each province was conferred on the bishops of the principal city, and these aspiring prelates, who soon acquired the lofty titles of Metropolitans and Primates, secretly prepared themselves to usurp over their episcopal brethren the same authority which the bishops had so lately assumed above the college of presbyters.[120] Nor was it long before an emulation of pre-eminence and power prevailed among the metropolitans themselves, each of them affecting to display, in the most pompous terms, the temporal honours and advantages of the city over which he presided; the numbers and opulence of the Christians who were subject to their pastoral care; the saints and martyrs who had arisen among them; and the purity with which they preserved the tradition of the faith, as it had been transmitted through a series of orthodox bishops from the apostle or the apostolic disciple, to whom the foundation of their church was ascribed.[121] From every cause, either of a civil or of an ecclesiastical nature, it was easy to foresee that Rome must enjoy the respect, and would soon claim the obedience, of

Ambition of the Roman pontiff

the provinces. The society of the faithful bore a just proportion to the capital of the empire; and the Roman church was the greatest, the most numerous, and, in regard to the West, the most ancient of all the Christian establishments, many of which had received their religion from the pious labours of her missionaries. Instead of *one* apostolic founder, the utmost boast of Antioch, of Ephesus, or of Corinth, the banks of the Tiber were supposed to have been honoured with the

---

118 We may appeal to the whole tenor of Cyprian's conduct, of his doctrine, and of his Epistles. Le Clerc, in a short life of Cyprian (Bibliothèque Universelle, tom. xii, p. 107–378), has laid him open with great freedom and accuracy.

119 If Novatus, Felicissimus, &c., whom the bishop of Carthage expelled from his church, and from Africa, were not the most detestable monsters of wickedness, the zeal of Cyprian must occasionally have prevailed over his veracity. For a very just account of these obscure quarrels, see Mosheim, p. 497–512.

120 Mosheim, p. 269, 574. Dupin, Antiquæ Eccles. Disciplin. p. 19, 20.

121 Tertullian, in a distinct treatise, has pleaded against the heretics the right of

preaching and martyrdom of the *two* most eminent among the apostles;[122] and the bishops of Rome very prudently claimed the inheritance of whatsoever prerogatives were attributed either to the person or to the office of St. Peter.[123] The bishops of Italy and of the provinces were disposed to allow them a primacy of order and association (such was their very accurate expression) in the Christian aristocracy.[124] But the power of a monarch was rejected with abhorrence, and the aspiring genius of Rome experienced, from the nations of Asia and Africa, a more vigorous resistance to her spiritual, than she had formerly done to her temporal, dominion. The patriotic Cyprian, who ruled with the most absolute sway the church of Carthage and the provincial synods, opposed with resolution and success the ambition of the Roman pontiff, artfully connected his own cause with that of the eastern bishops, and, like Hannibal, sought out new allies in the heart of Asia.[125] If this Punic war was carried on without any effusion of blood, it was owing much less to the moderation than to the weakness of the contending prelates. Invectives and excommunications were *their* only weapons; and these, during the progress of the whole controversy, they hurled against each other with equal fury and devotion. The hard necessity of censuring either a pope, or a saint and martyr, distresses the modern Catholics, whenever they are obliged to relate the particulars of a dispute in which the champions of religion indulged such passions as seem much more adapted to the senate or to the camp.[126]

The progress of the ecclesiastical authority gave birth to the memorable distinction of the laity and of the clergy, which had been unknown to the Greeks and Romans.[127] The former of these appellations comprehended the body of the Christian people; the latter, according to the signification of the word, was appropriated to the chosen portion that had been set apart for the service of religion: a celebrated order of men which has furnished the most important,

Laity and clergy

---

prescription, as it was held by the apostolic churches.

122 The journey of St. Peter to Rome is mentioned by most of the ancients (see Eusebius, ii. 25), maintained by all the Catholics, allowed by some Protestants (see Pearson and Dodwell de Success. Episcop. Roman.), but has been vigorously attacked by Spanheim (Miscellanea Sacra, iii. 3). According to father Hardouin, the monks of the thirteenth century, who composed the Æneid, represented St. Peter under the allegorical character of the Trojan hero.

123 It is in French only that the famous allusion of St. Peter's name is exact. Tu es *Pierre* et sur cette *pierre*. [You are Peter (Pierre) and on this rock (pierre)]. The same is imperfect in Greek, Latin, Italian, &c., and totally unintelligible in our Teutonic languages.

124 Irenæus adv. Hæreses, iii. 3. Tertullian de Præscription. c. 36, and Cyprian Epistol. 27, 55, 71, 75. Le Clerc (Hist. Eccles. p. 764) and Mosheim (p. 258, 578) labour in the interpretation of these passages. But the loose and rhetorical style of the fathers often appears favourable to the pretensions of Rome.

125 See the sharp epistle from Firmilianus, bishop of Cæsarea, to Stephen, bishop of Rome, ap. Cyprian. Epistol. 75.

126 Concerning this dispute of the re-baptism of heretics, see the epistles of Cyprian, and the seventh book of Eusebius.

127 For the origin of these words, see Mosheim, p. 141. Spanheim, Hist. Ecclesiast. p. 633. The distinction of *Clerus* and *Laicus* was established before the time of Tertullian.

though not always the most edifying, subjects for modern history. Their mutual hostilities sometimes disturbed the peace of the infant church, but their zeal and activity were united in the common cause, and the love of power, which (under the most artful disguises) could insinuate itself into the breasts of bishops and martyrs, animated them to increase the number of their subjects, and to enlarge the limits of the Christian empire. They were destitute of any temporal force, and they were for a long time discouraged and oppressed, rather than assisted, by the civil magistrate; but they had acquired, and they employed within their own society, the two most efficacious instruments of government, rewards and punishments: the former derived from the pious liberality, the latter from the devout apprehensions, of the faithful.

Oblations and re- venue of the church
    I. The community of goods, which had so agreeably amused the imagination of Plato,[128] and which subsisted in some degree among the austere sect of the Essenians,[129] was adopted for a short time in the primitive church. The fervour of the first proselytes prompted them to sell those worldly possessions which they despised, to lay the price of them at the feet of the apostles, and to content themselves with receiving an equal share out of the general distribution.[130] The progress of the Christian religion relaxed, and gradually abolished, this generous institution, which, in hands less pure than those of the apostles, would too soon have been corrupted and abused by the returning selfishness of human nature; and the converts who embraced the new religion were permitted to retain the possession of their patrimony, to receive legacies and inheritances, and to increase their separate property by all the lawful means of trade and industry. Instead of an absolute sacrifice, a moderate proportion was accepted by the ministers of the gospel; and in their weekly or monthly assemblies, every believer, according to the exigency of the occasion, and the measure of his wealth and piety, presented his voluntary offering for the use of the common fund.[131] Nothing, however inconsiderable, was refused; but it was diligently inculcated that, in the article of Tythes, the Mosaic law was still of divine obligation; and that, since the Jews, under a less perfect discipline, had been commanded to pay a tenth part of all that they possessed, it would become the disciples of Christ to distinguish themselves by a superior degree of liberality,[132] and to acquire some

---

128 The community instituted by Plato is more perfect than that which Sir Thomas More had imagined for his Utopia. The community of women, and that of temporal goods, may be considered as inseparable parts of the same system.
129 Joseph. Antiquitat. xviii. 2. Philo de Vit. Contemplativ.
130 See the Acts of the Apostles, c. ii. 4, 5, with Grotius's Commentary. Mosheim, in a particular dissertation, attacks the common opinion with very inconclusive arguments.
131 Justin. Martyr, Apolog. Major, c. 89. Tertullian, Apolog. c. 39.
132 Irenæus ad Hæres. l. iv. c. 27, 34. Origen in Num. Hom. ii. Cyprian de Unitat. Eccles. Constitut. Apostol. l. ii. c. 34, 35, with the notes of Cotelerius. The Constitutions introduce this divine precept by declaring that priests are as much above kings, as the soul is above the body. Among the tythable articles, they enumerate corn, wine, oil, and wood. On this interesting subject, consult Prideaux's History of Tythes, and Fra Paolo delle Materie Beneficiarie: two writers of a very different character.

merit by resigning a superfluous treasure, which must so soon be annihilated with the world itself.[133] It is almost unnecessary to observe that the revenue of each particular church, which was of so uncertain and fluctuating a nature, must have varied with the poverty or the opulence of the faithful, as they were dispersed in obscure villages, or collected in the great cities of the empire. In the time of the emperor Decius, it was the opinion of the magistrates that the Christians of Rome were possessed of very considerable wealth; that vessels of gold and silver were used in their religious worship; and that many among their proselytes had sold their lands and houses to increase the public riches of the sect, at the expense, indeed, of their unfortunate children, who found themselves beggars, because their parents had been saints.[134] We should listen with distrust to the suspicions of strangers and enemies: on this occasion, however, they receive a very specious and probable colour from the two following circumstances, the only ones that have reached our knowledge, which define any precise sums, or convey any distinct idea. Almost at the same period, the bishop of Carthage, from a society less opulent than that of Rome, collected a hundred thousand sesterces (above eight hundred and fifty pounds sterling), on a sudden call of charity, to redeem the brethren of Numidia, who had been carried away captives by the barbarians of the desert.[135] About an hundred years before the reign of Decius, the Roman church had received, in a single donation, the sum of two hundred thousand sesterces from a stranger of Pontus, who proposed to fix his residence in the capital.[136] These oblations, for the most part,

133 The same opinion which prevailed about the year 1000 was productive of the same effects. Most of the donations express their motive, "appropinquante mundi fine". [Since the end of the world is approaching]. See Mosheim's General History of the Church, vol. i. p. 457.

134 Tum summa cura est fratribus,
(Ut sermo testatur loquax)
Sestertiorum millia.
Addicta avorum prædia
Fœdis sub auctionibus,
Successor exheres gemit
Sanctis egens parentibus.
Hæc occuluntur abditis
Ecclesiarum in angulis,
Et summa pietas creditur
Nudare dulces liberos.

[And then, so everyone keeps saying, the brethren are most concerned with selling their properties and offering thousands of sesterces. The disinherited heir bemoans the fact that his grandfathers' estates have been infamously auctioned off and that he himself has been left in poverty by his saintly parents. All this wealth is tucked away in corners in the churches and it is thought to be the height of piety to leave one's dear children destitute.]
Prudent, περὶ στεφανων, Hymn 2.

The subsequent conduct of the deacon Laurence only proves how proper a use was made of the wealth of the Roman church; it was undoubtedly very considerable; but Fra Paolo (c. 3) appears to exaggerate when he supposes that the successors of Commodus were urged to persecute the Christians by their own avarice, or that of their Prætorian præfects.

135 Cyprian, Epistol. 62.
136 Tertullian de Præscriptionibus, c. 30.

were made in money; nor was the society of Christians either desirous or capable of acquiring, to any considerable degree, the incumbrance of landed property. It had been provided by several laws, which were enacted with the same design as our statutes of mortmain, that no real estates should be given or bequeathed to any corporate body, without either a special privilege or a particular dispensation from the emperor or from the senate;[137] who were seldom disposed to grant them in favour of a sect, at first the object of their contempt, and at last of their fears and jealousy. A transaction, however, is related under the reign of Alexander Severus, which discovers that the restraint was sometimes eluded or suspended, and that the Christians were permitted to claim and to possess lands within the limits of Rome itself.[138] The progress of Christianity and the civil confusion of the empire contributed to relax the severity of the laws; and, before the close of the third century, many considerable estates were bestowed on the opulent churches of Rome, Milan, Carthage, Antioch, Alexandria, and the other great cities of Italy and the provinces.

Distribution of the revenue The bishop was the natural steward of the church; the public stock was intrusted to his care, without account or control; the presbyters were confined to their spiritual functions, and the more dependent order of deacons was solely employed in the management and distribution of the ecclesiastical revenue.[139] If we may give credit to the vehement declamations of Cyprian, there were too many among his African brethren who, in the execution of their charge, violated every precept, not only of evangelic perfection, but even of moral virtue. By some of these unfaithful stewards, the riches of the church were lavished in sensual pleasures, by others they were perverted to the purposes of private gain, of fraudulent purchases, and of rapacious usury.[140] But, as long as the contributions of the Christian people were free and unconstrained, the abuse of their confidence could not be very frequent, and the general uses to which their liberality was applied reflected honour on the religious society. A decent portion was reserved for the maintenance of the bishop and his clergy; a sufficient sum was allotted for the expenses of the public worship, of which the feasts of love, the *agapoe*, as they were called, constituted a very pleasing part. The whole remainder was the sacred patrimony of the poor. According to the discretion of the bishop, it was distributed to support widows and orphans, the lame, the sick, and the aged of the community; to comfort strangers and pilgrims, and to alleviate the misfortunes of

137 Diocletian gave a rescript, which is only a declaration of the old law: "Collegium, si nullo speciali privilegio subnixum sit, hereditatem capere non posse, dubium non est". [There is no doubt that a corporate body, unless permitted by a special exception, is not able to inherit.] Fra Paolo (c. 4) thinks that these regulations had been much neglected since the reign of Valerian.

138 Hist. August. p. 131. The ground had been public; and was now disputed between the society of Christians and that of butchers.

139 Constitut. Apostol. ii. 35.

140 Cyprian. de Lapsis, p. 89, Epistol. 65. The charge is confirmed by the 19th and 20th canon of the council of Illiberis.

prisoners and captives, more especially when their sufferings had been occasioned by their firm attachment to the cause of religion.[141] A generous intercourse of charity united the most distant provinces, and the smaller congregations were cheerfully assisted by the alms of their more opulent brethren.[142] Such an institution, which paid less regard to the merit than to the distress of the object, very materially conduced to the progress of Christianity. The Pagans, who were actuated by a sense of humanity, while they derided the doctrines, acknowledged the benevolence, of the new sect.[143] The prospect of immediate relief and of future protection allured into its hospitable bosom many of those unhappy persons whom the neglect of the world would have abandoned to the miseries of want, of sickness, and of old age. There is some reason likewise to believe that great numbers of infants who, according to the inhuman practice of the times, had been exposed by their parents were frequently rescued from death, baptized, educated, and maintained by the piety of the Christians, and at the expense of the public treasure.[144]

II. It is the undoubted right of every society to exclude from its communion and benefits such among its members as reject or violate those regulations which have been established by general consent. In the exercise of this power, the censures of the Christian church were chiefly directed against scandalous sinners, and particularly those who were guilty of murder, of fraud, or of incontinence; against the authors, or the followers, of any heretical opinions which had been condemned by the judgment of the episcopal order; and against those unhappy persons who, whether from choice or from compulsion, had polluted themselves after their baptism by any act of idolatrous worship. The consequences of excommunication were of a temporal as well as a spiritual nature. The Christian against whom it was pronounced was deprived of any part in the oblations of the faithful. The ties both of religious and of private friendship were dissolved; he found himself a profane object of abhorrence to the persons whom he the most esteemed, or by whom he had been the most tenderly beloved; and, as far as an expulsion from a respectable society could imprint on his character a mark of disgrace, he was shunned or suspected by the generality of mankind. The situation of these unfortunate exiles was in itself very painful and melancholy; but, as it usually happens, their apprehensions far exceeded their sufferings. The benefits of the Christian communion were those of eternal life, nor could they erase from their minds the awful opinion, that to those ecclesiastical governors by whom they were condemned the Deity had committed

Excommunication

141 See the apologies of Justin, Tertullian, &c.

142 The wealth and liberality of the Romans to their most distant brethren is gratefully celebrated by Dionysius of Corinth, ap. Euseb. l. iv. c. 23.

143 See Lucian in Peregrin. Julian (Epist. 49) seems mortified that the Christian charity maintains not only their own, but likewise the heathen poor.

144 Such, at least, has been the laudable conduct of more modern missionaries, under the same circumstances. Above three thousand new-born infants are annually exposed in the streets of Pekin. See Le Comte, Mémoires sur la Chine, and the Recherches sur les Chinois et les Egyptiens, tom. i. p. 61.

the keys of Hell and of Paradise. The heretics, indeed, who might be supported by the consciousness of their intentions, and by the flattering hope that they alone had discovered the true path of salvation, endeavoured to regain, in their separate assemblies, those comforts, temporal as well as spiritual, which they no longer derived from the great society of Christians. But almost all those who had reluctantly yielded to the power of vice or idolatry were sensible of their fallen condition, and anxiously desirous of being restored to the benefits of the Christian communion.

With regard to the treatment of these penitents, two opposite opinions, the one of justice, the other of mercy, divided the primitive church. The more rigid and inflexible casuists refused them for ever, and without exception, the meanest place in the holy community, which they had disgraced or deserted, and, leaving them to the remorse of a guilty conscience, indulged them only with a faint ray of hope that the contrition of their life and death might possibly be accepted by the Supreme Being.[145] A milder sentiment was embraced, in practice as well as in theory, by the purest and most respectable of the Christian churches.[146] The gates of reconciliation and of Heaven were seldom shut against the returning penitent; but a severe and solemn form of discipline was instituted, which, while it served to expiate his crime, might powerfully deter the spectators from the imitation of his

Public penance

example. Humbled by a public confession, emaciated by fasting, and clothed in sackcloth, the penitent lay prostrate at the door of the assembly, imploring, with tears, the pardon of his offences, and soliciting the prayers of the faithful.[147] If the fault was of a very heinous nature, whole years of penance were esteemed an inadequate satisfaction to the Divine Justice; and it was always by slow and painful gradations that the sinner, the heretic, or the apostate was re-admitted into the bosom of the church. A sentence of perpetual excommunication was, however, reserved for some crimes of an extraordinary magnitude, and particularly for the inexcusable relapses of those penitents who had already experienced and abused the clemency of their ecclesiastical superiors. According to the circumstances or the number of the guilty, the exercise of the Christian discipline was varied by the discretion of the bishops. The councils of Ancyra and Illiberis were held about the same time, the one in Galatia, the other in Spain; but their respective canons, which are still extant, seem to breathe a very different spirit. The Galatian, who after his baptism had repeatedly sacrificed to idols, might obtain his pardon by a penance of seven years, and, if he had seduced others to imitate his example, only three years more were added to the term of his exile. But the unhappy Spaniard,

---

145 The Montanists and the Novatians, who adhered to this opinion with the greatest rigour and obstinacy, found *themselves* at last in the number of excommunicated heretics. See the learned and copious Mosheim, Secul. ii. and iii.

146 Dionysius ap. Euseb. iv. 23. Cyprian de Lapsis.

147 Cave's Primitive Christianity, part iii. c. 5. The admirers of antiquity regret the loss of this public penance.

who had committed the same offence, was deprived of the hope of reconciliation, even in the article of death; and his idolatry was placed at the head of a list of seventeen other crimes, against which a sentence, no less terrible, was pronounced. Among these we may distinguish the inexpiable guilt of calumniating a bishop, a presbyter, or even a deacon.[148]

The well-tempered mixture of liberality and rigour, the judicious dispensation of rewards and punishments, according to the maxims of policy as well as justice, constituted the *human* strength of the church. The bishops, whose paternal care extended itself to the government of both worlds, were sensible of the importance of these prerogatives, and, covering their ambition with the fair pretence of the love of order, they were jealous of any rival in the exercise of a discipline so necessary to prevent the desertion of those troops which had inlisted themselves under the banner of the cross, and whose numbers every day became more considerable. From the imperious declamations of Cyprian we should naturally conclude that the doctrines of excommunication and penance formed the most essential part of religion; and that it was much less dangerous for the disciples of Christ to neglect the observance of the moral duties than to despise the censures and authority of their bishops. Sometimes we might imagine that we were listening to the voice of Moses, when he commanded the earth to open, and to swallow up, in consuming flames, the rebellious race which refused obedience to the priesthood of Aaron; and we should sometimes suppose that we heard a Roman consul asserting the majesty of the republic, and declaring his inflexible resolution to enforce the rigour of the laws. "If such irregularities are suffered with impunity (it is thus that the bishop of Carthage chides the lenity of his colleague), if such irregularities are suffered, there is an end of EPISCOPAL VIGOUR;[149] an end of the sublime and divine power of governing the church, an end of Christianity itself." Cyprian had renounced those temporal honours which it is probable he would never have obtained; but the acquisition of such absolute command over the consciences and understanding of a congregation, however obscure or despised by the world, is more truly grateful to the pride of the human heart than the possession of the most despotic power imposed by arms and conquest on a reluctant people. *The dignity of episcopal government*

In the course of this important, though perhaps tedious, inquiry, I have attempted to display the secondary causes which so efficaciously assisted the truth of the Christian religion. If among these causes we have discovered any artificial ornaments, any accidental circumstances, or any mixture of error and passion, it cannot appear surprising that mankind should be the most sensibly affected by such motives as were *Recapitulation of the five causes*

---

148 See in Dupin, Bibliothèque Ecclésiastique, tom. ii. p. 304–313, a short but rational exposition of the canons of those councils, which were assembled in the first moments of tranquillity after the persecution of Diocletian. This persecution had been much less severely felt in Spain than in Galatia: a difference which may, in some measure, account for the contrast of their regulations.

149 Cyprian, Epist. 69.

suited to their imperfect nature. It was by the aid of these causes, exclusive zeal, the immediate expectation of another world, the claim of miracles, the practice of rigid virtue, and the constitution of the primitive church, that Christianity spread itself with so much success in the Roman empire. To the first of these the Christians were indebted for their invincible valour, which disdained to capitulate with the enemy whom they were resolved to vanquish. The three succeeding causes supplied their valour with the most formidable arms. The last of these causes united their courage, directed their arms, and gave their efforts that irresistible weight which even a small band of well-trained and intrepid volunteers has so often possessed over an undisciplined multitude, ignorant of the subject, and careless of the event of the war.

Weakness of Polytheism In the various religions of Polytheism, some wandering fanatics of Egypt and Syria, who addressed themselves to the credulous superstition of the populace, were perhaps the only order of priests[150] that derived their whole support and credit from their sacerdotal profession, and were very deeply affected by a personal concern for the safety or prosperity of their tutelar deities. The ministers of Polytheism, both in Rome and in the provinces, were, for the most part, men of a noble birth, and of an affluent fortune, who received, as an honourable distinction, the care of a celebrated temple, or of a public sacrifice, exhibited, very frequently at their own expense, the sacred games,[151] and with cold indifference performed the ancient rites, according to the laws and fashion of their country. As they were engaged in the ordinary occupations of life, their zeal and devotion were seldom animated by a sense of interest, or by the habits of an ecclesiastical character. Confined to their respective temples and cities, they remained without any connexion of discipline or government; and, whilst they acknowledged the supreme jurisdiction of the senate, of the college of pontiffs, and of the emperor, those civil magistrates contented themselves with the easy task of maintaining, in peace and dignity, the general worship of mankind. We have already seen how various, how loose, and how uncertain were the religious sentiments of Polytheists. They were abandoned, almost without control, to the natural workings of a superstitious fancy. The accidental circumstances of their life and situation determined the object, as well as the degree, of their devotion; and, as long as their adoration was successively prostituted to a thousand deities, it was scarcely possible that their hearts could be susceptible of a very sincere or lively passion for any of them.

The scepticism of the Pagan world proved favourable to the new religion When Christianity appeared in the world, even these faint and imperfect impressions had lost much of their original power. Human

---

150 The arts, the manners, and the vices of the priests of the Syrian goddess are very humorously described by Apuleius, in the eighth book of his Metamorphoses.
151 The office of Asiarch was of this nature, and it is frequently mentioned in Aristides, the Inscriptions &c. It was annual and elective. None but the vainest citizens could desire the honour; none but the most wealthy could support the expense. See in the Patres Apostol. tom. ii. p. 200, with how much indifference Philip the Asiarch conducted himself in the martyrdom of Polycarp. There were likewise Bithyniarchs, Lyciarchs, &c.

reason, which, by its unassisted strength, is incapable of perceiving the mysteries of faith, had already obtained an easy triumph over the folly of Paganism; and, when Tertullian or Lactantius employ their labours in exposing its falsehood and extravagance, they are obliged to transcribe the eloquence of Cicero or the wit of Lucian. The contagion of these sceptical writings had been diffused far beyond the number of their readers. The fashion of incredulity was communicated from the philosopher to the man of pleasure or business, from the noble to the plebeian, and from the master to the menial slave who waited at his table, and who eagerly listened to the freedom of his conversation. On public occasions the philosophic part of mankind affected to treat with respect and decency the religious institutions of their country; but their secret contempt penetrated through the thin and awkward disguise; and even the people, when they discovered that their deities were rejected and derided by those whose rank or understanding they were accustomed to reverence, were filled with doubts and apprehensions concerning the truth of those doctrines to which they had yielded the most implicit belief. The decline of ancient prejudice exposed a very numerous portion of human kind to the danger of a painful and comfortless situation. A state of scepticism and suspense may amuse a few inquisitive minds. But the practice of superstition is so congenial to the multitude that, if they are forcibly awakened, they still regret the loss of their pleasing vision. Their love of the marvellous and super-natural, their curiosity with regard to future events, and their strong propensity to extend their hopes and fears beyond the limits of the visible world, were the principal causes which favoured the establish-ment of Polytheism. So urgent on the vulgar is the necessity of believing that the fall of any system of mythology will most probably be succeeded by the introduction of some other mode of superstition. Some deities of a more recent and fashionable cast might soon have occupied the deserted temples of Jupiter and Apollo, if, in the decisive moment, the wisdom of Providence had not interposed a genuine revelation, fitted to inspire the most rational esteem and conviction, whilst, at the same time, it was adorned with all that could attract the curiosity, the wonder, and the veneration of the people. In their actual disposition, as many were almost disengaged from their artificial prejudices, but equally susceptible and desirous of a devout attach-ment; an object much less deserving would have been sufficient to fill the vacant place in their hearts, and to gratify the uncertain eagerness of their passions. Those who are inclined to pursue this reflection, instead of viewing with astonishment the rapid progress of Christianity, will perhaps be surprised that its success was not still more rapid and still more universal.

It has been observed, with truth as well as propriety, that the conquests of Rome prepared and facilitated those of Christianity. In the second chapter of this work we have attempted to explain in what manner the most civilized provinces of Europe, Asia, and Africa were united under the dominion of one sovereign, and gradually connected *as well as the peace union of the Roman empire* by the most intimate ties of laws, of manners, and of language. The Jews of Palestine, who had fondly expected a temporal deliverer, gave so cold a reception to the miracles of the divine prophet that it was found unnecessary to publish, or at least to preserve, any Hebrew gospel.[152] The authentic histories of the actions of Christ were composed in the Greek language, at a considerable distance from Jerusalem, and after the Gentile converts were grown extremely numerous.[153] As soon as those histories were translated into the Latin tongue, they were perfectly intelligible to all the subjects of Rome, excepting only to the peasants of Syria and Egypt, for whose benefit particular versions were afterwards made. The public highways, which had been constructed for the use of the legions, opened an easy passage for the Christian missionaries from Damascus to Corinth, and from Italy to the extremity of Spain or Britain; nor did those spiritual conquerors encounter any of the obstacles which usually retard or prevent the introduction of a foreign religion into a distant country. There is the strongest reason to believe that before the reigns of Diocletian and Constantine, the faith of Christ had been preached in every province,

Historical view of the progress of Christianity

and in all the great cities of the empire; but the foundation of the several congregations, the numbers of the faithful who composed them, and their proportion to the unbelieving multitude, are now buried in obscurity, or disguised by fiction and declamation. Such imperfect circumstances, however, as have reached our knowledge concerning the increase of the Christian name in Asia and Greece, in Egypt, in Italy, and in the West, we shall now proceed to relate, without neglecting the real or imaginary acquisitions which lay beyond the frontiers of the Roman empire.

in the East

The rich provinces that extend from the Euphrates to the Ionian sea were the principal theatre on which the apostle of the Gentiles displayed his zeal and piety. The seeds of the gospel, which he had scattered in a fertile soil, were diligently cultivated by his disciples; and it should seem that, during the two first centuries, the most considerable body of Christians was contained within those limits. Among the societies which were instituted in Syria, none were more ancient or more illustrious than those of Damascus, of Berœa or Aleppo, and of Antioch. The prophetic introduction of the Apocalypse has described and immortalized the seven churches of Asia: – Ephesus, Smyrna, Pergamus, Thyatira,[154] Sardes, Laodicea, and Philadelphia; and their colonies were soon diffused over that populous country. In a very early

---

152 The modern critics are not disposed to believe what the fathers almost unanimously assert, that St. Matthew composed a Hebrew gospel, of which only the Greek translation is extant. It seems, however, dangerous to reject their testimony.

153 Under the reigns of Nero and Domitian, and in the cities of Alexandria, Antioch, Rome, and Ephesus. See Mill, Prolegomena ad Nov. Testament, and Dr. Lardner's fair and extensive collection, vol. xv.

154 The Alogians (Epiphanius de Hæres. 51) disputed the genuineness of the Apocalypse, because the church of Thyatira was not yet founded. Epiphanius, who allows the fact, extricates himself from the difficulty by ingeniously supposing that St. John wrote in the spirit of prophecy. See Abauzit, Discours sur l'Apocalypse.

period, the islands of Cyprus and Crete, the provinces of Thrace and Macedonia, gave a favourable reception to the new religion; and Christian republics were soon founded in the cities of Corinth, of Sparta, and of Athens.[155] The antiquity of the Greek and Asiatic churches allowed a sufficient space of time for their increase and multiplication, and even the swarms of Gnostics and other heretics serve to display the flourishing condition of the orthodox church, since the appellation of heretics has always been applied to the less numerous party. To these domestic testimonies we may add the confession, the complaints, and the apprehensions of the Gentiles themselves. From the writings of Lucian, a philosopher who had studied mankind, and who describes their manners in the most lively colours, we may learn that, under the reign of Commodus, his native country of Pontus was filled with Epicureans and *Christians*.[156] Within fourscore years after the death of Christ,[157] the humane Pliny laments the magnitude of the evil which he vainly attempted to eradicate. In his very curious epistle to the emperor Trajan, he affirms that the temples were almost deserted, that the sacred victims scarcely found any purchasers, and that the superstition had not only infected the cities, but had even spread itself into the villages and the open country of Pontus and Bithynia.[158]

Without descending into a minute scrutiny of the expressions, or of the motives of those writers who either celebrate or lament the progress of Christianity in the East, it may in general be observed that none of them have left us any grounds from whence a just estimate might be formed of the real numbers of the faithful in those provinces. One circumstance, however, has been fortunately preserved, which seems to cast a more distinct light on this obscure but interesting subject. Under the reign of Theodosius, after Christianity had enjoyed, during more than sixty years, the sunshine of Imperial favour, the ancient and illustrious church of Antioch consisted of one hundred thousand persons, three thousand of whom were supported out of the public oblations.[159] The splendour and dignity of the queen of the East, the acknowledged populousness of Cæsarea, Seleucia, and Alexandria, and the destruction of two hundred and fifty thousand souls in the earthquake which afflicted Antioch under the elder Justin,[160] are so

The church of Antioch

---

155 The epistles of Ignatius and Dionysius (ap. Euseb. iv. 23) point out many churches in Asia and Greece. That of Athens seems to have been one of the least flourishing..

156 Lucian in Alexandro, c. 25. Christianity, however, must have been very unequally diffused over Pontus; since in the middle of the third century there were no more than seventeen believers in the extensive diocese of Neo-Cæsarea. See M. de Tillemont, Mémoires Ecclésiast. tom. iv. p. 675, from Basil and Gregory of Nyssa, who were themselves natives of Cappadocia.

157 According to the ancients, Jesus Christ suffered under the consulship of the two Gemini, in the year 29 of our present æra. Pliny was sent into Bithynia (according to Pagi) in the year 110.

158 Plin. Epist. x. 97.

159 Chrysostom. Opera, tom. vii. p. 658, 810.

160 John Malala, tom. ii. p. 144. He draws the same conclusion with regard to the populousness of Antioch.

many convincing proofs that the whole number of its inhabitants was not less than half a million, and that the Christians, however multiplied by zeal and power, did not exceed a fifth part of that great city. How different a proportion must we adopt when we compare the persecuted with the triumphant church, the West with the East, remote villages with populous towns, and countries recently converted to the faith with the place where the believers first received the appellation of Christians! It must not, however, be dissembled that, in another passage, Chrysostom, to whom we are indebted for this useful information, computes the multitude of the faithful as even superior to that of the Jews and Pagans.[161] But the solution of this apparent difficulty is easy and obvious. The eloquent preacher draws a parallel between the civil and the ecclesiastical constitution of Antioch; between the list of Christians who had acquired Heaven by baptism and the list of citizens who had a right to share the public liberality. Slaves, strangers, and infants were comprised in the former; they were excluded from the latter.

In Egypt   The extensive commerce of Alexandria, and its proximity to Palestine, gave an easy entrance to the new religion. It was at first embraced by great numbers of the Therapeutæ, or Essenians of the lake Mareotis, a Jewish sect which had abated much of its reverence for the Mosaic ceremonies. The austere life of the Essenians, their fasts and excommunications, the community of goods, the love of celibacy, their zeal for martyrdom, and the warmth though not the purity of their faith, already offered a very lively image of the primitive discipline.[162] It was in the school of Alexandria that the Christian theology appears to have assumed a regular and scientifical form; and, when Hadrian visited Egypt, he found a church, composed of Jews and of Greeks, sufficiently important to attract the notice of that inquisitive prince.[163] But the progress of Christianity was for a long time confined within the limits of a single city, which was itself a foreign colony, and, till the close of the second century, the predecessors of Demetrius were the only prelates of the Egyptian church. Three bishops were consecrated by the hands of Demetrius, and the number was increased to twenty by his successor Heraclas.[164] The body of the natives, a people distinguished by a sullen

---

161 Chrysostom. tom. i. p. 592. I am indebted for these passages, though not for my inference, to the learned Dr. Lardner. Credibility of the Gospel History, vol. xii. p. 370.

162 Basnage, Histoire des Juifs, l. 2, c. 20, 21, 22, 23, has examined, with the most critical accuracy, the curious treatise of Philo which describes the Therapeutæ. By proving that it was composed as early as the time of Augustus, Basnage has demonstrated, in spite of Eusebius (l. ii. c. 17), and a crowd of modern Catholics, that the Therapeutæ were neither Christians nor monks. It still remains probable that they changed their name, preserved their manners, adopted some new articles of faith, and gradually became the fathers of the Egyptian Ascetics.

163 See a letter of Hadrian, in the Augustan History, p. 245.

164 For the succession of Alexandrian bishops, consult Renaudot's History, p. 24, &c. This curious fact is preserved by the patriarch Eutychius (Annal. tom. i. p. 334, Vers. Pocock), and its internal evidence would alone be a sufficient answer to all the objections which Bishop Pearson has urged in the Vindiciæ Ignatianæ.

inflexibility of temper,[165] entertained the new doctrine with coldness and reluctance; and even in the time of Origen it was rare to meet with an Egyptian who had surmounted his early prejudices in favour of the sacred animals of his country.[166] As soon, indeed, as Christianity ascended the throne, the zeal of those barbarians obeyed the prevailing impulsion; the cities of Egypt were filled with bishops, and the deserts of Thebais swarmed with hermits.

A perpetual stream of strangers and provincials flowed into the capacious bosom of Rome. Whatever was strange or odious, whoever was guilty or suspected, might hope, in the obscurity of that immense capital, to elude the vigilance of the law. In such a various conflux of nations, every teacher, either of truth or of falsehood, every founder, whether of a virtuous or a criminal association, might easily multiply his disciples or accomplices. The Christians of Rome, at the time of the accidental persecution of Nero, are represented by Tacitus as already amounting to a very great multitude,[167] and the language of that great historian is almost similar to the style employed by Livy, when he relates the introduction and the suppression of the rites of Bacchus. After the Bacchanals had awakened the severity of the senate, it was likewise apprehended that a very great multitude, as it were *another people*, had been initiated into those abhorred mysteries. A more careful inquiry soon demonstrated that the offenders did not exceed seven thousand: a number, indeed, sufficiently alarming, when considered as the object of public justice.[168] It is with the same candid allowance that we should interpret the vague expressions of Tacitus, and in a former instance of Pliny, when they exaggerate the crowds of deluded fanatics who had forsaken the established worship of the gods. The church of Rome was undoubtedly the first and most populous of the empire; and we are possessed of an authentic record which attests the state of religion in that city, about the middle of the third century, and after a peace of thirty-eight years. The clergy, at that time, consisted of a bishop, forty-six presbyters, seven deacons, as many sub-deacons, forty-two acolytes, and fifty readers, exorcists, and porters. The number of widows, of the infirm, and of the poor, who were maintained by the oblations of the faithful, amounted to fifteen hundred.[169] From reason, as well as from the analogy of Antioch, we may venture to estimate the Christians of Rome at about fifty thousand. The populousness of that great capital cannot, perhaps, be exactly ascertained; but the most modest calculation will not surely reduce it lower than a million of inhabitants, of whom the Christians might constitute at the

In Rome

---

165 Ammian. Marcellin. xxii. 16.
166 Origen contra Celsum, l. i. p. 40.
167 Ingens multitudo is the expression of Tacitus, xv. 44.
168 T. Liv. xxxix. 13, 15, 16, 17. Nothing could exceed the horror and consternation of the senate on the discovery of the Bacchanalians, whose depravity is described, and perhaps exaggerated, by Livy.
169 Eusebius, l. vi. c. 43. The Latin translator (M. de Valois) has thought proper to reduce the number of presbyters to forty-four.

317

most a twentieth part.[170]

In Africa and the western provinces   The western provincials appeared to have derived the knowledge of Christianity from the same source which had diffused among them the language, the sentiments, and the manners of Rome. In this more important circumstance, Africa, as well as Gaul, was gradually fashioned to the imitation of the capital. Yet, notwithstanding the many favourable occasions which might invite the Roman missionaries to visit their Latin provinces, it was late before they passed either the sea or the Alps;[171] nor can we discover in those great countries any assured traces either of faith or of persecution that ascend higher than the reign of the Antonines.[172] The slow progress of the gospel in the cold climate of Gaul was extremely different from the eagerness with which it seems to have been received on the burning sands of Africa. The African Christians soon formed one of the principal members of the primitive church. The practice introduced into that province of appointing bishops to the most inconsiderable towns, and very frequently to the most obscure villages, contributed to multiply the splendour and importance of their religious societies, which during the course of the third century were animated by the zeal of Tertullian, directed by the abilities of Cyprian, and adorned by the eloquence of Lactantius. But if, on the contrary, we turn our eyes towards Gaul, we must content ourselves with discovering, in the time of Marcus Antoninus, the feeble and united congregations of Lyons and Vienna; and, even as late as the reign of Decius, we are assured that in a few cities only, Arles, Narbonne, Toulouse, Limoges, Clermont, Tours, and Paris, some scattered churches were supported by the devotion of a small number of Christians.[173] Silence is indeed very consistent with devotion, but, as it is seldom compatible with zeal, we may perceive and lament the languid state of Christianity in those provinces which had exchanged the Celtic for the Latin tongue; since they did not, during the three first

170 This proportion of the presbyters and of the poor to the rest of the people was originally fixed by Burnet (Travels into Italy, p. 168), and is approved by Moyle (vol. ii. p. 151). They were both unacquainted with the passage of Chrysostom, which converts their conjecture almost into a fact.

171 Serius trans Alpes, religione Dei susceptâ. [Later across the Alps, the worship of God was adopted.] Sulpicius Severus, l. ii. These were the celebrated martyrs of Lyons. See Eusebius, v. 1. Tillemont, Mém. Ecclésiast. tom. ii. p. 316. According to the Donatists, whose assertion is confirmed by the tacit acknowledgment of Augustin, Africa was the last of the provinces which received the gospel. Tillemont, Mém. Ecclésiast, tom. i. p. 754.

172 Tum primum intra Gallias martyria visa. [Then for the first time martyrdom was seen in Gaul.] Sulp. Severus, l. ii. With regard to Africa, see Tertullian ad Scapulam, c. 3. It is imagined that the Scyllitan martyrs were the first (Acta Sincera Ruinart. p. 34). One of the adversaries of Apuleius seems to have been a Christian. Apolog. p. 496, 497, edit. Delphin.

173 Raræ in aliquibus civitatibus ecclesiæ, paucorum Christianorum devotione, resurgerent. [Scattered congregations in other states appeared again, sustained by the devotion of a few Christians.] Acta Sincera, p. 130. Gregory of Tours, l. i. c. 28. Mosheim, p. 207, 449. There is some reason to believe that, in the beginning of the fourth century, the extensive dioceses of Liège, of Treves, and of Cologne composed a single bishopric, which had been very recently founded. See Mémoires de Tillemont, tom. vi. part i. p. 43, 411.

centuries, give birth to a single ecclesiastical writer. From Gaul, which claimed a just pre-eminence of learning and authority over all the countries on this side of the Alps, the light of the gospel was more faintly reflected on the remote provinces of Spain and Britain; and, if we may credit the vehement assertions of Tertullian, they had already received the first rays of the faith when he addressed his apology to the magistrates of the emperor Severus.[174] But the obscure and imperfect origin of the western churches of Europe has been so negligently recorded that, if we would relate the time and manner of their foundation, we must supply the silence of antiquity by those legends which avarice or superstition long afterwards dictated to the monks in the lazy gloom of their convents.[175] Of these holy romances, that of the apostle St. James can alone, by its single extravagance, deserve to be mentioned. From a peaceful fisherman of the lake of Gennesareth, he was transformed into a valorous knight, who charged at the head of the Spanish chivalry in their battles against the Moors. The gravest historians have celebrated his exploits; the miraculous shrine of Compostella displayed his power; and the sword of a military order, assisted by the terrors of the Inquisition, was sufficient to remove every objection of profane criticism.[176]

The progress of Christianity was not confined to the Roman empire; and, according to the primitive fathers, who interpret facts by prophecy, the new religion within a century after the death of its divine author, had already visited every part of the globe. "There exists not," says Justin Martyr, "a people, whether Greek or barbarian, or any other race of men, by whatsoever appellation or manners they may be distinguished, however ignorant of arts or agriculture, whether they dwell under tents, or wander about in covered waggons, among whom prayers are not offered up in the name of a crucified Jesus to the Father and Creator of all things."[177] But this splendid exaggeration, which even at present it would be extremely difficult to reconcile with the real state of mankind, can be considered only as the rash sally of a devout but careless writer, the measure of whose belief was regulated by that of his wishes. But neither the belief nor the wishes of the fathers can alter the truth of history. It will still remain an undoubted fact that the barbarians of Scythia and Germany who afterwards subverted the Roman monarchy were involved in the darkness of paganism; and that even the conversion of Iberia, of Armenia, or of Æthiopia, was not

Beyond the limits of the Roman empire

174 The date of Tertullian's Apology is fixed, in a dissertation of Mosheim, to the year 198.
175 In the fifteenth century, there were few who had either inclination or courage to question, whether Joseph of Arimathea founded the monastery of Glastonbury, and whether Dionysius the Areopagite preferred the residence of Paris to that of Athens.
176 The stupendous metamorphosis was performed in the ninth century. See Mariana (Hist. Hispan. l. vii. c. 13, tom. i. p. 285, edit. Hag. Com. 1733), who, in every sense, imitates Livy, and the honest detection of the legend of St. James by Dr. Geddes, Miscellanies, vol. ii. p. 221.
177 Justin Martyr, Dialog. cum Tryphon. p. 341. Irenæus adv. Hæres. l. i. c. 10. Tertullian adv. Jud. c. 7. See Mosheim, p. 203.

attempted with any degree of success till the sceptre was in the hands of an orthodox emperor.[178] Before that time the various accidents of war and commerce might indeed diffuse an imperfect knowledge of the gospel among the tribes of Caledonia,[179] and among the borderers of the Rhine, the Danube, and the Euphrates.[180] Beyond the last-mentioned river, Edessa waṣ distinguished by a firm and early adherence to the faith.[181] From Edessa the principles of Christianity were easily introduced into the Greek and Syrian cities which obeyed the successors of Artaxerxes; but they do not appear to have made any deep impression on the minds of the Persians, whose religious system, by the labours of a well-disciplined order of priests, had been constructed with much more art and solidity than the uncertain mythology of Greece and Rome.[182]

General proportion of Christians and Pagans

From this impartial, though imperfect, survey of the progress of Christianity, it may, perhaps, seem probable that the number of its proselytes has been excessively magnified by fear on the one side and by devotion on the other. According to the irreproachable testimony of Origen,[183] the proportion of the faithful was very inconsiderable when compared with the multitude of an unbelieving world; but, as we are left without any distinct information, it is impossible to determine, and it is difficult even to conjecture, the real numbers of the primitive Christians. The most favourable calculation, however, that can be deduced from the examples of Antioch and of Rome will not permit us to imagine that more than a twentieth part of the subjects of the empire had enlisted themselves under the banner of the cross before the important conversion of Constantine. But their habits of faith, of zeal, and of union seemed to multiply their numbers; and the same causes which contributed to their future increase served to render their actual strength more apparent and more formidable.

Whether the first Christians were mean and ignorant

Such is the constitution of civil society that, whilst a few persons are distinguished by riches, by honours, and by knowledge, the body of the

178 See the fourth century of Mosheim's History of the Church. Many, though very confused circumstances, that relate to the conversion of Iberia and Armenia, may be found in Moses of Chorene, l. ii. c. 78–89.
179 According to Tertullian, the Christian faith had penetrated into parts of Britain inaccessible to the Roman arms. About a century afterwards, Ossian,[18] the son of Fingal, is *said* to have disputed, in his extreme old age, with one of the foreign missionaries, and the dispute is still extant, in verse, and in the Erse language. See Mr. Macpherson's Dissertation on the Antiquity of Ossian's Poems, p. 10.
180 The Goths, who ravaged Asia in the reign of Gallienus, carried away great numbers of captives; some of whom were Christians, and became missionaries. See Tillemont, Mémoires Ecclésiast. tom. iv. p. 44.
181 The legend of Abgarus, fabulous as it is, affords a decisive proof that, many years before Eusebius wrote his history, the greatest part of the inhabitants of Edessa had embraced Christianity. Their rivals, the citizens of Carrhæ, adhered, on the contrary, to the cause of Paganism, as late as the sixth century.
182 According to Bardesanes (ap. Euseb. Præpar. Evangel.), there were some Christians in Persia before the end of the second century. In the time of Constantine (see his Epistle to Sapor, Vit. l. iv. c. 13), they composed a flourishing church. Consult Beausobre, Hist. Critique du Manichéisme, tom. i. p. 180, and the Bibliotheca Orientalis of Assemani.
183 Origen contra Celsum, l. viii. p. 424.

people is condemned to obscurity, ignorance, and poverty. The Christian religion, which addressed itself to the whole human race, must consequently collect a far greater number of proselytes from the lower than from the superior ranks of life. This innocent and natural circumstance has been improved into a very odious imputation, which seems to be less strenuously denied by the apologists than it is urged by the adversaries of the faith; that the new sect of Christians was almost entirely composed of the dregs of the populace, of peasants and mechanics, of boys and women, of beggars and slaves; the last of whom might sometimes introduce the missionaries into the rich and noble families to which they belonged. These obscure teachers (such was the charge of malice and infidelity) are as mute in public as they are loquacious and dogmatical in private. Whilst they cautiously avoid the dangerous encounter of philosophers, they mingle with the rude and illiterate crowd, and insinuate themselves into those minds, whom their age, their sex, or their education has the best disposed to receive the impression of superstitious terrors.[184]

This unfavourable picture, though not devoid of a faint resemblance, betrays, by its dark colouring and distorted features, the pencil of an enemy. As the humble faith of Christ diffused itself through the world, it was embraced by several persons who derived some consequence from the advantages of nature or fortune. Aristides, who presented an eloquent apology to the emperor Hadrian, was an Athenian philosopher.[185] Justin Martyr had sought divine knowledge in the schools of Zeno, of Aristotle, of Pythagoras, and of Plato, before he fortunately was accosted by the old man, or rather the angel, who turned his attention to the study of the Jewish prophets.[186] Clemens of Alexandria had acquired much various reading in the Greek, and Tertullian in the Latin, language. Julius Africanus and Origen possessed a very considerable share of the learning of their times; and, although the style of Cyprian is very different from that of Lactantius, we might almost discover that both those writers had been public teachers of rhetoric. Even the study of philosophy was at length introduced among the Christians, but it was not always productive of the most salutary effects; knowledge was as often the parent of heresy as of devotion, and the description which was designed for the followers of Artemon may, with equal propriety, be applied to the various sects that resisted the successors of the apostles. "They presume to alter the holy scriptures, to abandon the ancient rule of faith, and to form their opinions according to the subtile precepts of logic. The science of the church is neglected for the study of geometry, and they lose sight of Heaven while they are employed in measuring the earth. Euclid is perpetually in their hands. Aristotle and Theophrastus are the objects of their

Some exceptions with regard to learning

184 Minucius Felix, c. 8, with Wowerus's notes. Celsus ap. Origen. l. iii. p. 138, 142, Julian ap. Cyril. l. vi. p. 206. Edit. Spanheim.
185 Euseb. Hist. Eccles. iv. 3. Hieronym. Epist. 83.
186 The story is prettily told in Justin's Dialogues. Tillemont (Mém. Ecclésiast. tom. ii. p. 334), who relates it after him, is sure that the old man was a disguised angel.

admiration; and they express an uncommon reverence for the works of Galen. Their errors are derived from the abuse of the arts and sciences of the infidels, and they corrupt the simplicity of the Gospel by the refinements of human reason."[187]

with regard to rank and fortune Nor can it be affirmed with truth that the advantages of birth and fortune were always separated from the profession of Christianity. Several Roman citizens were brought before the tribunal of Pliny, and he soon discovered that a great number of persons of *every order* of men in Bithynia had deserted the religion of their ancestors.[188] His unsuspected testimony may, in this instance, obtain more credit than the bold challenge of Tertullian, when he addresses himself to the fears as well as to the humanity of the proconsul of Africa, by assuring him that, if he persists in his cruel intentions, he must decimate Carthage, and that he will find among the guilty many persons of his own rank, senators and matrons of noblest extraction, and the friends or relations of his most intimate friends.[189] It appears, however, that about forty years afterwards the emperor Valerian was persuaded of the truth of this assertion, since in one of his rescripts he evidently supposes that senators, Roman knights, and ladies of quality were engaged in the Christian sect.[190] The church still continued to increase its outward splendour as it lost its internal purity; and in the reign of Diocletian the palace, the courts of justice, and even the army concealed a multitude of Christians who endeavoured to reconcile the interests of the present with those of a future life.

Christianity most favourably received by the poor and simple And yet these exceptions are either too few in number, or too recent in time, entirely to remove the imputation of ignorance and obscurity which has been so arrogantly cast on the first proselytes of Christianity. Instead of employing in our defence the fictions of later ages, it will be more prudent to convert the occasion of scandal into a subject of edification. Our serious thoughts will suggest to us that the apostles themselves were chosen by providence among the fishermen of Galilee, and that, the lower we depress the temporal condition of the first Christians, the more reason we shall find to admire their merit and success. It is incumbent on us diligently to remember that the kingdom of heaven was promised to the poor in spirit, and that minds afflicted by calamity and the contempt of mankind cheerfully listen to the divine promise of future happiness; while, on the contrary, the fortunate are satisfied with the possession of this world; and the wise abuse in doubt

187 Eusebius, v. 28. It may be hoped that none, except the heretics, gave occasion to the complaint of Celsus (ap. Origen, l. ii. p. 77) that the Christians were perpetually correcting and altering their Gospels.
188 Plin. Epist. x. 97. Fuerunt alii similis amentiæ, cives Romani . . . Multi enim omnis ætatis, *omnis ordinis*, utriusque sexûs, etiam vocantur in periculum et vocabuntur. [Others showed the same folly, Roman citizens . . . for many of all ages, all social classes and both sexes are also being brought to trial and will be brought in the future.]
189 Tertullian ad Scapulam. Yet even his rhetoric rises no higher than to claim a *tenth* part of Carthage.
190 Cyprian. Epist. 79.

and dispute their vain superiority of reason and knowledge.

We stand in need of such reflections to comfort us for the loss of some illustrious characters, which in our eyes might have seemed the most worthy of the heavenly present. The names of Seneca, of the elder and the younger Pliny, of Tacitus, of Plutarch, of Galen, of the slave Epictetus, and of the emperor Marcus Antoninus, adorn the age in which they flourished, and exalt the dignity of human nature. They filled with glory their respective stations, either in active or contemplative life; their excellent understandings were improved by study; Philosophy had purified their minds from the prejudices of the popular superstition; and their days were spent in the pursuit of truth and the practice of virtue. Yet all these sages (it is no less an object of surprise than of concern) overlooked or rejected the perfection of the Christian system. Their language or their silence equally discover their contempt for the growing sect, which in their time had diffused itself over the Roman empire. Those among them who condescend to mention the Christians consider them only as obstinate and perverse enthusiasts, who exacted an implicit submission to their mysterious doctrines, without being able to produce a single argument that could engage the attention of men of sense and learning.[191]

Rejected by some eminent men of the first and second centuries

It is at least doubtful whether any of these philosophers perused the apologies which the primitive Christians repeatedly published in behalf of themselves and of their religion; but it is much to be lamented that such a cause was not defended by abler advocates. They expose with superfluous wit and eloquence the extravagance of Polytheism. They interest our compassion by displaying the innocence and sufferings of their injured brethren. But, when they would demonstrate the divine origin of Christianity, they insist much more strongly on the predictions which announced, than on the miracles which accompanied, the appearance of the Messiah. Their favourite argument might serve to edify a Christian or to convert a Jew, since both the one and the other acknowledge the authority of those prophecies, and both are obliged, with devout reverence, to search for their sense and their accomplishment. But this mode of persuasion loses much of its weight and influence, when it is addressed to those who neither understand nor respect the Mosaic dispensation and the prophetic style.[192] In the unskilful hands of Justin and of the succeeding apologists, the sublime meaning of the Hebrew oracles evaporates in distant types, affected

Their neglect of prophecy

---

191 Dr. Lardner, in his first and second volume of Jewish and Christian testimonies, collects and illustrates those of Pliny the younger, of Tacitus, of Galen, of Marcus Antoninus, and perhaps of Epictetus (for it is doubtful whether that philosopher means to speak of the Christians). The new sect is totally unnoticed by Seneca, the elder Pliny, and Plutarch.

192 If the famous prophecy of the Seventy Weeks had been alleged to a Roman philosopher, would he not have replied in the words of Cicero, "Quæ tandem ista auguratio est, annorum potius quam aut mensium aut dierum?" [Will this prophecy of yours eventually come about in years rather than months or days?] De Divinatione, ii. 30. Observe with what irreverence Lucian (in Alexandro, c. 13), and his friend Celsus ap. Origen. (l. vii. p. 327), express themselves concerning the Hebrew prophets.

conceits, and cold allegories; and even their authenticity was rendered suspicious to an unenlightened Gentile by the mixture of pious forgeries, which, under the names of Orpheus, Hermes, and the Sibyls,[193] were obtruded on him as of equal value with the genuine inspirations of Heaven. The adoption of fraud and sophistry in the defence of revelation too often reminds us of the injudicious conduct of those poets who load their *invulnerable* heroes with a useless weight of cumbersome and brittle armour.

and of miracles

But how shall we excuse the supine inattention of the Pagan and philosophic world to those evidences which were presented by the hand of Omnipotence, not to their reason, but to their senses? During the age of Christ, of his apostles, and of their first disciples, the doctrine which they preached was confirmed by innumerable prodigies. The lame walked, the blind saw, the sick were healed, the dead were raised,

General silence concerning the darkness of the Passion

dæmons were expelled, and the laws of Nature were frequently suspended for the benefit of the church. But the sages of Greece and Rome turned aside from the awful spectacle, and, pursuing the ordinary occupations of life and study, appeared unconscious of any alterations in the moral or physical government of the world. Under the reign of Tiberius, the whole earth,[194] or at least a celebrated province of the Roman empire,[195] was involved in a præternatural darkness of three hours. Even this miraculous event, which ought to have excited the wonder, the curiosity, and the devotion of mankind, passed without notice in an age of science and history.[196] It happened during the lifetime of Seneca and the elder Pliny, who must have experienced the immediate effects, or received the earliest intelligence, of the prodigy. Each of these philosophers, in a laborious work, has recorded all the great phenomena of Nature, earthquakes, meteors, comets, and eclipses, which his indefatigable curiosity could collect.[197] Both the one and the other have omitted to mention the greatest phenomenon to which the mortal eye has been witness since the creation of the globe. A distinct chapter of Pliny[198] is designed for eclipses of an extraordinary nature and unusual duration; but he contents himself with describing

---

193 The philosophers, who derided the more ancient predictions of the Sibyls, would easily have detected the Jewish and Christian forgeries, which have been so triumphantly quoted by the fathers, from Justin Martyr to Lactantius. When the Sibylline verses had performed their appointed task, they, like the system of the millennium, were quietly laid aside. The Christian Sibyl had unluckily fixed the ruin of Rome for the year 195, A·U·C· 948.

194 The fathers, as they are drawn out in battle array by Dom Calmet (Dissertations sur la Bible, tom. iii. p. 295–308), seem to cover the whole earth with darkness, in which they are followed by most of the moderns.

195 Origen ad Matth. c. 27, and a few modern critics, Beza, Le Clerc, Lardner, &c., are desirous of confining it to the land of Judea.

196 The celebrated passage of Phlegon is now wisely abandoned. When Tertullian assures the Pagans that the mention of the prodigy is found in Arcanis (not Archivis) vestris (see his Apology, c. 21), he probably appeals to the Sibylline verses, which relate it exactly in the words of the gospel.

197 Seneca Quæst. Natur. i. 1, 15, vi. 1, vii. 17. Plin. Hist. Natur. l. ii.

198 Plin. Hist. Natur. ii. 30.

the singular defect of light which followed the murder of Cæsar, when, during the greatest part of the year, the orb of the sun appeared pale and without splendour. This season of obscurity, which cannot surely be compared with the præternatural darkness of the Passion, had been already celebrated by most of the poets[199] and historians of that memorable age.[200]

199 Virgil. Georgic. i. 466. Tibullus, l. i. Eleg. v. ver. 75. Ovid. Metamorph. xv. 782. Lucan. Pharsal. i. 540. The last of these poets places this prodigy before the civil war.
200 See a public epistle of M. Antony in Joseph. Antiquit. xiv. 12. Plutarch in Cæsar. p. 471. Appian. Bell. Civil. l. iv. Dion Cassius, l. xlv. p. 431. Julius Obsequens, c. 128. His little treatise is an abstract of Livy's prodigies.

From CHAPTER XXXVIII

General Observations on the Fall of the Roman Empire in the West

The Greeks, after their country had been reduced into a province, imputed the triumphs of Rome, not to the merit, but to the FORTUNE, of the republic. The inconstant goddess, who so blindly distributes and resumes her favours, had *now* consented (such was the language of envious flattery) to resign her wings, to descend from her globe, and to fix her firm and immutable throne on the banks of the Tiber.[1] A wiser Greek, who has composed, with a philosophic spirit, the memorable history of his own times, deprived his countrymen of this vain and delusive comfort by opening to their view the deep foundations of the greatness of Rome.[2] The fidelity of the citizens to each other, and to the state, was confirmed by the habits of education and the prejudices of religion. Honour, as well as virtue, was the principle of the republic; the ambitious citizens laboured to deserve the solemn glories of a triumph; and the ardour of the Roman youth was kindled into active emulation, as often as they beheld the domestic images of their ancestors.[3] The temperate struggles of the patricians and plebeians had finally established the firm and equal balance of the constitution; which united the freedom of popular assemblies with the authority and wisdom of a senate and the executive powers of a regal magistrate. When the consul

1 Such are the figurative expressions of Plutarch (Opera, tom. ii. p. 318, edit. Wechel), to whom, on the faith of his son Lamprias (Fabricius, Bibliot. Græc. tom. iii. p. 341), I shall boldly impute the malicious declamation, περὶ τῆς Ῥωμαίων τύχης. The same opinions had prevailed among the Greeks two hundred and fifty years before Plutarch; and to confute them is the professed intention of Polybius (Hist. l. i. p. 90, edit. Gronov. Amstel. 1670).
2 See the inestimable remains of the sixth book of Polybius, and many other parts of his general history, particularly a digression in the seventeenth book, in which he compares the phalanx and the legion.
3 Sallust, de Bell. Jugurthin. c. 4. Such were the generous professions of P. Scipio and Q. Maximus. The Latin historian had read, and most probably transcribes, Poybius, their contemporary and friend.

displayed the standard of the republic, each citizen bound himself, by the obligation of an oath, to draw his sword in the cause of his country, till he had discharged the sacred duty by a military service of ten years. This wise institution continually poured into the field the rising generations of freemen and soldiers; and their numbers were reinforced by the warlike and populous states of Italy, who, after a brave resistance, had yielded to the valour, and embraced the alliance, of the Romans. The sage historian, who excited the virtue of the younger Scipio and beheld the ruin of Carthage,[4] has accurately described their military system; their levies, arms, exercises, subordination, marches, encampments; and the invincible legion, superior in active strength to the Macedonian phalanx of Philip and Alexander. From these institutions of peace and war, Polybius has deduced the spirit and success of a people incapable of fear and impatient of repose. The ambitious design of conquest, which might have been defeated by the seasonable conspiracy of mankind, was attempted and achieved; and the perpetual violation of justice was maintained by the political virtues of prudence and courage. The arms of the republic, sometimes vanquished in battle, always victorious in war, advanced with rapid steps to the Euphrates, the Danube, the Rhine, and the Ocean; and the images of gold, or silver, or brass, that might serve to represent the nations and their kings, were successively broken by the *iron* monarchy of Rome.[5]

The rise of a city, which swelled into an Empire, may deserve, as a singular prodigy, the reflection of a philosophic mind. But the decline of Rome was the natural and inevitable effect of immoderate greatness. Prosperity ripened the principle of decay; the causes of destruction multiplied with the extent of conquest; and, as soon as time or accident had removed the artificial supports, the stupendous fabric yielded to the pressure of its own weight. The story of its ruin is simple and obvious; and, instead of inquiring why the Roman empire was destroyed, we should rather be surprised that it had subsisted so long. The victorious legions, who, in distant wars, acquired the vices of strangers and mercenaries, first oppressed the freedom of the republic, and afterwards violated the majesty of the purple. The emperors, anxious for their personal safety and the public peace, were reduced to the base

4 While Carthage was in flames, Scipio repeated two lines of the Iliad, which express the destruction of Troy, acknowledging to Polybius, his friend and preceptor (Polyb. in Excerpt. de Virtut. et Vit. tom. ii. p. 1455–1465), that, while he recollected the vicissitudes of human affairs, he inwardly applied them to the future calamities of Rome (Appian. in Libycis, p. 136, edit. Toll).

5 See Daniel, ii. 31–40. "And the fourth kingdom shall be strong as *iron*; forasmuch as iron breaketh in pieces, and subdueth all things." The remainder of the prophecy (the mixture of iron and *clay*) was accomplished, according to St. Jerom, in his own time. Sicut enim in principio nihil Romano Imperio fortius et durius, ita in fine rerum nihil imbecillius: quum et in bellis civilibus et adversus diversas nationes aliarum gentium barbararum auxilio indigemus [For just as in the beginning nothing was stronger than Roman power nor more enduring, so in the end nothing was more stupid. Thus in civil war and against hostile nations we need the aid of barbarian peoples.] (Opera, tom. v. p. 572).

expedient of corrupting the discipline which rendered them alike formidable to their sovereign and to the enemy; the vigour of the military government was relaxed, and finally dissolved, by the partial institutions of Constantine; and the Roman world was overwhelmed by a deluge of Barbarians.

The decay of Rome has been frequently ascribed to the translation of the seat of empire; but this history has already shewn that the powers of government were *divided* rather than *removed*. The throne of Constantinople was erected in the East; while the West was still possessed by a series of emperors who held their residence in Italy and claimed their equal inheritance of the legions and provinces. This dangerous novelty impaired the strength, and fomented the vices, of a double reign; the instruments of an oppressive and arbitrary system were multiplied; and a vain emulation of luxury, not of merit, was introduced and supported between the degenerate successors of Theodosius. Extreme distress, which unites the virtue of a free people, embitters the factions of a declining monarchy. The hostile favourites of Arcadius and Honorius betrayed the republic to its common enemies; and the Byzantine court beheld with indifference, perhaps with pleasure, the disgrace of Rome, the misfortunes of Italy, and the loss of the West. Under the succeeding reigns, the alliance of the two empires was restored; but the aid of the Oriental Romans was tardy, doubtful, and ineffectual; and the national schism of the Greeks and Latins was enlarged by the perpetual difference of language and manners, of interest, and even of religion. Yet the salutary event approved in some measure the judgment of Constantine. During a long period of decay, his impregnable city repelled the victorious armies of Barbarians, protected the wealth of Asia, and commanded, both in peace and war, the important straits which connect the Euxine and Mediterranean seas. The foundation of Constantinople more essentially contributed to the preservation of the East than to the ruin of the West.

As the happiness of a *future* life is the great object of religion, we may hear, without surprise or scandal, that the introduction, or at least the abuse, of Christianity had some influence on the decline and fall of the Roman empire. The clergy successfully preached the doctrines of patience and pusillanimity; the active virtues of society were discouraged; and the last remains of the military spirit were buried in the cloister; a large portion of public and private wealth was consecrated to the specious demands of charity and devotion; and the soldiers' pay was lavished on the useless multitudes of both sexes, who could only plead the merits of abstinence and chastity. Faith, zeal, curiosity, and the more earthly passions of malice and ambition kindled the flame of theological discord; the church, and even the state, were distracted by religious factions, whose conflicts were sometimes bloody, and always implacable; the attention of the emperors was diverted from camps to synods; the Roman world was oppressed by a new species of tyranny; and the persecuted sects became the secret enemies of their country. Yet party-spirit, however pernicious or absurd, is a principle of union as well as of dissension. The bishops, from eighteen hundred pulpits, inculcated the duty of passive obedience to a lawful and orthodox sovereign; their frequent assemblies, and perpetual correspondence, maintained the communion of distant churches: and the benevolent temper of the gospel was strengthened, though confined, by the spiritual alliance of the Catholics. The sacred indolence of the monks was devoutly embraced by a servile and effeminate age; but, if superstition had not afforded a decent retreat, the same vices would have tempted the unworthy Romans to desert, from baser motives, the standard of the republic. Religious precepts are easily obeyed, which indulge and sanctify the natural inclinations of their votaries; but the pure and genuine influence of Christianity may be traced in its beneficial, though imperfect, effects on the Barbarian proselytes of the North. If the decline of the Roman empire was hastened by the conversion of Constantine, his victorious religion broke the violence of the fall, and mollified the ferocious temper of the conquerors.

This awful revolution may be usefully applied to the instruction of the present age. It is the duty of a patriot to prefer and promote the exclusive interest and glory of his native country; but a philosopher may be permitted to enlarge his views, and to consider Europe as one great republic, whose various inhabitants have attained almost the same level of politeness and cultivation. The balance of power will continue to fluctuate, and the prosperity of our own or the neighbouring kingdoms may be alternately exalted or depressed; but these partial events cannot essentially injure our general state of happiness, the system of arts, and laws, and manners, which so advantageously distinguish, above the rest of mankind, the Europeans and their colonies. The savage nations of the globe are the common enemies of civilized society; and we may inquire with anxious curiosity, whether Europe is still threatened with a repetition of those calamities which formerly oppressed the arms and institutions of Rome. Perhaps the same reflections will illustrate the fall of that mighty empire, and explain the probable causes of our actual security.

I. The Romans were ignorant of the extent of their danger, and the number of their enemies. Beyond the Rhine and Danube, the northern countries of Europe and Asia were filled with innumerable tribes of hunters and shepherds, poor, voracious, and turbulent; bold in arms, and impatient to ravish the fruits of industry. The Barbarian world was agitated by the rapid impulse of war; and the peace of Gaul or Italy was shaken by the distant revolutions of China. The Huns, who fled before a victorious enemy, directed their march towards the West; and the torrent was swelled by the gradual accession of captives and allies. The flying tribes who yielded to the Huns assumed in *their* turn the spirit of conquest; the endless column of Barbarians pressed on the Roman empire with accumulated weight; and, if the foremost were destroyed, the vacant space was instantly replenished by new assailants. Such formidable emigrations can no longer issue from the North; and the long repose, which has been imputed to the decrease of population, is the happy consequence of the progress of arts and agriculture. Instead of some rude villages, thinly scattered among its woods and morasses, Germany now produces a list of two thousand three hundred walled towns; the Christian kingdoms of Denmark, Sweden, and Poland, have been successively established; and the Hanse merchants, with the Teutonic knights, have extended their colonies along the coast of the Baltic, as far as the Gulf of Finland. From the Gulf of Finland to the Eastern Ocean, Russia now assumes the form of a powerful and civilized empire. The plough, the loom, and the forge, are introduced on the banks of the Volga, the Oby, and the Lena; and the fiercest of the Tartar hordes have been taught to tremble and obey. The reign of independent Barbarism is now contracted to a narrow span; and the remnant of Calmucks or Uzbecks, whose forces may be almost numbered, cannot seriously excite the apprehensions of the great republic of Europe.[6] Yet this apparent security should not tempt us to forget that new enemies, and unknown dangers, may *possibly* arise from some obscure people, scarcely visible in the map of the world. The Arabs or Saracens, who spread their conquests from India to Spain, had languished in poverty and contempt, till Mahomet breathed into those savage bodies the soul of enthusiasm.

II. The empire of Rome was firmly established by the singular and perfect coalition of its members. The subject nations, resigning the hope, and even the wish, of independence, embraced the character of Roman citizens; and the provinces of the West were reluctantly torn by the Barbarians from the bosom of their mother-country.[7] But this union was purchased by the loss of national freedom and military spirit; and the servile provinces, destitute of life and motion, expected their safety from the mercenary troops and governors, who were directed by the orders of a distant court. The happiness of an hundred millions depended on the personal merit of one or two men, perhaps children, whose minds were corrupted by education, luxury, and despotic power. The deepest wounds were inflicted on the empire during the minorities of the sons and grandsons of Theodosius; and, after those incapable princes seemed to attain the age of manhood, they abandoned the church to the bishops, the state to the eunuchs, and the provinces to the Barbarians. Europe is now divided into twelve powerful, though unequal, kingdoms, three respectable commonwealths, and a variety of smaller, though independent, states; the chances of royal and ministerial talents are multiplied, at least with the number of its rulers; and a

6 The French and English editors of the Genealogical History of the Tartars have subjoined a curious, though imperfect, description of their present state. We might question the independence of the Calmucks, or Eluths, since they have been recently vanquished by the Chinese, who, in the year 1759, subdued the lesser Bucharia, and advanced into the country of Badakshan, near the sources of the Oxus (Mémoires sur les Chinois, tom. i. p. 325–400). But these conquests are precarious, nor will I venture to ensure the safety of the Chinese empire.
7 The prudent reader will determine how far this general proposition is weakened by the revolt of the Isaurians, the independence of Britain and Armorica, the Moorish tribes, or the Bagaudæ of Gaul and Spain (vol. i. p. 280, vol. iii. p. 352, 402, 480).

Julian, or Semiramis, may reign in the North, while Arcadius and Honorius again slumber on the thrones of the South. The abuses of tyranny are restrained by the mutual influence of fear and shame; republics have acquired order and stability; monarchies have imbibed the principles of freedom, or, at least, of moderation; and some sense of honour and justice is introduced into the most defective constitutions by the general manners of the times. In peace, the progress of knowledge and industry is accelerated by the emulation of so many active rivals: in war, the European forces are exercised by temperate and undecisive contests. If a savage conqueror should issue from the deserts of Tartary, he must repeatedly vanquish the robust peasants of Russia, the numerous armies of Germany, the gallant nobles of France, and the intrepid freemen of Britain; who, perhaps, might confederate for their common defence. Should the victorious Barbarians carry slavery and desolation as far as the Atlantic Ocean, ten thousand vessels would transport beyond their pursuit the remains of civilized society; and Europe would revive and flourish in the American world which is already filled with her colonies and institutions.[8]

III. Cold, poverty, and a life of danger and fatigue, fortify the strength and courage of Barbarians. In every age they have oppressed the polite and peaceful nations of China, India, and Persia, who neglected, and still neglect, to counterbalance these natural powers by the resources of military art. The war-like states of antiquity, Greece, Macedonia, and Rome, educated a race of soldiers; exercised their bodies, disciplined their courage, multiplied their forces by regular evolutions, and converted the iron which they possessed into strong and serviceable weapons. But this superiority insensibly declined with their laws and manners; and the feeble policy of Constantine and his successors armed and instructed, for the ruin of the empire, the rude valour of the Barbarian mercenaries. The military art has been changed by the invention of gunpowder; which enables man to command the two most powerful agents of nature, air and fire. Mathematics, chymistry, mechanics, architecture, have been applied to the service of war; and the adverse parties oppose to each other the most elaborate modes of attack and of defence. Historians may indignantly observe that the preparations of a siege would found and maintain a flourishing colony;[9] yet we cannot be displeased that the subversion of a city should be a

8 America now contains about six millions of European blood and descent; and their numbers, at least in the North, are continually increasing. Whatever may be the changes of their political situation, they must preserve the manners of Europe; and we may reflect with some pleasure that the English language will probably be diffused over an immense and populous continent.

9 On avoit fait venir (for the siege of Turin) 140 pièces de canon; et il est à remarquer que chaque gros canon monté revient à environ 2000 écus; il y avoit 110,000 boulets; 106,000 cartouches d'une façon, et 300,000 d'une autre; 21,000 bombes; 27,700 grenades, 15,000 sacs à terre, 30,000 instruments pour le pionnage; 1,200,000 livres de poudre. Ajoutez à ces munitions, le plomb, le fer, et le fer blanc, les cordages, tout ce qui sert aux mineurs, le souphre, le salpêtre, les outils de toute espèce. Il est certain que les frais de tous ces preparatifs de destruction suffiroient pour fonder et pour faire fleurir la plus nombreuse colonie. [140 cannon had been brought up and, it is worth noting, each large mounted

work of cost and difficulty, or that an industrious people should be protected by those arts, which survive and supply the decay of military virtue. Cannon and fortifications now form an impregnable barrier against the Tartar horse; and Europe is secure from any future irruption of Barbarians; since, before they can conquer, they must cease to be barbarous. Their gradual advances in the science of war would always be accompanied, as we may learn from the example of Russia, with a proportionable improvement in the arts of peace and civil policy; and they themselves must deserve a place among the polished nations whom they subdue.

Should these speculations be found doubtful or fallacious, there still remains a more humble source of comfort and hope. The discoveries of ancient and modern navigators, and the domestic history, or tradition, of the most enlightened nations, represent the *human savage*, naked both in mind and body, and destitute of laws, of arts, of ideas, and almost of language.[10] From this abject condition, perhaps the primitive and universal state of man, he has gradually arisen to command the animals, to fertilise the earth, to traverse the ocean, and to measure the heavens. His progress in the improvement and exercise of his mental and corporeal faculties[11] has been irregular and various, infinitely slow in the beginning, and increasing by degrees with redoubled velocity; ages of laborious ascent have been followed by a moment of rapid downfall; and the several climates of the globe have felt the vicissitudes of light and darkness. Yet the experience of four thousand years should enlarge our hopes, and diminish our apprehensions; we cannot determine to what height the human species may aspire in their advances towards perfection; but it may safely be presumed that no people, unless the face of nature is changed, will relapse into their original barbarism. The improvements of society may be viewed under a threefold aspect. 1. The poet or philosopher illustrates his age and country by the efforts of a *single* mind; but these superior powers of reason or fancy are rare and spontaneous productions, and the genius of Homer, or Cicero, or Newton, would excite less admiration, if they could be created by the

cannon costs around 2,000 crowns. There were 110,000 bullets, 106,000 cartridges of one type and 300,000 of another, 21,000 bombs, 27,700 grenades, 15,000 sacks of earth, 30,000 digging tools and 1,200,000 pounds of powder. To these munitions must be added lead, iron, tin, ropes, everything for the use of miners; sulphur, saltpêtre and tools of every kind. There can be no doubt that expense of all these preparations for destruction would be sufficient to found and maintain the largest colony in a flourishing condition.] Voltaire, Siècle de Louis XIV. c. xx. in his Works, tom. xi. p. 391.

10 It would be an easy though tedious task to produce the authorities of poets, philosophers, and historians. I shall therefore content myself with appealing to the decisive and authentic testimony of Diodorus Siculus (tom. i. l. i. p. 11, 12, l. iii. p. 184, &c., edit. Wesseling). The Ichthyophagi, who in his time wandered along the shores of the Red Sea, can only be compared to the natives of New Holland (Dampier's Voyages, vol. i. p. 464–469). Fancy or perhaps reason may still suppose an extreme and absolute state of nature far below the level of these savages, who had acquired some arts and instruments.

11 See the learned and rational work of the President Goguet, de l'Origine des Loix, des Arts, et des Sciences. He traces from facts or conjectures (tom. i. p. 147–337, edit. 12mo) the first and most difficult steps of human invention.

will of a prince or the lessons of a preceptor. 2. The benefits of law and policy, of trade and manufactures, of arts and sciences, are more solid and permanent; and *many* individuals may be qualified, by education and discipline, to promote, in their respective stations, the interest of the community. But this general order is the effect of skill and labour; and the complex machinery may be decayed by time or injured by violence. 3. Fortunately for mankind, the more useful, or, at least, more necessary arts can be performed without superior talents, or national subordination; without the powers of *one* or the union of *many*. Each village, each family, each individual, must always possess both ability and inclination to perpetuate the use of fire[12] and of metals; the propagation and service of domestic animals; the methods of hunting and fishing; the rudiments of navigation; the imperfect cultivation of corn or other nutritive grain; and the simple practice of the mechanic trades. Private genius and public industry may be extirpated; but these hardy plants survive the tempest, and strike an everlasting root into the most unfavourable soil. The splendid days of Augustus and Trajan were eclipsed by a cloud of ignorance; and the Barbarians subverted the laws and palaces of Rome. But the scythe, the invention or emblem of Saturn,[13] still continued annually to mow the harvests of Italy: and the human feasts of the Læstrygons[14] have never been renewed on the coast of Campania.

Since the first discovery of the arts, war, commerce, and religious zeal have diffused, among the savages of the Old and New World, those inestimable gifts: they have been successively propagated; they can never be lost. We may therefore acquiesce in the pleasing conclusion that every age of the world has increased, and still increases, the real wealth, the happiness, the knowledge, and perhaps the virtue, of the human race.[15]

---

12 It is certain, however strange, that many nations have been ignorant of the use of fire. Even the ingenious natives of Otaheite, who are destitute of metals, have not invented any earthen vessels capable of sustaining the sustaining the action of fire and of communicating the heat to the liquids which they contain.

13 Plutarch. Quæst. Rom. in tom. ii. p. 275. Macrob. Saturnal. l. i. c. 8, p. 152, edit. London. The arrival of Saturn (or his religious worship) in a ship may indicate that the savage coast of Latium was first discovered and civilised by the Phœnicians.

14 In the ninth and tenth books of the Odyssey, Homer has embellished the tales of fearful and credulous sailors, who transformed the cannibals of Italy and Sicily into monstrous giants.

15 The merit of discovery has too often been stained with avarice, cruelty, and fanaticism; and the intercourse of nations has produced the communication of disease and prejudice. A singular exception is due to the virtue of our own times and country. The five great voyages successively undertaken by the command of his present Majesty were inspired by the pure and generous love of science and of mankind. The same prince, adapting his benefaction to the different stages of society, has founded a school of painting in his capital, and has introduced into the island of the South Sea the vegetables and animals most useful to human life.

Notes

1 'Richard of Cirencester' was a fictitious chronicler invented by Charles Bertram (1723–65).

2 Gibbon uses the word in its literal sense, to refer to the holding of power by one man; the implication of hereditary succession is a modern accretion.

3 The equites (or knights) were the wealthiest non-senatorial citizen class. The name is derived from their original military functions, but in the Early Empire they achieved increased importance in the civil administration.

4 Public official, drawn from the senatorial class.

5 The priests presiding over the State cults. The political implications of Roman state religion are shown by the fact that the Emperor himself held the office of Pontifex Maximus (Chief Priest or, as Gibbon translates it, Supreme Pontiff).

6 That is, Livy.

7 See note 1 above.

8 Here Gibbon refers to the powerful families of the senatorial ruling class of the Republic.

9 Official holding power on behalf of or in place of the consuls of the year. During the Republic this had been a means by which the Senate ensured that there were sufficient high ranking officials to administer the provinces.

10 That is by saying 'veto' (I forbid), hence the modern usage.

11 Of Gibbon's interpretation of *primum* Bury says: 'Gibbon's inference from *primum* is hardly tenable; but he is right in so far that Augustus had prepared the way for the change of Tiberius'.

12 A *colonia* was a town set up as an instrument of imperial policy and populated largely by Roman citizens, usually retired legionaries.

13 The change is a small one from 'be thoroughly discussed' to 'be discussed beforehand' (i.e. by the chiefs). No change is really necessary.

14 Gibbon may be wrong here. *Exigere plagas* (Tactitus *Germ.* 7) means 'to examine the wounds'. *Exugere* has the sense of 'to suck out', 'dry off'.

15 Hymen was the god of marriage. The marriage was actually between Manlius and Lavinia.

16 Young children were admitted free to the baths.

17 Origen (*c.* 184–254), with more enthusiasm than prudence, took Matthew 19:12 literally and castrated himself.

18 Ossian: a legendary Gaelic warrior and bard supposed to have lived in the third century. In 1763 James Macpherson (1736-96) published *Temora*, an epic in eight books, which he claimed was a translation of an original poem by Ossian. This fabrication was accepted by many although its authenticity had early been challenged by Dr Johnson and others. It is interesting to note that the growth of Antiquarianism in the late seventeenth and eighteenth centuries was accompanied by a rash of such literary and historical fabrications. The Ossianic poems, 'Richard of Cirencester' (see note 1) and the 'Rowley' poems by Thomas Chatterton (1752-70) are all examples of this phenomenon.

INDEX

Figures followed by an asterisk * refer to the notes following each extract; figures followed by n refer to authors' footnotes within the extracts. Where reference is made to a particular source etc. in the footnotes of several consecutive pages, the numbers are run together, as 191–5n; discrete references in the text are indexed as such.

Eugene de Savoie-Carignan, prince 129, 130*
Eumenius 225*n*
Euphrates 186, 189, 190
Euripides 12, 14*
Europe, condition of 328–30
Eusebius, *Chronicles* 274–5*n*, 277–8*n*, 286*n*,
    298*n*, 305*n*, 309–10*n*, 315–18*n*, 320–2*n*
Eutropius 189*n*, 242*n*
Eutychius 301*n*, 316*n*
evil
    alleviation 112–13
    mixture with Good 109
    natural 115–16
    physical *cf* moral 96, 98–9
    tolerated by God 92, 98
excess, distrust of 1
    in religion 32
    see also enthusiasm
exertion, personal, reasons for 173
exorcism 290, 291*n*
Ezra, Jewish reformer 285

Fabretti 221*n*
Fabricius 221*n*
Fénélon, archbishop 30*
Fielding, Henry 2, 25
    Joseph Andrews 30; preface 4, 25–30
    Tom Jones 25
Flavians 209, 241–2
    see also Domitian; Titus; Vespasian
Florus 200*n*, 215*n*
Fo (Buddha) 138, 138*n*, 139*
Folard, chevalier 196
Fortis, Abbate 201*n*
Fra Paolo 287*n*, 300*n*, 306–8*n*
France
    agriculture 167
    classicism 3, 4
    economy 155, 159
    government 167
    Revolution 131
    under Romans *see* Gaul
    universities 175
Freinshemius 257*n*
Freret 189*n*, 200*n*
Frontinus 197*n*

Galba, Roman emperor 241
Galen 229, 322, 323, 323*n*
Garrick, David 11, 44
Gaul 186, 199–200, 249
    Christianity 318–19
    cities 222
    Gauls 125, 141*n*, 200, 200*n*, 284*n*
    gods 207*n*
    religious persecution 208–9
Geddes, Dr 276*n*, 319*n*
Gellius, Aulus, *Noctes Atticae* 212*n*, 220*n*, 280*n*
George II, king of England 332*n*
Germanicus Caesar, Roman general 22, 124*,
    186*n*, 240, 241
    widow 247*n*
Germany, ancient 248–68
    addiction to drink 255, 256
    bards 263
    Batavians 265

Bructeri 265
character of people 255, 259–61
checks on progress 263–5
Cimbri 251*n*
climate 250–1
communications 250
confederation against M. Aurelius 266–7
culture 252–5
disunity of states 265
extent 249
government 157–9
lack of arms/discipline 264–5
liberty 257
magistrates 258–9
Marcomanni 266–7, 266*n*
M. Aurelius conquers 190–1, 266–7
militarism 255, 256, 258, 263
origin of peoples 251–2
origins of European civilization 249
people, generally 125, 142, 183, 185,
    199, 267–8
population 256–7
Quadi 266–7
religion 261–3, 261–2*n*
Sitones 257
Suiones 257
Ubii 253*n*
women 260–1
Germany, modern 129, 253, 329
Gibbon, Edward 2, 4, 5, 183–4, 333*
    *History of the Decline and Fall of the Roman
        Empire* 184–332
Gnostics 276–9, 277–8*n*, 297*n*, 315
Goethe, Johann Wolfgang von 1
Goguet 331*n*
Gothicism 184
government
    ancient Germany 257
    borrowing 153, 171
    duties of sovereign authority 170, 172
    Eastern 138–9
    economic policy 148
    and education of the people 181
    English 125–9, 131
    English *cf* Roman 122–3
    expenditure 152, 170
    form of, and trade 142–3
    French 167
    principles of Roman 206, 211
    purpose of 257–9
    sovereign authority essential 146–7
    types of 131
Greece 22
    Achaean league 202
    Christianity 314–15, 315*n*
    colonies in Italy 200
    education 175, 179–80
    games 180, 182*
    influence on Rome 213–14
    Jews reject religion 269
    military tactics 194
    military training 175, 179–80
    as Roman province 202
    scientists 228–9
    view of Roman success 325
Gregory of Nyssa, St 297*n*, 315*n*

Christian Jews 273–6
Essenians 306, 316
exclusiveness 271–2
exile from Jerusalem 275, 275*n*
Gnostic view of Judaism 276–7
Herodians 269–70*n*
and idolatry 279
and immortality of the soul 284–5
Messianic principle 272–3
not conquerors 271–2
and oriental beliefs 285
Pharisees 285
prophets 323, 323*n*
rebellions against Romans 190*n*, 193, 275
religious zeal 269–71, 285
Sadducees 285, 285*n*
tithes 306
John, king of England 126, 128*
Johnson, Samuel 2, 3, 9, 94*, 120*, 333*
    on authorship 119
    Life of Pope 16–23
    on optimism 108–20
    The Plays of William Shakespeare 11–14
Jonson, Ben 29, 30*
Jortin, Dr 285*n*
Joseph of Arimathea 319*n*
Josephus, Flavius 270*n*, 277*n*
    History of the Jewish War 193*n*, 196*n*, 197*n*,
        217*n*, 222*n*, 223*n*, 240*n*, 270*n*, 285*n*
    Jewish Antiquities 209*n*, 270*n*, 285*n*, 306*n*, 325*n*
Julian 188*n*, 238*n*, 309*n*
    Ceasars 186*n*, 188*n*, 239*n*, 244*n*, 294*n*
Julius Africanus 321
Julius Caesar, Gaius 122, 124*, 186, 186*n*,
        191*n*, 230*n*, 234*n*, 236, 239, 244*n*,
        253*n*, 283*n*, 325
    De Bello Civili 234*n*
    De Bello Gallico 141*n*, 207*n*, 211*n*, 250*n*,
        254*n*, 256*n*, 258*n*, 263*n*, 265*n*
    character 238
Justin 269*n*, 289*n*, 297–8*n*, 309*n*, 323
Justin Martyr 275–6, 276*n*, 279*n*, 287, 287*n*,
        290*n*, 292, 297*n*, 306*n*, 319, 319*n*, 321,
        321*n*, 324*n*
Juvenal 206*n*, 208*n*, 214*n*, 228*n*, 269*n*, 283–4*n*

Kant, Immanuel, *Was ist Aufklärung?* (*see* Vol II) 4
Keating, Dr 252*n*
Koran 34, 36*

Lactantius 279*n*, 286–8*n*, 287, 296*n*, 313,
        318, 321, 324*n*
Laelius 36*
La Font de Saint Yenne 4
language
    burlesque 25, 26–7
    and Christian writing 318
    and national characteristics 192*n*, 213
    Roman empire 213–14
    use in theatre 6–8, 12–13
Laodicea, council of 287*n*
Lardner, Dr 314*n*, 316*n*, 323*n*
Laugier 184
laws
    adaptation to climate 135–9
    barbarians and 262

'natural' 147
    and political liberty 132–4
    of trade 141–5
    unchangingness 138
Le Beau 193*n*
Le Blanc 184
Le Clerc 274–5*n*, 278*n*, 285*n*, 302*n*, 304–5*n*
Le Comte 309*n*
Leibniz, Gottfried Wilhelm 93, 94*, 96,
        97–8, 107*
Libanius 224*n*
liberty
    ancient Germans 257
    Augustus maintains illusion 239
    and effective economy 167, 170
    England 121, 122, 126, 129
    political, and types of government 132–4
    poverty and 142
    protection 230
    requires direction 301
    Roman loss of 246–8
life, desirability 99–100, 103
Ligue, La 123, 124*
Limborch 273*n*
Lipsius 235*n*, 266*n*
    De Magnitudine Romana 197–8*n*
    De Militia Romana 194*n*, 196*n*
    De Pronunciatione Linguae Latinae 213*n*
literature
    burlesque 25, 26–7
    epic 26
    Johnson on authorship 119
    novel 3, 25–30
    patronage 4
    prose romances 26, 30*
    Roman 213*n*, 228–9
    task of 3
    translation 22
    vanity as cause 110
    see also poetry; realism; theatre
Livy (Titus Livius), *Ab Urbe Condita* (History
        of Rome) 55, 60, 64*, 189*n*, 195*n*,
        209*n*, 232*n*, 317, 317*n*, 319*n*
Locke, John 24*, 31, 35–6*
    Essay concerning Human Understanding 19, 35*
Longinus 229, 229*n*
Louis XIV, king of France 3, 123, 129, 130*
Louis, father of Louis IX of France 126
love
    and climate 137
    as theme in literature 6–8, 12–13
Lucan (Marcus Annaeus Lucanus) 238*n*,
        262–3*n*, 325*n*
Lucian 54–5, 64*, 84, 87*, 191*n*, 207*n*, 228*n*,
        229, 295*n*, 309*n*, 313*n*, 315, 315*n*
Lucretius Carus, Titus 64*
Ludolphus 276*n*

Mably, abbé de 260*n*
Machiavelli, Niccolò 257, 257*n*
Macpherson, James 320*n*, 333*
Macqueen, Daniel 87*
Macrobius 209*n*, 281*n*, 332*n*
Maffei, marquis 211, 218*n*
Magna Carta 126
Mahomet *see* Mohammed

Oricellarius, Bernardus 220*n*
Origen 277–8*n*, 298, 298–9*n*, 306*n*, 317,
    317*n*, 320, 320–4*n*, 321, 333*
Orobio 273*n*
Orosius 230*n*
Ossian 187*n*, 320*n*, 333*
Otho, Roman emperor 241
Ottoman empire 202, 203, 205, 222*n*
Otway, Thomas 15*
Ovid (Publius Ovidius Naso) 17, 18, 19, 24*, 248*n*
    Ars Amatoria 209*n*, 260*n*
    Epistulae ex Ponto 250*n*
    Fasti 189*n*, 281*n*
    Metamorphoses 325*n*
Oxford, first earl 129, 130*
Oxford University 174

Palestine, under Romans 203
    see also Jews
Pantheon, Rome 218*n*
Paris, abbé 57, 61, 64*
Parthians 185, 185*n*, 188–9, 190, 191*n*
Pascal, Blaise 63, 64*
patriotism 191, 328
    Christian 299–300, 304
Pausanias 211*n*, 220*n*
Pearson, John 301*n*, 305*n*, 316*n*
Pelloutier 209*n*, 250*n*, 252*n*, 263*n*
Peregrinus 295*n*
Pericles, Athenian statesman 220
Persia 246–7, 246–7*n*, 248–9
Persian Gulf 188
Persius (Aulus Persius Flaccus) 284*n*
pessimism 43*, 89, 106
Peter, St 305, 305*n*
Peter, emperor of Russia 132*n*
Pharisees 285
Philip of Macedon 188, 202
Philo Judaeus 270*n*, 306*n*, 316*n*
philosophy
    Arab 110, 120*
    and bigotry 66
    contrary to common sense 42–3
    early Christians 321–2
    and facts 249
    freedom 65–6, 74–5
    Greek 65–6, 75*, 207, 247
    metaphysics 283
    and morality 66, 70, 207
    salary of a Roman philosopher 228*n*
    takes wide view 328
Philostratus 219–20*n*, 222*n*, 228*n*
Phoenicia, under Romans 203
physiocrats 146, 154, 167, 171*
Pignorius 216*n*
Pindar 17–18, 24*, 284*n*
Plato 93, 141, 145*, 229, 252, 283, 306,
    306*n*, 321
    Laws 145*
    Platonists 207
Pliny the elder (C. Plinius Secundus) 247,
    323, 323*n*, 324
    Historia Naturalis 185*n*, 195*n*, 201*n*, 209*n*,
        212–13*n*, 216–17*n*, 220*n*, 222, 222*n*,
        224–8*n*, 227, 241*n*, 247*n*, 249*n*, 324*n*
Pliny the younger (C. Plinius Caecelius

Secundus) 218, 294, 323, 323*n*
    Epistolae 188*n*, 210*n*, 218–19*n*, 224*n*, 235*n*,
        294*n*, 315, 315*n*, 322, 322*n*
    Panegyricus (on Trajan) 188*n*, 193*n*, 236*n*, 24?
Plotina, Roman empress 242
Plotinus 1
Plutarch 323, 323*n*, 325*n*, 332*n*,
    Parallel Lives 55, 57, 63*, 198–9n, 208n,
        212n, 215*n*, 251*n*, 256*n*, 261*n*, 325*n*
poetry
    bards, German 263
    and love 6–7
    Pope's 19
    and reality 12
Poland 134
Polemo 228*n*
politeness, social 6
    manners and trade 141
political boundaries, contemporary with
        Gibbon, of former Roman empire
        199–205
political economy *see* economics
politics
    existence of principles 4
    political body self-regulating 163–4
    political stability 167–8
    religious control 125–6
    and trade 144
    Whig philosophy 36*
Polybius 193, 194*n*, 196*n*, 208*n*, 234*n*, 325–6,
    325–6n
polytheism 206–7, 206*n*, 238, 271, 279, 312– 13
    and immortality of the soul 283–4
Pompey (Gnaeus Pompeius Magnus) 122,
    124*, 232–3, 232–3*n*, 272*n*
Pope, Alexander 6, 88–9, 94*, 96, 97–8, 101,
    109–10, 112–16
    Alcander 19
    Dunciad 24*
    Essay on Criticism 21, 24*, 120*
    Essay on Man 37, 94*, 96, 107*, 108, 120*
    Iliad translation 3, 17, 21–3, 207*n*
    influences on 18–20
    Life (Johnson) 16–23
    Ode on Solitude 18
    Pastorals 16, 19, 20
    Rape of the Lock 21
    on Shakespeare 13, 15*
    Silence 19
    Windsor Forest 21
Poquelin, Jean–Baptiste *see* Molière
power, abuse of 133
Prideaux 270*n*, 306*n*
Procopius 224*n*
Protagoras 66, 75*
providence 3–4, 113–14
    Hume on 65–75
    Rousseau on 96–106
provinces of Roman empire 199–205, 210–14
    Augustus delegates 233
    cities 221–3
    decline 228
Prudentius 289*n*, 307*n*
Ptolemy (Claudius Ptolemaeus) 203*n*, 229,
    253, 253*n*,
Puranas, the 34, 36*

342

Index by Ann Edwards